TURNAROUND

TURNAROUND

HOW AMERICA'S TOP COP
REVERSED THE CRIME EPIDEMIC

WILLIAM
BRATTON
with PETER KNOBLER

 RANDOM HOUSE NEW YORK

All rights reserved under International and Pan-American Copyright Conventions. Published in the United States by Random House, Inc., New York, and simultaneously in Canada by Random House of Canada Limited, Toronto.

Library of Congress Cataloging-in-Publication Data

Bratton, William.
   Turnaround: how America's top cop reversed the crime epidemic / William Bratton with Peter Knobler.
     p.   cm.
   ISBN 0-679-45251-6
   1.Bratton, William.   2.New York (N.Y.). Police Dept.—Officials and employees—Biography.   3.Police chiefs—New York (State)—New York—Biography.   4.Police administration—New York (State)—New York.   5.Public relations—Police—New York (State)—New York.
I.Knobler, Peter.   II.Title.
HV7911.B72A3 1998
363.2'092—dc21   97-28105

Random House website address: www.randomhouse.com

Printed in the United States of America on acid-free paper

9 8 7 6 5 4 3 2

First Edition

Book design by Caroline Cunningham

To my parents, Bill and June Bratton, my wife, Cheryl, and my son, David, for their unwavering support. To the cops for their unwavering commitment to making the streets of America safe.

—W.B.

To Jane and Daniel.

—P.K.

"The best executive is the one who has sense enough to pick good men to do what he wants done, and self-restraint enough to keep from meddling with them while they do it."

—Theodore Roosevelt

Day One

Don't stick your neck out. It's the first principle in running a police organization. Never say your goals out loud; you'll only look bad when you don't achieve them.

That's not me.

New York's newly elected mayor, Rudolph W. Giuliani, had chosen me to be police commissioner of the City of New York—the number one police job in America—and it was time to stick my neck out. The city was a mess. People were afraid of being mugged, they were afraid of having their cars stolen, they were afraid of the everyday assault on common decency and good conduct that had become standard New York behavior. Surveys showed that more than half the people who had recently left the city did so to improve the quality of their lives. And chief among the reasons they couldn't do that in the city was crime.

Although I was born and raised and had worked almost all my life in Boston, I knew New York. My two years as chief of the New York City Transit Police in the early 1990s had given me a full immersion in the way the city handled itself—a view from the underground up. Nothing changes fast in the city. There is the sense that this is the way it is, this is the way it's always been, and this is the way it always will be. New Yorkers respect strength and admire spirit, they pride themselves on their toughness—it's tough enough just to get by—but when I got there they had just about given up.

New Yorkers wanted a way out of the danger and lawlessness they saw around them. They couldn't walk from their apartments to the subway without getting aggressively panhandled or threatened or worse—"Hey, hey, hey, mister, gimme a quarter. That the best you got?" They couldn't walk to work without seeing men and women using the streets and sidewalks as outdoor toilets. They couldn't stop their car at a traffic light without some guy smearing their windshield with a filthy rag and demanding a dollar for his efforts. Squeegee men, these fellows were called, and to many people it seemed they just about ruled the city. I had joked frequently that they should replace the torch in the Statue of Liberty's hand with a squeegee—it was a more fitting symbol of the welcome many people received when they got here.

New York City felt it was under siege, and there was the widespread sense that no one was doing anything about it. In 1990, shortly after he was elected, Mayor David Dinkins and his entire administration took a major hit when, in response to a particularly bloody week in the city, the *New York Post* ran this tabloid headline in huge type on its front page:

"DAVE, DO SOMETHING"

Mirroring the local perspective, the story went national shortly thereafter. *Time* magazine had a cover story in September featuring "The Rotting of the Big Apple." In response to this challenge, Dinkins was able to pass "Safe Streets" legislation that increased the size of the city's three police departments by over six thousand officers.

But by 1994, even this ongoing infusion of personnel hadn't seemed to help. There was a sense of doom on the streets. The police department seemed dysfunctional. Several generations of corruption scandals had left it seemingly without the will to fight crime. The cops on the beat wanted to do their jobs, but the brass didn't trust them to do it. Corruption on a commander's watch can kill his career, so rather than aggressively attack the places where most crime occurred, particularly drug-related crime, police officers had been ordered by their superiors to stay out of them; the feeling behind many desks was that it was better for cops to stay away from criminals and steer clear of temptation than to chase them down and put them away.

Mayor Giuliani was a former federal prosecutor. He liked putting criminals in jail; it was what he had done for a living. Giuliani was elected mayor in 1993 largely on the quality-of-life and crime issues, and, impressed with my earlier record as transit chief, he brought me in to help clean up the rest of the city. I brought to New York a lifetime career in law enforcement and had led the turnaround of four major police departments, including the New York City Transit Police and the Boston Police Department. Like most American police departments, for the last twenty-five years the NYPD had been content to focus on reacting to crime while accepting no responsibility for reducing, let alone preventing, it. Crime, the theory went, was caused by societal problems that were impervious to police intervention. That was the unchallenged conventional wisdom espoused by academics, sociologists, and criminologists. I intended to prove them wrong. Crime, and as important, attitudes about crime, could be turned around. Using law enforcement expertise, leadership and management skills, and an inspired workforce, I intended to create an organization whose goal and mission was to control and prevent crime—not just respond to it. By turning around the NYPD, and reducing crime and fear, we would turn around the city. And, who knows, maybe even the country.

I believed that police could, in fact, be counted upon to have a significant effect on crime. With effective leadership and management we could control behavior in the street, and by controlling behavior we could change behavior. If we could change behavior we could control crime.

When I interviewed with Giuliani for the police commissioner's position, I told him we could reduce crime by 40 percent in three years.

On December 2, 1993, at the announcement of my appointment as the city's new police commissioner, a little more than a month before I took office, I stood beside the mayor and made this promise: "We will fight for every house in this city. We will fight for every street. We will fight for every borough. And we will win."

The turnaround had begun. Like Babe Ruth pointing his bat to the bleachers indicating where his next home run would land, I was confidently predicting the future. I was a leader who had spent my whole professional life seeking out and turning around low-performing, dysfunctional police departments. Now I had been given the challenge of a lifetime—the NYPD. One of my predecessors, Commissioner Lee Brown, when he led the department, likened the experience to trying to "turn an aircraft carrier around in a bathtub." I intended to turn it around with the speed of a destroyer.

I spent the next five weeks putting my team together. I interviewed men and women at all levels of the NYPD and matched people to positions; you can seriously undermine an organization by putting the right person in the wrong job. My team and I planned our strategies and prepared to hit the ground running.

On Sunday, January 9, 1994, the day before I was scheduled to be sworn in as commissioner, several members of my new team were to meet at the apartment of John Miller, who was going to be my deputy commissioner of public information (DCPI), to go over what we were calling the rollout, our first major changes. Miller, a television-news reporter for the local NBC affiliate, was best known for sidling up to organized-crime don John Gotti and getting him to talk. In his $2,000 suits, John looked fearless on the tube; in real life, he is a guy who loves being on the scene. Aggressively single, John was an excellent reporter with great contacts; he knew just about everybody in town, and the cops loved him. He was taking a $500,000 pay cut to become my DCPI because it was the job he had always wanted. As a reporter, he'd had a front-row seat to the New York circus; now, he was in the center ring.

Peter LaPorte, my new chief of staff, was there. So were consultant John Linder, chief of department and soon-to-be first deputy commissioner Dave Scott, and newly appointed deputy commissioner for crime-control strategies Jack Maple, whom I had brought with me from my years in transit. Maple is a barrel-chested Queens native who favors homburgs, double-breasted blazers, bow ties, and two-toned spectator shoes. He is a character out of *Guys and Dolls,* with a brilliant police mind.

My term as commissioner was to begin officially at midnight, and I was taking the five o'clock shuttle out of Logan Airport in Boston. After an early dinner in New York with friends, I was to join the gang at Miller's apartment before heading up to the 103rd Precinct in Queens for my first official act: attending roll call and addressing the officers as they began their shift.

Late in the afternoon, the phone rang at Miller's east-side apartment. Apparently, a situation was developing around a mosque in Harlem that looked like it could be potentially troublesome. Maple said to Miller, "I'm going to meet the Commish out at the airport. Why don't you go up and get a handle on this mosque thing?" Miller called down to police headquarters at One Police Plaza. The night sergeant gave him the rundown.

There had been a gun run; a phone call had come in on the emergency number, 911, saying there was an armed robbery in progress, two men with guns. Police had responded, and the location turned out to be the Nation of Islam Mosque Number 7, Louis Farrakhan's operation, at Fifth Avenue and 125th Street, on the third floor. The first officers to arrive, a male-female team, were met by Muslim security, which is usually very tight. Police officers are particularly focused when there is the possibility of a firearm involved at a scene, and New York City's Nation of Islam members are very sensitive about police issues. The Muslims didn't want the police entering their place of worship carrying weapons. When the officers evidently tried to brush by, a fight ensued, with some people rolling down a flight of stairs. The cops were overpowered, one of their guns and their radio were taken, and they were literally thrown out into the street.

It was snowing and blustery, the streets were icy, and the temperature had fallen to around fifteen degrees. Snow from the previous week was now rock hard. The fight in the street became one of those cartoon battles, except serious; you swung at somebody and ended up falling on your butt on the ice, which is how bones get broken.

A crowd started to gather. The cops called for backup, and so did the Muslims. Finally, there was a standoff, the cops controlling the outer perimeter and the Muslims controlling the inner. It was shaping up to be one of those New York confrontations, greater than the sum of its parts.

I wasn't even police commissioner yet—I was a civilian until midnight. My predecessor, Ray Kelly, had already resigned and was on a plane to Europe. John Pritchard, the first deputy, had also resigned. Dave Scott, who as chief of department was the number-three man, was up there running the show. That was fine. Scott had a foot in each administration; I had asked him to be my first deputy commissioner, and he was going to be the senior ranking uniformed officer on both sides of midnight. Miller ran up there with him.

Maple briefed me when I got off the plane. Welcome to New York. Without official authority until midnight, I didn't feel it would be appropriate for me to be on the scene, so we went to a restaurant and kept in constant contact by telephone. Our cellular phones didn't work inside, so Jack and I kept shuffling out to the car to talk to Miller and Scott and the mayor.

Early reports from the scene seemed to indicate that the cops had done nothing intentionally wrong. A report of a firearm is very serious, and the officers had every right—indeed, the duty—to investigate thoroughly. When you think of a mosque, perhaps you get the image of the splendor of Mecca or the Muslim equivalent of Saint Patrick's Cathedral. Mosque Number 7, however, sat in a commercial building, next door to a supermarket. Far from assaulting an imposing place of worship, the officers thought they were entering a commercial property. They never got near the third-floor mosque itself.

The mayor believed that where there is room for benefit of the doubt, that benefit should go to the police. I agreed completely. The first thing we asked was "Were our officers right?" When the answer came back affirmative, we were in the position to support our men and women. Our early comments to the press said just that.

This came as a surprise to the press and to the cops. For years, the brass had backed away in times like these, adopting a wait-and-see attitude that allowed the media to shout any damn thing they wanted without strong pro-police input from City Hall and One Police Plaza. When the bosses don't back you up, the attacks in the papers and on the air get very shrill and ugly. Cops had come to expect such softness from their superiors, and they resented it. That had to stop. The newly elected mayor believed that, and so did I.

Chief Joe Leake was borough commander of Manhattan North. Leake, himself black, was on the scene, trying to broker a deal in which the police would search the mosque to obtain the gun and radio in exchange for letting the people who were inside leave. Everyone in the mosque was a potential suspect, and they were going nowhere without being identified. The Muslims were refusing to give anything up or anyone over.

Of course, the mayor was involved. He had been sworn in ten days earlier as a law-and-order mayor, and he had made it clear during the campaign that he was not going to give special treatment to any group—black, white, Asian, Hispanic. And race was an issue. African Americans in particular feared that his administration would be insensitive to them. For twenty-five years, they and other groups in the city had been treated gingerly by City Hall. Now Giuliani had come in and said, Everybody's going to be treated the same. In addition, the black community felt injured by the fact that they had lost David Dinkins, an African American, as mayor. For several years, New York had had a black mayor and a black police commissioner, Lee Brown. Now they had a white police commissioner from Boston and a white mayor whom they really did not trust.

Furthermore, much of the overwhelmingly white constituency that had elected Giuliani felt that the black community in particular had gotten away with too much already. The black community knew this and resented it. Farrakhan's Muslims had gone out of their way to depict Islam as "the black man's religion," and this current situation, cops in a mosque, had the potential to become a community rallying point. Add this to Giuliani's impulse to support cops when they were doing the right thing and you could understand why the tension was high.

I don't know that the incident would have been treated very differently

if it had happened at a Catholic church. Giuliani felt previous administrations had backpedaled too much in dealing with many special-interest
groups around the city, and he was going to put a stop to it. Giuliani saw
this as purely a police-and-order issue, and he was determined to put his
stamp on the city right away.

All this was in play on this bitterly cold, windy, snowy Sunday night,
with the leadership of the police department still in the hands of men who
for twenty years had been taught and had learned through bitter experience to respond in a very low-key, sympathetic manner to many of the
city's special-interest groups—in a nutshell, never to stick their neck out.

Giuliani was not happy with the standoff. His position, basically, was:
You've got criminals in there. Go in and get them.

Relying on Scott and Leake and my own sensitivities to this issue, I felt
that would exacerbate the situation. No one in New York law enforcement
was unaware that in the 1970s a police officer had been shot during a
standoff at a city mosque, and we didn't want another seventies-style
situation on our hands. I had worked for two years as transit police chief
and was mindful that sometimes negotiations are appropriate.

This wasn't sitting well with the mayor. He kept calling me and Scott
and Leake. "You have police officers injured," he said. "You have stolen
police property. Why aren't you going in?" It was a legitimate question,
but it was asked continually. The command post was in a supermarket
next to the mosque, and Leake kept getting pulled out of negotiations to
talk to someone from City Hall. He told them essentially, with grace and
tact, "Nothing has changed because every time we go to negotiate, we get
pulled back into the supermarket to talk to you."

The Muslims, meanwhile, had none of these problems; they weren't
answering to Farrakhan every five minutes. They had a chain of command
and were making decisions. We had a level-three mobilization of cops and
they had a level-four mobilization of Muslims. We were being outflanked.

"There ought to be arrests tonight," the mayor insisted. "No one is to
be D.A.T.'d." (A D.A.T. is a desk appearance ticket, known to cops as a
"disappearance ticket" because most people who get them don't show up
in court.) "I want arrests!"

Giuliani seized upon this incident to draw his line in the sand; here's
how he was going to be different from Dinkins. He was going to be aggressive, hands-on. Giuliani would have preferred to keep everybody
locked inside the building until they surrendered the people who assaulted the officers and stole the radio. However, Scott and Leake were

handling the situation masterfully. They had been field commanders for many years in the department and knew the community—were *of* that community—and felt that the tensions were so high that to make the point that we, the police, were in charge would have raised the potential for bloody consequences.

Leake had two jobs that night; one was to catch the guys who assaulted the cops, and the other was to prevent a riot. His view was, "Let's prevent the riot first, and then we'll get down to getting these mugs. We have a description, we know where they come from. Detectives have caught a lot of people on a lot less than that. We'll get them." I concurred.

I used the weather conditions to bring the point home to the mayor. "It's a very tenuous situation up there," I told him. "We have a lot of police, and if we attempt to, if you will, assault the place—to go in using force—there is the potential to have this escalate. We ought to step back and allow the negotiation process to work."

Ultimately, a deal was worked out in which Scott and an aide went into the mosque, searched the premises, and retrieved the radio and the gun. Then there was a walk-by; although many people involved in the incident had left the scene, the individuals who remained in the building were brought out in a long line so the officers who had been assaulted could make identifications and arrests. A promise was obtained from the Muslims that the next day they would surrender the people they knew to be involved in the assault and theft. The Muslims agreed, Scott and Leake agreed, I agreed, and finally, so did the mayor.

I still wasn't commissioner.

Eight officers had been hurt, and the mayor and I went to the hospital to visit the most seriously injured. The cops were very glad to see us and to hear the mayor's early comments supporting their actions. We could use the incident to get out dual messages. To the cops: I'll support you with the benefit of the doubt. To the city: There's a new sheriff in town, and we're not going to tolerate disrespect for the police.

Leaving the hospital, Miller, Maple, and I headed up to the 103rd Precinct in Jamaica, Queens, for roll call. (In the peculiarity of New York police jargon, the 103rd Precinct is not pronounced the "one hundred and third," it is the "One-oh-three." This is for radio purposes; the "Three-oh," the "Three-three," and the "One-one-three" are more likely to be understood and less likely to cause confusion over static-filled airwaves than the "thirtieth," the "thirty-third," and the "hundred-and-thirteenth." By now, it's just the way cops talk.)

The 103 was a microcosm of the city: Multiethnic and multiracial, it had good neighborhoods, bad neighborhoods, and some in-between. It was Governor Mario Cuomo's home precinct, but it had all kinds of crime problems. John Miller was very conscious of New York history and symbolism and had suggested we go to the 103 because it was an example of the city being out of control. The 103 was the precinct where Eddie Byrne had been killed.

In February 1988, Police Officer Ed Byrne was sitting in his patrol car, guarding the home of a man who had informed on a drug dealer, when he was shot to death by drug dealers. It was a vicious and cold-blooded murder, and they did it to send a message: This was their turf, their world, they had the power. But massive police response to that homicide had changed that perception of the 103. We now intended to change it for the rest of the city.

I might not have told the 103 I was coming. Tradition held that before a police commissioner visited a precinct a call would be put in saying he was coming. It was a not-very-subtle message that if the commanding officer was working, he'd better be there; that if he wasn't working, he might think about working; that if he still wasn't working, then the executive officer better be there; that the broom better be taken to the place; that the girlie pictures go down and the color photos of the brass get straightened. Three parking spaces were to be cleared in front for the commissioner's car, his advance car, and his backup car. It was expected to be expected.

I preferred it another way. I was a cop going to visit a police station, no advance notice. All my advance guy would do was make sure there wasn't total pandemonium.

I walked in before the midnight shift.

It's funny about the world of police; there are the cops of the day and the cops of the night. Cops of the night are a different breed. Their uniforms tend to be a little less neat, they're a little more unkempt. They look like people who belong in the dark. As I entered the muster room of the beat-up old station, twenty-odd pairs of eyes turned to size up their new leader.

"This is my first official act as police commissioner," I told them. "I came a long way to get here. I know you're thinking: Who's this guy who talks funny, this guy from Boston who's the new commissioner.

"It's odd that this is a department I've dreamed of my whole life. I don't know why a kid from Dorchester was dreaming of being a New York City cop, but I do remember a picture book I kept checking out of the library that had illustrations of all the units and divisions of this department, and I know how I used to feel about the traditions of the NYPD. I want you all to feel the same way that I do.

"I said when I took this job that we would take this city back for the good people who live here, neighborhood by neighborhood, block by block, house by house. But I'm going to need your help in doing that. I'm going to need all of you in the game.

"I want my cops to be cops. I want them to be assertive. I don't want them walking by or looking the other way when they see something. No matter what the old rules were, I expect you to see something and take proper police action.

"I expect you to be honest. I expect you to uphold the oath that you took on the first day. If you get into problems doing your job, and you're doing it right, I'll back you up. If you're wrong, I'll get you retrained and back to work. If you're dirty or brutal, I'll see to it that you're arrested, you're fired, and you're put in jail.

"I like cops. I've been with cops most of my adult life. I want to bring three things to this department: Pride, Commitment, and Respect. I want you to be proud of your city, of your department, and of yourselves. Proud that you're cops in the greatest police department in the world. I also want you to take pride in your appearance, in your uniforms, and in how you wear them."

I looked out at these guys. The 103 was a good place to start in terms of improving appearances. They as much as said, You couldn't have given us an hour's notice? We could have gotten a haircut or something.

"I want you to have commitment," I told them. "Commitment to do the job. Oh, yes, we are in for some rough times here. We've seen what the Mollen Commission found"—the Mollen Commission was investigating corruption in the NYPD—"and I'll tell you now there's more to come. It's not enough just for you to uphold your oath. When that man or woman next to you is brutal or corrupt or stealing, it is part of your oath that you just can't stand by, that's not enough.

"You all have families back home, wives and kids who depend on you. Mothers and fathers who love you." There were two generations of officers in front of me; some were kids who went home and lived with mommy and daddy, others were men in their forties who went home to kids. "When some cop that you work with is robbing drug dealers or beating people, that puts you all in danger. Because then we're asking the criminals to be able to tell, Is that the good police coming through the door or the bad police?

"What happens when a cop gets shot because some drug dealer thought that cops weren't coming to arrest him but to beat him and rob him?"

The 103 stared at me.

"I want you all to know right now, I know what I'm asking of you, and I'll tell you what I intend to give you in return.

"If you do your jobs, I will back you to the hilt. We had an incident tonight which we're looking into. And if I find the officers acted properly—and it appears they did—then I will back them up publicly. We will be sailing in harm's way as we take back this city together."

Miller was watching the cops. He remembers, "A third of the cops were saying, 'This guy's too good to be true.' Another third were saying, 'Uh oh, this guy's going to be trouble.' And a third were wondering which way to go." Cops had heard the brass say they were going to get tough on cops before, but they had never heard a commissioner come in and say he was going to back them up. The old brass had come through a long police culture in which the assumption was that if there was an "incident," the officer must be guilty, and even if he wasn't guilty, it was easier to hang him out to dry than to fight the public and the press. So the cops were listening to me and figuring, "Break our balls *and* back us up, that might not be a bad deal; we'll take that."

I also talked to them about respect, both for themselves and for the public they serve. "We're going to work very hard to take this city back, but all our good work can be undone by one cop who treats a citizen disrespectfully," I told them. "We have to keep the public's respect for us. If we do our job brutally, if we do it criminally, if we do it thoughtlessly, then we're going to lose the public's respect and all the good work you do will be overshadowed by the sense that we're a brutal, corrupt force. Pride, Commitment, Respect."

Leaving the roll call, Maple, Miller, and I crammed into the back of my department-issued four-door Mercury. In the front sat my security detail, Detective Al Powlett and Detective Jimmy Motto, who was driving. There's no sight in the world quite like the New York skyline all lit up, if you stop and pay attention to it. We were in the center lane, cruising over the Triborough Bridge from Queens into Manhattan, when the digital clock on the dashboard hit 12:00. "It's midnight, Commissioner," said Detective Motto. "Raise your right hands," I said to Maple and Miller. We all laughed. "Okay, we're onboard now." It had been a long day and a longer night, and as we passed through the toll booth, I was finally commissioner. Life was going to change and I was ready.

———————

I had called the first meeting of the super chiefs for seven the next morning in the police commissioner's conference room on the fourteenth floor of One Police Plaza. The super chiefs were the chiefs of department, patrol, detectives, personnel, and the Organized Crime Control Bureau— the highest uniformed officials in the NYPD. These men were in place when I came into the department. Between them, they had in the neighborhood of two hundred years of police experience. I had appointed my aides, but I had not yet made any command-staff personnel changes, except for Dave Scott.

The police commissioner's office is located in One Police Plaza—One PP, as it's more commonly known—or the Puzzle Palace, as it's sometimes referred to by the cops. It's a red-brick monolith that sits in lower Manhattan overlooking the East River and the Brooklyn Bridge. The super chiefs were all seated on one side of a long conference table facing the tall windows. The building had been outfitted with vertical blinds, which were open, the morning sun rising over the Brooklyn Bridge and blasting the room with yellow light.

John Miller, party animal that he was, usually prowled around Manhattan till all hours of the night. He hated to get up much before ten, so it was a measure of his devotion to his new job that he had dragged himself out of bed to attend. He and Maple sat with their backs to the windows as the chiefs squinted at them.

It is the custom and practice of the New York Police Department that, when coming to the police commissioner's office, all police personnel wear the dress blue uniform. It's a matter of respect for the office and the commissioner himself; when you're on the fourteenth floor, you dress the part. The chiefs of detectives and organized crime control, since they are not routinely in uniform, are permitted to wear suits. All these men in their crisp white shirts looked at Maple. "Who is this fat guy with the bow tie, this transit lieutenant who sits at the right hand of the commissioner, who now we're all a-scared of, who a week ago we wouldn't have given the time of day off our watches?" they must have wondered.

They looked at Miller. "And this hump over here. Some reporter!" And slowly it began to dawn on them: Oh my God, could the nightmare be true? Could *that* be the inner circle? Is it possible that the New York Police Department, the greatest law-enforcement institution in the world, is being run by some guy from Boston, a TV reporter, and a transit cop?

"Good morning, gang." I walked in and sat down. "Some of you know me from the transit police; some of you don't know me." I knew them. I had spent most of the past month going over everyone's files, which had been gathered by my transition team through both formal and informal sources. "Let me give you a few rules," I said. "The way I operate is, I'm not into screaming and yelling and throwing things. I want input from everybody. I'd like to hear it." There is the temptation to yes bosses to death, which doesn't do anybody any good. I wanted to put that out of the way first thing.

I went through an agenda of specific issues we would be dealing with early in my tenure.

"As far as your demeanor in the office," I said, "I don't have a big fondness for cursing. I think we can communicate without doing that."

With the formalities out of the way, I turned to the pressing business of the morning.

"Now, this mosque thing. Where are we on that?"

My new first deputy commissioner, Dave Scott, led the discussion. "We're looking for this Brother Jared," I was told. One of the suspects now had a name. He had left the scene in all the hubbub before he could be detained, and the Muslims were in the process of reneging on their agreement to turn in those involved in the assault. "We have a description, and we're working on a sketch."

After the meeting, some of my staff and I walked over to City Hall. I could have jumped into a car and had my security detail drive me, but it's not a long walk, and I enjoy getting around the city by foot. We went down the commissioner's private elevator, through the front lobby of One PP, out onto the brick concourse, past the United States attorney's office on the right. Walk around the back of the Municipal Building, past the hot-dog vendor who's always ready with a quick snack, and you're at the foot of the Brooklyn Bridge. We waited for the light to change.

The media had been after the mayor all morning, as would be expected. This kind of confrontation is big news. Reporters and news people were bundled in winter coats, toting notepads and battery packs, shouldering cameras and lights. As we came around the parking lot to the front of City Hall, they spotted us and converged, peppering us with questions as we walked.

"What does this mosque thing mean?"

"What's the response?"

"Black leaders are saying you are insensitive to their community!"

"Look," I told them as I kept moving, "our police officers were responding to a call. They were doing their job, and they were attacked. We're conducting a full investigation."

Without comparing notes, the mayor and I had said the same thing: There was a controversy, it got messy, and we are backing the cops up. In some ways, the mosque incident was a gift; for a department who had heard my roll-call speech at the 103 and wondered, "What's he really like?" here was the answer. I knew cops, I liked cops, I trusted cops. I would back up my force until I learned something different.

The next day I was officially sworn in at City Hall. Mayor Giuliani was very gracious in his private office prior to the ceremony as I introduced him to members of my family and friends. The room where I was sworn in was filled with over four hundred people. A baseball fan, Giuliani told the gathering, "Wade Boggs, we got him from Boston. And Babe Ruth." I was flattered.

I'm usually much better when I ad lib, but that day I had some prepared remarks. "The people in the neighborhood," I said, "the people on their beat, the tourists who make this city so great—they have to work together with police officers. They must share a common commitment to making individual blocks and whole neighborhoods safer. The public and police are partners."

We police, I said, "are obliged to act against disorderly conditions and behavior that cause fear, no matter how trivial. We are obliged to deliver police services with the highest degree of professionalism possible. We are obliged to forge the strongest possible ties to the neighborhoods we protect. And we are obliged to stand by our police officers whenever they make honest, good-faith efforts to enforce the law.

"I am reminded of what John Paul Jones, the great American naval hero, said about being given an important command. He asked for 'a ship that sails fast, for I intend to go in harm's way.' You have given me a fast ship, Mr. Mayor, the most powerful in my profession, with the finest crew on earth, and we are prepared to go in harm's way. To do our duty to keep the peace, to make New York a safer place for all of us.

"That is my commitment to the men and women, the citizens of Boston . . .

"Excuse me." I stopped. *"Boston!"* The whole room erupted in laughter, me most of all. "Just teasing you. I was getting a little too somber there."

I quoted Dr. Martin Luther King, Jr.: " 'The ultimate measure of a man is not where he stands in moments of comfort and convenience but where he stands in times of challenge and controversy.' That," I said, "is how we should be measured." I shook hands with the mayor, kissed Cheryl, and was presented with the shield of the police commissioner of the City of New York.

This gold ceremonial shield is absolutely beautiful. Eighteen-karat gold, it has five platinum stars and is filled with NYPD history and symbolism. It was presented to the first New York City police commissioner in 1901 and has been to every one since. I was the thirty-eighth.

My day was full of ceremonial activity and police routine. I tried to ab-sorb the excitement, the pomp and circumstance, and also get down to work. In mid-afternoon, the woman who had custody of the shield was looking for it. It was normally kept in a vault and taken out only for spe-cial occasions, and she wanted it back. I couldn't find it. My first day in office, I had lost the $10,000 commissioner's shield that had been passed down for more than ninety years. "I'll get it down to you," I told her. I didn't have a clue where it was.

At home that night, I asked my wife, "Cheryl, do you have any idea what I did with that badge? They're looking for it and can't find it."

"Oh, I have it. You gave it to me at the ceremony." Thus was New York City history preserved.

Two days later, Charles Hynes was getting sworn in as Brooklyn district attorney. I wanted to attend, but bad weather and heavy traffic had the Brooklyn Bridge all tied up. You could see from my office window that even with a siren blaring it would take an age for a police car to get across. I didn't want to miss the ceremony, so I told my security detail, "I'm going to take the train."

They were aghast. They were brand new bodyguards for a brand new commissioner and they had the basic city cop's attitude about the subway: You don't go down there unless somebody's already dead. Plus, they didn't know how to get to Brooklyn. "It's only a couple of stops, guys," I told them. "Let's go."

We took the elevator downstairs and jumped on the number 4 train to Borough Hall.

My detail and I were standing in the car like any group of straphangers when a panhandler came through. It was, unfortunately, a common oc-currence, a man walking through the cars with an aggressive spiel. While a series of lawsuits had established that begging for money is a constitu-tionally protected right, aggressive panhandling in an enclosed space like the subways has been judged to be illegal. The city had been overrun with exactly this kind of behavior underground, and I had spent two years getting rid of it.

This guy's story was that he had tuberculosis; something communicable. He looked awful in a threatening and unhealthy way, and he was demanding money. No one wanted to be near him, no one would make eye contact. People ducked behind their newspapers or moved away. Anyone who has ever ridden the subway knows the sense of unpleasant resignation this scene brings: You're underground, there's no escape, and here he comes. The panhandler had taken over the car.

I moved toward him. "I'm the police commissioner," I informed the man. "You're not allowed to do that. Get off the train." I think I startled the guy. Civilians hardly ever stand up and take on the underground population. He objected, but he had no grounds; you can't intimidate people in the confined space of a subway train and expect to get away with it. This was exactly the quality-of-life violation I had been brought in to take care of. At the next station, I gave the guy the heave-ho. Now, we were taking back the city not only block by block but car by car.

My security detail closed in. God Almighty, not only is he riding the subway but now he's ejecting panhandlers! Who is this guy?

District Attorney Hynes was sworn into office in an ornate oak-paneled room in Borough Hall. Traffic had let up, and my detail convinced me to take the car back to the office, but before I headed over the bridge, I called in. Peter LaPorte, my chief of staff, told me, "The good news is that Minister Don Muhammad is here with his chief of security, Shariff Muhammad, and Minister Conrad Muhammad from the mosque." Minister Don Muhammad—known as Minister Don—was head of the Boston chapter of the Nation of Islam and, I believe, Farrakhan's senior northeast representative. The Boston Black Muslim community had gotten along very well with the Boston police when I'd been there, Minister Don and I had a good working relationship, and when this situation broke, he had called me in New York and asked to set up a meeting. I'd said sure.

"Al Sharpton and C. Vernon Mason are with them," LaPorte told me.

"What's Sharpton doing there?" I said. "I didn't agree to meet with him."

I had never met Al Sharpton, but I was well aware of him. He was one of New York's most recognizable figures and injected himself into every New York racial issue, as he was now attempting to do in this one. He had counseled Tawana Brawley in a bogus case alleging abuse of a young black woman by six white men that, after months of salacious race-baiting by him and his cohorts, turned out to be a hoax. His rabble-rousing around a black boycott of a Korean grocery store was shamefully destructive to the city's race relations and had seriously undermined the administration of Mayor Dinkins and his police commissioner, Lee Brown. While Sharpton has some following in certain segments of New York's population, his effect on the city has not been a positive one.

Sharpton is flamboyant and media savvy. He is a rotund man, his hair processed in the manner of James Brown. His attire of leisure suits, turtle-necks, and gold medallions, often worn simultaneously, had given way over the years to double-breasted suits and a more mainstream appearance. His whole persona was calculated for TV coverage.

He lived in New Jersey, but there was no denying his influence in New York. Because he was so visible, there were many people with legitimate leadership roles in the black community—businesspeople, religious people, elected officials—who were really not in the position to take him on except at great risk to themselves. Whatever risk I faced was more than made up for by the possibility of negating his influence as self-appointed community leader during my term. He had no role in this situation, and I wasn't about to let him get on his soapbox and use this issue to establish himself as a player with this administration.

"Have Dave Scott take Sharpton and Mason in his conference room and meet with them about whatever their concerns are." This was entirely appropriate. "My meeting is scheduled with Minister Don. I'm not opening this to a mini–town meeting for whoever they've decided to bring along. I will meet with the principals involved, not self-appointed leaders."

A few minutes later, LaPorte came back on the line. "They say you meet with all of them or you don't meet with them at all."

"Well, Pete, then we don't meet with them. I will meet with the principals involved."

Minister Don Muhammad could not be seen disrespecting such a loud and highly visible community figure by meeting with me alone, so the whole group left and held a press conference downstairs in the lobby of police headquarters. "We are extremely disappointed that this meeting did not take place," announced Minister Don, "but it would not have been right and proper if we didn't have the entire group we have here."

"Everyone in the community is upset," said C. Vernon Mason. "Some of us believe the mayor has already made a deal to let the police be unrestrained."

"Who is Bratton to say he will not meet with me?" wailed Sharpton. "[Ray] Kelly came to Brooklyn to eat grits with me."

Minister Don had probably not had extensive dealings with Sharpton up to that point, and now he'd gotten a good look. Sharpton, he saw, was just looking to keep the pot stirred up. Minister Don knew me to be a fair guy he could work with. Now here was an opportunity to represent the Black Muslims in New York and build a relationship in places where he had never before had access, and I think he didn't want to squander it. He called later to set up a secret meeting.

In the meantime, Dave Scott had pulled the tapes of the 911 call that had reported the disturbance in the first place plus the transmission from the cops' radios on the scene. It's important to work with the facts. They were revealing.

The 911 call was anonymous. The voice said two men, armed with guns, had entered Mosque Number 7 to rob it. As we examined the tape more closely, it became apparent that the call was a hoax, but the officers who responded didn't have the luxury of that analysis. They'd had to assume the call was for real and respond quickly.

The radio transmission documented a pitched struggle. It was clear from listening that the officers were being assaulted by a group; they were screaming bloody murder for help. The Muslims' claim that the police had come in force, invaded their mosque, beaten everyone, and left was simply untrue.

But a serious mistake had been made. The department has a protocol when dealing with incidents at what are called "sensitive locations," such as mosques, churches, and synagogues. There were over six hundred sensitive locations on the books at the time, and they were to be approached with more restraint than normal locations, with a supervisor required to respond with the officers. In fact, this protocol had been developed in response to that 1972 confrontation at Mosque Number 7 in which a police officer had been shot and killed while responding to a false report of a robbery. It was clear from the tape that the dispatcher who received the 911 call had not informed the officers that the disturbance was at a sensitive location.

John Miller wanted to release the tapes to the news media and get a jump on the debate over who started the fight because it wasn't going our way. Radio news reports had begun evenhandedly enough with phrases such as "Charges that police stormed into a Harlem mosque," but as the story wore on, it got shortened to "*When* police stormed into a Harlem mosque." Then it devolved into "stormed," as in storm troopers, as in police, as in Harlem. It was turning into a disaster, and Miller felt we had to reverse the trend.

Chief of Detectives Joe Borrelli wanted no part of playing any tapes. "This tape could be evidence," he said. "And we're going to need it."

We decided that we would play the tapes in-house for the press. They could take notes and describe what they heard, but the tape would remain in our hands. It was at this point that ex-reporter Miller learned his first lesson about how the press looks from the other side. Articles in the next day's papers said, "Police, in an attempt to gain spin control of the mosque incident, played a three-minute tape on which cops could be heard screaming. The cops who stormed into the Harlem mosque . . ."

My staff and I met secretly with Minister Don and his entourage, minus Sharpton and Mason, in the conference room of a Wall Street brokerage firm, five days after the incident. The Muslims felt the police hadn't shown sufficient respect for their house of worship, that we had rushed inside and would not have been as aggressive to the congregants at a Catholic church or a Jewish synagogue. The point had some legitimacy; the officers could have shown more sensitivity, and perhaps if they had entered a religious location they were more familiar with, they would have. We explained, however, that they had not been informed by their dispatcher that this was a sensitive location, that they were trying to protect the community from what they were told were armed robbers, that despite whatever appearance of disrespect, their intentions had been entirely honorable.

We discovered that the entire incident had been deliberately created by local drug dealers who had been chased away from the area around the mosque by the Muslims. In retaliation, they had made the call to provoke a confrontation between their two enemies, the Muslims and the police.

At the meeting that afternoon, we all agreed, in good faith, to disagree. The Muslims refused to turn over any suspects, and the police department told them we didn't need their help, we would catch the criminals on our own. Which we did after an extensive investigation by the department's detectives that took many months to complete.

The Black Muslims are a complex group that must be reckoned with. They espouse many high ideals, including family values and pride in black heritage and culture, and they are often a very strong force for good in terms of securing black neighborhoods from drug dealers and other criminal elements. Unfortunately, as much as Louis Farrakhan tries to deny it, their good is often more than washed away by the phenomenal amount of racism, prejudice, and hatred of whites they espouse, particularly toward Jews. In Boston, their rhetoric did not seem to be on the scale that Farrakhan uses on the national level, but race is a major issue in New York—as it is around the country—and ultimately the effect on the city of Farrakhan's rhetoric and efforts is problematic.

I felt it was important that the police department be understood by the black and other minority communities, particularly because the actions the mayor and I believed necessary could be misconstrued as putting down blacks or Hispanics. Our statistics told us clearly that a large percentage of the crime in New York was being perpetrated by blacks and Hispanics. This was a fact. But what also needed to be understood was that most of the victims were also blacks and Hispanics. They were the chief victims of crime and of police ineffectiveness in reducing crime. They had a right to be protected.

I had selected David Scott as my second in command in the NYPD, making him the highest-ranking black officer on the force. He was sworn in the day after my meeting with the Muslims. Dave was a thirty-three-year veteran of the department and would help me become an insider. He was respected up and down the organization, he deserved the job, and I was not unaware that this appointment would demonstrate my recognition of good work regardless of color and my desire to involve the minority community. I intended to make him the most powerful first deputy commissioner in the history of the NYPD, unlike Ray Kelly's first deputy commissioner, John Pritchard, also black, who had been largely a figurehead.

I planned to be assertive in stopping crime throughout the city. We had to make a particular effort in minority neighborhoods, where the crime was felt most. It would be difficult to do our job if we were viewed as doing it in a negative or disrespectful way. As I had told the cops at the 103, it was essential to treat all communities and all residents of the city with respect. It was important to win the respect of citizens—white, black, or Hispanic—in all of New York's neighborhoods. We could not be successful in the long run if we were seen only as an occupying force. This was critical because we were going to be much more assertive than previous police administrations, and we knew that maintaining our presence as firm but fair and respectful would present a continuing challenge, perhaps our most important one.

At the beginning of his term, the commissioner has a golden opportunity to influence the media, the public, his own police force, and the bad guys. We planned to use the press to market our message. It wasn't enough simply to bring about change, we had to sell a better image of the department, and we had to market the change as it came. In fact, we had to market the change *before* it came. "Get ready, things are about to get better. Things are getting better, see? Things are already better." We wanted to capture the press early and build momentum.

The press, of course, will not be complicit in a police department's marketing plans. They don't view themselves as an arm of our public-relations department, and they're right. But the police commissioner is a mayor's most important appointment, and any new person in the job can expect a series of honeymoon articles about who he is and how he intends to attack crime. Crime sells newspapers, and the commissioner is the living symbol of the city's attempt to deal with crime, so it's only natural that reporters will gather round and attempt to get a handle on him. It was our job to focus this attention properly. That's why I hired Miller, who came from that world.

Many police commissioners aren't comfortable with the press. In all large organizations, there are plenty of areas that a leader doesn't want made public, and a commissioner can feel vulnerable to being exposed, to being made a target. At the same time, exposure can be a bonanza, and I welcomed it. I admit it, I don't mind seeing my name in the papers. But, more important, I wanted to get the message out that change was here and we were serious. The media was the best and quickest way to do that. In some respects, what I was trying to do was similar to what Lee Iacocca had done with Chrysler: to make my identity synonymous with the organization's.

The cops read the papers, they listen to radio, they watch the evening news. Departmental memos can establish formal guidelines, but headlines give cops the feeling. We can issue directives telling them we're changing procedure, and they'll take it as an order; let them see the commissioner on the tube talking about taking back the streets, and they'll get the picture. It will affect their lives. When cops' friends start talking about the news—"I see that you're going after criminals from now on"—they bring it home.

Bad guys read the papers too. They'd had it pretty good in New York, but now we put them on notice: The party was over.

The public wanted results. They wanted less crime; they wanted to feel safer in the streets. The first step to reducing fear is to tell people we're on the case. The cavalry is coming.

Events in the city and the influence of John Miller ensured that I was all over the papers, the radio, and TV my first week as commissioner. On Friday, on my way from police headquarters to a television interview, I met with New York *Daily News* reporter Patrice O'Shaughnessy, who was doing a piece for the Sunday paper. "My number-one priority," I told her, "is fear reduction." We discussed the mosque incident and another shooting that also had happened that week. "I got a quick crash course in how to deal with crisis in New York under scrutiny," I said. "It also allowed myself and the mayor to spend a lot of time together, and now I know how we'll work together. . . . The mayor trusts what I'm about. For a guy everybody suspected would be intrusive in police matters, he hasn't been; he lets me run the department."

I also wrote an article for the *Daily News* opinion page explaining department thinking on the mosque incident and outlining my thinking on race relations.

That Sunday, the reporter's quick profile gave me and the mayor high marks for our handling of the difficult situation. It was a nice piece. The *Daily News* saw fit to run a full-page picture of me on the front page. The headline read "Top Cop William Bratton: I'LL END THE FEAR."

Well, that just started the fear.

Miller got a call from Cristyne Lategano, the mayor's communications director. "When was this *Daily News* thing set up? Who knew about it? Why was the commissioner talking to the *Daily News*?"

"It was a routine request," he told them. "They wanted an interview about his first week in office. You know, where did you go, what did you do?" The public-information office had been going its merry way, trying to pump out good stories about the NYPD and its new commissioner, trying to get people involved in this new turnaround. Apparently that wasn't what City Hall had in mind.

The issue was who was supposed to get the credit. Any time that week a positive story had appeared that was focused on me, or on both the mayor and me, the Hall's position was that it should have focused solely on the mayor. Miller was left with the distinct impression that, as far as City Hall was concerned, the *Daily News* had a photo of the wrong man on the front page.

No one had told us the game was rigged. As smart as we all thought we were, it took a while for this fact to register.

Jack Maple and I got summoned unceremoniously to City Hall. "Be in Peter Powers's office at five o'clock" was the way they put it. It was Sunday night. I'd been on the job seven days. We weren't told what the meeting was about, just show up.

After hours, you come into City Hall through the front door. You have to ring a buzzer to get in, unless the cop on guard duty is on the ball and spots you coming up the steps. Once inside, you go through a marble entranceway, pass two columns, and make a left until you hit a waist-high gate that is manned by a New York City police officer twenty-four hours a day, seven days a week. Straight ahead are a pair of French doors in front of which sit a pair of receptionists, but at five o'clock on a Sunday the desk was empty.

Go through the doors, and you're in a small rectangular office. It's not an office filled with the trappings of power, not an intimidating office, unless you know the Hall and that its placement is meaningful. This is the seat of power, the office where Peter Powers does business.

Powers was Giuliani's deputy mayor for operations. He had overall charge of the operations of the New York City government. Most of the city commissioners reported directly to him. I didn't. Unlike his predecessor, Rudy Giuliani had certain commissioners reporting directly to him, particularly the police commissioner; he wanted it clearly understood that he was hands-on and would be very involved with his police commissioner. One of Giuliani's campaign criticisms of Mayor Dinkins was that he was too distant; Commissioner Brown had reported to the deputy mayor for criminal justice. Rudy wanted no such buffer. I was a direct report and we had hot lines linking our offices.

Powers was a lifelong friend of Giuliani, as close as they come. While he had never worked with him in the U.S. attorney's office, Powers had run both of Giuliani's mayoral campaigns and had been one of the Giuliani inner circle who, about seven weeks earlier, had met with me prior to my appointment. In his late forties, a little stooped over, with hair combed straight back and glasses on the end of his nose, hearing aids in both ears, Powers had been a tax attorney and cultivated the scholarly look of a kindly schoolteacher. Appearances can be deceiving.

When Maple and I got to his office, Powers was not in a good mood. He was seated with Denny Young, the mayor's counsel and confidant who had worked with Giuliani when he was U. S. attorney.

"You guys are going way too high profile," he informed us. "This business with the press and the TV shows and the interviews and the front-page profiles, these are going to cause problems. We are trying very hard not to raise expectations or to have everyone out in the media. What we want to do is put our nose to the grindstone, achieve our goals, and then announce them. The mayor has a carefully controlled agenda. We can't have people taking control of that agenda and pushing it anywhere they want."

I knew he wasn't joking, but I was nevertheless somewhat incredulous. Here we had had a remarkably successful first week, we were moving forward with an agenda that I had presented to the mayor and had discussed fully with him before I'd been appointed; we had gotten excellent press and showed every sign of having an immediate positive effect on the city of New York and the police department.

Maple sat there, his hands folded, expressionless.

"We need to be aware of these stories," Powers went on. "The mayor is very concerned. *We* will control how these stories go out. The mayor has an agenda, and it's very important that everybody stay on message and that the message come from the mayor."

Powers's point was clear. The mayor wasn't in these stories.

Some mayors—some bosses, some managers—have the personal strength and personality to take pride and pleasure in the accomplishments of the people working under them. New York's former mayor Ed Koch, for instance, was well known for sharing credit for the successes of those in his administration. There is something simultaneously gracious and self-sustaining about a person who has the ability to say, "Look at this guy, isn't he doing a great job! Aren't I a genius for hiring him?" Rudy Giuliani, it was becoming clear, was not that kind of leader.

Powers continued, his anger barely concealed. "I've known Rudy since we were kids, okay? I'm his best friend, and *I* couldn't get away with this. If I was doing this stuff, he'd get rid of *me*. If this keeps up, we'll have to look elsewhere, it's that simple." He wrapped it up with a cold warning: "If you can't work that way," he said simply, "he'll get someone else."

I understood the mayor's desire to take credit for the successes on his watch. At the same time, I didn't take kindly to being threatened. This was the mayor speaking; Peter Powers was clearly doing Rudy Giuliani's dirty work. What kind of a guy would issue these threats? What kind of a guy would pass them along? One part of me was saying, "Go ahead, fire me. How are you going to explain that to the city?" Another part wanted to do this job, a job I had pointed toward my entire life. I was finally in a position to have a significant impact on American policing, and I didn't want to give it up one week in. I told myself, Keep your eyes on the prize, advance the agenda, think of the greater good. I bit my tongue.

It wasn't a very long meeting. Powers impressed his point upon me and Maple, and we left.

As we walked down the icy marble steps of City Hall, Maple pulled up his collar, wrapped his Burberry overcoat around him and said, "Commissioner, have I thanked you for this job lately?"

TURNAROUND

Chapter 1

My mother couldn't find me.

I was only a year and a half old, barely a toddler, and there were a very limited number of places I could be. My parents and I lived in a small basement apartment in Cambridge, Massachusetts, it was the dead of winter, and she and I had been playing in the yard out back. She went inside for only a moment. When she came out I was gone. My mother was just starting to panic when she heard cars honking. For a second, she paid no attention; her son was missing, that's all that mattered. I had been born with a collapsed lung and had been given last rites at the hospital when I was two days old. I had survived, and my mother never wanted to risk losing me again. When the honking grew as frantic as she was, she ran up the alley and out onto the street.

There I was, in my snowsuit and cap, standing a foot and a half tall in the middle of Massachusetts Avenue, directing traffic. Cars were stopped. There was a crowd around me. She ran across four lanes and swept me up in her arms.

I don't remember any of this, but family lore has it that that's when they knew I wanted to be a police officer.

My father, Bill, and my mother, June, had been high school sweethearts in the Charlestown projects in Boston. They were married when my father got out of the service after World War II, and I was born on October 6, 1947. My father was Big Bill; I was always Little Billy. He worked as a long-shoreman on the Boston docks. Two years after I was born, he used bene-fits he had coming to him through the G.I. Bill and, with my mother's father, Joe DeViller, bought what was called a three-decker house at 62 Hecla Street in the Dorchester section of Boston.

Three-deckers were a Boston housing phenomenon—entire neighbor-hoods were made up of them. They were three-story, wood-frame houses, with each story a five-and-a-half-room floor-through apartment, the equivalent of what in New York are called railroad flats. They were inex-pensive and functional.

Dorchester was a working-class neighborhood. We didn't think of our-selves as poor, but no one in the neighborhood had a lot of money. My mother, father, my younger sister Pat, and I lived on the second floor. If we wanted hot water, we had to heat it in pans. For years, my mother cooked on a four-legged cast-iron stove, one of those old black monstrosities that today are retro and all the rage but back then were just old-fashioned. I was already a teenager the day they hauled that huge, smelly thing out and put in a hot-water tank and a real gas stove. We didn't get hot run-ning water in our home until the early sixties, and that was a big day for the Brattons.

The house was heated by coal. Once a year, a truck backed up to the side of the building and tilted five tons of it into the chute. At five o'clock every morning, my father had to go down to the basement and temper the flames in the furnace to get it going for the day. He did the same thing as soon as he came home at night and then again at eleven o'clock before he went to bed. It was quite an art just staying warm.

Wednesday was ash day, when the city came to pick up the ashes that a week of coal had produced. This was different from Ash Wednesday, when Catholics would ponder their mortality. This was Wednesday ash day, when a cloud of soot rose all over the neighborhood. An old truck with wooden slats on the side showed up, and a city employee, the ash man, shoveled us out. That was a job.

Coal ceased being the municipal heating fuel of choice in the 1950s, and at some point its use had dwindled to the point where the city wouldn't pick up ashes anymore; there wasn't enough work to support the ash men. But we had the coal furnace well into the 1960s, and for about ten years the men of the three families in our building—my father, my grandfather, and Mr. McNulty, who lived on the first floor—began spreading the ashes under the back porch. After a couple of years, the whole underside of the porch was packed in solid. We lived near the corner with an empty lot on one side and an alley on the other, and when we filled up our porch, we arranged with other houses on the alley to take them. We shoveled our own soot for a decade.

For extra heat we had a kerosene stove. It was a fire hazard, but it was necessary. Everybody had one, and throughout the neighborhood everybody's back hall smelled of kerosene because when you poured it from the can to the heater, the fuel would spill over and seep into the linoleum.

When you entered our apartment, you came into a hallway that ran the length of the creaky wood house. First door on the right was the bathroom with an old cast-iron claw-foot tub and pull-chain toilet with a wooden seat. Diagonally across from that was my room. It had two entrances: a door from the hall on one side but only a curtain between me and the kitchen. I never understood that.

Everything revolved around the kitchen with its cast-iron stove and black stone sink with the big brass fittings. The washing machine was in there as well, with a wooden hand-operated wringer and the revolving tub that shook wildly and made a thumping racket as it spun. My grandparents lived upstairs, and every morning my grandmother Ann would come down and hang out in the kitchen with my mother. They'd have coffee or tea, and the next-door neighbor, Dot Gorham, would come over and sit. Dinner, supper, all the important moments of the day happened there.

If you went left down the hall, my sister Pat's room was on the right. She is a year younger than I am. From there, you had to pass directly through my parents' bedroom to get to the living room at the front of the house. The living room had three windows facing out on the street; it was the perfect place to keep an eye on what was going on in the neighborhood. That was where I waited for my father.

From the time I can remember, my father worked a couple of blocks from home at a chrome-plating firm on Freeport Street. He would be out the door first thing in the morning for the eight o'clock shift and every afternoon at five past four I would look out that window, see my father walking up the block, and go running out to meet him.

I didn't have much time with my dad. In 1951, he got a full-time job as a mail sorter at the post office and from then on worked two jobs for the rest of his life. This was a much-coveted civil-service position, the kind a working-class family counted on for security, but it also meant I didn't see him a lot. My dad came home for supper, which we ate at four-thirty in the afternoon, and then either went off to work the six-to-two shift at the post office or went to bed so he could wake up at eleven-thirty and head over there at midnight. From the post office, he went directly to the plating plant.

Money was always tight. I don't think my parents to this day have a checking account. My father brought home his pay in cash and gave it to my mother, and she gave him some money back. They worked out of envelopes. My father kept his in the top bureau of their five-drawer dresser; my mother kept hers in the lower. There was an envelope for the egg man, who delivered every week and came up the back stairs on Friday nights to collect. An envelope for the milkman, who came every day. We had accounts at some of the local stores at the Field's Corner shopping area about a half-mile from the house, and a dollar or two a week went into those envelopes.

Like a lot of people in the neighborhood, my parents played the numbers each week, and once in a long while my father's number hit and he came home with three or six hundred extra dollars in his pocket. He was making forty or fifty dollars a week at the time, so you can imagine what that was like. The only reason the old *Boston Record-American* sold every day was that people all over the city needed it to find out the winning number.

Our neighborhood didn't have a large department store, we had Mr. Brown, who came and sold clothes on Saturday mornings. His appeal was that you could pay him just two dollars a week on account.

Sometimes on Fridays after work, if he had a little extra money, my dad and I would drive to a lounge/restaurant over on Upham's Corner called Haley and McGuire's and order a pizza to bring back home. We would wait in the little lounge and I would have a Coke, and my dad would get a beer. I think my father enjoyed going to Haley and McGuire's. That fifteen minutes was almost like a little night out. My dad didn't eat pizza, he was a meat-and-potatoes man; pizza was a treat for me and my mom and sister, so he would get some French fries for his dinner. Of course, I had to have some, and from then on I was addicted to French fries with my pizza.

One night as we were leaving, I saw my father put fifteen cents on the bar. I took it. "Dad," I said, "you left this money on the counter."

"No, no, no, son," he told me. "That's a tip." Three slices of pizza were sixty cents, the fries were probably twenty, with the beer and Coke, the bill probably came to a dollar five. "For the waitress." He put it back. I had never heard of such a thing.

Sunday was the one day my father had off, and Sunday dinner was the best meal of the week. It was usually turnips and mashed potatoes and meat. (Meat in the Bratton household was done when there was no longer a hint of red in it. I had gray corned beef until I left home.) I ate the leftovers in sandwiches at school until Thursday. Albert du Plain's bakery nearby made bread for restaurants, and on Sundays my mom would send me there on my bicycle for a loaf of French bread, which was a real treat.

After dinner, we would take a drive. We would all pile in my father's car and head off for four or five hours. It was an inexpensive way to spend the day together.

We always had an old car. The first one I remember was a 1951 two-toned Ford—black bottom, white roof, standard shift. I loved that car. My dad ran that Ford until the floorboards rotted out. In 1958, we got a silver '56 Chevy Impala with a white roof. We called it the Silver Bullet. My father would drive me, my mother, and my sister all over New England—down the Cape, up to New Hampshire. Fifteen miles outside of Boston was very rural, so driving the Silver Bullet to the suburb of Canton was like going out into the country. That was a big thrill. A lot of kids in my neighborhood never got to do that.

We always made it home in time to watch Walter Cronkite on *The Twentieth Century.* For Sunday supper, my mom took the mashed potatoes and turnips from dinner and made potato patties and sometimes fried up some baloney with it. At eight, we watched *The Ed Sullivan Show,* and then it was off to bed.

But no matter what the financial situation, every week my mother put away a dollar for vacation. And every summer we had fifty-two dollars, enough to take a cottage at the beach or go to a lake for a week.

We were a family that loved each other, but we were not outwardly emotional. There was no hugging or kissing. It was just something we didn't do. I don't think I've ever seen my father hug or hold my mother, apart from when they're dancing, but these are two people who are very much in love. Some people are great backslappers, quick with an embrace, a peck on the cheek, or a pat on the butt. I didn't grow up with that.

Dorchester was a lace-curtain Irish neighborhood, but not first-generation right off the boat. Besides the Brattons (we were Scottish and Irish and French-Canadian) you had Walshes and Quinns and McNultys and Devines. When I was growing up, there were still gas lamps in the street, and once in a while a city worker would come down the block with a ladder, climb up, and fiddle with the gas fixtures. Eventually, we got electric streetlights. The rag man was around with his horse-drawn drays, and the fruit vendor with his pushcart, and Charlie the ice-cream man in the Good Humor truck with no top on the cab.

We lived one house off the corner of Hecla and Adams streets, two blocks from the Edward Southworth School, where I went from kindergarten through third grade. Edward Southworth was a twelve-room brick-and-granite public school built at the turn of the century. It looked and felt like a fortress and was located on Meeting House Hill, one of the highest points in the city, which George Washington occupied when Revolutionary troops drove the English out of Boston.

I always did well in school, never had to work very hard, and was kind of a teacher's pet. Whenever a note had to be run over to the Mather School next door, I was the one chosen to run it. When it came time to clap the erasers—don't ask me why we thought that was such a great honor, you'd just get chalk dust all over yourself; maybe it was because you got out of class for a couple of minutes—I got the job.

I moved across the courtyard to the Mather School, a much larger building constructed in the 1930s, for grades four through six. The separation of church and state wasn't very wide in those days, and one of my strongest memories is that every Tuesday afternoon at one o'clock, every student was marched out of Mather for two hours of religious instruction. The very few Protestants went right next door to the Universal Church of God in Christ. Almost all the rest of the school went to catechism class at Saint Peter's Church and School down the block. (I don't know if we had any Jews at Mather.) We lined up two by two, flanked by the school traffic monitors and the school crossing guards and the nuns in habits, the whole bit, and off we marched.

Saint Peter's was a gorgeous old church with a high spire and a beautiful interior. It would have been inspiring if I hadn't wanted to get out so bad. I went to church there on Sundays and then had to hang around afterward for Sunday school. I got a good education and a good moral grounding, but I could not wait for eighth grade to come so I could be confirmed and not have to go to Sunday school anymore.

One afternoon when I was about eight years old, a half dozen of us were out playing ball in front of the Edward Southworth School when we caught the attention of a local gang called the Parksmen. Local kids, twelve-year-olds, they were the big neighborhood bullies, and they used to fight with another gang called the Red Raiders all the time. We'd been playing ball, and the Parksmen broke up the game and took us hostage. They put us on the front steps of the school and wouldn't let us go. They were much bigger than we were, so there was no chance of us fighting our way out. We were stuck. It started getting late.

Four-thirty came and went, and they wouldn't let us go. Finally, they let their guard down and I ran home.

"Where were you?" my father demanded. He and my mother weren't particularly worried about my safety—kids hung out in the streets all the time. What had him riled was that it was five o'clock and I had missed supper. There were rules—the family eats together was one of them—and I had broken one.

"The Parksmen held us hostage," I panted. "They wouldn't let us go. They've still got some of the kids."

My father hopped up from the table, grabbed my arm, and off we went. He stormed up the hill to Edward Southworth. "We'll see about this," he muttered. I had to run to keep up.

I thought my father was the toughest guy who ever lived. He was a little guy, five foot eight, thin, about 130 pounds, but, boy, you didn't want to see him mad.

My friends were still huddled on the stone steps. They looked very glad to see us. The Parksmen were slouching in front of them, smoking cigarettes, on guard duty, a bunch of tough twelve-year-old boys. My dad walked right through the pack. He never laid a hand on them, he just put the fear of God in those kids.

"Who the hell do you think you are?"

The Parksmen backed off immediately. First, they fanned out in a semicircle, but my father gave them a look that told them he'd rip their heads off. Then they bolted. Our guys were free. That gang never bothered us again.

I don't know if my father has ever had a fight in his life, but he was a scrapper as a kid. His mother died young, and he and his four brothers were split up among the relatives. Somewhere along the line, my father developed the confidence that he could handle whatever came along. You could tell in the way he carried himself. He never swaggered, but he didn't back down. In my parents' social circle, he was looked up to as the solid one, the good, hard-working, decent guy, the best at what he does, the rock, with a nice way about him. My sister and I were crazy about him.

One weekend afternoon, we were all up in the balcony of the Strand

Theater in Upham's Corner watching a movie. The Strand was a beautiful old ornate theater, and on those Sundays when we didn't take a family drive sometimes we went to the movies. Behind us, a bunch of older kids were acting up, talking and laughing during the show. Tough kids. My father asked them once, politely, please to be quiet. That worked for a minute, then they started up again.

My father stood up, gave them the look, and growled, *"If you don't shut up, I'm going to throw your ass the hell out of here!"* They shut up, of course. And there was something about the toughness of that expression that stayed with me.

Once in a while, Pat and I would get it, too. We fought all the time, over everything, it didn't matter what. Coop two kids in a car on a Sunday afternoon drive and sometimes we got out of hand. Finally, he would have enough. He'd pull over, slam on the emergency brake, throw his right elbow over the front seat, and shout. *"Goddamn kids, knock it off!"*

The hand would go up, but he never hit us. It was just a threat. His anger would flare up and then be gone.

My mother, who spent more time with us, was the real enforcer. When Pat and I would go crazy, she'd come after us with a belt. Today, we'd all probably be in family court, but then we got a quick whack and were banished to our rooms.

At the same time, I was very protective of my sister. When I was in my teens, Pat got into a fight with Gene Stanley, the kid next door. Gene was about my age. He was one of the neighborhood tough guys, and he pushed her down into a wet puddle of mud. It was a cold March day, and she came running up into the house all scared and screaming. I went storming down the stairs after him.

I didn't think of myself as a tough kid—in fact, I was Caspar Milquetoast. I don't think I've actually had a real fight in my life. But I went after him.

Gene Stanley was still out in the street. He certainly wasn't hiding from me.

I grabbed him by the shirt.

"If you ever do that to her again, I'll kill you!"

It was so unexpected, I think I scared the hell out of him and he surprised the hell out of me. He apologized immediately. He wasn't a bad guy.

What I enjoyed most was staying in the back room at home and making clay figurines. I built whole scenes out of clay. I began with Dr. Seuss;

I read his books, loved his characters, and re-created in modeling clay what he depicted on the page. I built a little world.

As I grew older, my figures and settings became more elaborate. I created replicas of entire Civil War battlefields with hundreds of figures, Union and Confederate, detailed down to the straps across their chests and the insignias on their hats. I read everything I could get my hands on about the Revolutionary and Civil wars. When the family visited Fort Ticonderoga, I came home and made a model of what I'd seen, complete with troops. I was fascinated with uniforms and armies. I saw the movie *The Fighting 69th,* starring James Cagney, on television and built an elaborate diorama, including trenches and four hundred soldiers, and refought World War I in clay miniature.

Our downstairs neighbors, the McNultys, had four kids. Two of them, Bobby and Franny, were my age. They were twins, and Franny was an albino with significantly limited vision. He always had his right arm crooked over his eyes to shade them from the sun. He had white hair, purple eyes, and thick, thick glasses. Because of his condition, Franny couldn't play sports, and because he was kind of an odd duckling, he didn't have a lot of friends. But I liked him, and we used to hang out a lot. When we got to be about eleven years old, Franny and I took Saturdays and went off to ride the trains and buses and explore the city. You could ride all day for a nickel. The McNultys had less money than we did, but Mrs. McNulty was so grateful that I would take Franny with me that she'd slip us both a quarter, and sometime during the day we'd buy Cokes and candy bars.

We'd start the day by walking down Adams Street to the train station at Field's Corner—Fieldsie, we called it—and look around inside the barn that housed the trackless trolleys. Then we'd board the train, get a little paper transfer, and we'd be off. I got out of my neighborhood and really came to learn the entire city.

The trains were old rattlers, olive green, with bare lightbulbs, porcelain strap handles, and a little cab on the right-hand side in front, where the operator sat. We could see him hunched over the control levers through the glass in his door. We watched these men for hours. Franny and I stood in the first car and looked out the glass front windows as we went through the tunnels. Franny always got sunburned because of his pale skin, so when we were riding in sunlight, we had to be careful.

We explored the whole city and the surrounding area for a nickel. Subways and trains and trolleys and buses, we rode them all. I was always fascinated by the old buses, which were much better than the new ones that were coming in. I'd jot down their numbers and keep track of the routes. It was big news when the old green trains were painted red or green or blue according to the lines they were on. When the first new cars came in—the Blue Birds, all sleek and modern but without the beat-up warmth and character of the originals—it felt as if a whole world was ending, as if good friends were moving away.

We'd ride till the end of the line and then get off and roam through the bus yards, go into the barns. A couple of times, the attendants showed us around. That was a thrill.

Over time, new kids began moving into Dorchester. We all hung on the corner, which was right up the block from my house. Every couple of years, a new generation of kids claimed that corner, and sooner or later it was our turn.

As the sixties began, there were two distinct social types in teenage Boston, the collegiates and the rats. The collegiates wore madras shirts and khakis and loafers with no socks; that was the look. That was *colleeege*. The rats wore leather jackets with buckles and chains and combed their hair in ducktails. Most of our corner was in between. We were twelve or thirteen years old, and we were so benign there was no phrase for us. Nerds hadn't been invented yet, but that's what we were.

We hung on the corner and had weeklong Monopoly games. We built scooters out of roller-skate wheels and milk boxes and two-by-fours. We didn't drink, we didn't disturb anybody, we didn't act up, we'd just be there hour after hour until eleven or twelve o'clock at night. The cops never once asked us to leave.

Our group on the corner was pretty much a democracy, but I did like to be in control. I was always trying to rise above the pack, especially in wartime. There were three or four wooded areas within a couple of blocks of our corner where kids could just go off and disappear; we were in central Boston, but as far as we were concerned we were on Iwo Jima. These Dorchester jungles were perfect for the kind of World War II fighting we saw in the movies on TV, and we saw a lot of combat. I was Captain Billy—or "Captain Billy Bones," as my sister called me because I was so skinny—and I was always in charge.

One Christmas, Franny and Bobby McNulty showed up with new ordnance. We all had new toys, but Franny and Bobby came out with a very realistic .50-caliber machine gun with dual handles and a tripod. We all took turns shooting off a few rounds. When you triggered it, the batteries made the gun go *rat-a-tat-tat,* and the muzzle flashed with red-and-white firepower. It was only plastic, but this cool new weaponry had the flat green color of Army materiel, and it looked to us like the real thing.

Of course, we had to take it to the "jungle" and put it to good use. For weeks, and then months afterward, we staged battlefield sieges, and it seemed like I was always the guy manning the machine gun, getting attacked by nine or ten kids and mowing them all down.

If we weren't on the corner of Hecla and Adams, we were down the other end of Hecla on Dorchester Avenue, near the plating shop where my father worked. It was a little seedier, a little poorer, a little more adventuresome. It seemed like a mile from one end of Hecla to the other, but in fact it was only a few hundred feet; the distance was cultural. There was a barroom on the corner of Dorchester, and a First National variety store, Johnny's butcher shop, a gas station, and Murray's drug store. Some old Irish guy actually tried to set up a restaurant for a while. That lasted about six months; nobody in that part of town had any money to eat out with.

If you walked the other way and took a left down Adams, the world was very different. That was on the way to Field's Corner, the commercial center of the neighborhood. The barbershop where I got my hair cut was at Fieldsie, as was the Peerless Market. Meyer's Delicatessen held a special place in my heart. I was a finicky eater and refused to eat Wonder Bread or Tip-Top or any white bread at all. Meyer's sold bulkie rolls, my favorite. Crusty on the outside, fluffy in the middle, I had my Sunday dinner leftovers on a bulkie roll for lunch almost every day at school, except for Fridays. Back then, Catholics couldn't eat meat on Fridays, so my lunch would consist of Saltines with jam. I think some of the kids thought we were so poor we couldn't afford sandwiches, but I just would not eat white bread.

At the corner of Arcadia Street was a beautiful red brick structure dating back to the turn of the century that held both Boston Police District 11 and a branch of the Boston Public Library. I knew my way to the library like a homing pigeon.

I could get lost in books for hours. I found a series of seven or eight Civil War novels designed for kids, no pictures, and I whipped through them. I was only sorry that there weren't more. When I was about eleven years old, I found one of the most influential books in my life on the shelf.

It was called *Your Police,* and it was a child's history of the New York Police Department. I couldn't read it often enough. It was a picture book, published in 1956, with photographs of the NYPD motorcycles, police cars, emergency trucks, helicopters, the equipment a police officer carried, the phone boxes, all the details and minutiae that you could want to know about a police department, everything I'd put onto my figurines. I was completely fascinated. I took that book out of the library regularly for years. Sometimes I would just go there and read it over and over.

I always wanted to be a police officer. I didn't know any police officers, no one in the family was a police officer—I just always wanted to be one. The influences were mostly from television and the movies, *Badge 714* and *Dragnet.* I watched *Dragnet* on TV every week, and when the movie came out, I saw it with my dad. I still remember the opening: A guy gets killed with a shotgun, and the detectives come to the scene to check the body out. Those shows and *Your Police* captured my imagination.

It also helped that the library shared the building with Police District 11. Sometimes I went outside, stood on the corner, and watched the cops file out for four o'clock roll call.

The officers marched out of the station two by two and piled into open-back blue paddy wagons to be delivered to their walking posts. The wagons had no rear doors, and you could see all these uniformed cops packed inside. The few police cars were all two-toned, gray top and blue bottom. The cops had gray shirts. I sat there and watched as they drove away.

But as often as I watched this daily parade, I never got up the nerve to walk inside. Some curious kids wander into firehouses; I think I was too much in awe to do anything but look.

Finally, I got my chance.

I don't know why my father had to go to the police station—maybe he needed a report for insurance or a claim number—but when he asked if I wanted to come with him I jumped.

We were going in.

My father ambled to the big desk on the left-hand side of the room. "What do you want?" the cop behind it asked. My father told him, and I just stood there and gaped. One of the cops must have noticed my fascination.

"You ever been in here before?" He was looking down at me from some height.

"No, sir."

"Like to take a look around?"

"Yes, sir!"

He took me downstairs to the basement, to the cell block. Iron bars, cold cement floors, the whole place painted flat gray, the clanging of everything in the room—I was in another world. There were no prisoners down there that day, but the place had its own particular odor.

It smelled of urine.

Cell blocks all smell that way. The waste sits there until someone comes to flush it down. The place smelled of unwashed human funk, deep, unavoidable, foul. It's one of those smells that stays with you. A cop can walk in blindfolded and know, yup, I'm in a cell block.

"You got to stay out of trouble," the uniformed officer told me, "or this is where we'll put you." He didn't seem to be joking.

Then, he took me upstairs to the detective room. I remember cigars and big hats. Detectives in those days were known as the Big Hats because they all wore fedoras. The building had been built in 1890, and seventy years of stale smoke had built up in the room—you felt it in your chest when you came in. The walls were green and peeling. Four men were lounging behind old oak desks. Irish faces. I couldn't place it, but there was something unfriendly about these guys. They didn't react to a kid, and they didn't interact with the uniformed cop. We were out of there pretty quickly.

After my father's business was finished, we walked home. I was thrilled that I had gotten inside. The only exposure we had to police, the only time they arrived at the house, was every few years when they came around to take the census. In Boston in the fifties, hundreds of cops were assigned to go door to door and fill out census cards. Sometimes, they'd show up to verify and validate voter registration.

There just wasn't any crime to speak of in our neighborhood. Maybe now and again something was broken into or vandalized, but I don't remember anyone's car ever being stolen, and my group of kids certainly wasn't the kind to give them any trouble.

When we got to an age where we had begun to earn some money doing odd jobs or were being given our first small allowances, the kids on the corner started playing cards and gambling—seven-card draw and five-card stud poker with our pennies and nickels and dimes, all the time and into the night. Once, we had a card game going, and from working and my allowance and my winnings I amassed the considerable sum of one dollar and sixty cents. My sister's friend Ann Marie Anderson had a penny. She was a tall blonde girl, kind of gangly, and she sat in with a bunch of us. I was going to win that penny.

She won the first pot, and now she had a nickel. She won the next one.

And the next. I got in deeper and deeper. Eventually, she won my entire buck-sixty. Taught me a lesson. I lost everything trying to win a penny.

I remember sitting under the new electric light pole on another evening, four or five of us in the game, and I thought I had been treated unfairly, cheated. I stood up and started swearing a blue streak. It was the thing to do at the time, to use rough language, and I was just getting good at it.

Our apartment was on the second floor, and it looked directly over the corner. It was springtime and my mother was sitting by the window, taking in the breeze, looking out at the night. Next thing I knew, she came charging down the stairs, grabbed me by the ear and dragged me into the house.

"I don't ever want to hear you use that language again!" she yelled at me. My friends were all watching. She gave me a few whacks and kicked me upstairs. That nipped it in the bud. I would use certain words for emphasis, but I seldom truly swore from that time on.

While I could be completely happy sitting in my room and reading, I definitely liked getting attention. I was in my glory in sixth grade when they made me school crossing guard and gave me a white strap to wear across my chest (I always kept it spotless) and a shiny silver badge. My post was the corner of East Street and Adams, and I would stand there with my book bag and my metal lunch box—Hopalong Cassidy, Wild Bill Hickok, Zorro, Davy Crockett, whoever was the latest craze—and I would stop traffic and cross the kids from one side of the street to the other. Everybody stayed between the white lines while I was on duty. Maybe I took it a little too seriously; a gang of girls used to chase me home at the end of the day.

That year, I really started to shine. If there was a center stage, I sought it. When I brought my clay figures into school and talked about my hobbies, the teacher was so impressed she sent me to see the principal, who assigned me to be master of ceremonies for our celebration of Flag Day. I stood in the auditorium in front of the whole school in my Boy Scout shirt (we didn't have enough money to buy the pants) and my good school trousers, which always seemed to be too short. I graduated with honors and passed the exams to get into the most prestigious public school in the city, Boston Latin.

The best part of Boston Latin was getting there. I walked up Meeting House Hill and then down to Kane Square, and every day I passed the same police officer at the same crossing. His car was always parked in ex-

actly the same spot and was one of the first I'd seen with the new-style rotating gumball-machine light, so that fascinated me. Every morning, this
red-faced Irish cop with a cigar in his mouth had the police radio running
through his loudspeaker so he could hear his calls while he was on his
post. I'd hear the crackle as I crossed the street. I never talked to him.

Kane Square was a turnaround for the trackless trolley. I got on and
rode through Upham's Corner and into Roxbury, the all-black neighborhood of Boston, to Dudley Street station, a big hub of trolleys, trains, and
buses. At Dudley Street, I fought a thousand other kids to get onto rickety
old Mack buses, the oldest and most dilapidated in the fleet. Those buses
were already riding on their rims and were serving their final days jam-
packed, creaking, and chugging up and down hills, shuttling schoolkids to
Boston Latin and to English High School. English was for rough-and-
tumble types, dead-end kids; Boston Latin was for us smart guys, and
those rides were filled with hard rivalries.

You had to study hard at Boston Latin. I was used to getting good
grades and not putting in much effort, but that didn't work here. I did okay
in most classes, but I found I had absolutely no proficiency with foreign
languages, particularly Latin, which was a requirement. I just could not
pick up the language, and in eighth grade I flunked out.

It was humiliating. I had been the boy wonder, off to conquer the world,
and now I was back at Grover Cleveland Junior High School with the rest
of the kids from the corner. The only saving grace was that Boston Latin
had been all boys but Grover Cleveland was coed. Having girls in class
was a big improvement.

Not that I was a great success with the girls. I spent one full school year
pining for Camille Grasso. Camille was a pretty girl who lived around the
corner, and I passed her house every day. I'd see her and never know what
to say. I never got up anywhere near the nerve to ask her out.

In ninth grade, I passed the exams and got into Boston Technical High
School. Boston Tech was so named because it was a multiple-career-path
school. You could graduate with technical engineering and shop skills, or
you could take an academic curriculum with machine shop and engineering on the side. I chose academics.

Boston Tech was in Roxbury, and this was my first significant exposure
to black people, or Negroes as we called them in those days. I had seen
blacks on my train expeditions with Franny McNulty and out the window
on the trolley to Boston Latin, but if a black person walked past our corner in Dorchester, all of us really took note. We didn't see black people

often because there were no black residents in the neighborhood and little-to-no work for outsiders.

Boston Tech was about 10 percent black, and while there were tensions and a growing awareness of race conflicts—this was 1962 to 1965, a volatile time in race relations—by and large we all got along pretty well.

Race was never really an issue for me. While I was not one of the white kids who hung out with a black crowd, I had enough black friends to the point that it didn't make a difference. A lot of the people I grew up with didn't have the opportunity to interact with blacks, which sometimes led to unfortunate generalizations and misunderstandings. I didn't think of it at the time, but going to high school in the middle of Roxbury turned out to be a positive influence.

On occasion, I walked home from school, about a mile total. It was a distressed area, and I did feel uncomfortable—even in those days Roxbury was a high-crime neighborhood—but I never had an incident. Mostly, I looked forward to passing the Drake's Devil Dog factory and smelling the sweet little chocolate cakes. From there I'd pass the famous Kasonoff Bakery and breathe in the rye bread. It was a tantalizing walk home.

We were Catholics, but not very observant, my father more involved in religion than my mother. I had a brother who died shortly after birth, and although they never discussed it with me, I always had the feeling his death might have distanced them from the church. We went to church for the holidays, but other than that my mother almost never went, except for weddings. At the post office where my father worked, there was a chapel where a fifteen-minute quickie service was performed each Sunday without a sermon, so he tried to get there. After I made my first communion and got confirmed, my parents left the decision whether to continue to go to Sunday school up to me. I had no interest, and I stopped going.

So one day here comes Father Carney up the front stairs.

Father Carney was a young priest, kind of a Bing Crosby type, popular with the kids, the sort who was put in charge of the Little League. I answered the door when he knocked. I hadn't seen him in a while.

"Hello, Billy. I'd like to see your father."

My dad was in the living room, reading. He didn't invite Carney in; he left the good father standing in the hall. Not to invite a priest into your home was unusual in our neighborhood. If we went to Mass, we'd hear buzzing in the pews about that one.

"You son's not been attending our Sunday school courses," Father Carney told him.

"Well, Father," said my dad, "I told him once he got confirmed that it would be his choice to go or not, and I guess he's made it."

"You know, it's your obligation as a Catholic father to make sure your son is all right in the eyes of the Lord. Our courses . . ."

"There's nothing wrong with my son."

They went at it pretty good. My father had made a commitment to me, I was old enough to make my own decisions, and no matter how the priest invoked the Lord and Scriptures, my dad was never one to bend to unreasonable authority. Father Carney never got his foot in our door, and I never set foot in Sunday school again.

Very early one hot and quiet summer Sunday morning when I was about fifteen, my father took me out in the car to teach me to drive. I didn't have a learner's permit, so I guess he was at some risk on his insurance, but he put me behind the wheel and off we went. There was not much traffic in Dorchester on Sundays.

We drove by the corner of Morrissey Boulevard and Freeport Street with the windows rolled down, and there was a cop at a call box, swearing a blue streak. Every other word out of his mouth was f-ing this and f-ing that, so routinely. It rubbed me the wrong way. For some reason, that stuck with me.

After I got my learner's permit, my father and I routinely spent Sunday mornings driving around Codman Square, a business district of Dorchester. One morning, we stopped behind a cop car at a red light. We were the only two cars at the intersection. The light turned green, and the two cops were busy shooting the breeze. They weren't moving. We waited.

"Toot the horn," my dad said finally.

"What?"

"Toot the horn, get 'em going."

So I tooted the horn.

Cops being cops, they pulled out, let us pass, and then pulled us over. Both officers got out of the cruiser and sauntered toward us.

"You honk your horn?"

"The light changed, you weren't moving." My father was immediately on his high horse. "Yeah, we honked at you. How'm I supposed to let you know that it turned green?" They straightaway got into a pissing contest.

I was sweating there with just a learner's permit, fearing that any confrontation would end my driving career. One officer was leaning at the window, an arm cocked on the roof, the other at his gun belt, talking over me to my father on the passenger side. My father never let up. I just kept both hands on the wheel and my eyes on my dad.

Fortunately, it was toward the end of the morning. If they'd met up with us in mid-tour, they probably would have busted my father's chops a little, but these guys had been riding around for eight hours and all they were interested in was getting home. My father couldn't have known that. He was interested in not getting pushed around.

Chapter 2

But that run-in didn't make much difference. When I graduated from Boston Tech in 1965, I knew I wanted to be a cop. I was eighteen years old. The City of Boston wouldn't hire police officers under the age of twenty-one. How was I going to get through these years?

I had a part-time job stocking shelves at the Finast Market, but I lost it and then dropped out of Boston State College after the first semester because I couldn't afford to continue. The tuition wasn't high, but I was living at home, and I needed to earn a living. That winter, my uncle, Peter Boyle, helped get me an interview at the phone company, which was a fairly good-paying company. I got the job. It was steady, very secure, the kind of job a blue-collar guy searched for, the private-sector equivalent of the civil service.

The first couple of months, I worked in the money room counting coins, which was awful work, but after a while they put me on the road. They gave me a little Ford station wagon to drive around in, and off I went, picking up the coin boxes from pay phones. We never had a robbery; who was going to lug around a couple of thousand pounds of stolen dimes and nickels? But after a while, I was assigned "specials." I'd go out and handle jammed or overloaded boxes, and in certain rougher neighborhoods of the city the company didn't want to leave the car unattended, so they hired traffic cops, on duty, with the white hats and gloves. I had a police escort, a cop in the backseat eight hours of the day. I thought that was great.

It was a soft detail for the cops, and mostly they would sit back there and read the newspaper. I wanted to be a cop, and here was a real live one in the backseat. I'd try to strike up a conversation.

"Jeez, I want to be a cop someday."

"Oh, yeah, kid, that's good." They would go back to reading their newspapers. All they were interested in, basically, was the overtime.

Late that summer, I was promoted into the central office as an installer/repairman. I was on night shift from five to midnight with two or three old-timers, and in the daytime I got a job working with my father in a plating shop in Roxbury Crossing.

Holding down two jobs, putting in sixteen hours a day, I began to understand how hard my dad had worked all his life. Plating was tough— dirty, grungy, straight labor. With all the acids and fumes, it wasn't the greatest of working conditions, and there was no workplace regulation. There was no OSHA in those days. Still, I liked working with my father. We didn't work side by side, but we had lunch every day in a little cafeteria-style neighborhood restaurant, which was as much concentrated time as I had spent with him in my entire life. I really enjoyed and appreciated just how hardworking, how straightforward, how good a man he was.

One of the few side benefits of working at the plating shop was that every so often cops at the adjacent Roxbury Crossing station house came in to get their badges shined—on the arm, of course. I talked with them every chance I got.

I had no social life, but I was happy to have two paychecks. I put some into savings and gave some to my folks.

Toward the fall of 1966, I decided to enlist in the army. The Vietnam War was heating up, and guys my age had two options: get drafted and serve two years in the service of the government's choosing or enlist in the regular army for three years and pick your own spot. The way I looked at it, this would be a good way to spend my time until I could take the civil-service exam to become a cop. More important, I could pick the military police. If I couldn't be a Boston cop, I could spend three years working on something that would be enjoyable and might also prepare me for becoming a police officer.

I had seen MPs around Boston. There were several military bases in the area, and along with large influxes of sailors on the weekends I saw the shore patrol in the streets alongside the city cops. They were strong and efficient and looked good in their uniforms. I went up to the army recruiting station at Codman Square and signed up.

I was to be sworn in on November 30, 1966.

My mother wouldn't see me off. She was crying. My father drove me to the old Boston Army Base in South Boston, where I was going to get shipped down to Fort Dix, New Jersey, for basic training. It was the only time I had ever seen a tear in his eye. We sat in the car, and he gave me a firm handshake. "Good luck, Bill. We're going to miss you." I got out, and he drove off.

I was processed, and then about five-thirty in the afternoon a caravan of Greyhound buses full of recruits headed south. Other than vacations in New Hampshire, a trip to Canada, and a visit to New York City with my parents, I had never been out of the Boston area.

We arrived at Fort Dix about one in the morning. They marched us over to a beat-up two-story wood barracks with ladders on both sides for fire escapes, just like I'd seen in World War II movies, and issued us our gear for the night. It was cold, and when I went to use the facilities, I found twelve toilet bowls fanned out in a circle—no separation, no privacy whatsoever—and a dozen guys sitting around looking at each other. I have always been a very private person, and I was aghast.

Then, they lined us up and marched us into the mess hall for a meal. Liver, lima beans, and mashed potatoes. This mess had probably been sitting on the steam tables since they fed the troops at five that afternoon. I was a persnickety eater to begin with. I had stayed clear of a lot of foods, and liver was one of them. Lima beans? Forget it. Thus began my army career.

For the next few days, we went through indoctrination, got our uniforms, filled out papers, received shots, took placement tests. After the aptitude exam, I was called into the sergeant's office. I stood at attention, and the sergeant said, "Bratton, looking at your test here, it appears that you would make a pretty good candidate for Officer Candidate School. We can sign you up. In fact, we would like to sign you up right now." He told me that upon finishing basic training, I would be shipped off to OCS and would graduate from there as a second lieutenant.

"Sir. When I enlisted I was guaranteed that I would be assigned to the military police, sir. If I go to OCS, will I still be an MP?"

"No, soldier. You go to OCS and you can request a specialization, but the army cannot guarantee that your request will be answered in the affirmative. You might be needed in other areas." He wanted me to make a decision right there.

I liked the fact that I was being invited to move to the top of the pack. I always wanted to stand out, and a second lieutenant far outranked a private. I was only in the army three days, and already I was being singled out.

But I was hooked on the dream of being a military policeman and then a cop. That's all that was on my mind, and this promotion, while seemingly a step forward, would interrupt that ambition. I respectfully declined.

For some reason, my company was an equal mix of New Englanders and Mississippians. My squad in particular was very well mixed. Just deciphering the accents was a job and a half. My best friend turned out to be Bill Campbell, a black kid from Roxbury. I could at least understand his accent.

My first drill instructor, Sergeant Rush, was a big, black, Smokey the Bear–type guy with a gruff voice who was trying to grow us into soldiers. He was a decent guy underneath the shouting, and about a week into basic he appointed me squad leader, which got me a semiprivate room.

We had a private first class named Gomer. Gomer spoke with a heavy southern accent and had only recently been through basic himself. When the drill instructors went home at night, this was the character they left in charge of the place. Perhaps it was because I was Rush's guy, perhaps it was because he didn't like northerners; in any case, Gomer was all over me.

Some guys you know are trying to shape you up, others are trying to break you. Gomer went out of his way to make things tough on me. When we had hand-to-hand training with cudgels that look like giant Q-tips, I was the one he pulled out and pummeled. Every morning at reveille, we woke up, showered, and ran several miles carrying an M-14 rifle. I wasn't in good enough shape, not immediately. I kept lowering the rifle.

"Bratton, you little pansy." I had never heard drawling and shouting at the same time. "Get that rifle up!" Gomer loved to chase me down and chew me out. Because of his dislike for me, my entire squad was taking the brunt of his attacks.

Weekly barracks inspection was a major preoccupation in basic training. Each member of the squad had to operate as part of a unit, and we all had to pull together, otherwise we would all fail, and none of us would receive the Holy Grail of boot camp, a weekend pass. When we succeeded, we all had a great sense of accomplishment. Toward the end of basic training, we faced inspection by the post commander, and Gomer was even crazier. Before I'd arrived at the barracks that evening, he and Campbell had gotten into it, and for some time I had the sense that Gomer didn't really like blacks, either.

I came into the room and everybody was in T-shirts, slaving away getting the place ready. We had already been indoctrinated on the importance of shiny floors; that was a big deal in the army, floors so polished that you could see your reflection in them. (To this day, I like to see a shining floor.) We had a heavy metal buffing machine that we lugged around especially for this purpose. It was large and bulky and not easy to maneuver, but it got the job done. Gomer, just to ride Campbell, had told him to buff the ceiling. Then he had left.

We couldn't stand this guy. As respectful as I am of authority, when that authority is abusive or foolish, I will rebel.

I looked up. "He wants us to buff the ceiling? We'll buff the damn ceiling. Let him explain it to Rush."

Campbell and I climbed up and stood on the top of a double-decker bunk. The metal frame sagged and creaked but held us. It was a shame to put our boots all over a freshly made bed, but it had to be done. I leaned over. "Hand that thing up here." Three guys shouldered the buffer, which teetered as we tried to hoist it. Campbell and I grunted it to shoulder level, the bed shifting under the weight. Two guys on each side were spotting, another made sure the electric cord didn't get tangled. The rest of the squad was looking on, ready to help.

"What the hell are you doing?" Gomer had come back.

"You ordered us to buff the ceiling, we're buffing the ceiling. Those were your direct orders. You're insisting that things be done your way, here it is."

Gomer was flustered. A buffed ceiling was way out of bounds. There was no way he could justify it to his superiors, and he knew it. "You knew I didn't mean it!"

Hey, we had a direct order. If there was hell to pay for it from the drill instructors, well, we were ordered to do it, and it was Gomer's order.

Gomer went storming out of there. He didn't last much longer.

I finished basic training and got shipped off to Fort Gordon, Georgia, for MP school. The highlight of those two months was when my high school sweetheart from Boston, Linda Gowen, the first girl I ever dated, snuck down to visit me for a weekend in Augusta. If her parents had known, there would have been bloody murder.

There were four thousand MPs in training at Fort Gordon. We learned police tactics and techniques such as prisoner handling and handcuffing; we learned military codes and responsibility and protocol; we learned how to drive jeeps. We practiced enforcing military law.

The whole idea of the military police was spit and polish. At five o'clock reveille, we all put on our uniforms and gathered to salute the flag. The uniforms were pressed so heavy with starch, you had to peel the pants apart and put your foot in slowly to separate the legs. I loved that sound and feeling as I slid in and the fabric came open. MPs bloused their pants at the boot, put on a shirt, pistol, belt and shiny helmet liner, and then walked around like robots, not bending knees or arms until after inspection so nothing got wrinkled. Those outfits were hot. This was in Georgia in ninety-five-degree heat (or hotter), and there were easily 1,200 of us running around the quadrangle chanting and singing in cadence. I loved the parades and formations, the pomp and circumstance.

I did well in all areas of training except sidearms: I could not shoot a .45 pistol. I had trouble disassembling it, and once it was apart I had the damnedest time putting the thing back together again. Of course, a sidearm is vital for an MP, and this was something you had to do in order to graduate. There was a course and a final exam that I failed the first time, miserably. I was a bad mechanic and a lousy shot. I took the course over and flunked it again. I walked through it a third time. Failed. They were going to wash me out.

The week before graduation, I asked to speak to the range instructor, and I pleaded my case.

"Gee, Sarge," I said, "more than anything I want to be a military policeman. I signed up for an extra year to do it. I turned down OCS." If I wasn't an MP, I still had two and a half more years in the army, and they could put me anywhere. I didn't even want to think about that. "Can you do something for me?"

"Okay, come on, one more time," he said. "This is your fourth time through. Normally, we don't do more than two."

I finally managed to fumble my way through.

I had usually been able to sneak by on native ability, but here I'd almost lost something very important to me. From then on, I put in the effort on everything. Even though I'd passed, I went back and worked on that weapon until I could disassemble and assemble it blindfolded. I developed my marksmanship until it was acceptable.

I worked for eight weeks and then got my assignment. I had visions of putting on my spiffy uniform with the white hat and MP armband and cross straps and providing military escorts in Europe or patrolling the streets of Saigon.

My entire one-hundred-man company got assigned to the 212th Sentry Dog Company, Eighteenth Military Police Brigade. It turned out that someone, somewhere in the annals of U.S. Army history, decided that handling sentry canines was a military-police function. K-9 Corps. For the next two and a half years, I was going to be walking a dog.

This was not my idea of military policing. I tried everything I could think of to get out of it, but I didn't have a hook. I was one in a million in the army, there was nothing I could do about it. I would gladly have traded with anyone else in the MPs, but there weren't too many people rushing to get into this line of work.

We trained for six weeks in Okinawa, where I met my dog, Duchess, a sixty-pound female German shepherd. Because we were going to be doing exclusively perimeter work, the dogs were trained to alert on motion and human scents. They were highly trained and highly skilled. They had one handler a year, and then they'd break in a new one. I learned how to handle Duchess and then, in May 1967, we got shipped out to Vietnam.

There was no air conditioning on the C-130 cargo plane we flew in on. There weren't any passenger seats, either. We all sat on canvas webbing along each wall of the fuselage and listened to the engines drone. This was one of those huge transport aircraft with the back door that lowers and it wasn't built for noise suppression. The dogs were cooped up in stainless steel crates, and they yelped nonstop.

It had just rained, and Tan Son Hut Air Force Base was thick and humid. As we stood on the tarmac, the country smelled moldy. Flatbed baggage carts were clattering to the outbound aircraft, pulling pallets of stainless steel coffins. Planes and helicopters were landing and taking off. The noise was phenomenal, and we were all sweating like crazy.

We took the dogs to the temporary kennels, where they were going to be housed for the few days before we got shipped to our final destination. The kennels were terrible, the dog runs were beat to hell. They were tough accommodations for the dogs. Then, my company climbed onto the back of some trucks and rode through the streets of Saigon to our compound. Our accommodations weren't much better than the dogs'.

Saigon was buzzing. I had never heard Vietnamese, and words in the street sounded very rat-a-tat-tat. Traffic was everywhere, nonstop and shrill. Our truck was surrounded by a convoy of Vespa scooters with little carriages attached at the rear to accommodate four passengers. They trailed in our wake like pilot fish. People all around us rode bicycles, and the taxicabs were these crazy little French cars that looked like something the Three Stooges would ride around in.

My senses were overloading, everything bombarding me at once. Saigon had a powerful and inescapable smell all its own. The heat lay on me like a wool coat I couldn't shed. There was no breeze. I didn't feel danger, just excitement and a very fast pace.

But more than anything, the basic overriding presence in Saigon was military. Military trucks and gun jeeps, American military police in fatigues, Vietnamese police with their white hats, soldiers carrying weapons in the street, all the official buildings sandbagged, bunkers. It was a wartime capital.

There were easily a thousand of us stationed in the compound, a grouping of Quonset huts and barracks ringed by barbed wire, sandbags, and gun towers, sitting right in the middle of a Saigon neighborhood. We were issued new clothing, jungle fatigues very different from the formal uniforms we'd had back in the States. We were issued helmets and bulletproof vests and received several days training on the new M-16 rifles that were just coming into use. I spent about four days getting acclimated and then received my orders to report to company headquarters at Long Binh.

In 1967, Long Binh was the largest military installation in Vietnam and growing. From the time I got there until I was transferred out in 1968, its military population grew to the tens of thousands and its size grew to twenty-five square miles. Long Binh was about thirty miles outside of Saigon and sat up on a plateau with a good view of the surrounding area, which is probably why the army chose the location. We were assigned to guard the ammunition dump.

It was the largest ammunition dump in the country, a mile on each side. Long Binh supplied all the bombs for the planes, all the napalm, all the military hardware, you name it; if it exploded, it was at Long Binh.

The ammunition was housed in gigantic berms designed to contain explosions, thirty feet high on three sides with an opening on the fourth. Roads led in and out from one berm to another, and trucks were constantly driving back and forth, restocking the hardware as the war demanded more inventory. The entire dump looked like a series of giant, lethal anthills. Our compound sat right across the road, but on three sides the Long Binh dump butted up against the jungle.

The ammunition dump was ringed by twenty-six equally spaced guard towers, each with searchlights and sixty-millimeter machine guns and teams of soldiers manning them. Vietnam is a beautiful country, but the army had knocked down every tree in sight. In daytime there was no shade—the whole area was a dust bowl. During the rainy season, the place turned into a swamp.

This was not a highly dangerous area. Military police and personnel were everywhere, and no guerrilla activity had been reported. There was a war going on, but that was someplace else. The town of Bien Hoa was a couple of miles down the road, and we ran around there without our weapons. A lot of guys had Vietnamese girlfriends and ended up spending most of their time in town. It was pretty easy duty.

Within the first few months, I achieved the rank of specialist four, was chosen soldier of the month, and drew the assignment to escort a lieutenant on a pay run as he delivered monthly pay to the 212th in a dozen locations around the country. I got a fine tour of Vietnam. We flew cargo planes and helicopters the length and breadth of the country, from the beaches of Cam Ranh Bay and Vung Tau up to the awe-inspiring mountains of the Central Highlands, then down to the Mekong Delta, south of Saigon. I fell in love with the beauty of the place.

I saw the Bob Hope Christmas show. Twenty-five years earlier, my father had seen Bob Hope entertain the troops during World War II, and I felt a good connection. But mostly my tour of duty was pretty boring.

Our job was to walk the dogs on the perimeter of the ammunition dump between the guard towers. Between the dump and the jungle tree line was about 150 yards of no-man's-land, completely flattened and covered with row upon row of concertina wire and trip lights. It looked like something out of World War I.

Each shift we lined up with our dogs, passed inspection, and were issued our ammunition. (We were supposedly in a war zone, but when we were not on guard duty all our ammunition was locked up.) The supply sergeant counted out seven clips of ammo, and when each tour was over, he counted them back in.

We patrolled three sides of the dump; there was so much activity on the side facing our compound that it didn't make sense to have the dogs there. Fifteen of us were assigned to the posts: Whisky, X-Ray, Yankee, each with five substations. The handler and his dog were dropped off at their post, relieving the sentry before him, and six hours later were themselves relieved. The guy who had the good job was the driver: All he had to do was tool around in the truck. That plum duty was rotated.

Patrolling the perimeter meant that we and our dogs walked back and forth for six hours along a lighted road with the jungle on one side and a drainage ditch on the other. Of course, we stopped by the towers and shot the breeze with the guys behind the guns. Every one of us had our own little AM radio with an earpiece, and, though we weren't supposed to, we tuned in to Armed Forces Radio just to pass the time. Once per shift, a truck came by with coffee and Kool-Aid.

One time, Duchess caught wind of something out at the perimeter. She stopped and alerted, and I got very nervous. I looked out there and . . . some crazy porcupine was just walking along the line.

Occasionally, a two-man perimeter jeep patrol rode by and lobbed a couple of grenades from an M-39 grenade launcher into the jungle just to try to catch whoever might be out there off guard. Sometimes, they shot off flares to light up the area, but nothing ever came of it.

Someone in charge decided we dog handlers should go out on patrol. Without any warning, one afternoon they led a group of us outside the post and into the woods. This was real foolishness. We weren't trained as infantry. The noncommissioned officer who was leading us had the same training we did. We were out there in the jungle—it wasn't very deep jungle, but it was jungle—toting our M-16s, twenty-five guys with animal training. We were moving along in a line without our dogs, but we didn't know what we were looking for.

We spent six hours wandering around in the woods. God forbid we ever encountered anything. We weren't trained as infantry. What were we going to do if we ran into some Vietcong, arrest them?

I had just finished the six-to-twelve shift at Whiskey Four one midnight in late January 1968. My replacement had hopped down with his dog. I had just heaved Duchess onto the back of the truck and been relieved when the world lit up. Mortar rounds screamed, rockets came tearing in from the jungle, and the ammunition dump started to blow. The noise was incredible, it shook inside you. Everything was bedlam. The machine guns in the guard towers opened up, men were hollering and firing. I looked behind me, and I could see Vietcong sappers coming through holes in the concertina wire.

My replacement and his dog jumped back on the truck, and we took off. We weren't dropping off dog handlers anymore, we were barreling sixty miles an hour down the pocked and dusty road, picking them up.

Berms were blowing up as we shot by them. The sky was orange. Night had become day. As each new handler pulled himself onboard, he started cursing; the explosions were so near that the metal truck was heating up, and guys burned their hands as they grabbed onto the sides. In the back, we had to muzzle the dogs so they wouldn't go after each other, everything was so crazed. They were jumping and howling; the bed of the truck was so hot the pads on their feet were frying.

We were being rocked by the explosions. Flying down the road, I thought I heard stones rattling around the floor of the truck, maybe debris from the berms that had blown hundreds of feet in the air. I looked down and saw three U.S. Army issue grenades rolling on the metal truck bed like giant pinballs. They must have come loose from someone's belt, and now they were careening against the sides of the truck. This wasn't the movies, no one fell on them.

We roared around the side of the ammunition dump and into the main post, unloaded the dogs into the kennels, and ran to our battle stations in the bunkers. We spent the rest of the night sitting there, locked and loaded, watching the dump blow up, listening to the mortars and machine guns. Gunships flew overhead and pounded gunfire wildly past the perimeter, out into the jungle.

The camp itself was not attacked, only the ammunition dump. We waited all night for an assault that never came.

I didn't feel fear, which was strange. The noise, the heat, the flash of the rockets exploding—there was certainly enough to be scared of. What I felt was excitement, exhilaration, a great rush of adrenaline. Afterward, when I had time to consider what might have happened to me, that was scary. Too much time to think will do that to you. While it was going on, I was simply doing what I was trained to do.

The kid at the post next to mine got killed. He was new to the company. I don't remember his name. I should, but I don't. I've always felt kind of guilty about that. Ours were the posts farthest from the compound and closest to the jungle. The Vietcong had concentrated their resources to get into the dump and do their damage. They had set their charges, trained their mortars, and overrun the Whiskey Three guard tower. I was one guy removed. That kid was the only dog handler we lost, at that time the only dog handler killed in Vietnam.

The next morning on Armed Forces Radio, we heard that the embassy in Saigon and bases up and down the country had also been attacked. It was Tet, the Vietnamese New Year, and the Vietcong had launched the Tet Offensive.

We were issued a lot more ammunition the next night when we went out one more time to patrol the perimeters. As we drove by on the way to our posts, I saw Whiskey Three all torn up, the wire down, the floodlights out. I was assigned to Yankee Two, and this was a very different experience from the stroll with my dog I had been taking each night for months. We expected to be attacked.

Nothing came of it. We spent several weeks on heightened alert, but we saw nothing more. Even as the rest of the country was being torn by this most significant assault in the war, our area stayed quiet. But the nature of the war had now changed. We no longer went down into Bien Hoa for recreation. For the remaining five months I spent in Vietnam, no one felt quite as secure or comfortable moving around.

Tet was the extent of my combat experience. In my entire eleven months in country, I spent only two or three nights under fire. Otherwise, I had a relatively sheltered Vietnam experience. My tour ended in late April 1968, and I flew home in one piece. I was very lucky.

———

I had shipped a whole trunk of my Vietnam gear home to Boston via the U.S. Army—jungle fatigues, T-shirts, boots, all the daily wear from my year in Vietnam. When my parents opened it, the stench was so bad they had to throw the whole thing out. Perhaps I had gotten used to it in Vietnam; maybe everybody in the army smelled the same over there. Perhaps, even if it smelled foul to the outside world, once there you simply learned to accept it. Perhaps that was Vietnam in a nutshell.

After I finished my thirty-day leave upon returning from Vietnam, the army assigned me to Homestead Air Force Base in south Florida. My parents hadn't seen me in more than a year, and they decided to drive down with me. I set my MP helmet in the back window of my father's green 1968 Mustang, figuring it would help with the speed traps, and we headed south.

I must have been the only soldier in army history to arrive for duty a day early. My parents and I checked into a Howard Johnson's, had a nice meal, and drove to the base, where I reported the next morning. The army told me I was being assigned to Company A, Fifty-second Artillery Battalion, an antiaircraft battery deep in the Everglades.

The U.S. government had positioned a significant portion of its Nike Hercules antiaircraft missile system at various sites in south Florida in response to the fear that Russian MiG jets would come winging over from Cuba and overwhelm American defenses. It was my responsibility, for the next two years, to walk my dog and guard these installations.

The Army van drove through a lot of farm country and into Everglades National Park. Then it kept on driving and driving down a straight concrete road that went on for miles. We passed nothing, just Everglades and overgrowth. Finally, we saw radar towers and Battery A, a series of one-story cinderblock buildings containing a barracks, mess hall, and supplies facilities, surrounded by a chain-link fence. Two years here? I felt like Cool Hand Luke doing hard time.

Farther into the Everglades, down another concrete road, around a bend, was the missile site. Once again, big berms, and in the berms they've got the barns, and in the barns they've got the missiles, long white things with little wings coming out of them, just like I'd seen in newsreels as a kid. They were antiaircraft missiles; these weren't nuclear warheads or anything. The dogs were kept in an eight-dog kennel not far from the missiles. The whole place was guarded by two towers and surrounded by another double row of chain-link fence topped with barbed wire.

All the soldiers who worked targeting, controlling, and maintaining the missiles left at the end of the shift. Our duty consisted of driving down to the missile site at the end of the workday and walking patrol.

My dog's name was Shep. Shep was a big old-timer and would alert on the alligators, whose eyes glowed at night. The site had been built on a landfill, and you'd be out there walking the perimeter in the awful heat and thickening humidity with a million mosquitoes. If you shined your flashlight out into the Everglades, you'd see alligator eyes. All I could think of was *Peter Pan* and how Croc used to spend every waking hour trying to get another taste of Captain Hook. Never smile at a crocodile.

Our biggest fear was that the damn alligators would burrow in under the fence line and be in the run with us. The fence posts were set into concrete, but that might not stop an alligator with an appetite. Each new arrival was told the legendary tale about the K-9 handler who came around the corner one evening and found himself nose to nose with a big snapper. He and his dog took off like a bat out of hell, with the alligator chasing after them. We never lost a handler, but we saw a lot of alligators.

The base never had any action. Not one national-security alert in the two years I served there. It was easily the most boring assignment you could possibly have.

In the fall, 1968, my girlfriend Linda and I were married. Married soldiers could go home at night when they weren't working, so Linda got a job in a store in Homestead and I drove seventy miles round-trip when I went off duty to be with her. Homestead was a sleepy little southern town with a small nonmilitary population. It was a long two years. Money was tight, and I was just marking time.

I made sergeant and got a leadership role running the K-9 security detail. I was finally discharged on November 29, 1969. Linda and I loaded our cat and what few possessions we had into my prize possession, a 1966 burgundy two-plus-two Ford Mustang, and drove back to Boston. As 1970 came in, I went back to work full-time for the phone company and was also working four nights a week behind a cash register in a Curtis Farms convenience store.

Chapter 3

I BASICALLY MISSED THE SIXTIES. WHEN I WAS IN VIETNAM, SOME OF THE GUYS wore beads, smoked marijuana, and listened to antiwar rock and roll, but I never had much interest in that. As far as the antiwar movement goes, after watching the Vietnamese Army and people, many of us began to feel they just wanted to be left alone. We began to ask what were we doing there. I knew enough history to know that the Vietnamese had been fighting a civil war for fifty years and that the French had been there before us. But I was nineteen years old and did not try to understand the overall scope of it. I was there, there was a war to be fought, my country was involved, and I had a small piece of the action. Two years of enforced isolation in the Everglades put me even further from the cultural upheaval that affected a lot of my generation.

I was fresh out of Vietnam at the time of the assassinations of Martin Luther King, Jr., and Robert Kennedy. Looking at hippiedom, Woodstock, the drug culture, the style of dress, the music, Jimi Hendrix, Abbie Hoffman, the 1968 Democratic National Convention, from where I stood it was as if the country had had a national nervous breakdown. I disliked everything about the sixties.

I didn't particularly mind serving in Vietnam, I felt it was my obligation and I was proud to serve. I thought the war was justified, that our intentions were honorable. I believed in the domino theory about communism, that we had to draw a line in the sand. (Later, like so many others, I came to question the wisdom of the war and the loss of lives; I came to believe there might have been a better way.)

I always loved my country and loved our system of government. When it became fashionable to be anti, I never bought into that. I never felt disenfranchised. I didn't harbor the anger and mistrust toward the government that other people did. I believed in order and conformity and the need for everyone to abide by social norms. There was behavior that was accepted and behavior that was not. Even as kids on the corner, we knew you didn't drink in public and you didn't use the street as a toilet. There were rules, there were reasons for these rules, and I understood and accepted those reasons.

I always liked to be in control, which is why drugs never appealed to me. I didn't need drugs for escape. If I wanted to escape, I went to a movie or read a book. I didn't have to shoot up to get away from anything, and I had little tolerance or understanding for people who did.

In the three years since I'd left the corner of Hecla and Adams, the whole neighborhood had changed. The area had been redlined by real-estate agents and targeted for rental and sale to minorities. It was astonishing, as if my entire hometown had disappeared. Some of my friends still lived there, but I found that by and large most of my neighborhood—my parents included—had moved out to the suburbs and been replaced by a largely Hispanic and black community. Right after Christmas 1969, after spending a month living with her parents in Duxbury, Linda and I moved into a one-bedroom apartment outside of Boston in Weymouth.

The City of Boston didn't give a civil-service exam every year, and when they did, the Boston Police Department didn't always hire from it. Depending on budget and politics, some years no one got hired at all. That was out of my control. I had waited all my life to take the Boston police exam, and when one was finally scheduled for early 1970, I was ready.

I set my alarm very early the day of the test. The rest of my life would depend on this, and I wanted to give myself plenty of time. I'm the kind of guy who likes to get places early, settle in, and get comfortable. I woke up that morning to find that it was snowing like crazy. It was February, and a blizzard had blown in, a real nor'easter. The roads were icy and piled high with snow. It was going to be slow going.

The exam was being held at Boston Latin, the old school I had flunked out of. It was a fifteen-mile drive from my home, and I allowed an hour and a half to make the trip. Half a mile from my apartment, just as I was heading onto the Route 3 expressway, the car died. I was on the ramp, in the middle of a blizzard, and the most important test in my life was going to begin in exactly ninety minutes.

I slammed the door, ran up the ramp, and was lucky enough to find a pay phone that worked. I called my father. No answer at the house. Where were they at eight o'clock in the morning? In any event, by the time he got down from Milton, I'd never make it.

I called my sister Pat. She lived the next town over in Quincy. She was home. Down she came, boots and a winter jacket over her pajamas, in her '61 Ford Falcon. Pat was a bit of a character, she had a presidential seal on the side of her car; it wasn't exactly the Seal of the President of the United States—it had some cockamamie saying on it—but it looked official. I left my Mustang on the side of the ramp and hopped in with her. When we could get up any speed at all, we skidded and plowed and slogged into the city. I was a complete basket case: Am I going to get there? Am I going to get there?

We pulled up in front of the school two minutes before they locked the doors. I ran inside, sweating and crazy, and took the test. I passed.

By the end of August, Boston's newly elected mayor, Kevin White, announced he had signed a contract with the recently formed police union that guaranteed the force two-man cars and a "four-and-two" work shift, four days on and two days off. Before this time, Boston cops had worked horrendous schedules with no overtime and no paid time for court appearances, conditions that had in large part contributed to the creation of one of the country's first police unions. Mayor White, new in office and eager to make an impression, was looking to enhance the police department, and he met many of the union's demands. To staff it, he was going to have to hire a lot of new police. Hallelujah!

As well as passing the written exam, to become a member of the Boston police, you had to pass a physical. It was pretty demanding; being a cop is a strenuous job. You had to climb a rope to the ceiling; you had to run a mile in a qualifying time; you had to climb a ladder, pick up a 150-pound dummy, throw it over your shoulder, and climb back down; you had to jump in a pool and swim one hundred yards—all in the space of one hour.

I went to the Cambridge YMCA and trained rigorously, except for the swim. I was then and still am deathly afraid of water, and I had never learned how to swim. I desperately wanted to be a police officer, but I didn't see how I could pass.

When I got the notice to report for my physical, I was in a panic. There was no way out. At the last minute, I went down and got the thing postponed. Then I went to my sister Pat again.

Pat was trained as a lifeguard. She took me to the Quincy Y and taught me to swim. Well, not exactly; whenever I got in water over my head, fear overwhelmed me and my breathing went all haywire and I hyperventilated and struggled even harder and got tired out and sank. Pat taught me to flounder in a straight line.

When I got to the Cambridge YMCA on the day of the physical, I was anything but calm. The nerves, the anxiety jolted through me. Thank God, the pool at the Cambridge Y was only four feet deep. It was a lap pool; if it had had a deep end and a diving board, I would never have made it. I had to swim four laps back and forth, and as I looked down the lane before I dove in, I didn't see how I could do it.

Fortunately, the officer monitoring the exam was drunk. He had a reputation for being four sheets to the wind and I had trained in anticipation of this. I eased myself into the water.

I was flapping my arms, doing everything I could to stay above water, and I made one turn, then another. I could hear myself grunting—it was the sound of unmistakable panic, and with one lap to go I didn't think I'd make it. I was pulling up the rear, splashing, gurgling, and the last ten yards I don't know if I walked or swam. The attendant never noticed. He passed me. I immediately got out of the pool, ran into the locker room, and threw up.

On October 7, 1970, one day after my twenty-third birthday, I was hired onto the Boston police force. There were 157 of us in that class of officers, with three blacks and no women. Of the 2,800 cops on the Boston force in 1970, only fifty-five were minorities, with no women. In December, the Boston police hired an additional fifty or so officers, and then the lawsuits began. The discrepancy between a civilian population that was 20 percent minority and a police force that was 2 percent minority was so clear that various groups began to protest it in court. No one was hired on the Boston Police Department for the next several years while these suits concerning discriminatory hiring practices were moving through the system, ultimately resulting in federal consent decrees controlling minority hiring. I had just made it.

As a prospective candidate, I was interviewed by the number-two man in the department, Superintendent-in-Chief Bill Taylor, who said to the person with him, "This is a kid who's going to go far in this job. This kid could be commissioner." So I got on the Boston police and began pulling down the magnificent sum of $153.85 a week. First thing they did was send me and the rest of my class to the police academy.

We were supposed to be trained for twelve weeks, but just before Thanksgiving, in order to beef up the downtown area and save on overtime pay for regular officers, they interrupted our training and put us out in the street. These were the days when people from all over the area came downtown to do their holiday shopping and see the Christmas lights on Boston Common, and Boston was gridlocked from Thanksgiving through Christmas. We were rushed through qualifying with firearms, given what we needed to know for the short term, and put out on traffic duty, undercover, and pickpocket details. We changed from our khaki academy uniforms into our dress blues. I was so proud to put on that blue uniform. About seven weeks after coming into the Boston Police Academy, there I was, a gun on my hip, directing traffic and freezing my rear end off in front of Symphony Hall. I had finally made it. I was a Boston cop on the streets of Boston! Merry Christmas. Happy New Year.

I enjoyed traffic duty. (I had started at age one and a half!) I was in control, like when I was a crossing guard at Edward Southworth, except the girls weren't chasing me home anymore. I was standing in the street in charge of the flow of huge numbers of people and vehicles, all stopping and starting at the sound of my whistle, the movement of my hands.

The traffic division to which we were assigned temporarily was a plum assignment for regular officers for other reasons as well. The regular traffic cops had steady posts, and at Christmas time shop owners and business owners were very free with the Christmas envelopes to the cops they saw every day. Like the mailman with a steady route, the cop on the beat developed friendships with the merchants, and it was a very commonplace practice to accept a bottle or an envelope with a five-dollar bill as a holiday gift. The downtown posts were particularly lucrative because of all the big businesses. Maybe you'd get a deal on a stereo system or a deep discount on a suit of clothes. One captain in the downtown district was famous for keeping the front doors of the police station open as people carted in the gifts; legend had it that the station was overflowing. It wasn't legal, but it was widely accepted, and nobody—not the police, not the merchants, not the media—thought that accepting these gifts was a crime or a sin. For a brand-new young officer, it was an eye-opener.

But taking that envelope could potentially lead to more significant forms of corruption. If you could excuse taking a gratuity, next thing maybe you could take care of a ticket. And once you've taken care of a ticket, maybe you could take care of an arrest. Benign neglect could turn into indifference, which could develop into a corrupted enforcement of the law.

And what if a store owner decided not to participate? What if he had a bad year or didn't get along with the cop on his beat? Would he feel he did not get the same protection as the guy down the block who was offering the envelope? Would ten dollars get you better service than five? It was a legitimate concern; it did work that way over time.

The distinction was made between "grass eaters" and "meat eaters," terms used by the Knapp anticorruption commission investigating systemic police corruption in New York City in the early 1970s. Grass eaters were officers who took a few bucks to not issue a citation or to not enforce a Sunday-closing blue law—basically, to look the other way. Meat eaters were more aggressive: They were the cops who demanded money in exchange for allowing an illegal activity; they saw a violation and went in and threatened a businessman with police action unless he paid up.

At the academy, this kind of moral theorizing was talked about in platitudes, but because of our early assignment to the streets, we were quickly schooled in the ways of the real world of policing before the lessons of the academy could sink in. One of our instructors was a uniformed officer named Charlie Dunford, a nice guy, a real character. He came in once in a while and gave us a sense of what to expect when we got back out there. One day, he came to the front of the class and said, "Hey, fellas, I'm here to give you dugout training."

A dugout is a place where cops go to get off their feet for a while, to get out of the weather. Every traffic cop had a dugout on his post. When I was assigned to traffic detail down by the old Park Plaza office building, a room in that building was outfitted with chairs and couches, where cops could take lunch out of the public eye. If they wanted to take a quick nap, that's where they'd go. The favorite dugout was a firehouse; there was always a card game going.

Dunford described for the class in graphic detail how you would get into the dugout. "You get close . . ." He pressed his back and palms against the wall and slid along furtively, "make sure nobody's looking . . ." He swiveled his head both ways like you see in prison-break movies, "and then you *duck* in."

We were laughing, he was kidding, but he gave us more tips. The streets of Boston, we knew, were broken up into walking beats, and every couple of blocks there were police call boxes. Walkie-talkies weren't standard issue in those days. The first few we had were as big as suitcases; there were only four in the whole district. Walking cops were on their feet eight hours a day, and guys ran out the door after roll call so they wouldn't have to lug these things around all shift. Once you left the station, you were out of communication. It was still a time when a cop felt safe walking the neighborhood by himself without a radio.

The call boxes were stand-alone metal containers that opened with a police key. Inside was an old telephone, the kind where you held the earpiece to your ear and spoke into a separate mouthpiece. Some of the old drunks used to hide their bottles inside; a call-box slot fit a pint of liquor perfectly. The telephones connected to switchboard operators at the station who plugged in the calls. On top of the call box was a long pole with a red light, and when that light was blinking it meant you were to call in. Dunford told us, "Watch the lights." Every cop with any time on the force knew what that meant. The ideal dugout was one where you could look out the window and see the light.

Having had more than a month in the street, once my class got back to the academy, we were seasoned veterans, or at least we thought we were. We were uncontrollable; you couldn't tell us anything. After about a month, they gave up trying. There's an old Irish folktale about a band of patriots who were driven out of Ireland under British rule and roamed Europe as mercenary soldiers under the name the Wild Geese, never to return. One of our instructors, Detective Bernie Hurley, nicknamed our class the Wild Geese. He also looked at the assembled talent and said, "This is going to be the class the stars will fall on." (Stars were the Boston Police insignia used to designate top brass.)

A lot of cops coming on the job have some connection within the department. For many it's family: a father or cousin or stack of uncles who have been on the force for generations and who can put in a good word and get you a placement. I didn't have a hook. (In New York, that kind of contact is known as a "rabbi," someone who can get you through the system with divine guidance.) I was coming in alone. As befitting someone with no access to the strings being pulled, my first assignment was to Police District 3, Mattapan, one of the toughest districts in the department and thought to be a dumping ground.

For many years, the Mattapan area had been a predominantly middle-class Jewish community. It had a very famous neighborhood delicatessen, the G&G, a favorite campaign stop for presidential candidates. In the late sixties and early seventies, Mattapan, like my old neighborhood, had been a victim of redlining; in three or four years, a neighborhood that had been almost 100 percent middle-class and Jewish became 90 percent poor and black. Crime shot up, law enforcement went down, corruption took root.

Corruption in the Boston Police Department in the early 1970s was thought to be widespread in the detective bureau and rumored to be run by the detective sergeants. While many detective sergeants might well have been honorable, hardworking police officers, a large number were thought to be corrupt. They controlled the detectives and the vice investigations. If there were deals to be made with the courts, if you were going to try to put in a fix, word was that the detective sergeants were the group to go to. They were the source of many allegations. They were also, as you might expect, very powerful people.

I have to say "allegedly" about all of this because a lot of these allegations never resulted in indictments. Unlike the Knapp Commission investigations in New York, in Boston in the 1970s no major police corruption scandal broke that resulted in cops going to jail.

The detective sergeants allegedly collected the protection money in each district and distributed it to other levels in the department, allowing bosses to stay on the take and above the fray. A story made the rounds that the home safe of one of the superintendents had been robbed of several hundred thousand dollars. This was at a time when superintendents were making about $20,000 a year. There were so many of those stories, they had become department folklore.

As a young cop, I never witnessed payoffs. I was told, "Stay away from these locations, kid." You knew, but you didn't know. It was all scuttlebutt, done with a wink and a nod, just beneath the surface.

Boston was a puritanical city that by law closed its liquor-licensed premises at one o'clock in the morning and prohibited the sale of liquor on Sundays. Of course, a significant amount of drinking and dancing as well as illegal gambling got done on weekends and after closing time at any number of after-hours joints. Licensed or not, these places were often allowed to remain open after-hours, but as young police officers we understood that we weren't to go near them. The bosses told us, "We've got an investigation under way, and we don't want you going in there and screwing it up." In reality, these places were probably paying good money every week for the privilege of having the cops stay away.

As kids on the corner, we knew where these joints were—we knew where to get a six-pack when the grocery store wouldn't sell to us—and we always assumed that if we knew about it, the cops must know about it, and they must be getting taken care of not to disrupt it. Once I got in the station house, I soon understood how it worked. It was pretty much commonly understood that we stayed away from there.

But many of these joints were storefronts or people's apartments in the middle of residential neighborhoods, and they were the source of problems. With drinking and gambling going on late at night, this is where the knife fights and the shootings occurred. The area's legitimate residents wondered, rightly, why the police couldn't do anything about it. Plus, as idealistic young newcomers a few of us wanted to do something positive. This looking the other way was not what we joined the department for. The after-hours hangouts were in our sectors and they were our responsibility; if something went wrong, we would be blamed.

What helped some of these places stay in business were department policies and procedures and the law itself that precluded police from entering without a complaint. Occasionally, when the violations became too egregious, some unknown upstanding citizen (or cop) would put in a dummy call: There's a man with a gun. There's a fight inside. Officer in trouble. (The call came through the central switchboard and was untraceable.) This gave the police a reason to enter the premises and break things up. Cops were shocked, shocked, to find out what was going on. That sort of thing put people's noses out of joint back at the station, but they couldn't do much about it.

As well intended as these dummy calls might have been, they set a very bad precedent. You can't commit a crime to prevent a crime. In those days, there wasn't a young cop in Boston who thought he was doing anything wrong when he made these calls; he thought he was pursuing the greater good, but his world wasn't big enough to understand it was a downward spiral. It might seem that your cause is just, but you can't tell a lie to get to the truth. If you can justify illegally entering a premises, next thing you know you can justify planting evidence, then you can condone arresting a civilian on a trumped-up charge just to get him off the street. Break one law, break them all. Once you start chipping away at the legalities, you lose all force of law. The end does not justify the means.

My partner, a kid named Olson, and I were sent out one evening with one of the longtime sergeants, a guy I'll call Jones. Jones was from the old school; he still carried a claw. A claw is a "come along," one of those devices that is designed to encourage a prisoner to move. It looks like a rowboat oarlock, but when you slap a claw on a prisoner's wrist and turn it, you can snap bones. The claw was not issued by the department, but Jones still carried one.

It was a Friday evening tour, four to midnight, and right after roll call, Jones told me and my partner, "Come with me, we're going up to Franklin Field." This was an all-black public-housing project, a tough part of a tough district.

It turned out that a friend of Jones's owned a riding stable at the Franklin Park Zoo, adjacent to the projects, and evidently a saddle had been stolen. A kid had rented a horse and stolen the saddle, and now we were going up to retrieve it.

Franklin Field was a typical cinderblock and glazed-stone housing development of three-story multiunit buildings. We banged on the door of the boy's home, and inside were the mother, the son, and other family members. The son was a big kid, and he was visibly nervous. The saddle was there, and we moved to arrest him for possession of stolen property. The kid didn't want to go, the family was all excited, words were exchanged, and we ended up in a real donnybrook. We were wrestling around with this kid, falling on the floor, Jones got his hat knocked off and his glasses sent flying. It was a real good scuffle.

Finally, we got the kid out into the hall, and Jones was going to get his licks in. He had the claw out and wrapped around the kid's wrist. He was twisting it, and the kid was screaming in pain. I grabbed Jones and pushed him away.

"Stop!"

"What do you mean, 'stop'?" Jones came after me. "Who the hell do you think you're talking to?"

"Hey, he's under arrest!" I shouted. "You can't do this."

"Get the hell out of my way."

"The kid's out. It's over!"

That little break in the action stopped Jones for the moment. The boy was subdued. People were sticking their heads out into the corridor to see what all the ruckus was. To turn the screw again in public would have been too obvious. Jones backed off.

From that time on, Jones absolutely hated me. He went out of his way to make my life miserable. He gave me the worst fixed-post assignments, rotten areas where I would have to stay for long periods of time. He went back to his colleagues and pretty soon word got around about me: Watch this kid, he's not part of the program.

The Boston Police Department was perceived as brutal, but as hard to believe as it might be, with the exception of that incident, I never witnessed wanton brutality. In the old days, legend had it, it was kind of a tradition in the department that if you fought with a cop, you paid for it; once they got you back at the station, you had to run the gauntlet, with everybody giving you a whack. Talk like that used to disturb me, all the clerks—station house warriors—taking whacks at the prisoners. They were clerks because they couldn't handle it in the street, but they were going to get their licks in. But I never witnessed any of this.

Certainly, I had donnybrooks in which both sides exchanged a lot of blows. The worst always seemed to revolve around family fights. In the seventies, the cops were called increasingly to referee domestic disputes, and one of the reasons Mattapan was considered such a lousy house to work was that you had so many domestic-violence runs. We were continually being brought in to deal with husbands and wives fighting or kids fighting with their parents.

One night, my partner Henry Berlo and I got called to a husband-and-wife disturbance on the top floor of a three-decker, which was itself built on a ledge; there were three flights of stairs to climb before you got to the front porch. The fellow was all bulked up. I was no power lifter at five foot ten, 160 pounds; Berlo was two inches shorter and the same weight. We got to the top floor and asked the guy to leave the house, which was the common practice. He refused. After some discussion and more heated refusals, we grabbed him by the arm and tried to move him along. It ended in an incredible fight, all of us tumbling down three flights of stairs.

Neighbors heard the disturbance and called the cops. We couldn't have done so; we had no radios and no time. When we fell out onto the porch, the backup had run the three flights to assist us. It took about a half dozen cops to subdue him, but once he was cuffed and tossed in the back of the wagon that was the end of it. We didn't take him back to the station house and whack him around.

I was riding with a fellow cop, Billy Celester, one hot Friday night when another domestic-disturbance call came in, again on the third floor. They always seemed to be on the third floor. A seventy-year-old Haitian grandmother and a whole passel of kids were in the house, and she wanted her grandson out; he was wanted on a warrant, and she was fed up with him. He wasn't going, we started rolling around with him, and the next thing we knew, the grandmother had changed her mind. "Leave him alone! Leave him alone!" She came roaring out of the kitchen swinging a machete over her head.

Celester and I hit the door at the same time. He was pretty rotund, and neither of us made it on the first pass. We stepped back in a flash, and then crashed through the storm door, smashing it to smithereens. We rolled down the stairs and ran like crazy, with her in pursuit.

Another time, a cop named Bob Crowley and I were called to a disturbance, a problem with a grandfather. When we got there, the old man started acting up and took a swing at us, so we moved in to arrest him. The whole family got in on it. Crowley was a good-sized kid who worked out, but here was this sixty-something guy bouncing both of us all over the living room. When the public reads newspaper stories about grandfathers and grandmothers giving cops a hard time, they never believe it, but it's true. In times of crisis, some people get superhuman strength. I lived it.

Mattapan was tough duty. At a little past midnight, on January 1, 1974, someone called the station house and said there was a baby lying out in the middle of the street. Happy New Year. My partner Paul Griffin and I found a six-month-old boy with foam coming out of his mouth. His drug-addicted mother had poured Drāno down the baby's throat because, she said, voices were telling her that the devil possessed him. Griffin scooped the boy up, wrapped him in his coat, and cradled him in the backseat while I raced to the hospital. We were both crying; we couldn't believe what people did to each other. The baby died. It was the first murder of the new year.

Next January 1, the first call concerned a fight over a twenty-five-cent pot at a poker game. One guy had chased another out into the hallway and shot him dead. I was standing over the body with a couple of other cops when we felt something falling on our heads. With one of his neighbors dead on the floor, some character three floors above was looking down the stairwell and shoveling Chinese food in his mouth. The rice spilled over the rail.

I was called to a scene where a mother had killed her two mentally retarded teenage girls because she was ill and didn't know who would take care of her girls after she was gone. The teenagers were propped up against the wall. There was blood everywhere because she had stabbed them to death. It looked like there had been quite a struggle. I stood guard over these two young girls for a full tour of duty, waiting for the medical examiner.

All cops have these stories. The good ones don't forget, when they read crime reports, that there are people involved.

The corruption in District 3 and the city, both rumored and real, was very troubling. Most of us sought out and worked with partners we had confidence in, who were not corrupt and wanted to work. I was fortunate to find two: Henry Berlo and Paul Baker. Berlo and I had come on the job and gone through the academy together, so we knew and liked each other. Baker was in his thirties, had been a cop for about ten years, and had spent several years in Mattapan. His partner had recently gotten a transfer out of District 3, and I was lucky to be assigned to work with him my first summer. I had been bouncing from partner to partner for a while before he and I were assigned fairly steadily.

Baker knew the ropes. The best word to describe him was "conscientious." He was as quick with a sardonic comment as anyone, but he took his job seriously.

We were sitting in Dunkin' Donuts once when a breaking and entering call came in. "Put the cover on your coffee," he told me. "Let's go."

"It's just a report," I said. "We can finish the coffee."

"When a call comes in," he said firmly, "you go."

That had not been the practice with some other cops I'd ridden with. If it wasn't an emergency, you basically took your time getting there. Baker was a different breed. "When somebody calls, they want us. That's what we're getting paid to do, and that's what we're gonna do." He was a straight shooter. He handled the issues of corruption, treatment of prisoners, and everything the same way. At a very critical time in my career and life, Baker was the perfect partner.

Not everyone treated the job with such respect. I was riding once with an old-timer down Blue Hill Avenue, Mattapan's main thoroughfare, and passed the Blue Hill Cleaners. Cops got a discount at the Blue Hill, so it tended to get a little extra attention. As we rode by, the place looked different. Nothing I could put my finger on, just a feeling. I said to my partner, "It doesn't look right in there."

The last thing this old-timer wanted to do was get involved. "Nah, nah. Nothing, kid. Nothing, kid." We kept on rolling.

We got down to Mattapan Square and in came the 911 call: robbery at the Blue Hill Cleaners.

It was my own fault for listening to him. Putting aside the fact that I was a young cop who would have loved a robbery pinch, I should never have accepted the attitude. Don't get involved? Why else would we do this job?

Mattapan had gone rapidly from a largely Jewish to a largely black neighborhood, but some of the elderly Jewish people either couldn't or wouldn't move and were, unfortunately, subject to a lot of harassment and intimidation. One woman's home had its windows broken repeatedly, and one of my partners and I were assigned to guard the property. One day, a young black kid came walking up the street, and my partner wouldn't let him pass in front of the house. "You can't walk here," the cop said. "You'll have to cross the street."

"What do you mean, I can't walk here? Why can't I walk here?"

" 'Cause I told you you couldn't walk here, that's why. Get the fuck out of here." It didn't end up well, but finally the kid left.

A little later that evening, my partner was on a break, and I was standing in front of the house when the same kid came walking on the same side of the street. I didn't say anything to him, just let him walk by. He came up to me and said, "Why'd that cop do that? What was that all about? I wasn't doing anything." I didn't have an answer. It was such an unnecessary altercation, so verbally abusive. The kid was very upset about being treated badly, and he had every right to be. I suspect he didn't grow up liking or respecting the police. I learned early on the importance of respect, and the great damage a cop can do with his mouth and his attitude.

One of the more enlightened innovations the Boston Police Department did have in the early seventies was a program that encouraged police officers to go to college. The department had done a search and found that fewer than twenty-five cops had college degrees. The benefits of an education are obvious, and so the BPD offered scholarships to Boston State College. It was quite a deal. During the school year, an officer worked four nights a week from six to midnight and had the rest of his time free for classes and study. Twenty-five scholarships were available that year. I took the exam, got accepted to the program, and in 1971 started college. I had dropped out of Boston State six years before. Now I was back.

One of the things that happens to cops when they go into the police business is that they very quickly get wrapped up in the "blue cocoon." All your friends are cops, all your talk is cop talk about cop issues, all the war stories are cop stories, all you hear are cop ideas. Outsiders are not allowed in; they haven't been through your life, they can't speak your language, they can't understand the stress you live with every day of your life, and because they don't understand and you can't make them understand, you can't respect them. Police officers had a very insular view of the world; from the moment we entered the academy, we were taught that it's us cops against the rest of the world. Everything about the police culture reinforces the idea that we are different. We drink in cop bars, we go to cop parties, we dance at cop weddings and cry at cop funerals. Being a cop is all you know, and because it is a potentially life-threatening job every day, it becomes all you care about. I was very lucky. Early in my career I was given other options.

At Boston State College, I took some law-enforcement courses, but I also studied urban geography and began to learn the importance of cities and how they develop. I took an American government course and met Michael Dukakis when he spoke as a guest lecturer. I took two semesters of art appreciation with a Professor Arvinites and went on field trips to the nearby Gardiner Museum and the Boston Museum of Fine Arts. Personally, I was more drawn to the realism of Norman Rockwell than the wilder side of Pablo Picasso, but I came to understand what was so compelling about Picasso's colors and bold strokes. Arvinites taught us to see art not only for its individual beauty but also in the context of the society in which it was created. I was not attracted to Renaissance art, for instance, but I was fascinated to learn of the political significance of a painting's lighting or use of objects. We were also taught to explore what might have been in the artist's mind, which was not something we had been encouraged to consider at the police academy. College taught me to look at things differently than my contemporaries did and to really appreciate what I was looking at. It's good for cops to go to college.

We were a good class. Jack Gifford, Al Sweeney, Paul Evans, Joe Saia, Tom Maloney, Bob Dunford, and I had started in the department together, and now we were breaking out of the cocoon together.

And college was not only classroom study. I had been away in the military for three years and then in uniform at the department for one more. Probably the most beneficial aspect of going to college was the opportunity to talk to other students who had had, and were having, different experiences.

This was 1971. Richard Nixon was president. The war in Vietnam was going strong, and so was the antiwar movement at home. Between classes, we police students hung around the cafeteria and talked with our classmates. Boston State was a more conservative school than Harvard or Yale or Berkeley, its students mostly came from blue-collar families like mine, but even these working-class kids were beginning to question the war. Most of the students didn't see things my way. At twenty-four, I was older and more experienced than most of my classmates and very patriotic, a firm believer in answering when your country called. We faced off against whole tables full of longhaired college kids, book bags draped over the plastic stacking chairs like sacks of ammunition, and we discussed politics and society. There was no shunning, no spitting, no one called me a pig, and I didn't clap them in cuffs. The more we were exposed to each other and interacted, the more we began to understand each other.

Some fellow students felt the war was dead wrong, and we spent long hours over coffee hashing out the state and direction of America. These kids couldn't understand why I had gone off to war and why I felt it was the right thing to do. To them, this was clearly an inappropriate war: How could I defend it? I tried to make them understand the concept of obligation to your country. Even the protests they were engaged in were protected by the First Amendment: How could they not love the country that allowed them to protest? I had no problem with the protests as long as they were done legally.

There were major demonstrations pretty regularly in Boston, antiwar activists either blocking inductees from leaving the army base where I had been inducted or disrupting business at the JFK Federal Building to prevent people from registering for the draft. The radicals were growling, the crowd carrying signs and chanting antiwar slogans. Some days, thousands of people were in the street.

I was right in the middle. I'd be in the cafeteria during the morning, talking with my classmates, and in the afternoon I'd put on my uniform, strap on my funny-looking riot helmet, grab my nightstick, and go to work to maintain order at these rallies. I saw kids across the picket lines with whom I had been talking politics a couple of hours before. Without my college experience, I might have been tempted to see the demonstrators as one solid bunch of longhaired, hippie-looking pot smokers. But college taught me to think differently.

The demonstrators saw the police as parallel to the armed forces: The army was out there fighting this unjustified war, we were back here protecting the Establishment. What I found important about college was my ability to put a face on the police. I was very proud to be in uniform. I tried to make it clear that the police were not the enemy. All these faceless demonstrators suddenly had faces for me; I understood their motivations. Now the police had a face, too: mine. I had relationships in both worlds.

The kids learned about the cops, the cops learned about the kids. We become humanized in each other's eyes.

In the summer of 1972, Linda and I found out we were going to have a baby in February. At the time, we were having trouble making ends meet, and when the baby arrived we would lose Linda's income as well. With very little opportunity to make money outside my salary, I was considering leaving the Boston police. My frustration with the job at District 3 certainly played a part in my considerations. I was getting crummy assignments, I wasn't making enough money, and the organization that I had spent my entire youth dreaming about had turned out to be less than I'd imagined. I wanted out. The suburban Quincy Police Department was closer to home and had more paid details on which I could make some side money. It didn't have the size or traditions of Boston, but it had a good reputation, and it was my intention when my name was called from their list to leave the Boston police and join the Quincy force.

In February 1973 we were overjoyed to have a son, David. Unfortunately, Linda and I had begun to grow apart. The job had changed me. Linda and I separated about six months after David was born, and we were later divorced.

In the spring of 1973, Robert di Grazia was named Boston's police commissioner.

Mayor Kevin White, like John Lindsay in New York, was a progressive in liberal times. In 1972, White was talked up as a potential vice-presidential running mate for George McGovern. Like so many others, he had heard rumors of corruption within the Boston Police Department; it was widely believed that a large number of the old guard was on the take. While the rumored corruption predated White, a police scandal on his watch could obliterate his political aspirations. So when police commissioner Ed McNamara's term expired in late 1972, White organized a national search for his replacement. Bob Kiley, White's deputy mayor for public safety, was instrumental in locating reform police candidates.

Bob di Grazia had begun in a ten-person police department in California and rapidly moved up the ladder. He had been a protégé of future FBI Director Clarence Kelly when Kelly was chief of police in Kansas City. He was police chief of Saint Louis County when he was hired to turn Boston around.

Di Grazia was brought in very specifically as an outsider, with no allegiances to the old-boy network that had been running the department. He was there to break up that network and replace it with fresh management ideas and fresh faces. An insider's strengths and weaknesses are known throughout an organization, and often, because of the relationships he has formed over time, he does not have the wherewithal to make drastic changes, something clearly needed in the BPD. This is particularly true in the small world of police organizations, where broad experience outside the department is discouraged, and parochialism and in-breeding prevent old allegiances from being challenged. The office is, by law, a civilian position, so while the commissioner might not have come from within the police department, he was at least from the Boston area. For the past thirty years all police commissioners had been Boston products.

Di Grazia was one of the new breed of police leaders that was beginning to evolve in the early 1970s. He was a progressive police thinker, full of new ideas. He came in with the mandate from the mayor to reform the police department, and he went right to it, a million directions at once. He pumped up the excitement level. The BPD, which had been sputtering in idle, was kicked into gear and gunned.

Probably the most important change that di Grazia made was in personnel. He understood the potential corruption problems and administrative inefficiencies in the Boston department and that he couldn't go after everybody—the most he could hope for was to reform the system so that those who had sinned in the past would sin no more. He went after the most significant players, the meat eaters, and he went after them all at once.

The corruption appeared to be concentrated among the detectives. Very shortly after he came on the job, di Grazia wiped out the detective sergeants. It was called the Saturday Massacre. These legendary powers—the men who actually ran the department, the rumored bagmen—one Saturday morning found themselves without commands or transferred to assignments so far out of the way that they could have no influence. The message went through the department like a shock wave: It's over. This is a new day.

The senior commanders had been active in the department way of life since they had come on the force. People have a tendency to go along with whatever is in place, and cops are no different from anybody else; there are only so many Frank Serpicos in the world. Di Grazia's dilemma was that he was aware of the allegations of widespread corruption but probably couldn't prove them. He was also under time pressure; he didn't have the luxury of instituting months-long investigations. So di Grazia tried to eradicate the department's most abusive members by taking them out of positions of power and hoped to reform the rest. He created a Special Investigation Unit to investigate past corruption and, as important, to prevent new abuses from occurring in the future.

Now everyone in the department was faced with a choice. Some who were honorable responded to the new era and became successful in it. Some immediately went into retirement. Others waited out their pensions. For young officers like me, frustrated by what we saw around us, di Grazia was a godsend.

The sudden overhaul and its rash of retirements left a lot of openings for promotions. But di Grazia didn't want to fill positions with newer versions of the same old gang; he quickly changed the system for selecting sergeants. In the old system, seniority counted for around 75 percent of the mark, with the written exam counting only about 15 percent. What that meant in real terms was that you couldn't get promoted to sergeant unless you had between fifteen and twenty years on the job. By the time you had twenty years on the job, you weren't going to buck the system, which made for one class after another of old sergeants steeped in the old-boy practices. When I entered the force, the average age of a sergeant was approximately fifty-five, and the average age of a police officer was forty-three. (In New York City, most cops are retired by their early forties.)

The sergeant's exam itself hadn't changed much in twenty years. It was one-hundred-question straight civil-service memorization out of the Blue Book of police procedures. Word was that 85 percent of the questions never changed. Under di Grazia, everything changed. Seniority now counted for only 10 or 15 percent of your grade, the written test was another portion, and he added two new criteria: performance in the Assessment Center and before the Oral Board. The Assessment Center was a series of written exercises taken under time pressure; the Oral Board consisted of people from outside the department.

The written test was redeveloped and now involved information and concepts that could be found in seven or eight new books on police management, practice, and theory. Some of the works we studied were the Kerner Report on police handling of the riots of the 1960s, the American Bar Association report on police practices, and police management books by N. F. Iannone and Paul Whisenand. Instead of straight memorization, the new test evaluated your oral skills, your ability to perform under pressure, and your knowledge. You also received extra points if you had a college degree. The exam leveled the playing field and opened the sergeants' ranks to younger officers.

Di Grazia recognized the need for both the department and the public to be aware of this new approach to policing. He set goals. Among his innovations, the new commissioner began improving the department's training practices. He upgraded the department's rules and regulations for the first time in many years. He completely reorganized the department and significantly improved the Police Academy, both in terms of training recruits and in-service training for police officers. He demanded accountability from his district commanders. Di Grazia developed many programs to reach out to Boston's communities. He understood the importance of public relations, and to give the BPD a new image he changed the department's logo. In a system that was working on shoe leather he began designing new patrol cars. He brought in advanced technology, including computers.

Di Grazia hired civilian experts to introduce these new advanced policing ideas to an organization that was extremely comfortable doing exactly what it had been doing for the last fifty years. This was a topic of great controversy. His "whiz kids" were mostly academics in their twenties and thirties. They included Bob Wasserman, Gary Hayes, Mark Furstenberg, and Phil Marks. Some had full beards and mustaches and hair down over their ears. In some respects, they looked like the radical element we faced at those antiwar demonstrations, and both the city council and the police union were up in arms, thinking, Who are all these strangers—these outsiders, these *civilians!*—coming in to run one of the greatest police departments in the world? We don't need these people with their newfangled ideas. What do they know about policing?

Rules and regulations are what drive a bureaucracy, and di Grazia and his team went to work rewriting everything. One of di Grazia's basic policing philosophies was that the police workers themselves should be involved in the creation of the system, and to that end he opened the committees reviewing the rules and regulations and invited officers to help work on them. I volunteered. The Boston Police Department had never had a planning unit. What was there to plan? You go out and do your job. All of a sudden, a unit of forty-five cops and civilians was literally replanning the BPD. Newsletters began to go out, specialized training in areas such as hostage negotiation, supervisory practices, and modern management techniques were instituted. The BPD was on the move.

But it wasn't all rosy. The police union, which had been formed recently because officers had been abused by management for generations, was strong and militant. Even before he came to town, di Grazia had made a grave mistake in dealing with them. Commenting on a specific officer who had done an honorable job, he had said words to the effect that if he had fifty cops like this guy he could clean up Boston once and for all. The union took this and other early missteps as a slap at the other 2,800 officers on the force and immediately cooled to the new commissioner. Rather than making an effort to include the union, di Grazia had created an incredibly powerful enemy that was looking to flex its muscles.

Because di Grazia's new committees were dealing with changes in working conditions, the union held that union delegates should be appointed to these committees. Cops knew the rules and regs; through the decades, they had learned how to manipulate them, and the union brass didn't want all that changed. The union didn't want anything changed at all unless they could get something in their contract in return. When di Grazia didn't consult the union immediately, its leaders felt left out all over again. It was a classic confrontation over who was going to run the show, and neither was willing to bend. Di Grazia was, in fact, trying to eliminate exactly this kind of mindless resistance.

Di Grazia himself was a strapping guy in his early forties, six foot three, Italian, handsome, and a very imposing presence. He set an example. The entire system of corruption was going to be addressed, starting with the smallest details. That sent out a message right away.

Di Grazia's predecessor used to ride around Boston in a chauffeured black Buick limousine with the distinctive three-digit plate "386." Di Grazia requisitioned a baby-blue Dodge and drove it himself. He very quickly became a celebrity, a darling of Boston society, appearing at all types of charitable events and society functions. At the same time, unlike his predecessors, he attended community meetings throughout the city. Di Grazia understood he had many audiences to play to and moved gracefully through all strata of Boston society.

We had never seen his predecessor in the field and most community groups had never seen him in their school basements. A cop in the district station never saw anybody with stars on their shoulders; the brass never got out of headquarters. Di Grazia went out and did roll calls. He wanted to listen to cops, to find out what was on our minds. One afternoon at the four o'clock roll call at District 3 in Mattapan, the commissioner came striding in with the captain of the districts and some of the sergeants.

There were about twenty of us local officers lined up, and di Grazia addressed us from the podium.

He spoke for about five minutes. He talked about his plans for the Boston police, the advances he was putting through, his vision of the department and its future. We stood at attention and listened. This was not a normal day at work.

The commissioner concluded by saying, "I need to hear from you. I want to know the things you need in order to do your job. Tell me, and I'll try and get them for you. Now, do you have any questions?"

Dead silence. Between the union suppression and the fact that all these bosses were standing behind him staring at us, no one was going to stick his neck out. So up goes my hand.

Commissioner di Grazia was delighted. You always want an icebreaker. He brightened and pointed to me.

"Yes, Officer?"

"How do I get out of here?"

I could see the bosses stiffen. Was this some third-year patrolman busting the commissioner's chops?

"What do you mean, 'How do I get out of here,' Officer?"

"How do I transfer out of here, sir?"

The roll call was getting a little uneasy. A few of the guys chuckled, the brass started fidgeting.

Di Grazia turned to the bosses behind him. "Isn't there a blue form . . . ?"

I was very familiar with the notorious blue forms. They were the sheets of blue paper on which you requested a transfer, but if you didn't have a hook they ended up in the circular file. I had turned a few of them in, and nothing ever happened.

I don't know whether di Grazia thought I was busting his chops or not. I wasn't. I had heard many good things about the man that had made me rethink leaving the department, but I was desperate to get out of Mattapan, and I didn't know how. Whatever he thought, di Grazia didn't engage me in much of a dialogue. I figured my chances were nil when, after the event, a sergeant brushed by me and muttered, "Smart-ass."

A few days later, I was walking my beat in Mattapan Square when I ran into a cop I had become friends with at the academy, Frank Corbosiero. Di Grazia had just organized a Special Investigation Unit (SIU) to investigate police corruption. The police union had gone nuts, of course, at the thought of cops investigating cops, but the commissioner knew there was corruption in the department and had put together a small squad of volunteer officers. Corbosiero and I had worked together in District 3. He was a very moral guy, as frustrated as I was with what he had seen on the force, and when he heard about the SIU, he had volunteered and gone over.

"So," I asked him, "how's it going?"

"It's tough. A lot of cops turn their backs. You're kind of a pariah. But, you know, I'm kind of liking the work."

I told Corbosiero about the commissioner's visit. We had a few chuckles about that. I told him I was considering leaving the job and working in Quincy. He knew what I was talking about.

Two weeks later, I came into the precinct at four o'clock and saluted the desk sergeant, an old-timer named Danny Green.

"What are you doing here, Bratton?"

"Reporting for duty, Sarge."

"You don't work here anymore."

"What do you mean, Sarge?"

"You been transferred. The orders come down today. Report out to District 14."

District 14 was in Brighton. Boston College was out there, a lot of nightclubs, a lot of paid details. It was a very nice area. I cleaned out my locker, got into my car, and reported to my new post.

I assumed that di Grazia had taken note of my transfer request and moved it through the bureaucracy, but I found out years later that Corbosiero had been responsible. He had told his superiors, "We're about to lose a good cop," and asked that they move me. If I had not received that transfer, I would probably have gone to Quincy and disappeared. I owe Frank a great debt.

Chapter 4

When I got to District 14 in September 1973, I found they didn't have much use for cops who were going to Boston State College on the department's release program. Most of the leadership hadn't gone to college, and there was a certain amount of resentment toward the dozen District 14 officers in the program. Whenever possible, the sergeants gave us the crummy assignments, the "fixers," which involved standing at a fixed post for eight hours at a time, usually from six in the evening till two in the morning. I'd be placed on some corner in a residential neighborhood, and all they wanted me to do was stand there so some rowdy kids couldn't stand in the same place and make noise. They went out of their way to supervise us and came by regularly to make sure we were on post. I spent so much time on Appian Way, I felt I owned the place.

Two blocks away, another college guy was standing on his private corner. His name was Mickey Roache, and when a two-man sector car became available, he and I partnered up and rode together. Roache was in his thirties, married with several kids. He was a staunch Catholic who went to church every day. He was honest, sincere, respectful, and somewhat naive.

Roache and I worked well together. I liked to drive and hated doing reports; Mickey was an awful driver and didn't mind doing the writing. I was a gung-ho, conscientious young cop; Mickey didn't mind working.

Mickey was among the most honest men I've ever met. One particularly small corrupt practice was commonplace at the time: At the scene of every accident or towing violation, cops would accept two dollars from the tow-truck operator. Mickey did not take the two bucks. Most cops thought, "What's the harm?" We didn't control which company was called; there was a list of authorized tow companies that the district called in sequence; we had nothing to do with it. Two bucks wasn't a lot of money, just a sign of good will from the tow companies, kind of a tip. People thought of cops like waiters and taxi drivers and doormen; you tipped them. There was also a pie company in our district, and every cop who showed up at their bakery got two pies for Christmas. Mickey did not participate. He felt that we were being paid a salary to do a job, and we should neither solicit favors to do that job nor accept gratuities for doing what we were supposed to do. I hadn't thought much of it before, but these values made sense to me, and when I partnered up with Roache, I didn't accept gifts or tips either. These were exactly the values that di Grazia was attempting to ingrain in the department as a whole.

Mickey was having a tough time making ends meet. He drove an old, dilapidated car and was always short of money, but he was very committed to getting his education, and he did not take time away from his studies to take paid details, which only compounded his money problems. I finally convinced him to take a paid detail with me down at Sammy White's bowling alley in Brighton. Sammy White's had a lounge adjacent to it that featured live entertainment. It had so much activity, they put two officers on paid detail. The job paid twenty-seven dollars cash at the end of the night, which was big money when you were making $150 a week; a day's pay for four hours of hanging around, watching the crowd, and having some fun yourself.

The night went along without incident till two o'clock, closing time, when one drunken woman didn't want to leave. As nice as we could be, we tried to get her out, but sooner or later it ended up in a major donnybrook, with Mickey and me and this woman screaming and wrestling on the floor. It was an incredible scene—they had to call the wagon. It was also the last detail Roache ever worked. This was exactly the kind of encounter he wanted to avoid on the job, and he certainly didn't want to go through it during off-hours.

On New Year's Eve 1975, in the whole Brighton area with its 70,000 residents—one of the largest police districts in the city—the total police presence was two cars and a patrol wagon. Mickey and I were teamed up along with a couple of old-timers in the wagon and two young cops in the other car. The first call of the night was a family fight in a housing development. As we were coming out of that, we heard an outrageous noise, like a train throwing on its brakes. The screeching got louder and louder. It sounded like a tank. We stepped away from the brick building and saw a car plowing down the street with sparks flying from all four wheels like a fireworks show. We got closer and saw it had no tires! The drunk behind the wheel had burned them off completely—God knows how long he'd been driving this way—and was speeding on the hubs.

We chased him for a little while and finally pulled him over. We got him to the station, booked him, then had to take him downtown to police headquarters for a Breathalyzer test. Commonwealth Avenue is a four-lane road separated by trolley tracks, and as we cruised down it we passed the City Club, a large nightclub packed with 1,500 young people. From across the street, we saw a big battle going on outside. We had our prisoner in the backseat, but these people were whacking away at each other. We put out the call for assistance, swung around, and tried to break things up.

At least fifty people must have been fighting on the sidewalk, all these different brawls going on up and down the block. The two bastards in the patrol wagon drove by the other way and kept on going. The other car showed up with Tommy Clifford and his partner, but cars from other districts had to be brought in: The Metropolitan Police arrived, and the state police headquarters down the street sent some cars in.

I was breaking up fights and scanning the mob for my partner. I looked up the street and saw Mickey facing off with about four guys. He had his arms around one of them in a bear hug—evidently this kid had a knife and had attempted to stab another. Roache had wrapped him up tightly, chest to chest, and the kid was struggling, trying to punch him in the ribs.

Clifford ran up with me, and we finally got that crew under control. Now we had another set of arrests. It was only one o'clock—the night was just starting.

Down at headquarters, Roache took off his jacket. He was black and blue from this kid using him like a heavy bag. Mickey had accepted that punishment; he refused to carry a club. He had been a boxer, and he couldn't bring himself to smack the guy. It was his own code of honor.

As much as di Grazia tried to clean up the pockets of alleged corruption and inefficiency, in some places the word didn't get out. District 14 still had some old-timers in their supervisory leadership who had been around the department for twenty-five years and weren't going anywhere.

They had all the power, and they ruled the roost. Many of them were intent on waiting di Grazia out. You came in, saluted them, went out, and did your job. They sat inside.

One night, Roache and I had a major jam, a *West Side Story*–type knives-and-fists gang fight at nearby Ringer Park and playground. Forty kids were going at it, and when we put out the word, all the cruisers responded. But even with twelve or fourteen cops on the scene, we were still having a hard time getting it under control. We kept calling for the sergeants—they had the experience and ability to put this scene in order right away, and we needed all of it. The station was only a half mile from the playground, but these two bastards, the patrol supervisor and the desk sergeant, did not come out. They didn't want to get into anything, and they left us on our own.

This was all wrong. When you've got a dozen cops in one police action, you need leadership. Without someone clearly in charge, you have no ability to organize the scene, and it can fall apart. But these guys just refused. That one incident typified what was wrong with the department: lack of leadership and supervision.

I liked being in uniform and getting out into the neighborhood; it was fun to patrol business districts, to interact with people. Most cops dream of becoming detectives and investigating crimes. The best of them have what I can only describe as a sixth sense about when something is wrong and can get to the heart of it right away. While interrogating suspects, they have an inquisitiveness and a special ability to find out what they need to know. It's hard to explain but easy to recognize. I knew very early that I didn't have that ability, and I never would. I was pretty good at picking up when something was amiss in the street, but the really good detectives went beyond that to something I couldn't even touch. I wanted very much to move up in the organization, but it became clear to me that I wouldn't do it in plainclothes. If I was going to have a good career in the police department, it would be in the supervision-management field. In the spring of 1974, I began to study for the sergeant's exam.

I had four years on the job; normally, I would have had to wait another ten years or more before I was even eligible. But di Grazia had changed the line of succession, and I was determined to take advantage of the opportunity. I was still going to college at night, and eight or nine of us put together a study group. I was going to outstudy the bastards and get ahead of the Sergeant Joneses of the world. I read all the textbooks, underlined the important passages, and transcribed them onto three-by-five flash cards. Whenever I had a spare moment, I would pull out my three-inch-thick stack of cards and quiz myself.

Captain Hanley at District 14 was a tough-talking old-timer who didn't have much use for di Grazia or this new policing. During a lull at one police action, when twenty officers were assigned to guard a high school as a result of a series of disturbances, and everyone else was hanging out, hats off, smoking cigarettes, I began going through my flash cards. The captain zeroed in on me.

"What are you doing, Bratton?"

"There's a sergeant's exam coming up, Captain; I'm just keeping myself fresh."

"Put 'em away," he barked. "You're on duty here." You'd think the department would encourage a constructive use of an officer's time, but no one had told this guy there was a new day coming.

I studied for almost a year. It was a particularly good year because not only was I pursuing a significant goal but I remarried. Her name was Mary Doran, and I had met her several years earlier while walking my beat in Mattapan. She was working as a secretary in a local bank. We were married in May 1975.

Mickey Roache wasn't going to take the exam. His priority was getting his college degree, and he just didn't feel he had the time to study. He wasn't even going to sign up, but I talked him into it. We were riding around in the sector car all the time, and I kept after him till he agreed.

My good friend Al Sweeney, whom I had known since kindergarten, had already graduated from college. I joked with him that while I was in Vietnam, he was getting his college degree and serving his country as a park ranger, patrolling Boston Common during the height of hippiedom. Sweeney was one of the few of us who was not a veteran, and he was sweating the promotion exam because he wasn't going to get the two-point veteran's preference; he would have to do two points better than all of us just to stay even.

I aced the exam. I came in first on the written test and placed second overall. I remember very clearly coming home after work and finding a letter on very beautiful new stationery from the Office of the Police Commissioner, Boston Police Department, congratulating me. I was very impressed that Commissioner di Grazia sent this letter to my home rather than handling it through department sources and having news of my promotion handed to me by a sergeant at the station. I thought that was a terrific personal touch. I still have the letter.

Even the promotion exercise was special. It was held in John Hancock Hall, July 3, 1975, and Mary pinned my badge on my uniform. The involvement of an officer's family in the police world was another significant di Grazia innovation. My father took the official family photographs, but he wasn't familiar with the camera, and when we got the photos back there were no heads—all we got were shots of us from the neck down.

We were the largest class of sergeants ever promoted in the history of the Boston police. Eighty of us, including a large number of young officers with only three or four years on the job—I was twenty-seven years old—moved into leadership positions. In our ranks were Al Sweeney, Jack Gifford, Tom Maloney, Paul Evans, Joe Saia. Mickey Roache made it. A lot of the Boston State College guys. Three police commissioners ultimately came out of that class. We were a new generation of police but very different from the "youth generation" that was rocking and rolling in the streets. Our training began immediately.

It was a time of great change for the city. What had been kind of a drab, backwater city was being reinvigorated. Exciting public spaces such as Faneuil Hall and Quincy Marketplace were being developed; Kevin White was an activist mayor who had hired a dynamic young police commissioner; the whole city seemed vibrant. I was excited to be a part of it.

Rather than send us right out into the field, the department put the whole class of sergeants through three weeks of postpromotion training at Boston University. Di Grazia wanted to make sure we were well guided when we went out to spread his word. Our teachers built upon the progressive policing books we had been expected to master for the exam. A lot of our training had to do with leadership. We were taught management-supervision techniques and how to discipline people. We had anticorruption seminars and discussed ethics issues, things a police officer would never otherwise hear about. We had classes on how to give public presentations and speeches because we were expected to speak persuasively on behalf of the department.

The most important effect of our new training was to show me and the rest of my class that there were ideas and approaches to policing beyond the narrow confines of the Boston Police Department. Our teachers were very smart, very capable, and very much in touch with the world outside. To his everlasting credit, di Grazia took us out of the blue cocoon.

In his continuing effort to eliminate the corrupt practices of the old regime, di Grazia used his newly promoted sergeants to effect a turnaround in the department. He had eighty new sergeants, and rather than send eight each to every district and risk our being tainted, if not corrupted, by the old guard, he chose four districts and completely changed the leadership. The only problem with this method was that the layer above us was still made up of old-style lieutenants. From district to district, this clash of cultures caused problems.

I was raring to go. After three weeks of cutting-edge police training, my enthusiasm was skyrocketing. I was going to do everything right, make the changes from day one, bring the Boston Police Department into the future.

My first assignment as a sergeant was to District 6 on Athens and D streets in South Boston. "Southie" was a very insular, parochial, lower-middle-class Irish and Polish community. They did things their own way and were not too hospitable to anybody from the outside. When my new fellow sergeant Joe Saia and I showed up our first day at our first roll call, we found the cops were like that, too. Everything was laid back, kind of a wink and a nod.

My first roll call was the day shift. I had planned my presentation the night before. Maybe I had practiced it out loud. I was ready. I had bought a brand-new gray Samsonite briefcase to hold the Polaroid camera I had bought to take pictures at crime scenes, along with my tape recorder and my cuffs and clubs and ticket books and all the department forms I thought I'd need. As safety monitor on the corner of East Street and Adams, I'd had a Hopalong Cassidy lunchbox; now I had my new briefcase.

There were fifteen to twenty cops slouching in front of me and Sergeant Saia, and when we looked at their faces, we saw some of them had not quite recovered from hard drinking the night before. Alcohol abuse was a big problem in the department in those days. But they were going to hit the streets.

Every cop there seemed to have in excess of thirty years in the department. Most had spent all of them in South Boston, and many lived in the neighborhood. Every one of these men had been on the job longer than I'd been alive.

I introduced myself. I knew they were suspicious of this young kid who was going to upset their world, but that's what I was there for. "Here's some of the things we're going to be looking at," I told them. "Response time. I don't want you hanging around the station, I want you out there on your sectors, chasing your calls. And expect to see us." I wasn't going to be one of those District 14 supervisors who stayed cooped up indoors. When my officers needed me, I was going to be there.

There was a stirring. The idea that a sergeant might be out in the street could be unnerving; the assumption was that we were there to catch someone at an infraction. It's in a cop's nature to assume that anyone above him in the chain of command will go out of his way to catch him doing something wrong. Because there are so many rules, and those rules were disregarded so routinely, the cops weren't too pleased with anyone looking over their shoulder. "That's as much to assist as to supervise," I assured them.

The day lieutenant at District 6 was a guy named Barney Ryan, old school, about forty years on the job, gawky, six-three, glasses on the end of his nose. He looked like Ichabod Crane, and I think he'd been in the district station since they built the place. Barney was the duty supervisor and a great guy, but one of his principal interests was the ever-present domino game in the back room.

District 6 continued my education. I was alone in the station one night on a midnight-to-eight shift, having let my clerk grab a few winks while I covered the front desk, when a guy came in and gave himself up on a warrant. He'd been accused of beating up his girlfriend, and he was turning himself in. The guy admitted he'd hit her, but he was showing remorse, and he didn't seem like such a bad guy. I took down the information, called it in to headquarters, and got a booking number to make the arrest official. The guy asked if he could make a phone call, and I said sure. He talked into the receiver for a couple of minutes, and then he bolted. Apparently, he and his girl had kissed and made up, and now he was making a break for it.

But if he got away he was an escaped prisoner, *my* escaped prisoner. The paperwork alone would have cost me days of work, plus, losing a prisoner was next to a sin and that kind of thing stays with you forever. I chased the guy four blocks before I caught him and dragged him back to the station house kicking and screaming.

Fortunately, District 6 was led by Captain Morris Allen. Captain Allen's previous command had been the Boston Tactical Patrol Force, an aggressive unit that every cop wanted to get into. It was the crème de la crème. Allen was a great leader, an honest guy who cared about his troops. He was one of my first mentors.

We had been taught the importance of morale in our postpromotion training, and Allen was very involved in the physical condition of the station and its effect on the people who worked there. He was in the process of remodeling the station, literally out of his own pocket. You couldn't get money out of the city government, but in the two years I worked there, building materials came in from all over, and the place was gutted and put back together. We actually had a multitiered garden fountain in the middle of the lobby!

Captain Allen was particularly interested in the cleanliness and condition of the district's cars. I'm convinced that every Christmas someone in fleet management got an envelope from Allen, because his district always had the best cars.

But Allen's best attribute was that he encouraged those under him to be creative. Di Grazia saw to it that overtime pay was budgeted so sergeants and lieutenants could come in for a couple of hours a week and meet with the commanding officer to discuss the problems in the district and what we could do about them. Captain Allen built the police in District 6 into a team.

We had many nightclubs in our district, and one in particular was a problem. It was called the Channel, and every Thursday and Friday night they'd get 1,500 kids down there, and it would be a bloody mess—underage drinking, fights, stabbings. I was night supervisor, and Allen gave me the responsibility of dealing with this club. This was exciting. I designed a plan in which we put undercover cops inside the place and cops in uniform outside. We got the club's floor plan and drew up diagrams for contingencies. Then, I brought in the cops and detectives and worked on the strategy. "Okay, who's going to be inside in the undercover? Where are the uniformed cops going to be?"

The cops ate it up. Police work requires officers to work alone much of the time, and this coming together in a group created a lot of excitement. Even the old-time cops got into it, and the action was a success. Allen encouraged this type of creativity and gave his young supervisors enough leeway to make our own decisions. It was a far cry from District 3 in Mattapan, where the nightclubs had been protected and I'd had to steer clear of them.

One sunny summer morning, I was out on patrol by myself in Boston's standard-issue Matador station wagon. (In a well-intentioned effort to upgrade our transportation, di Grazia had made the Matador our patrol car. Cops hated the big square clunkers because they didn't maneuver well, but we were stuck with them.) I was halfway over the Broadway bridge on the very edge of my patrol area when a call came over the radio: holdup alarm at the New England Merchant's Bank on Dorchester Avenue. I was about a half mile away. I radioed that I was nearby and immediately looped around.

As I was responding, another call came in. The holdup man was identified as a black male, six feet two inches tall, in a red leisure suit.

This was South Boston, 1975, at the height of the notorious school-
busing crisis, when racial tensions were incredibly high. South Boston was
a white neighborhood so hostile to black people that most blacks would
not go there if they could in any way avoid it. One major employer, the
Gillette razor-blade company, hired a lot of blacks, but even those workers usually walked or drove only through areas that were very well policed. The idea that a large black man in a red leisure suit would rob a bank
in South Boston just didn't make any sense.

Further radio transmission: the suspect fired a shot in the bank, has
now exited the bank, and is dragging with him a white female, either a
teller or a customer.

Dorchester Avenue is a major artery through South Boston. The
bank was situated directly next to a railroad track, at the base of a four-
lane steel bridge. The bridge had no overhead wires or girders; it just
rose and humped over the railroad track. Across the street was a big bus-
maintenance garage. On one side of the bank was an empty lot and on the
other the Doughboy donut shop.

I took a right onto Dorchester and had to stop about seventy-five yards
from the bridge. Traffic wasn't moving because this screwball was dragging
a young woman up the street with a gun to her head. Bus drivers and
garage workers had emptied into the avenue; a couple of guys had
hopped off a dump truck and joined the posse; it was a Thursday, big pay-
day in a busy area, and a crowd had gathered and surrounded the man
and his hostage. They were hanging back, giving the guy about ten yards
breathing room because he was waving a gun at them. He's got a paper
bag full of money and a black revolver and he's got his arm around this
woman's neck and he's got an angry crowd of thirty-five to forty white
people around him. Where's he going to go? For some reason, he starts up
the bridge. The crowd moves with him.

I was the first unit on the scene, so I radioed, "We've got a black
male dragging a white female onto the Broadway bridge. I'm moving up."
There were no other police units in sight. I took out my gun and moved
through the crowd, which, strangely, was not moving back from the man's
threatening gestures.

The gunman continued to drag the woman onto the bridge. An office
building overlooked the bus yard, and its windows were filling with workers coming to see what the big deal was. On the far side sat a sandwich

shop and the D Street public-housing development, overflowing with poor white people, the heart and soul of South Boston. Word was spreading quickly, and folks had begun to pour out of the projects. The bridge had low, pebbled concrete sides and a walkway behind the huge water pipes that served as a railing, and people were craning their necks to watch the action from the street. The man and his hostage were now at the center of the bridge. It was as if he were onstage.

After becoming a sergeant, I had volunteered for hostage-negotiator school. One of the things you learn is: Never give up your cover. If I had been thinking straight, I would have remembered, but the crowd moved backward, I walked forward, and all of a sudden I had gone past the stopped cars and the dump trucks and the buses and found myself out on the bridge, in front of the gunman, my own weapon aimed directly at him, only five yards away.

Two minutes earlier, I had been a happy guy riding in my car; now I was facing off with this black guy in a red suit. I didn't know if he had already shot someone, only that a shot had been fired. I didn't know if he had an escape plan or an accomplice, but I could see the fear in the man's eyes. I suspect he could see the fear in mine.

The hostage kept collapsing, and the gunman struggled to keep her upright as his shield. He waved the gun at her, at the crowd, at my face. The crowd wasn't moving in on us, but it wasn't going anywhere either. I heard police sirens and knew the cavalry was coming. I heard the crowd growling in waves, but at the same time everything had gone silent. It seemed like an eternity while the three of us stared at one another. Then the hostage-school training started to kick in: Talk to the guy, get a dialogue going.

"Hey, look, calm down," I told him. My gun was pointed at his head. "You haven't hurt anybody yet. Look, you can see you can't get away, you're going to have to give it up. You're going to face jail time but, you know, you hurt her or you hurt me and you're going to make this a lot worse situation."

"Stay away! Stay away!" he shouted. At least he was talking to me. The idea was to keep him involved.

"Look, don't hurt her. She's got nothing to do with this. Why don't you let her go?"

I don't know how long this went on. It seemed like forever; it might have been a couple of seconds. Meanwhile, I could see other police on both sides of the bridge beginning to make their way forward, starting to get into position. In particular, I saw a couple of old-timers, Officers Gene Kelly and Bob Dumas, two cops who had worked Southie for forty years. They were both big, robust, the kind who would jump right in. Out of the corner of my eye, I saw them trying to sneak up in back of this guy.

They were scaring me to death. The man was jittery. He was pointing the gun at me. He was scaring me to death. "Stay back!" I yelled to Dumas and Kelly. One of the new sergeants, George Kenney, was on the scene now, and I began talking to him on my walkie-talkie. "Get them back! *Keep them back!*" I was trying to maintain a dialogue with the gunman and reduce his panic. Kelly and Dumas probably figured they could tackle him. He'd shoot me, then he'd shoot her, and with the cops behind him, I wouldn't be able to do anything for fear of shooting both of them. Kenney finally coordinated with the other units, and they backed off.

On either side of the bridge, as traffic got more and more backed up, people were getting out of their cars and walking toward this show. They didn't have to come too far, because wherever you were you had a great view.

We were dancing around, the gunman and I, me trying to stay in front of him, not allow him to focus anywhere else and get any more excited or anxious. More of my hostage training kicked in. I realized that what was causing him the most tension was my gun; he couldn't keep his eyes off it. It's the nature of people faced with a weapon: You always end up focusing on it. I was doing the same thing, my eyes kept going back to his gun, particularly when he had it pointed at me.

I am the world's worst shot. I had proved that fact in the army and on the firing range. I couldn't shoot this man anyway because I'd end up shooting the hostage, so my weapon was really of no use to me. A ton of other cops were around by now, and any of them could take this guy out better than I could, if it came to that.

"Look," I said, "I'm going to lower my weapon. I'm not going to harm you." I bent my arm and slowly dropped my pistol to my side. I could see him thinking, "What's going on here?" Then it must all have come to him: I can't get out of here; the most immediate threat is gone for now; maybe I can live through this.

I was standing stock-still with a gun pointed at me.

"Okay, it's up." He dropped his gun hand and then the hand holding the money and the woman. She slumped and crawled away. Cops came swarming from all directions and tackled him.

There is one inexplicable aspect of human nature that all cops share:

We are attracted to danger. We get paid to run toward danger rather than away from it. Standing on that bridge was all the excitement any cop could crave. I have to admit, once I had lived through it, it was exhilarating. I had met the cop's ultimate challenge; I had put my life at risk for another, and I'd won.

News traveled fast. A witness called the police station and told the clerk, Charlie McLaughlin, "Jeez, this cop was amazing. He went right up and faced this guy off. He's gotta have balls as big as cannonballs!" So when I came through the door with the prisoner to do the paperwork, McLaughlin said, "How you doin' there, Cannonballs?"

The nickname stuck. Jack Gifford gave me two gold-painted golf balls. I kept them on my desk.

In police circles, one thing cherished above all else is heroism, facing down fear, courage. From then on in the police world, no matter what department I went to, I had credentials: cannonballs. I had faced off with a guy and rescued a hostage. That carries a lot of weight with cops; you're not an armchair soldier, you've made your bones.

Captain Allen nominated me for the Schroeder Brothers Medal, the BPD's highest award for valor, given for a singular act of heroism, and I was selected. I received the second Schroeder Brothers Medal ever awarded and accepted it with pride.

It's funny how things work sometimes. The office building overlooking the Broadway bridge was the home of the International Brotherhood of Police Officers (IBPO) and the National Association of Government Employees, two big unions representing hundreds of thousands of workers. Its president, Ken Lyons, happened to catch the whole hostage drama as it unfolded out his window. Through Lyons, the IBPO honored me at their annual luncheon as their Person of the Year. Commissioner di Grazia had been invited to assist in the presentation, and his office called and asked if I would meet the commissioner at his office and drive with him to the luncheon. I jumped at the opportunity to spend even a moment with him.

It was raining like crazy on the day of the presentation, and by the time I parked my car and walked to headquarters, I was drenched. I wanted to make a good impression, but the rain was squeaking in my shoes.

The commissioner's office was on the sixth floor of police headquarters. I tried not to gawk, but I soaked up the atmosphere—who knew when I'd ever get back? The doors to all the offices were framed in beautiful old oak, the windows in these old doors were etched glass, even the doorknobs were engraved with the Boston Police Department seal. The entire place had a special aura of authority, the weight of tradition and history. Everything I wanted to be was here. Just breathing sixth-floor air was a privilege.

Di Grazia had a black woman secretary, which was unusual in the BPD, and she was legendarily tough on everybody. When I was finally allowed to squeeze past her and was ushered into the commissioner's private office, I was floating.

The commissioner drove us to the lunch—imagine, a police commissioner driving a sergeant!—and when it was over took us back to headquarters. As he drove, he talked about what he was looking to do with the department and asked me for my perspective as a new sergeant. I was flattered to be asked my opinion, and I tried to be as politic as possible. I was slightly in awe and only said I was enjoying the direction in which he was taking us.

I saw di Grazia one other time that year, after fellow sergeant Jack Gifford and I wrote him a letter. In order to ensure that sergeants were checking up on their troops, a directive had been issued by the department's chief uniformed officer, Superintendent-in-Chief Joe Jordan, requiring that police dispatchers, who were all patrolmen, *at their discretion* assign patrol supervisors to go on certain calls. The new sergeants had no problem checking up on the troops; renewed vigilance was a major component of what we saw as our job. Gifford and I thought the directive put the responsibility in the wrong hands. By giving control of the assignments to the dispatchers, it eliminated our ability to go in unannounced. We wanted to decide which calls to monitor and when to roll in silently without tipping off the cops that we were coming.

If they know supervisors will be on the scene, cops will naturally show up and be on their best behavior. If they know we are not coming, they may act differently. We wanted them to be on their best behavior all the time, not just when their bosses were watching. This directive was a prime example of old-style police thinking; rather than motivate the force to do the right thing, it motivated them to learn how not to get caught. Rather than correct the actions of the few, we were effectively penalizing the many.

Gifford and I, as resident gadflies, wrote di Grazia a letter making this case. Mo Allen signed off on it and sent it over. There are a million ways for a letter like this to get sidetracked, but it reached the commissioner, and Gifford and I were invited in to discuss it. We were sitting quietly in front of di Grazia's secretary when the door opened and who came walking out but Joe Jordan himself. Jordan always looked like a million bucks in full dress uniform. He was a handsome man, careful about his appearance, who wore his hat kind of cocked to one side like Douglas MacArthur and had taken to wearing tinted aviator-style sunglasses. He saw two of his uniformed sergeants sitting, hats off, at the commissioner's door and said, "What are you two doing here?" You could see him thinking, What the hell are these two doing jumping the chain of command? While our letter went through his office to get to the commissioner, likely he hadn't seen it.

"We have an appointment with the commissioner, sir."

"Who are you?"

"Sergeant Bratton."

"Sergeant Gifford."

"Oh, well, how're you doing?" He left.

In we went and made our pitch. Di Grazia listened and said, "I think that makes sense. Let me talk to the superintendent." Some time later, the order was rescinded.

My effort to get di Grazia's attention was not without calculation. Responsibility for assignments was an issue about which I had strong feelings, but I did also consider how making this case could enhance my standing and increase my access to the top man in the department. I wanted to rise in the Boston police organization, and I was always trying to get noticed.

The major issue facing Boston in the early and mid-seventies was race. In 1974, a federal court ruled that Boston's public-school system was intentionally segregated and, as a remedy, ordered the city to bus students, white and black, to achieve integration. Many of Boston's neighborhoods erupted in outright rebellion that went on for six years.

Rather than accept desegregation, white parents began to send their kids to private schools. What had once been a mostly white public-school system was soon filled with minority students; money spent on security and busing was money not being spent on the schools themselves, and the quality of education began to decline. The whole system deteriorated. The public's anger was phenomenal, and the police were right in the middle of it.

Each morning, black children were bused from their own neighborhoods in Boston to central points, where they were placed onto different buses and driven to individual schools around the city. Black children who were being driven to schools in South Boston first went to Bayside

Mall, an abandoned shopping center at the edge of the neighborhood. The streets of South Boston are narrow and lined with shingled bay-windowed houses, the sidewalks are not wide, and a bus takes up a lot of space in such tight quarters. As these convoys made their way to their schools, they were often ambushed by groups of screaming white residents of Southie throwing rocks and bottles and brandishing signs reading "Niggers Go Home!" It was pure bigotry, pure hatred. Increasing numbers of cops had to be assigned to escort the buses.

South Boston High School and Charlestown High School became the principal battlegrounds of the efforts to resist integration. South Boston and Charlestown were very insular white residential areas with large public-housing populations. With white parents screaming outside, full-fledged riots often broke out inside the schools, and every day hundreds of patrolmen were stationed inside schools. There were daily fights and often stabbings. Conditions grew so bad that South Boston High became a virtual prison and the Boston police, assisted by the Metropolitan and state police forces and for a time the U.S. Marshals, worked literally around the clock to keep order. It was a terrible time for the city. The wounds caused during that era still have not healed.

Disturbances came anytime, day or night; the police got intelligence that a band of demonstrators was forming outside the school at midnight to graffiti the building or put up signs, and we'd have to show up and handle it. The situation got so out of hand that one Sunday, the District 6 station had to be evacuated; a rumor went around that it was about to come under attack by the antibusing forces.

Cops were on standby for the entire school year. Police stations began to look like flophouses. The Tactical Patrol Force spent the entire year, twelve hours on, twelve hours off, camped out on cots in the gym in the Marine reserve center in South Boston or by the Metropolitan District Commission (MDC) sewage-pumping station; cops spent so much time there, they didn't even smell the raw sewage anymore.

There was not much chance for police officers to get a break from the rebellion. Cops could visit relatives in the area, but in many cases that put them right into the neighborhood they were policing. Most of the police were from those neighborhoods—Joe Jordan, for instance, had been a star quarterback at South Boston High. It was their kids in these schools and their neighbors throwing the rocks. As with the antiwar demonstrations, the cops were in the middle. Officers looked across the barricades and saw the screaming faces of their sisters, their brothers, their cousins and nephews. Many would go home at night and have to hear their friends saying, "Hey, we saw you up at the heights today. Why did you arrest Johnnie Jones?" The antibusing people could not understand why we were arresting them, why we weren't letting the rock and bottle throwers go.

Which is not to say that some cops didn't turn a blind eye to a lot of what was going on. They agreed with it. Not only was the city divided against itself, the department reflected those divisions. It, too, became a basket case.

On May 12, 1977, several sticks of dynamite were found inside South Boston High School, and seven arrests were made. The fighting grew fierce. Ultimately, the federal government brought in hundreds of U.S. marshals in their riot helmets to preserve order. It reminded me of Little Rock in the fifties.

On Father's Day 1977, a protest march was scheduled by the anti-busing forces. They'd had a lot of these marches. This time, it was the fathers of South Boston who were going to parade. We brought in extra personnel for crowd control, but we were not prepared for the size of the demonstration, and very soon the scene got out of hand. The men began throwing rocks; bottles were crashing in the street. What had begun as a Father's Day parade quickly broke out into violence, and inside the crowd the word went out: "Take the high school!"

The best we could tell, they were going to seize the building. Word buzzed through the crowd, phones started ringing, people started coming from all over.

Calls were starting to come into headquarters that the march had turned violent, and the cops stationed at the high school were being over-run. I wasn't assigned to the parade, but I was patrol supervisor, responsible for policing the area. Basically, I was like a scout out hunting for marauding war parties of demonstrators.

I was about to swing down toward the L Street Bath House, South Boston's equivalent of an Irish-only country club, and then up to the school to join the troops, when I turned right onto East Sixth and came face to face with a loud and angry crowd of renegade marchers. Dozens of screaming protesters filled the two-lane street and were moving up the hill toward the school. They saw my cruiser and started cursing and hurling bottles. The language was unbelievable. This was no community protest, this was a mob, and they turned on me. These people were running at me, letting loose a rebel yell, a hateful sound like I had never heard.

I hit the brakes, threw the Matador in reverse, and backed up Sixth Street like a wild man. I was looking frantically over my shoulder, trying to keep the car straight, trying not to hit anything.

By the corner I hit forty miles an hour, backward. I did a two-point turn, came out spinning like you see in the movies, and raced up the hill. A boiling angry crowd was assembling on the top of Sixth Street. I felt like Davy Crockett fighting through Mexican lines to get into the Alamo. I made it to South Boston High only slightly ahead of the mayhem.

The call was going out to cops all over the city: Send reinforcements to South Boston. But it was Sunday, and, despite the ongoing conflicts, we were on minimal Sunday staffing, so cops were being called at home. Now all we could do was try to hold the fort and wait.

The brass started showing up. Of course, Commissioner di Grazia was there. The crowd hated him. With his liberal new policies and the police's insistence on not backing down to the mob, he was the archenemy. Joe Jordan arrived to direct the troops in double-breasted full uniform with gold buttons. Meanwhile, a pitched battle started up. The police assigned to the school had parked where we could find spots, and when the mob found a police car they trashed it. The windows in all our cars and vans were being staved in, the glass lying in shards on the seats and the pavement.

South Boston High sat on the top of a hill at the end of Sixth Street, and whoever held the high ground was going to win this battle. We were confined behind the metal fencing that surrounded the school property. With our helmets and riot gear, we could rush through the school's black iron gates and take the streets, but we didn't have enough manpower to hold them. All we could do was foray out and push the crowd back and then, when they surged, retreat behind the gates and regroup. Charge, retreat, regroup, all the while hearing the mob screaming and cursing us. Rocks and bottles flew out of the crowd. They didn't have very far to fly—it was only a couple of feet from the street to the steps of the building; any drunk could brain you.

Joe Jordan had had enough. Bostonians are supposed to be civilized people, and this behavior was beyond disgrace. Jordan was so angry, he reached down, picked up a rock that had smacked up next to him and threw it back at the mob like he was lobbing a grenade. We had no shields and we couldn't shoot them; it was a gesture of complete frustration. That's an absolute police no-no: A police professional doesn't attack a crowd with a rock. But I understood the feeling entirely.

I was ducking the incoming in the high-school courtyard and found myself standing in the school's doorway next to the commissioner, who was surveying the scene.

"Well, good afternoon, Sergeant Bratton!"

I thought that was the funniest thing. We're under fire, and he's talking to me like we're on a buffet line.

"You know," he said, "we've been talking about a new initiative to bring some of you young sergeants into headquarters to work on my staff and get a feel for the place."

"That's great, Commissioner." My eyes darted between his face and the sky. I didn't want to be disrespectful, but I didn't want to take a bottle on the head. It was a cold and overcast day, and my shoulders hunched like I was out in the rain.

"Would you be interested in coming up?"

It was as if the clouds had lifted. "I would love it!" I had been in South Boston for more than a year. The idea of going up to the commissioner's staff was very appealing, particularly at that moment.

"Good. I've got Dunleavy and Wasserman working on the program." Steve Dunleavy was di Grazia's civilian director of informational services and Robert Wasserman was his civilian director of the Police Academy. They were high up in his brain trust. "We'll talk to you."

If we lived. The insurrection at South Boston High went on for several hours before we finally got enough manpower to put an end to it.

It was anarchy. Racial animosity in Boston had spurred several horrendous beatings and murders. A white fisherman was beaten to death by several black kids over by the Columbia Point housing project. A black motorist was dragged from his car by a white mob in South Boston and severely beaten. They were going to kill him. One of the cops assigned to the school had to cut into the crowd, grab the man by the collar, and hold the mob back by firing shots in the air—all of it recorded on film by the media for the five o'clock news.

Through this whole period, we still had to handle our regular 911 calls. Not only were we policing the busing battles, we had to go into these people's homes and deal with the regular run of domestic disturbances. Of course, there was held-over animosity. From that time on, we ran up against a lot of cop fighters in Southie, guys who would go at a cop rather than accept his authority. It used to be that a police officer arrived on the scene, broke up a situation, told someone to move on, and they did it. Not anymore. Cops were the image of enforcement, and Southie degenerated into a small-minded world of its own. Sooner or later, we hauled these guys away. When they got dragged into court, these yahoos and their attorneys had a constant refrain: "South Boston boy, your honor." The judges heard that twenty times a day.

South Boston is a very close-knit community with some great strengths and tremendous pride. They played in their own ballpark and by local rules. They sought dispensation, and sometimes they got it. Every Boston cop who ever worked Southie can tell you about the "South Boston boy, your honor" defense. But when they used it to defend their actions during the school busing era, I'm not sure it's something I would have bragged about.

Chapter 5

BEFORE I COULD GET TO THE COMMISSIONER'S OFFICE, DI GRAZIA RESIGNED.

Sometime after the Father's Day riot, he announced he had accepted a job in Montgomery County, Maryland, which surprised everybody, especially me. One day he's talking to me about coming to headquarters, the next thing he's leaving.

Di Grazia was a meteor who burned out too quickly. He brought excellent new ideas to the profession but was very outspoken and made deep cuts in the old-guard workforce. He once referred to America's police chiefs as "pet rocks," which didn't endear him to his peers. He was also undermined by the mayor who had hired him.

Kevin White was very charismatic and well respected when he took office, but the school-busing issue had cut into his popularity. No one in the administration wanted to be the guy out front of the busing issue—there was too much potential for being hated. Di Grazia didn't seem to mind; this was his job, and he was the front person for the city's attempt to maintain order. He took some of the heat for the policing of the desegregation busing and was roundly hated in Southie, Charlestown, and Hyde Park, wherever the police protected the schools. In many other areas, however, di Grazia was a very popular figure.

Di Grazia was very smooth, tall, handsome, with a head of longish curly hair. (This was the seventies; hair mattered.) In a department traditionally dominated by people of Irish heritage, di Grazia was the city's first Italian-American police commissioner. The elderly loved him, and with that head of hair he could even relate to the young. Polls showed he was the most popular public figure in the city of Boston. Then he made a mistake; he started to tell people, "I could run for mayor." The phrase got back to Kevin White, and the mayor cut him off. He prevented di Grazia from receiving a pay increase, he canceled a job di Grazia had lined up for his wife, he did everything he could to stick it to him. Mayors, I have found, are very concerned about popular police commissioners.

Di Grazia was gone too soon.

The busing issue had also chewed up the department. Cops were worn out by the constant pressure and long hours, but because of all the overtime they began making a fortune. Many officers became very dependent on this extra money: They bought homes and boats and ran up mortgages and began to live lifestyles they wouldn't be able to afford once the crisis ended. Money became the god. We had bred a generation of cops who were motivated more by the money than by the job.

White appointed Joe Jordan as acting police commissioner to fill out the last year of di Grazia's five-year term. Where di Grazia had been innovative and progressive, Jordan was personable but conventional. He had broken free of the old guard, but, while he didn't renege on di Grazia's creative legacy, he did not push it forward as aggressively. White attempted to keep Jordan under his control, and Jordan could serve the next full term only if White appointed him to it. The commissioner's term ran five years and overlapped mayoral administrations precisely to avoid situations in which an appointee might be beholden to the mayor who appointed him. Under Mayor White, however, City Hall became increasingly influential in all matters affecting the police department.

A bit of Boston Police Department history is important here. The commissionership was a political patronage plum, and because of concern over the level of corruption in Boston, for about thirty years after the election of Boston's first Irish mayor, control of the appointment of the police commissioner remained in the hands of the governor. The Brahmins on Beacon Hill, old-time Yankees, controlled the state house and didn't want to lose control of the city to the Irish. It wasn't until 1962, following a major police corruption scandal, that the mayor of Boston regained that right. Even then, restrictions were imposed. The police commissioner would be a civilian, and to insure his independence, his term woud run for five years, overlapping the mayor's four-year term. The men who actually ran the department on a day-to-day basis were the superintendents, all of whom had come up through the ranks.

Di Grazia had brought together a band of civilians who became known as his "whiz kids": Gary Hayes, Mark Furstenberg, Phil Marks, Steve Dunleavy, and Bob Wasserman. Civilians. It was unheard of. To have a civilian in a position of actual power in the Boston Police Department was like the pope appointing a Jewish bishop. After di Grazia left, Dunleavy and Wasserman convinced Jordan to implement the former commissioner's plan to bring in young sergeants from this new class and establish a mentoring and development program. Jack Gifford, Al Sweeney, and I were tapped to work with them.

A lot of people wouldn't take the job. "I'm not working for a friggin' civilian; we'll be here long after they're gone." In fact, some officers were blackballed for working with these guys. Some people wouldn't talk to us. You were supposed to go up through the ranks, you didn't break the blue line. We became "headquarters people." You had to be a risk taker just to work in the commissioner's office.

For example, Al Sweeney was known as the start-up person; he was the tactical logistics person they sent in to lay the proper foundation for many new initiatives. He was assigned temporarily to the tow lot to set up the Denver boot program, in which officers clamped boots on illegally parked cars. "Captain," Sergeant Sweeney said when he got there, "I'm reporting as ordered."

"Oh, really. Who ordered you?"

"The commissioner's office."

"The commissioner's office ordered you."

"Yes, sir."

"Well, the commissioner's office has walls and ceilings and floors. Does the commissioner's office talk to you?"

"No, sir. The commissioner sent me here."

"Ah, very good, Sergeant. And your name?"

"Sergeant Sweeney."

"Ah, ha." He stopped. "You talk to the police commissioner?"

"No, sir. He talks to me."

It seemed to Sweeney that the captain was incensed. The department was controlled by World War II veterans and run like the military. You followed the chain of command and were not allowed to think until you reached a high enough rank. It was clear to Sweeney that, as far as this captain was concerned, sergeant wasn't high enough. Sergeants were gofers. It was bad enough Sergeant Sweeney was at headquarters. How dare he talk to the commissioner when the captain couldn't?

Sweeney was sent to Alabama to take a Civilian Disturbance Orientation course. Upon his return, he found himself at a meeting with white shirts, superintendents; he was a young sergeant, the only light-blue shirt in the room. He made some comment, and one of the superintendents said, "Who is that wiseass kid down there?" From then on, Sweeney was known as the Wiseass Kid.

Sweeney, Gifford, and I were young wiseass kids walking around headquarters talking on a first-name basis with superintendents and the civilian whiz kids. What made us so special? Dunleavy and Wasserman identified us as guys with potential, and they encouraged us. We got a taste of headquarters and learned its inner workings at a very early stage in our careers.

The most important benefit of working at headquarters was that it exposed us to the idea of looking at the city as a whole. As beat cops or sergeants assigned to individual districts we were inclined to deal with the situations immediately at hand, but in the commissioner's office we were taught to approach problems citywide.

Dunleavy, now Jordan's director of administration, was very involved in the development of the professional policing model of that era, with a strong emphasis on centralized control. His strength was in his systems, and he believed strongly in research, reports, and grunt work in the service of a professional goal. Until di Grazia arrived, the Boston police were bereft of modern techniques and management practices, but Dunleavy, who saw his powers and influence greatly expand under Jordan, sought to bring us up-to-date and to market us. I was assigned to be his staff assistant. It was a good deal: a private office in the commissioner's suite and a marked take-home car with the unit designation "Commissioner's Staff" on the front fender. I had arrived.

In the late sixties and early seventies, American policing evolved significantly. In November 1976 when I was assigned to the commissioner's office, the latest concepts were rapid response, mobility, technology, and professionalism. The emergency number 911 had come into being in the early seventies and completely changed the face of American policing, putting a premium on "the three R's": rapid response, random patrols, and reactive investigation. The cutting edge of policing theory in those years was all about response time and arrest clearance rates, the faster the better. If we got to the scene in a hurry, we could either arrest the criminal or pick up his warm trail and hunt him down. American police forces began to measure their impact not on what crime they were preventing but on how fast they were responding to it. (This was more fiction than fact; studies showed that police made an arrest in only 2.9 percent of all 911 calls involving serious crime.) Increasingly, money and manpower were devoted to responding after the fact. Rather than preventing crime, we were in the business of chasing crooks.

One of the strengths of the old system had been that the beat cops knew the neighborhoods they policed, and their presence in and knowledge of the community prevented many crimes from occurring. Under the new system, in city after city, cops were pulled out of the neighborhoods and put into sector cars from which they responded whenever there was a call.

When officers were not chasing 911 calls, they were expected to patrol their assigned sector and, by the visibility and randomness of their patrol, deter criminals from committing other crimes. Because criminals never knew where the cops were, the thinking went, they lessened the risk of getting caught by committing fewer crimes. Advanced police thinkers and managers of the time were answering questions such as: How many cops should be in cars? How many should work in the stations? How many in one district? How many in another? The disposition of manpower was controlled not at the district level but from the commissioner's office. Unfortunately, one of the results of this new professionalism was that we got isolated in our cars and lost contact and familiarity with the neighborhoods and their residents.

Driving around the streets is very different from walking on them. In a patrol car, the only time you talk to people is after a crime has occurred. You're not a fixture in people's lives. You're an authority, not a friend; an occasional presence, not a personality. You become "them," not "us." The noted theorist George Kelling called it "stranger policing."

Even the concept of the ideal cop was transformed. The friendly cop on the beat, known by good and bad alike, was replaced by the "Adam-12" impersonal model, very efficient, very stern. That bleeding assault victim or the seriously injured rape victim wasn't going to be offered an arm around the shoulder or a word of comfort. "Just the facts, ma'am." Jack Webb on *Dragnet* had twenty-two minutes between commercials to solve the crime and make the arrest; he didn't have time to be concerned about prevention.

We also, for the first time, had modern technology, and we wanted to use it. Police were going to be a modern crime-fighting machine. To support the technology and the new mobile policing style, we had procedures for everything, and a lot of my time at headquarters was spent researching and writing these procedures and developing new accountability systems. Dunleavy, for instance, pushed the idea of measuring response time by computer, and under his direction we developed a Standard Beat Plan that recorded the comings and goings of every police officer on patrol— on paper, every shift, every day. I'm a systems-oriented person, and this assignment suited me. We designed a program to measure and record what time each car logged in, what time it logged off, the number of calls it handled, the average time in service. It was the kind of management control that the Boston police had been sadly lacking, and it encouraged accountability. Every morning, the superintendent in charge of the bureau of field services reviewed the sheets and saw how we'd done the day before. Then he'd call around and quiz the district captains. "You were supposed to put out eight cars, you only put out seven. Why?"

We also designed the first computerized vehicle inventory. The department, as best we could tell, had never done a vehicle inventory. We had six hundred or so cars, but we didn't know where a lot of them were. One morning, we sent staff out and actually inspected every police car in the fleet in order to come up with a complete, standardized vehicle report. It took us over two weeks to find them all—at least, all that we could. The previous records and accountability forms were so bad that to this day I believe some are still missing. We also discovered an interesting scheme in which low-mileage cruisers were being sold and then repurchased by police personnel at very reduced prices.

Dunleavy was also a great one for imagery. Boston police cars had been blue and gray, a drab, awful-looking combination that reinforced the public image that the BPD never seemed to change. Our logo was all block letters, staid, old. Dunleavy redesigned them both. The logo was modernized, the cars were painted white with a distinctive-looking blue stripe to make them more visible and professional looking. The words "CALL 911" were printed in large letters on the back of every car. This proved to be a mistake, since the public started to call 911 for everything. The wording was then changed to "EMERGENCY CALL 911," but even later versions eliminated 911 altogether.

Walking around Boston, you couldn't help but notice these new cars, which gave the average citizen the sense of increased, more modern, and better police presence. Interestingly, cops initially didn't like the new colors; they thought it made them too visible. They even described the patrol wagons as "ice-cream trucks."

Dunleavy was very attuned to the political nuances of policing and to Mayor White's concerns. He pushed hard for increased police visibility in the neighborhoods, not only to maximize the impact of the force but to satisfy the political demand for it. As a former reporter, he understood the press's ability to deliver our message, and he trumpeted our response time, our technology, and all our advances.

Inside the department, however, Dunleavy was universally hated. He was tough and smart as a whip, but he had an awful personality. All he knew was one way: straight ahead. If the commissioner, or more important the mayor, said, "We're going to paint every street in the city of Boston purple tomorrow," the streets would be painted purple tomorrow, even if it was snowing and there was ice on the ground. Nothing got in his way. He was a royal pain in the ass to work for, but I learned a lot from him.

Dunleavy was the most obsessive perfectionist I have ever known. When the prototype for our new fleet of police vehicles was delivered, Dunleavy was unhappy. "We didn't order that black plug," he said. The department hadn't ordered AM radios in the cars, and the dealer had put a black rubber plug in the hole where the antenna was usually mounted.

"Well," the guy told Dunleavy, "you didn't order the radio, so that's what we put there."

"No," Dunleavy told him, "that has to be filled in and soldered over." This was the type of thing that drove people crazy. In some respects, Dunleavy and I were a good match. We both put great stock in getting things done and getting them done right. (You don't sit in your room as a kid making hundreds of clay figures without putting great value on attention to detail.) But working with Dunleavy also taught me what can happen when you drive it to the extreme and when you don't allow people to have input into the process. Largely as a result of my experiences with him, I have come to believe that the best leaders and managers are those who instill creativity but who take satisfaction in seeing their own ideas so embraced by their subordinates that the subordinates ultimately come to believe they were the original source.

Where Steve Dunleavy was almost entirely concerned with politics, technology systems, and imagery, Bob Wasserman, now director of operations, was more involved in the emerging philosophy of neighborhood policing and substantive changes to implement this philosophy. Guys didn't like Dunleavy because he was a know-it-all and a nitpicker; they didn't like Wasserman because he was smart and irascible. Wasserman seemed to be impersonal and demanding, but, in fact, much more than anyone I have ever met in policing, he consciously went out of his way to be a mentor, to develop and implement not only his own ideas but those of others as well. He became a close friend.

Wasserman was an academic and a practitioner. He had a scholarly appearance, a mustached overbite, an occasional beard, and talked with a bit of a stammer. There were a lot of Bugs Bunny jokes flying around the department. His political leanings were progressively liberal; his police beliefs and practices were also progressive, which put him outside normal department thinking.

I was first introduced to Wasserman by Al Sweeney, who had met him when Wasserman was director of the Police Academy. Sweeney, whose opinion I held in very high regard, said Wasserman was an important thinker, but when I first met him, I wasn't impressed. He was curt; his reputation gave you reason to respect the man but his manner didn't give you a lot of reason to like him.

When I met him again at headquarters, he had become Joe Jordan's civilian director of operations. Both Wasserman and Dunleavy's offices were right outside Jordan's door, and mine was right next to theirs. They were constantly battling each other for the soul of the BPD.

Wasserman went out of his way to identify talent and work with people in whom he saw potential. That's his style and his enduring legacy. I came well recommended, so he took a look at me. Once I got past his gruff exterior, he turned out to be not only a brilliant thinker and a doer but a good guy with a warm personal side.

Wasserman approached policing not as an imposition of will but as problem solving. Wasserman first exposed me to the writings of Herman Goldstein, *Policing a Free Society,* and the idea that police have discretion. It seems simple, but the fact is often overlooked: It's not all black and white. The law says, You shan't do this, you shall do that, but society has given the police officer broad discretion in enforcing these laws. Police management tends to tell officers what not to do, not how to do it. Not every civilian gets a ticket for going through a red light; you can give an oral warning, you can give a written warning, you can write out an actual ticket. When used appropriately, an officer's discretion can be very effective; when used inappropriately, it can lead to abuse and corruption.

Wasserman explained that police can't be an island, that we have to work in partnership with the community. Cops, he told me, should not be allowed to roam all over the place; they need defined areas of responsibility. To prevent crime and fear and not just respond to it, the same cops should consistently be in the same places at the same time, so they can know people and know problems and develop a sense of neighborhood and make a difference. Responsibility didn't rest just on the sixth floor, it should be pushed down to much lower levels. We needed to be proactive, Wasserman explained, not sit and wait for things to happen. He was one of the first in the profession to understand and define the elements and potential of what we came to know later as community policing.

Many cops see the Miranda ruling, which states that a suspect must be advised of his rights, as an intrusion on their job; Wasserman understood that we needed to embrace the Miranda law to make certain our arrests become convictions. He was constantly telling us that we have to work with the law. You can't break the law to enforce the law. Wasserman's most firmly held professional belief was that police must be more progressive and tolerant than we had ever thought and, indeed, should help to lead the way for the rest of society. His views on the importance of education, training, and the desegregation of the police (both racially and sexually) gave us all new perspectives.

Wasserman stressed that a good manager has to have a handle on how he or she uses personnel. Early in our relationship, he signed me up for two courses that had a great influence on my thinking: managing police investigations and managing police patrol practices. These three-day conferences were held under the auspices of the Law Enforcement Assistance Administration (LEAA), a federal organization formed in the 1970s to support and educate the police and other members of the criminal-justice system in the aftermath of the Kerner Report, which attributed some of the causes of the violent racial outbreaks in America to racial prejudice and police abuse. One of the LEAA's goals was to gather a body of knowledge about policing in areas where there was very little.

Dunleavy was not too enthusiastic about my going to these conferences, but Wasserman insisted. With police from around the country attending, it would be a great place to network, to share ideas, and to break out of the parochialism of our own department. I was excited about expanding my policing horizons, and I was honored that the department let me represent them. Wasserman's lesson stayed with me; we need to constantly look beyond the department, and indeed the police profession, for new ideas.

The Dunleavy/Wasserman, imagery/substance feast was a gourmet smorgasbord of police theory and practices. Some police professionals are concerned only with systems, some only with marketing and the press, others only with crime. I was first in line to taste everything, while so many others got only the usual blue-plate special.

In September 1977, Wasserman approached me about taking over an innovative neighborhood-policing project called the Boston-Fenway Program that he was proposing to Commissioner Jordan. It was to be located in District 4, probably the most interesting district in the city. District 4 encompassed the working-class, mixed-population South End, a gradually gentrifying neighborhood; the Back Bay area, for all practical purposes Boston's midtown Manhattan; plus the East Fenway and West Fenway, a diverse neighborhood home to many of the city's educational and cultural institutions, such as the Museum of Fine Arts, Symphony Hall, the First Church of Christ, Scientist, Northeastern University, Boston University, beautiful Frederick Law Olmsted–designed parks, and Fenway Park. It also included Kenmore Square, the heart of the city's nightclub district. District 4 was filled with college kids and was probably Boston's most racially, culturally, and economically diverse area.

In the late seventies, the decision to pull the police off the streets was beginning to take its toll. It was an anything-goes era. Marijuana and hallucinogen use was widespread. Under the banner of freedom of expression, society was becoming increasingly tolerant of aberrant behavior, with the cultural pendulum on a wide swing toward permissiveness. Instead of setting higher goals, we lowered standards. Aberrant behavior became so commonplace that society excused it. We were, as Senator Daniel Patrick Moynihan said, "defining social deviancy down," not understanding that all these little things, because they weren't being addressed, emboldened some in society to take what they saw as the next step.

Although not fully aware of it at the time, as a young officer I was experiencing three revolutionary social experiments that radically changed the quality of life in cities. As described by Professor George Kelling in one of his essays: "The first was the official recognition—indeed, the virtual blessing—of an anything-goes ideology on the streets. The second was the 'depolicing' of the crime problem. The third was the depolicing of urban streets and public spaces. The last two are similar yet distinct.

"Permissiveness grew out of the idea of 'victimless crimes' such as prostitution, aggressive panhandling, drug-induced and drunken behavior, creating graffiti, and squeegeeing. After all, the argument goes, who is really hurt by such crimes? Many, like prostitution, are consensual, agreed upon by and affecting only seller and buyer. Why should the state and its criminal justice apparatus be concerned when nobody is hurt? Police have enough to do just handling serious crime, let alone nonviolent deviance. This argument went further: Much behavior considered deviant is really acceptable under other cultural standards—ergo, enforcing laws against minor crimes is really imposing white middle-class standards on minorities, the poor, and, later, the homeless. And the argument was extended further still: Society is enriched and ennobled by much nonviolent deviance. Graffiti is seen as a valid artistic expression by society's victims and should be appreciated as such, and aggressive panhandling is an important political message about social inequities.

"A similar ideology in the seventies shaped public policy regarding mental illness and drunkenness. To be sure, mental commitment and drunkenness laws had been abused, and many facilities were outrageously inadequate. Yet to some radical psychiatrists and civil libertarians, the problem was not sick individuals but a sick society. People weren't ill, society was, and the mentally ill were pointing this out to the rest of society. Thus, in the name of their 'liberty interests,' even the most seriously emotionally disturbed individuals, chronic schizophrenics, were turned out to the streets to receive 'community treatment'—an unrealized fiction. Likewise, drunkenness was decriminalized without adequate treatment facilities, despite the well-known links among drinking, crime, and violence.

"The second experiment was in depolicing the crime problem. The axioms that defined the crime problem and its solution went something like this: Poverty, racism, injustice, and family breakdown cause crime. Crime must be dealt with by dealing with its causes. Police can do nothing about poverty, racism, and injustice; ergo, they can do nothing about crime. Police can, of course, arrest people who commit crimes—and through incarceration prevent crime—but short of that, all police can do is displace crime. Crime prevention can be achieved only by vast social change: either by eliminating poverty, racism, and injustice or by restoring family values, primarily by eliminating welfare.

"The third experiment was that of depolicing city streets. In the name of police efficiency, elimination of political influences and corruption, and the assumed anticrime benefits of rapid mobility, police were being sequestered in cars throughout the United States. The old model of diffusing police among citizens so that police could prevent crime by their presence and by reducing opportunities for crime was replaced by mobilized, reactive police who were remote from communities.

"Lost in all of this for decades were the enormous consequences to communities of uninterrupted disorderly conditions in neighborhoods. Johns might or might not be victims or criminals, but neighborhoods certainly lose out. Aggressive schizophrenics, drunken youths, promiscuous and scantily clad prostitutes, and all sorts of other 'nonviolent' deviants might enjoy their 'liberty interests,' but neighborhood residents who could not move were virtually imprisoned in their homes. Most tragically, such conditions affected those with the least resources to deal with it: the poor, minorities, elderly, and other inner-city residents. The idea that behaviors like public urination and defecation, drunkenness, drug dealing, aggressive panhandling, and other such forms of illegal loutish behavior were somehow a sign of cultural pluralism was a cruel mockery; it represented condescension toward both the poor and ethnic and racial minorities, and it forestalled official efforts to restore order and reclaim neighborhood streets. Disorderly, crime-breeding conditions were allowed to exist in inner cities that simply never would have been tolerated in middle-class areas. The nurturing institutions of society—family, religion, schools, and commerce—could not function under such circumstances."

As a young cop, I became aware of the growing lack of respect for police. On the corner, instead of moving along as you asked them, people would sass you or push back. I'd listen to the old-time cops talking about the old days, and I'd know what they meant. I could see firsthand a diminishing of respect for the police and our symbolic authority.

Of course, the good old days weren't always so good; in Boston, you couldn't go into a police station to make a complaint about a cop—you'd get your head handed to you. If you were black, you couldn't go into a police station at all. There was no Miranda warning, and the interrogation of prisoners was an anything-goes proposition. It was the time of the third degree.

From time to time, proposals are made to do away with the Miranda warning and the exclusionary rule on the grounds that they inhibit good policing. That's a bunch of nonsense. We can operate effectively with the Miranda warning and the exclusionary rule. Many of the statements police get are from suspects who admit to crimes after they have been advised of their rights and have chosen not to invoke them. Until they say the magic words, "I want a lawyer," we're free to talk to them. The whole idea is to keep them talking, keep them from getting "lawyered up." You don't want them to seek an attorney until you're able to elicit the information you want. So now, rather than beating it out of them, we become much more calculating in our approach, more adroit in the use of mouth and brain than foot and stick, while at the same time ensuring that their constitutional rights are respected. That's how times change for the better. You don't want a totalitarian state, you want a society that says, "We are willing, in order to maintain law and order, to tolerate this much interference in our lives and no more." Society has to define the appropriate balance, and the police have to understand that that's as far as we go.

One result of this diminished police control and presence was a rising tide of crime in the streets of District 4. As well as the neighborhood residents, the people who were coming down from Lexington, Concord, and other suburban areas to the city's cultural institutions were now becoming victims of crime. Fenway was becoming dangerous, and the community's leaders were very concerned that patrons would stop attending exhibits, performances, and ballgames, that their buildings and physical plants would be vandalized, their workers hurt and terrorized. The eroding conditions severely threatened the vitality of this important neighborhood.

In an attempt to deal with this problem, a not-for-profit consortium of businesses and private institutions banded together as the Boston-Fenway Program, under the leadership of Claire Cotton, a writer and editor and former vice-chancellor of Boston University. They basically said, "We either need to control this situation or we need to move." But how do you move Symphony Hall, Northeastern University, and the Christian Science Mother Church? You don't.

The Boston-Fenway Program's primary purpose was to develop a partnership among private institutions and the police and the neighborhoods to address the area's deteriorating situation. Cotton approached Wasserman and said he had the funding. What they needed was the expertise, the vision to get the job done.

Wasserman wanted to move me to District 4 to take over this initiative, but Dunleavy didn't want me to go. I was desperate for the opportunity to get back in the field and practice what I'd been learning. A deal was struck: If I could find a suitable replacement, I could take the assignment. I went to my old college classmate and sector-car partner, Mickey Roache, who was working in District 4 as a patrol supervisor. "Mickey," I said, "here's an opportunity to come up to headquarters." I worked on Roache and soothed Dunleavy, and they went for it.

Roache came to headquarters at a time when, spurred by the busing rebellion, Wasserman and Jordan were grappling with the issue of race violence. Wasserman, with Jordan's approval, came up with an extraordinarily creative unit, the Community Disorders Unit, to investigate race crimes.

There were no volunteers from the Boston police for this very controversial unit. Wasserman thought highly of Roache, and since he couldn't find anyone else to accept it, he cajoled him into taking the job. Very moral, very straight, smart, hardworking, and, most important, free of prejudice, Roache was absolutely the right guy.

Cotton, Wasserman, and I worked hard on the Boston-Fenway Program. We knew we couldn't target the cultural areas of Fenway alone—that wouldn't sit well or be fair to the entire community. We devised a plan to address crime districtwide. In some respects, this was one of the first community-policing initiatives in the nation, fifteen years before that term gained currency.

First we had to establish exactly what the problem was. We planned to go into each neighborhood to find out.

The commander of District 4 was Captain James McDonald, a hail-fellow-well-met who disappeared for a couple of hours every day to play handball. Cops loved him. Old-time, old-school captain, easygoing, smart, he managed the district quite well but also understood he was working for a guy who was very hands-on: Deputy Superintendent James "Mickey" MacDonald.

Mickey MacDonald was always puffing on a cigar. He had a silver mane of hair, piercing blue eyes—guys called him Old Blue Eyes—a barrel chest and a constant tan. Just a rugged, handsome Irish guy. He belonged to the Old Colony Yacht Club in South Boston and spent much of his off-duty time playing cards there with the boys. Like much of the leadership of the Boston police at that time, he was one of the old-guard generation; many of his contemporaries had been hooked into the era's corruption and inefficiency.

You can appreciate the awkwardness of my situation. The police commissioner told the commanding officer of District 4, "I'm sending this young sergeant from my staff down to redesign your district." Here's this kid, working for the civilian whiz kids Wasserman and Dunleavy, and he wants men twenty-five years his elder to work with him and with this consortium from Fenway. Both MacDonald and McDonald, as you might expect, initially looked at me a little askance.

But MacDonald had seen the light. When di Grazia came in, he had gone from old school to new school. In many ways, he was out in front, leading the charge.

Several older men in the department resented that di Grazia and his outsiders had to come in and make the changes they knew should have been made. These men had great pride in the BPD. They were not necessarily resistant to di Grazia's ideas, only that they were being made so publicly. Did we need to do it in full view, with so many people's lives and reputations being ruined? With lesser men, this resistance could have presented me with a serious problem.

Mickey MacDonald and I hit it off. Like Mo Allen before him, he quickly became my mentor. I like to believe he learned something from me as well. He set me up in an office right outside his own and soon recognized that I was going to work to his betterment and bring in some additional resources. I rode around the district for a couple of hours every day, just to get a feel of the territory, and MacDonald and I spent a lot of time patrolling together, chasing calls, observing. He understood the importance of being there to observe conditions for himself, to instruct or correct if necessary, but to be a leader. He was a walk-around manager years before they coined the phrase.

MacDonald loved being a cop. He loved strutting. He loved being out on the street. He always wore his dress uniform, crisp white shirt, and was neat as a pin except when he was dropping cigar ashes on himself, before he finally gave stogies up after a heart-bypass operation. He had command presence. When he walked into a room, in uniform or plain clothes, you knew: Here is the guy who's in charge. I loved and respected Mickey MacDonald and learned a lot from him about the importance of a commander leading. In that district, he set the tone. He went through his paperwork every day; nothing went on in that district that he was unaware of. We were going to work on crime, we were going to develop the hot spots, we were going to work on systems. He had a temper and a half, and he could rip you up one side and down the other, but he was fair, and the cops loved him. Most important, they worked for him. And together, we did redesign that district.

MacDonald was a great believer in using crime statistics to target hot spots and staying on top of his detectives, but he also understood the importance of working with the community. When I arrived, the district had been divided up like any other into sectors comprised of a number of federal census tracts, each with approximately the same calls-for-service workload and each assigned a police car. There were seventeen sectors and seventeen sector cars, each ostensibly spending most of their time in their own area. But the way 911 calls came in, particularly in the more troublesome areas, all seventeen cars could conceivably be in the South End catching calls. One emergency could empty all the other sectors and leave most of the district essentially unpoliced.

According to the statistical tracking and computer systems of our professional police model, we were responding to incidents quickly and were eminently successful. From the management side, we were doing a hell of a job. But from the operational or philosophical side, there was a lot to be desired. The public wasn't happy. "Sure, you get there within six minutes, but what good is that? The crime has already been committed. And what do you do when you get there? You come in, take a report, and leave. You haven't solved our problems." Crime was going up, the fear factor was rising, and people weren't even getting to know who their cops were because the guys in the cars were coming and going all the time.

A classic 911 story came up back when I was working in Southie at District 6. In one year, 1,300 calls came in regarding the corner of I Street and East Seventh Street. A gang of kids was hanging out on that corner, and an old-timer was living in an apartment with a window right next to where these kids were drinking and acting up. The old man called constantly. We would send a two-man sector car, get there in five minutes, kick the kids off the corner, notify the dispatcher, and leave. The kids would come back, the old man would call—always anonymously—we would arrive . . . 1,300 times. Nobody ever tried to locate the caller or solve the problem.

That was the essence of professional policing. By department standards, we were doing a great job. Meanwhile, no one was happy and nothing changed. The kids hanging out felt harassed, the guy calling was not pleased, and the cops in the car were pissed off at the constant futility of shooing away these disrespectful kids. It would have been more economical to have put a police officer on the corner twenty-four hours a day holding a lamp. At least he could have provided some light for the neighborhood.

In District 4, the situation was much the same. The assaults, the drug dealing, the prostitution, the public drinking, the graffiti, and the loud parties were not being dealt with effectively by the police. Conditions didn't get better, the public got more and more aggravated, some people moved out, and the quality of life in the neighborhood went on a downward spiral. So I was given an extraordinary opportunity: power, money, resources, staff, attention, and the mandate to create a program that would take into account the various needs in order to find a new and better way of policing. There were two factors in this equation: the neighborhood's needs and the cops'. We addressed them simultaneously.

In order to solve problems, you must know what and where they are. Boston-Fenway Program funding allowed me to hire several staff people, including Julie Rossborough, a former Amtrak policewoman, and Donna Taylor, a Northeastern University criminal-justice student intern, to identify the community groups and the issues. In the early 1970s, while still a captain, Mickey MacDonald had been one of the first Boston commanders to hold community meetings in his district. It was this initiative that first brought him to di Grazia's attention and had led to his promotion to deputy superintendent.

District 4 was huge, and you couldn't expect people to traipse over from the Back Bay to the district station in the South End. Boston is a city of neighborhoods, and people tend to stay in their own. So we leafleted communities and advertised. For the first time in the history of the Boston Police Department, we took the police department to the people.

If there were groups with organized meetings, we went to those. Otherwise, we set up our own in schoolrooms, community halls, whatever was available. We provided refreshments and a little show-and-tell.

Instead of the deputy superintendent who would tell them about the grand scheme of things, I brought the cops, the detectives assigned to that sector, and the sergeant who was working that night. Meet your police. We talked about our perspective of the neighborhood's specific problems and gave crime-prevention tips. And we listened: "What are your problems? What is the biggest issue here?"

It turned out that the police had one perception of the largest problem in an area and the neighborhoods had another one altogether. Ours was usually serious crime. Theirs was usually a lot more mundane. This was a major problem of the professional model: different priorities.

Because so much of our time was consumed chasing 911 calls, we were focusing what little time we had left on solving major crime. If we handled that, we figured, we would ease the public's fear. Meanwhile, the public felt plagued by a constant invasion of little things, exactly the day-to-day annoyances that had been handled in previous eras by the beat cop. Or at least he gave that impression. Who hasn't heard the old story about the cop dragging a kid home by the ear and telling his mother, "Johnny's been acting up"?

At one of the community meetings, the police focused on a string of burglaries: This was important, a major thief breaking into people's homes. The community, on the other hand, was upset that the streets were filthy and cleaning couldn't take place because cars were clogging the streets and cops weren't tagging them to be towed. The officers took this to heart, and the next day we began writing tickets. In the process of tagging and towing the cars, the officers started talking to the people, and it didn't take long before they found residents who had seen the burglar on the street. The burglary was solved, the case cleared. Had we not addressed the sweeping of the street, we wouldn't have opened the dialogue that solved the larger crime. It taught a valuable lesson: Seemingly unrelated problems can be responded to so that each positively affects the other.

It wasn't the easiest lesson in the world to absorb. I was still a young cop. We all wanted to make the good pinch, the gun pinch. We wanted to disarm felons, we didn't want to be wrestling with drunks. But as I went to these community meetings, it quickly began to sink in. Though both searching for the same destination, police and community had been going in opposite directions.

Officers walked away from the community meetings saying, "I heard your complaints about noise and vandalism, and we will address them. But here's our problem: We've got a cat burglar breaking into houses. Here's what we can do; here's what you need to do." We made our promises back and forth. Then the phones started ringing. We opened up a tremendous amount of communication that had been cut off before because the police always had an us-versus-them relationship with the community. We were beginning to become accountable to the community and their priorities.

We held these community meetings three or four nights a week for the entire year. Julie Rossborough took notes as people raised their hands and named their issues. In the average meeting, we fielded thirty or forty questions, some of them very tough. People's anger and built-up frustration over not having their needs met for many years came to the surface. But once they understood that we were actually going to act on these problems, they were very grateful.

Rossborough developed a matrix chart of approximately twenty key issues that were raised consistently, and it was a surprise. As a percentage of the population, very few people are actually robbed at gunpoint. Even in the worst neighborhoods, if there is a shooting on the street while you are at work, you don't know about it. It could happen in your own building, and you might not be aware of it. People were complaining about the so-called signs of crime, the constant irritants, the stuff in their faces every day: prostitution, graffiti, filth in the street, noisy parties. It became clear that the system Steve Dunleavy and I had designed and implemented and believed in was not meeting the needs of the public.

Bob Wasserman brilliantly recognized this and began to put systems into place to deal with it.

The issues we had to face were:

- How do we motivate the cops?
- How do we get cops to respond to the identified concerns of the public?
- How do we get the cops to work with the public?
- How do we get the operational philosophy of the Boston Police Department more in sync with the needs of this district?

We developed the Neighborhood Responsive Police Plan. We designed a sector map for District 4 that was not based on the traditional census tracts. Instead, we tried to develop sectors that were clearly identifiable geographically in the public's mind as their neighborhood and worked from there. Within the four large quadrants that were the Back Bay, the South End, East Fenway, and West Fenway, we identified sixteen distinct neighborhoods. We assigned one sector car to each.

Wasserman was familiar with a British policing model called the Two-Car Plan. Two-officer rapid-response vehicles were sent when a problem call, for example, a robbery in progress, came in. The more routine, leisurely policing of the neighborhoods was done by the bobby on the beat, on a bicycle, or in a one-man service car. Two cars handling two different responsibilities. Wasserman suggested using two types of cars in District 4.

There were 212 cops in the district. I had worked with them, spent a lot of time riding around with them, and I felt I knew them. As a young cop, I always complained that we never were given any information and were not asked for our comments, so when I got into a position of some power, I shared information with my officers, and I asked what they were doing. It was a policy of inclusion, not exclusion.

I came to see that a lot of cops in that district were not averse to meeting with community groups; they liked it. They listened to the complaints and went about the business of handling them. Other cops were perfectly happy to take their regular calls but said, "Don't bother me with that other stuff, I don't want anything to do with it." As a manager, I adjusted to the reality of my workforce. They're not all clones, they had different personalities and professional perspectives. I surveyed my cops and tried to match assignment with temperament. I had to understand what turns cops on.

Most cops want their patch, their own territory. They want to do the job. The basic idea is: Give me an area, and I'll take care of business. Others want to go all over the place. I was one of those. I would have chased calls all over the district. But a lot of the guys had grown up being beat cops, particularly the old-timers, and then in the sixties and seventies had been put into patrol cars. Many of the car teams in District 4 were made up of cops who had been on the job for thirty years, who missed their old beats. We'd find them, in their new two-man cars, gravitating back to their old haunts, where they knew everybody, where they got their cup of coffee, where they got their dry cleaning. They had their patch.

I surveyed the cops about the system I was planning to propose to the police commissioner and gave them the choice: "Pick what you'd like to do and where you'd like to do it." I needed approximately 50 cops to staff up the rapid-response cars and 150 to staff up the neighborhood-service cars. We based the number of rapid-response cars on the previous year's Priority One emergency calls. If we had fifty calls on a Friday night from four to midnight, that meant three cars would be needed. If the numbers went down from midnight to eight, we might need only one car. We adjusted the manpower to the need. Similarly, the sectors for the neighborhood service cars were designed around identifiable neighborhoods and calls for service.

In exchange for service cars missing out on some action, accepting additional responsibilities to deal with neighborhood residents, and being held accountable for responding to their priorities, I offered those officers a carrot: "Very rarely," I told them, "under the new system will I take you out of your neighborhood. We'll keep you on your beat. We'll try to reduce cross-sector dispatching to a minimum by holding nonemergency calls until you are free to handle them." They liked that. South End cops didn't want to work in the Back Bay, and Back Bay cops didn't want to work in the South End. I tried to accommodate them all; if people are working jobs they want to work, it stands to reason they will do a better job. I also made a conscious effort to assign the same officers to the same beats on all shifts. I wanted to establish continuity within the neighborhood and create a sense of growing order and control in the streets.

Fortunately, the numbers worked out. I had around 60 cops who wanted to go around chasing calls, and 150 who wanted to stay in one area. Most of the cops got their choice.

The next hurdle was to alter the basic philosophy with which the Boston Police Department and every other police department in this country embraced 911. Clearly, the idea behind 911 was speed; the police were supposed to dispatch a car to deal with a 911 call as fast as possible. You didn't stack calls. Robbery in progress, cat in a tree, didn't matter; if there was a car free, whether around the corner or three miles away, you sent him over. Psychologically, a dispatcher wanted to move the calls from "pending" to "dispatched" and get them off the screen.

We proposed a sea change in the use of 911. A robbery and a stranded cat were not equal in the public's need for service; why should we respond to them as if they were? Under our computer-aided dispatching system, the call taker would enter the 911 information into a computer, which would analyze and automatically classify it by priority, according to public risk. (The system was humanized by the dispatcher, who could look at the information and override these designations if he felt it was necessary.) Under our proposed system, instead of giving the next call in the stack to the first available unit, we authorized stacking of nonemergency calls to await the availability of cars assigned to the sector of the call. Rapid-response quadrant cars would zoom in from all over the quadrant for a Priority One call, but Priority Twos and Threes would be stacked in order of seriousness for the neighborhood service cars. This was a much more efficient use of our resources: It would get the job done, it would never leave any part of the district unpoliced, and it would satisfy both the civilians and the police.

To put this program into practice, I had to sell it to the police commissioner. Since Mickey MacDonald had helped develop it, he was enthusiastic. Bob Wasserman, who had come up with the idea, was naturally an ally. It was up to me to sell it.

The meeting took place in the commissioner's office with Commissioner Jordan and some of the top brass. As if they weren't enough, Wasserman had invited former New York City Police Commissioner Pat Murphy. Murphy was a policing icon. He had also been the head of police in Washington and Detroit. He had cleaned house as the reform commissioner in New York City and broken the old pattern of corruption. He was the guy everybody wrote about, the leader in our field. He had written a book. Now he was heading up the Ford Foundation–sponsored Police Foundation, a private organization that conducted research, studied police initiatives in cities around the country, and made recommendations about police practices.

So, don't you know, I woke up the morning of my presentation with laryngitis.

Wasserman and Dunleavy were in the room to back me up. Although

Dunleavy was still not happy about my leaving his staff to go to District 4, he understood that this initiative could make a difference. Mickey MacDonald also stood with me. Some superintendents in his position might have been offended, but he was an exception in those days, encouraging and supporting creativity. If he and I hadn't gotten along, it would have killed the plan.

This was radical change, and change wasn't readily accepted in the Boston police. Some naysayers, choosing conformity over creativity, said we couldn't make one district different from all the rest.

I had prepared. I'd developed flip charts with color maps of each newly defined geographical sector, and demonstrated where each car would go and how our manpower would be allocated. I had rehearsed the most persuasive ways of making my case, and I croaked my way through it.

Murphy thought it was great, the latest in police thinking! Jordan signed off on it. We were in business. I was twenty-nine years old and in charge. I was ecstatic.

Back at the District 4 station house, an old brick-and-stone Depression-era building on the corner of Berkeley and Warren streets in the South End, the walls of my office looked as if someone had splattered paint all over the city. I had requisitioned gigantic maps of the district from City Hall and papered all four walls with them. I covered the maps with acetate and assigned a young civilian employee named Tommy Santry to put up dots: red dots for burglaries, blue dots for robberies. Each dot got a date inside to note when the crime took place. We updated the wall every night. Once we got our information organized, you could see exactly where District 4 crime was clustered. We put duplicate maps in the guardroom where officers turned out for roll call, prepared their reports, and took their meals. That way, when my office was closed, the crime information would be available to them twenty-four hours a day. The maps were also right next to the paid-detail board where off-duty extra-money assignments and rosters were posted. This area of the guardroom was known as the Wailing Wall, and the linoleum had long ago been worn away by the shuffling of many feet as officers pored over the board.

At first, the officers laughed. They gave me the nickname Lord Dots. Cops couldn't be bothered with dots, they were out there on the real streets. What's a pin map going to give them? But it didn't take long to get their interest.

After the initial ribbing and sarcasm that is so much a part of policing, the cops began to use the information. They had the entire district in front of them, and they checked out their own sectors and everybody else's. I made a point of being there as much as I could. I wanted to make contact.

I got the cops interested by giving them timely, accurate, easy-to-digest information. I didn't order them in and show them, I made it available, and the cops bought in. Then they went about solving some crimes and preventing others.

In each neighborhood sector, Julie Rossborough, now joined by her sister Cynthia Nichols, set up neighborhood panels and encouraged people in the community to work with their sector officers on a regular basis. When I brought neighborhood people into the office and they talked about their complaints, I had a visual to show them. That robbery on the corner of Massachusetts Avenue and Columbus? Right here. Their concerns were on my wall in blue and red; they could see we were on the case; they were recognized. It was a combination of acknowledgment and showmanship.

The Boston-Fenway Plan increasingly put me in the public eye, and I found I enjoyed it and was good at it. Back in the early days of VCRs, when one videotape cost twelve bucks, I taped my first television appearance off the local Channel 7 news announcing the beginning of this program. I got a big kick out of that. I began meeting notable and influential people at the various institutions that were a part of the Boston-Fenway Consortium. These were people I had read about in the newspapers, seen on the news and in the society pages. They were CEOs of corporations, academics, and patrons of the arts. Not only was I listening to their concerns and advice, they were listening in turn to me and taking my advice. For a Dorchester boy who didn't get hot water plumbing in his home until he was fourteen, this was heady stuff.

The Boston-Fenway Program worked. We targeted crime clusters in wealthy, middle-class, and working-class neighborhoods throughout the district, sent officers in, and an entire area of the city that had been threatened with decay and destruction rebounded. With crime declining, development could begin.

There was one notable weak link in the 911 system. We had approximately fifty police dispatchers working at headquarters, but they were rotated: Some were regulars, some floaters, but they weren't always working District 4. Despite our constant attention, they consistently took sector cars out of one quadrant and sent them to another on minor calls. I recognized our plan wasn't going to work unless I went up to operations and took control of the dispatch end as well. I spent time in what's called the

Turret, the 911 command center, and wasn't shy about getting on the air and telling a dispatcher, "That call's not on his beat. Find another car." While I put together a training program for the dispatchers, gave them special maps showing the newly designed District 4 sectors, and told them, "We do it differently," I couldn't break their psychology of getting rid of calls. I didn't have the consistency of control, and as a result some of our cars were still sent flying all over. Nevertheless, the program was judged a success.

I was not only running the Boston-Fenway Program, I was a manager within District 4, and I took that responsibility seriously. The things that drove me crazy when I was a beat cop, I now could take care of. For instance, in a patrol car, it made me completely nuts when I'd come to work and the lights wouldn't go on or the windshield wipers didn't work; I felt that no one was taking care of me, that my work was taken for granted. So every Sunday, I had all the District 4 cars brought in, and I personally inspected them. Then, during the week, we got them repaired. It made an impression on the cops that I took that much time on their behalf, and it forced the other supervisors in the station to respond. I was determined to be a new kind of boss.

Along that line, shortly after my arrival, Wasserman asked if I would be willing to assume additional duties as the Boston police's first liaison to the city's growing gay and lesbian population, many of whom lived in District 4. The relationship between the police and the gay community in the seventies was tenuous and had worsened when, in response to complaints from the Boston Public Library, District 4 undercover officers had arrested a large number of gay men for solicitation in the public restroom of the library's main branch at Copley Square.

Concerned that the gulf between the department and the gay community was widening, Wasserman responded to a request from David Brill, a gay reporter for the alternative *Real Paper*, for the department to meet confidentially with gays to hear their complaints. Since most of these complaints were being made against District 4 officers, Wasserman felt I would be the appropriate intermediary.

Mickey MacDonald was a conservative, church-bred Irish Catholic, and homosexual activities went against everything he believed in. If they were breaking the law, as they were in the library, he was going to enforce the law. But MacDonald was also a police officer, and he understood his obligation to protect that community under the law. We were able to find common ground. Solicitation at the library was clearly illegal and would not be tolerated. At the same time, however, a gay cruising area in a park in the Fenway area was being plagued by a series of muggings and robberies. We put officers in the park and made several arrests but purposely didn't interrupt the other behavior.

It was a delicate balance. Society was changing, and there was a lot of tension between gays wanting to come out of the closet and flex their muscles and a general public still not fully prepared for these activities, whether in a public men's room or a nightclub or a park at night after dark. We police found ourselves very much in the middle. Laws were being broken by gays, and we had to enforce them. At the same time, we also had to protect gays against the homophobic attacks of gay-bashers.

The experience highlighted how difficult policing can be in a time of great social change. We were somewhat successful in that we were able to walk through the legal, cultural, and social minefields without major explosions. I don't know that we changed anybody's minds or attitudes, but we changed the behavior of the police. We even established an annual softball game between the cops and the gay community, though we did not have a gay liaison until several Boston cops came out of the closet in the mid-1980s.

In March 1978 I made lieutenant. I was on my way up.

Chapter 6

In the summer of 1980, word shot around police headquarters that *The Boston Globe* was preparing a multipart series on the deficiencies of the Boston Police Department, story after story hammering away at the incompetence and ineffectiveness of the department and its leadership. Headquarters got word that the *Globe* might even call for the commissioner's resignation.

Joe Jordan was an honest, hardworking guy, a career cop, the first ever to make it up through the ranks to commissioner. One of his great strengths was his willingness to try new initiatives and to go in new directions. However, the *Globe* series would charge he was not a very effective manager. Jordan had fallen into the trap of appointing a lot of his cronies to the command staff, some of whom weren't all that competent and a few of whom were thought to be corrupt. He also found himself in the middle of a bitter feud between his two top superintendents, Executive Superintendent John Doyle and Chief of the Bureau of Field Services (BFS) Eddie Connolly.

Despite this, Jordan had been in office about five years, having completed di Grazia's term and begun his own. Mayor White was up for reelection for his third term and was still high on Jordan, as was Steve Dunleavy, who had moved over to City Hall as director of public safety, with oversight responsibilities for the police and fire department. One of the reasons White supported Jordan so strongly was that, through Dunleavy, the mayor influenced everything that went on in the department.

By the time you've been in office ten years, scandals are brewing, and White had lots of headaches. Crime was still a major problem in the city. He had union troubles; as a bargaining tactic, the police union was saying that the best thing civilians could do to fight crime in Boston was to move out and save themselves. Sure enough, people were moving out of the city. The mayor didn't want to get rid of Jordan, but he didn't need any police department problems, either. And the department had quite a few.

To head off this potentially devastating *Globe* series, they had to do something big. Between them, the commissioner, the mayor, and his political operatives decided to completely change the leadership and operational practices of the Boston Police Department. They were going to reorganize the command staff, make sweeping personnel changes, and take citywide the neighborhood policing program that I had been developing in District 4.

John Doyle was the number-two man in the department and had been Jordan's best friend for many years. The highest rank Doyle had achieved prior to his appointment as executive superintendent was detective, but by running the police squad in District Attorney Garrett Byrne's office, he had blossomed into a J. Edgar Hoover—he had all the confidential files, he knew where all the bodies were buried. He was a very smart, Machiavellian character.

Fortunately, Doyle liked me. In the mid-seventies I had been selected to work undercover as part of a district attorney's investigation of organized crime in the strip joints in Boston's infamous "Combat Zone," and Doyle had identified me as an up-and-comer. When I was promoted to sergeant, he had told my family, "Your son's got a great future ahead of him in the police department." Doyle worked closely with Dunleavy, and between them they were the power behind the throne.

The number-three man was Eddie Connolly, who was in charge of all patrol officers. Connolly was a hero cop. He had been head of the original drug squad in the sixties and been much beloved as an area commander in Jamaica Plain and West Roxbury before moving up in the late seventies. He had, unfortunately, moved one step too high. The chief of BFS must be good in the streets *and* at headquarters. Connolly was a great street cop, but he was not an administrator.

Connolly hated me. The reason goes back to an incident on a hot summer day in 1979. There had been a hostage situation in the working-class neighborhood of Jamaica Plain. A distraught man was holding his family hostage and was believed to be armed. Connolly responded to the scene with a civilian assistant, Chuck Wexler. In conformity with department procedures and protocols, the area had been cordoned off by the area commander, Deputy Superintendent Stanley Dirsa. I, along with Sergeant James Cox, had been summoned to the scene as hostage negotiator.

It turned out that Connolly knew the shooter. Arriving at the scene before Cox and I did, he immediately took charge. The man was holed up in his house with his wife and one or two of his kids. It was a two-family, two-story house next to the elevated train tracks, two doors facing out onto a small porch. Connolly went in the front door by himself and stood at the hallway door leading to the second-floor apartment. He called up to the man.

The department's procedures and protocols for hostage negotiations were quite specific. You closed off the area, evacuated civilians, brought in the Tactical Patrol Force and hostage negotiators, who would be responsible for negotiating with the perpetrator. Dirsa had done all of that. But before the negotiators could arrive, Connolly tried to open a dialogue. He pounded on the door and called the guy's name. "It's Eddie Connolly," he announced. "I want to talk to you!"

Boom, boom. The guy shot Connolly in the chest, right through the door.

Connolly staggered out of the hallway, bleeding profusely. "Jesus, he shot me. He shot me!" There's a famous photo of Connolly being walked off the porch by Wexler, one hand on his chest wound, the other over Wexler's shoulder, blood spewing out of him. You can see the terror on Wexler's face and Connolly not believing he's been shot. He nearly died.

All hell broke loose. You can imagine the atmosphere, the number-three person in the Boston Police Department shot in uniform. For the rest of the day, it was like a war zone. They stopped the trains. Finally, after hours of negotiation, the man surrendered without harming anyone else.

In my role as a hostage negotiator, I had to write the after-action report. I labored over it, but finally I could do nothing but criticize Eddie Connolly. In department jargon, all the subsequent actions were precipitated by his deliberately taking a police action in direct violation of department procedure and protocols, putting the lives of police officers and civilians in jeopardy.

Connolly convalesced for months and then finally came back to work. When he saw the report, he went crazy. He ordered me into his office.

"Who the fuck do you think you are to criticize my actions?"

"With all due respect, my role was to critique this. You were wrong. It almost cost you your life. Here's all the procedures of the department. You violated every rule. It endangered the lives of other officers who had to deal with the situation generated by this guy shooting you." It was a pretty knock-down-drag-out fight. From that point on, Connolly hated me.

In September 1980, Lieutenant Jack Geagan and I were sent out to Detroit for three weeks on a loaner program to serve on promotion panels for that department. I missed my flight coming back and had to stay over on a Friday night. I checked into the Hyatt in Dearborn, Michigan, close to the airport and found it filled with college kids. Maybe it was a back-to-school celebration or perhaps a football weekend, but the place was a zoo.

I was taken to my room and found the door next to mine wide open. I smelled marijuana smoke, saw kids swilling beer, the whole bit. Naturally, I didn't want to hang around that scene, so I went downstairs and complained to the management. "I'm a sergeant in the Boston Police. I can't be in a situation where you've got all this type of activity going on. You, as a manager, shouldn't allow it." They were very apologetic and ended up putting me in their penthouse suite.

It was amazing. The glass in the penthouse window had to be twenty feet from floor to ceiling. A king-sized bed lay on a raised platform and from it you looked out at the city skyline. Management sent up wine and fruit. I was this thirty-two-year-old Boston kid. I had probably not stayed in a hotel more than half a dozen times in my life. It was incredible. I patted myself on the back for my good fortune and went out to have dinner—McDonald's, I think. When I came back to my suite, the message light was blinking. Call Jack Geagan.

"You're coming back tomorrow, Bill, is that right?" he asked.

"Yeah, I'll be in in the morning."

"The commissioner wants to see us in his office at noon. He asked me to call and make sure you'll be able to make it back in time."

"Of course. Do you know what it's about?"

"I don't know, but the place is abuzz with rumors."

Everybody knew the *Globe* series was imminent, and the scuttlebutt around the department was that a big change was coming. Geagan was rumored to be making superintendent. I had been getting some good reviews for the neighborhood-policing initiative in District 4, and it was widely speculated that I was going to be moving up to deputy superintendent.

After a restless night I flew back to Boston and was home by nine-thirty. I changed, speculated with Mary about what was going on, and headed into the commissioner's office. Joe Jordan, John Doyle, Jack Geagan, District 1's Lieutenant Detective Frank Coleman (a close friend of Jordan's), and Steve Dunleavy were already there. Commissioner Jordan began.

"As you're well aware, the *Globe* has this story coming out, and we've decided to make some changes in the leadership and structure of the department. We're here today to put it all together." Between Jordan and Dunleavy, working from an organizational chart, they started laying out the reorganization.

Lieutenant Coleman, they announced, was going in to replace Eddie Connolly as chief of BFS. Geagan was being made a superintendent, head of labor relations. I thought, "Jack and Frank got a triple promotion out of this one!" They were both lieutenants and were skipping right over the ranks of captain and deputy superintendent. In the Boston Police Department, the police commissioner was authorized to promote anybody from any rank into the command staff positions of deputy superintendent and superintendent. They were outside the civil service system, which stopped at captain.

It quickly became clear that this organizational change would just about double the size of the department's command staff. They were moving all these people around, taking suggestions, matching names to positions down to the rank of deputy superintendent. They asked my opinion of who should go where. I was a lieutenant—this was way above my station. I thought, "Wow, here I am in this inner circle completely reorganizing the Boston Police Department. It's the opportunity of a lifetime!" Jack Gifford moved up to deputy superintendent, and I tried to get Al Sweeney considered for a deputy superintendent slot, but they shot him down. The "Wise-ass Kid" had made a few enemies in the department, and it was payback time.

In the most controversial aspect of this reorganization, they were going to divide the city into north and south zones, another layer of bureaucracy, and put a superintendent in charge of each. These people would be sort of ambassadors without portfolio. Dunleavy and Jordan were somewhat vague about the positions, but it was understood that these positions were not going to be very powerful. They would report directly to the commissioner but would not have any control over the other superintendents. They were going to put Connolly in charge of the south zone, so they wouldn't have to break him from superintendent.

As the afternoon went on, the slots started to fill up; all the substantive positions were being taken. Meanwhile, there was still no discussion of the north zone and no discussion of where I might fit into all this. I thought, "Jeez, maybe I'm going to get the north zone." I supposed that would be all right—it would be a superintendent rather than a deputy superintendent, but it would be a figurehead position.

John Doyle's office was right next door to the commissioner's, and he had to step out to take a phone call. When he had left I said, not being shy, "Well, pretty much everything's filled here. Who are you putting in the north zone?" Without batting an eye, Jordan said, "John Doyle's going in there."

Doyle, the executive superintendent, was being slipped into what was, by general consensus, a nonentity position. All of a sudden, this shuffling of the deck was even more significant than I'd thought.

"Well, who's going to replace John Doyle?"

Joe Jordan looked at me and said, "You are."

"As superintendent?"

"Yeah. You'll be the executive superintendent. You'll be the number-two person in the department."

I was thirty-two years old, I'd been a lieutenant for a year and a half. Every other superintendent in the department was in his fifties. Almost all of them had been on the job longer than I'd been alive.

Doyle walked back in the room, and the discussion went on as if nothing had happened. After a couple of minutes, Jordan said to the rest of us, "Will you excuse me, I need to talk to John." Outside, I was so nonplussed I had to make sure I'd understood what had just happened. I asked Geagan, "Did Jordan mean what I think he means?"

"Yeah."

About three minutes later, Doyle came out, ashen. He walked right by us, went into his office, and closed the door. I think we all worried that we were going to hear a gunshot.

Press speculation was going wild. Eddie Corsetti of the *Boston Herald* had always been spoon-fed news of promotions and transfers by Steve Dunleavy. Usually, you could read Corsetti in the Saturday morning edition and know what was going to happen before it came out in personnel orders on Monday. This time, the mayor must have said clearly to Dunleavy, "There will be no leaks," because even Corsetti didn't have it.

Early the following week, a press conference was called to discuss personnel transfers and the reorganization of the department. The press was jammed inside, rumors were buzzing, nobody knew what was going on. We marched into the fourth-floor conference room and Commissioner Jordan introduced his new command staff. In size and scale, it was the most significant change in the history of the Boston Police Department. When my name was announced as executive superintendent, jaws dropped. I couldn't help stealing a glance over at Corsetti, who was the most incredulous of all.

There was no shortage of speculation as to what had happened. The most widely disseminated rumor had it that Doyle and White were very close and that, over the years, Doyle had consistently fed the mayor inside information on the workings of the department and its personnel. As a result of the rumbles about the *Globe* series, the rumor went, he had gone to the mayor and made a move on the commissioner. Whatever the real story, which may never be known, Doyle was effectively removed.

It was made crystal clear to me: The Boston Police Department plays a mean game of hardball. Jordan and Doyle had spent every day of the past few years together. They were golfing buddies. The coldheartedness of it all was what struck me. Jordan had let Doyle sit through most of the morning, through all the placements and planning. Doyle steps out to take a call, and when he comes back his career, for all practical purposes, is over.

Meanwhile, I was suddenly the top uniformed person in the Boston Police Department. I now outranked Eddie Connolly.

For the next several weeks at meetings that included the new command staff, Steve Dunleavy, and the mayor's press people, we began to design the presentation of our new policing plan to the city council. We met at City Hall, police headquarters, and the Parkman House, the mayor's brick-front town house on Boston Common. Using our success in District 4 as a model, we expanded it to the entire city. The beat cop was coming back through neighborhood policing. We could bring down crime by developing a partnership between the population and the police. We developed maps, graphs, and pictures in a professional, comprehensive presentation. We were going to get this job done. Then disaster struck.

The principal funding for municipal government was the state property tax, and throughout Massachusetts those taxes were exorbitant. In Boston, a city filled with colleges and religious institutions, 50 percent of the property was owned by tax-exempt institutions, and thus untaxable. The city could not convince the state legislature to implement a city sales tax and, as a result, more than anywhere else in the state, Boston relied on the property tax for revenues. Ultimately, this worked as a disincentive, driving the middle class and businesses out of the city. Voter resentment around the commonwealth led to the passage of Proposition 2^1/$_2$, the Tregor Bill, which capped the growth of any city's tax base at 2^1/$_2$ percent per year.

For Boston, this was catastrophic. In 1972, Kevin White had hoped to get the vice presidential nod and, failing that, was now trying to regain his stature as one of the leading mayors of America. He had preached the gospel of expansion and growth, and in spite of the school-busing issue, which cost the city tens of millions of dollars, had spent a lot of money to regenerate interest and development in Boston. One of his plans was to grow and finally professionalize the police department. But the money for this was going to come from property taxes. With this spending cap, these funds vanished and the city faced a revenue shortfall of about 25 percent. In an attempt to increase the amount of money allocated by the state to Boston, Mayor White cut back city services. He proposed laying off one-fourth of the police department and one-fourth of the fire department. He was going to close half of the city's police stations. It was a game of municipal chicken, and in the end, everybody lost.

I spent the next year as the department's point man, laying off police. Month after month, a hundred cops, a hundred more cops, a hundred *more* cops. It was my job to attend large public meetings and tell the good people of Boston why this cutback was going to give them better police service. "You've closed our neighborhood station, you're going to lay off 25 percent of the Boston Police Department, how the hell are you going to police the city?" Try answering that with a straight face.

What was meant to be a period of new philosophy, new initiatives, and great expansion degenerated into a time of retrenchment and stagnation. Needless to say, the neighborhood-policing programs we had planned were completely derailed. The public fear level increased. There were significant demonstrations against these cutbacks throughout the city. Some of the most serious were in East Boston, which is connected to the rest of the city by the Sumner and Callahan tunnels. It seemed like every night, its residents were closing the tunnels off in protest. We were arresting citizens who wanted more police protection; it almost got as crazy as school busing.

Fortunately, there was no appreciable rise in crime. We tried very hard to keep a lid on it, though all we were doing was chasing 911 calls. We managed to keep response time to a minimum, but there were no cops available to do anything else.

It was a devastating time for the department and the cops themselves. The years of school-busing overtime had encouraged cops to live beyond their means, and a lot of them now fell into both psychological and financial distress. Not only did they have large mortgages they could no longer afford, now they were out of work. The Civil Service Commission hearings were held in the guardroom at Area A-1 on New Sudbury Street, and all the officers who were subject to layoffs attended, often with their wives or husbands. It was my job to get up in front of the commission and testify that the city had no money, that we had to lay these men and women off. I was the face of the cutbacks.

It was terrible. You take a civil-service job, and you assume nothing's ever going to happen to you, you have a job for life. And these weren't newcomers getting laid off, these were men and women with ten, eleven years on the job.

Many of the cutbacks, done for symbolic purposes, cost the department dearly in terms of its traditions. In an attempt to give citizens a sense of continuing police presence while still making budget cuts, support facilities were consolidated into neighborhood station houses. That sounded like a good idea—additional officers would be seen on the streets going to and from work instead of being invisible inside out-of-the-way police buildings. But when the police academy was closed and moved into one room in a closed police station in East Boston, that was a disgrace. This was where you learned how to be a Boston police officer. The educational component of the Boston Police Department was decimated. The department I loved so much was in freefall.

I had difficult personal issues to deal with. As executive superintendent, I was exempt from the layoffs, but they hit my class hard. We laid off half the class, and I had the terrible responsibility of sealing people's fate. I had to testify at the civil-service hearings of my friends and colleagues, guys I came on the job with. On several occasions, I had guys out to my house in Canton for pizza and sodas to talk about what they were going through and how I could do a better job of communicating with them. I tried to be completely evenhanded, but I felt terrible, and there was really nothing I could do to help.

The damage caused by Proposition $2^1/2$ cannot be overestimated. During that era, the department shrank from 2,173 officers to 1,544. Coming on the heels of the school-busing turmoil, it was easy to understand why Boston cops were so angry. They had been badly abused. It would take a generation to repair the damage.

As bad as things were, I was charged with helping Joe Jordan run the department during this time of great crisis, and I took my job as executive superintendent seriously. The resectoring plan that Dunleavy and I had designed was now taking hold. I had day-to-day operational control and administrative responsibility for the BPD. I kept track of the department's money and judged whether it was being spent wisely; I stayed on top of the superintendents' budgets, reductions, and statistics.

My office was on the hallowed sixth floor of police headquarters, connected to the commissioner's by a small corridor and a private bathroom, and I'd go back and forth all the time. I had a computer terminal on my desk in the days before the computer revolution, but all it could really tell me was where the patrol cars were. More important was the cobalt-blue bulletin board I had installed, which ran nearly the length of one wall. On it, fourteen clipboards hung from metal hooks, each with a different heading: Crime Index, Clearance Rate, Overtime, Response Time, Personnel, Sick Time, Deactivated Calls, Bureau Stats, District Stats, 911 Calls, Total Calls, Zero Car Availability, Homicide, and Workload Analysis. I had at my fingertips timely, accurate information, the entire department's statistics from the previous day, such as how many calls we had answered, how many cops were out sick, and how much money was left in our overtime account, particularly critical information during the Tregor period. My staff was in early each morning collating and presenting the information to make an immediate picture of what had happened the day before. The intelligence was accurate; it was there to be analyzed and acted upon quickly. The clipboards were both functional and symbolic: I had a profile of the whole city and I wanted to show everyone who came into my office that I was staying on top of it. Al Sweeney nicknamed this the "Billy Board," and ultimately I installed Billy Boards in districts around the city.

I was working hard, but I was not part of the old-boy network. Most of the headquarters superintendents had worked with Commissioner Jordan for twenty or twenty-five years. Jordan was a great one for putting his feet up on his desk, and at five o'clock they would all gather in his office to smoke pipes and tell war stories. It was "choir practice" without alcohol, and among the choirboys in there most nights were Jack Geagan, Frank Coleman, chief of the Bureau of Administrative Services, Tony Leone, and Chief of Detectives Joe DiNatale. Even John Doyle would drop by. I'd stop in on occasion, but I wasn't really part of their crowd. I was nowhere near done with my work by five, so often I'd be in my office taking care of business, and I'd hear the group laughing about old times. I wasn't smart enough to understand that I should have been in the room with them. I probably should have done more schmoozing than supervising.

Part of the difference was generational. These were older men
longed to the VFW Post and bowled in bowling leagues. They di
tion wagons and went out only to the local bar and grills in the
neighborhoods. They were very parochial in their views, and the world of
policing did not extend beyond the geographic boundaries of the city of
Boston. My world was wider, and I drove a Cadillac El Dorado.

It was about three years old when I bought it, but it was a gorgeous car.
My father bought a used car every five or six years, and I can trace our economic development from a two-toned, two-door, 1950 standard-shift
Ford that my dad ran till the floorboards rotted out, to the silver '56 Chevy
Impala with the white roof—the "Silver Bullet"—to the aqua '61 Bel Air,
to the green '67 Mustang, to the ugly green midsize Plymouth, to the ma-
roon compact Chrysler, two of which I managed to smack up in the
process. Every once in a while, I drove my Cadillac to work and that drove
them crazy. My secretary, Kay Leary, once caught Jordan, Geagan, and
Coleman looking at it out the window. "Him and that goddamn Cadillac,"
she heard one of them say. "Who the hell does he think he is, parking that
thing in front of headquarters?"

All these superintendents in their mid-fifties technically answered to
this kid. I don't know that they liked it, although in reality they all had
direct access to Jordan. I chaired weekly meetings of all the superintendents at which we reviewed all relevant police matters and made decisions
for the future, such as budgets, overtime, and personnel changes. Jack
Gifford gave me a sign that I displayed prominently on my bookcase, so
every time the old guard came into my office they couldn't help but see it.
"Youth and skill," the sign read, "will win out every time over age and
treachery."

I was by far the youngest man ever to ascend to the number two spot.
In the late seventies, Dunleavy finally annoyed Jordan sufficiently that the
commissioner, with the mayor's acquiescence, forced him out of headquarters. Dunleavy was hard to take even on his best day, and I think
Jordan eventually got tired of him in his face. But instead of being fired,
Dunleavy was promoted up and out of the Police Department and assigned to the mayor's office in the newly created position of director of the
Office of Public Safety. They thought they had gotten rid of Dunleavy, but
they were wrong. The fox had moved into the henhouse. He became
closer to the mayor, ended up with a palatial set of glass-enclosed offices,
and effectively ran the Boston Police Department—and the fire department for that matter—out of City Hall.

Dunleavy and George Regan of the mayor's press office arranged for

Boston magazine to profile me. I think they intended the article to increase my visibility and start paving the way for people to think of me as Jordan's successor. As you might expect, I was not unhappy about being profiled.

The writer spent several weeks with me and Sergeant Bob O'Toole, a former member of the Tactical Patrol Force who served as my staff assistant. When I went on patrol, O'Toole was always at the wheel. The Tregor times had finally ended, and the reporter attended the official ceremony held by me and Jordan at Police District 11 welcoming back forty of the previously laid-off police officers. At some point, the writer asked about the future. "When Joe Jordan is ready to leave," I told him, "he'll be able to leave with his head held high and with flags flying. My personal goal," I said, "is to become commissioner. Be it one year or four years, that's what I want."

The article came out in April 1982, while I was attending a three-week conference sponsored by the Police Executive Research Forum (PERF), an organization of progressive police leaders that conducts research and develops advanced thinking about the police profession. It was an excellent program that brought top-notch police instructors and attendees from around the country and provided me an opportunity to network and learn from my peers. Gary Hayes, one of di Grazia's original whiz kids, was PERF's executive director.

I got back to my office after three weeks away, and I could feel some kind of undercurrent, an odd sense that things were not what they had been when I'd left. Kay Leary's desk was right outside the commissioner's office, and occasionally, when voices were raised, she could hear some of what was going on inside. It was her distinct impression that some of the superintendents had been ganging up on me, using the *Boston* magazine article as ammunition.

The long knives were out.

Chapter 7

I HAD OFFENDED BOSTON POLICE DEPARTMENT SENSIBILITIES. IN MOST ORGA-
nizations, you'd want a guy with the ambition and drive to become a
leader. Not in the BPD of the early 1980s. I was too brash, too arrogant. I'd
made my ambition clear and for all the world to see. "My personal goal is
to become police commissioner" got translated within the department as
"I am going to be the next police commissioner." No one in the history of
the department had ever said that out loud.

The Boston Police Department was steeped in Boston Irish culture. Irish
Alzheimer's: You forget everything except the grudges.

Joe Jordan was coming to the end of his term. He had a hidden drinking problem that would soon become very public, and with a mayoral
campaign around the corner, it was unlikely that he would accept reappointment. The people standing in line for his job sure as hell didn't want
a thirty-four-year-old kid around. They weren't getting any younger, and I
could be commissioner for a long time. And worse, I was one of those
di Grazia whiz-kid types. In my capacity as superintendent, they'd had a
taste of what it would be like to work under me, and they didn't relish the
thought.

Ever since the *Boston* magazine article had come out, Jordan's cronies
had hammered him day in and day out: You've got to get rid of this kid,
he's killing you.

Rising quickly in your profession is a universal career goal, but one of the negatives about getting ahead at an early age is that you don't acquire the instincts that come with experience. I had not been around long enough to appreciate the level or intensity of the plotting.

Mary and I lived in a nice split-level house in the bedroom community of Canton. I was on vacation not long after coming back from PERF, outside on a hot day, pulling up weeds in the yard, when Mary came out and said Lieutenant Donald Devine, my staff assistant, was on the phone.

"Super," he said, "do you know anything about an Inspector of Bureaus position?"

"No. What are you talking about?"

"Well, there's a car in the back alley of headquarters, an old, beat-up, marked cruiser, and it's marked 'Inspector of Bureaus.' Supposedly, it's going to be your car."

"What?!"

"Yeah. The rumbles around here are that you're being transferred."

I thanked Donald for the heads-up. My mind was spinning. What do I do? Who do I call? I called Dunleavy over at City Hall. I told him what I'd heard and said, "What's going on?"

"I don't know," he told me. "Let me find out."

A short time later, Dunleavy called back and said Jordan was planning to move me. They were creating this position, Inspector of Bureaus, so I'd keep my rank, but I was out of there. The car was meant as an intentional slight. When Eddie Connolly and John Doyle were transferred, each was given the trappings of power, an unmarked car and a driver. (In the department, an unmarked car was a status symbol.) The fact that I was being given a marked car, and a clunker, was meant to embarrass me. Jack Geagan, one of the conspirators, had jumped the gun by having it sent over early. They were playing hardball again. They intended to bury me.

I started wheeling and dealing to save my neck. Dunleavy said he was talking to George Regan, who was feeling bad for having arranged the magazine article, and that Regan was talking me up to the mayor. From a media perspective, how would it look for the public face of the department, the superintendent who embodied its renewed energy and youth and whom the press liked and supported, to take this fall? Dunleavy and Regan apparently convinced the mayor that it wouldn't play well, and Mayor White decided to put his arm around me.

I was still out as executive superintendent. But to give my new position more substance and to make it seem like a lateral transfer, I was also made liaison to the city's various community groups dealing with minority and gay issues.

When my vacation ended, I went back to my office and was notified that the commissioner wanted to see me. I went next door into his office. Jordan was kind of rocking in his chair, his unlit pipe in his hand.

"I suppose you know what I want to see you about," he said.

"Yeah, word's out."

"It's just reached a point where it's causing too much friction up here. The other superintendents feel they can't get along with you. To bring some order to this organization, I think it's important that I move you." He pointed to the chair he was sitting on. "I can't have you lusting after this seat."

I didn't say anything. This was his show.

"Well, I'm sorry it didn't work out," he said. "As you know, I'm going to be reassigning you as inspector of bureaus. Your office will be down in District A."

"Thank you, Commissioner," I answered. "I'll attempt to serve you well in that position." Then I left.

What a difference a day makes. I had moved from the plush offices of the sixth-floor police headquarters to a small corner office on the fifth floor of one of the city's police districts, with no secretary and a five-year-old car. Mine was the only office on the floor—the rest of the space was used for locker rooms. Instead of plain clothes, I was back in uniform. Message to the organization: Bratton's dead.

The next day, I started packing up. Bob O'Toole, Kay Leary, and a bunch of cops from District 4 volunteered to help me move my furniture, my Billy Board, my potted plants, and all my memorabilia, including a collection of hats from each of my police jobs, over to District A. We ended up getting silly, laughing like crazy, and having a miniparty.

I packed my sign, "Youth and skill will win out every time over age and treachery." Boy, was I wrong. Their plotting and intriguing had certainly paid off. Jack Geagan moved up from superintendent of labor relations into Frank Coleman's job as chief of the Bureau of Field Services; Geagan now ran all field operations. Coleman moved into my position as executive superintendent and eventually to a five-star post as superintendent-in-chief.

I was miserable, but my friends in the department did everything they could to soften the blow. Bobby O'Toole had been a motorcycle cop on the Tactical Patrol Force, and through his friends at the auto shop took that old clunker and made it into the best-looking car in the department. It came back looking like it came off the showroom floor. It was an in-your-face gesture to the guys who'd moved me out, and in a time of pain, a gesture of real friendship I appreciated tremendously.

But O'Toole paid for it. Joe Jordan asked him, in essence, to take a loyalty oath. He was brought into the commissioner's office in front of Coleman, Geagan, and DiNatale, and told, "Things are going to change here. We know you've been very friendly with Bratton, and we want to know how that is going to affect you." O'Toole said, "If you're asking me if I will do my job, I will continue to do my job. The position of police commissioner, no matter who is in there—whether it's you or a monkey—I will honor that position. If you're asking me to now say, 'Bill Bratton is out and I will have nothing to do with him, I don't like the guy anymore,' no, that's wrong. I'll do whatever I can to help him. I'll do it on my own time."

Jordan was very straight with him. "Why don't you take a day off," said the commissioner, "and we'll notify you where you're going."

They sent O'Toole to the Police Academy. Coleman called Al Sweeney, who was director of the academy, and said O'Toole was to have no contact with the recruits. He wasn't to teach a class. They were basically sending him down there to be an errand boy.

We were laughing when I piled the rest of my things into my shiny marked car and headed home. We were laughing, but we were hurting.

Jordan, Geagan, and Coleman were in the commissioner's office looking out the window. Kay Leary heard Coleman say, "I hope when my time comes to go, I can do it with as much class as he's doing it."

It was front-page news in all the Boston papers. The police department's number-two whiz kid was out on his ear. Maybe it seemed classy to the guys on the sixth floor, but no matter how calm a face I put on it, to me it was a complete humiliation.

At age thirty-four, I felt my career was over. My dream to become commissioner of the Boston police was finished. It had been made clear to me that I had enemies, and as long as these men were in power I had no significant place in the department. My whole life, my entire vision of my future had been wrapped up in the Boston Police Department, and the men who ran it didn't want me around. I didn't know whether I could stay, and I really didn't know where I could go.

I wasn't the first guy in the history of the department to get pushed aside. The internal politics were fierce, and you had to be good at it to survive. I'd been accused of being Machiavellian, but I probably wasn't

Machiavellian enough. I had seen some of my peers in similar situations, and they had lain down and died. All I'd ever wanted to be was a cop, and I decided not to let these guys kill me.

Joe Jordan had done me one favor; I was out of power, but I still had my rank. I stayed visible, I stayed active, I did my job. I tried to remain gracious in the face of humiliation and to keep on going. Out in the field, the troops liked me, and I listened to them and tried to make whatever changes I could. I used my experiences with the Boston-Fenway Program and with the gay community in District 4 to respond to minority and gay communities during a summer I hoped would turn out to be long but not hot.

I got an interesting call from Jim O'Leary, the newly appointed general manager of the Massachusetts Bay Transportation Authority (MBTA). He had come into his position in an unusual way. While in his previous MBTA job, he had received an envelope containing $10,000 in cash. It was intended for the general manager, Barry Locke, and had been delivered to O'Leary by mistake. O'Leary went to the state attorney general, Frank Bellotti, and in the investigation that followed, Locke was indicted for graft. Massachusetts had just elected a new governor, Michael Dukakis, who was interested in transportation issues, and O'Leary, because he was such an honest guy, was named the MBTA's new general manager.

O'Leary then set about rebuilding the transit authority with Dukakis's aggressive support. The new governor rode the Green Line trolley from his home in Brookline to the State House every day, calling when he got there about any deficiencies, such as graffiti, he had noticed along the way.

O'Leary invited me to lunch at the St. Botolph Restaurant. "I understand fully what went on over there," he told me, "and it doesn't diminish what I think you're capable of doing." The MBTA police were a mess, he said. They were taking constant hits in the paper, with news headlines such as "Terror Trains" and a *Globe* series on police incompetence. He had to get rid of the guy who was in there and make some changes. Would I be interested?

I'd thought my career was over, and here was a good man tossing me a life raft. I thanked him and said yes, definitely.

"I have a lot to do," he told me, "but I'll get back to you."

Months went by, and I didn't hear from him. Meanwhile, after four months in abject exile in the wilderness of my fifth-floor office, in the fall I was brought back to headquarters, to the sixth floor, as the new superintendent in charge of labor relations. I'd like to think it was because they recognized my talents, I'd like to think it was because they needed me back, but in reality it was to use me as the point man arguing the case for one-officer cars, a continuing residue of Proposition 2½ and the reduced size of the BPD. This was not going to be a popular position with the rank and file, and neither Coleman nor Geagan wanted to be out front on it. I'd been the fall guy in closing all the police stations and laying off the cops, so they passed it on to me.

The union, the Boston Police Patrolmen's Association (BPPA), was not happy with my return. They remembered my serving on the rules and regulations committee against their wishes when I was a police officer, and as one of the hotshot whiz kids developing accountability systems for Dunleavy and Wasserman. Most particularly, they remembered my being the voice of the BPD laying off five hundred of their members. Now, I was going to argue the case for one-officer cars.

The cabal of superintendents certainly broke Machiavelli's first rule of police politics: If you're going to kill somebody, kill him. If you're moving people, don't put them where they can come back and haunt you. I consciously turned what could have been a continuing embarrassment into a plus by involving myself wholeheartedly in the union world. I had no background in union issues, and union president Bob Guiney and legendary BPPA attorney Frank McGee were formidable adversaries. But the union's view was an important perspective for a police manager to acquire. Ultimately, one-officer cars were approved for the department.

There was an added symbolic bonus—I was back in the big house. My new office was right next door to the commissioner's. I got the unmarked car. I was working in plain clothes instead of uniform. Symbols are important in policing, and once again I had all the symbols and trappings of power.

A few months after we won the one-officer car battle, they transferred me to the Operations Division. They wanted to straighten out the 911 system. I went upstairs to the Turret and worked with a large unit of civilians and police officers.

O'Leary called. "I'm ready to make the move. Are you still interested?"

I wasn't sure. I'd gotten back into the department game and was slowly regaining power within the organization. I was enjoying the challenge, and I was working creatively. I was feeling pretty good. Who knows, maybe I could still get to be commissioner. They hadn't killed me, they'd wounded me, and now I was recuperating. The Boston Police Department had been my life's work. The idea of taking over the sixty-five-person MBTA Police wasn't as appealing as it had been a few months before. I stalled for time with O'Leary and told him I'd get back to him.

For the next week, I agonized over what to do. Then one morning, while reading the *Boston Herald* at my desk, I came upon a blurb in one of the gossip columns that said that the MBTA Police were in a terrible way and suggested I was being looked at to take it over.

I had heard stories of thunderbolts from the sky, lights going on above people's heads. This was that dramatic. I knew instinctively what I should do. I decided while reading the *Herald* that I wanted to do this. With Joe Jordan and his crew around, I'd never run the show. At the MBTA, I could.

I interviewed for the MBTA chief, and in the process I found that my old friend Al Sweeney had also applied and was a finalist as well. At the time, Sweeney was working at the Boston Police Academy and had been by-passed twice for deputy superintendent; he was my friend, which was going to be held against him at the BPD, and he was outspoken and thus had his own set of enemies. It was ironic that he was applying to become a chief; his father, Dan Sweeney, had been the much-loved and respected second president of the Boston police union.

There wasn't a captain's test on the horizon. Back in the seventies, in a very public dispute with the Superior Officers Federation, Joe Jordan had refused to promote anyone to the rank of captain. Instead, he relied on the commissioner's ability to promote anyone he wished to the higher rank of deputy superintendent. Over the years, through attrition, the number of captains plummeted. (This grudge was carried for sixteen years. By 1993, the date of the next captains' civil-service exam, there were only three captains in the BPD, down from twenty-six in the seventies.) This "grudge match" had a critical impact on countless careers. If you wanted to advance in the BPD, the only opportunity was to get promoted politically.

Sweeney considered himself politically dead in the organization. I called him at home and said, "I got a deal for you."

"What's the deal?"

"Jim O'Leary wants to hire us both."

"Two chiefs?"

"No. I'll be the chief, you be the deputy chief. I'm going to work on special projects, you run the day-to-day operations."

"I'll take it."

In May 1983, I took a leave of absence and was appointed chief of the MBTA Police.

I was sworn in on Boston Common, at the Park Street MBTA station kiosk by Governor Dukakis. For the governor to swear in the MBTA chief of police was very significant. The power of the state was being placed behind my small department.

Dukakis was a great believer in mass transit and had campaigned on the issue of rebuilding it, making it safe and efficient. His transportation secretary, Fred Salvucci, was mandated to rebuild the infrastructure of the whole state. Salvucci lay the groundwork for the new Ted Williams Tunnel under Boston harbor, reengineered the Central Artery that went through the center of the city so the ugly elevated structure could be put below ground, and coupled it with the significantly modernized and expanded MBTA. These are Dukakis's legacies. Boston's fast, clean, and efficient commuter rail and subway systems are the result of the leadership of Dukakis, Salvucci, and O'Leary.

I had apprenticed under Steve Dunleavy and so was able to help design the swearing-in ceremony for maximum effect. Such occasions develop momentum within an organization. They build pride and morale in people who might otherwise just put in their hours and go home.

When Joe Jordan was sworn in as police commissioner, Dunleavy had orchestrated a huge celebration, in part to trumpet the significance of Jordan's being the first commissioner appointed to his own term ever to have come up through the ranks, but also to move the organization forward. Most police ceremonies are small affairs held in conference rooms at headquarters. We held Jordan's at the bandstand on Boston Common. Hundreds of people were invited, bands were playing, bunting hung everywhere; it looked like an inauguration. I had helped design that event and now used it as a model.

When I was sworn in, it was front-page news in all the papers. Television stations from around the region sent crews to follow me onto the subway, where I was photographed straphanging with the president of the police union.

My wife, Mary, was not happy with any of this. She never took to public life and had not been particularly excited when I was made executive superintendent. She remained a very private person. She was extremely loyal and supportive during my ouster from the Boston Police.

Mary brought her mother to my swearing-in ceremony along with the rest of my family. I was center stage on Boston Common, surrounded by cameras and microphones and politicians, and I was pretty happy. Mary was not. "Bill," she told me, "I don't feel good about this. I think this is going to end our marriage." She could see us drawing apart. I was in the spotlight; she preferred us to be together in the shadows. That was a problem.

The job itself was great. Dukakis committed six million dollars to a seven-point anticrime plan, and Bob Wasserman worked with me on its development. Sweeney and I worked as a team. I created goals and asked him, "How can we get this done?" He offered three options, each with assets and debits. I chose one, he asked me to consider another; we went back and forth amiably. Sweeney was easy to work with, and ultimately we came away with a plan. I wasn't too proud to listen to his advice, or to anybody else for that matter, or to change my mind; I cared very much about making things happen. We built that small organization into a real force.

The MBTA Police had received nothing but negative publicity for many years, mainly because no one seemed to be in charge. Ranking officers arrived at a crime scene wearing sport coats and asking quietly, "What's going on?" I changed that. I arrived at crime scenes in full uniform and expected to be approached by the officer in charge and given a complete briefing.

Al Sweeney and I were riding the subway in full uniform the day he was hired. An inspector came walking down the train shouting to everyone, "You have to get off, we're changing cars. The next train is going to take you all the way through. This car is going out of service!"

We stood there.

"Gentlemen, you're going to have to exit the vehicle." He came closer and looked at us.

"Jesus Christ, I thought you were admirals! You're the chief of police? We've never seen the chief of police or a deputy chief down here. What's wrong?"

You can't overstate the effect of the chief of police showing up in a subway station. Symbolically, it means that every station is going to be policed, and every station will have to be policed correctly. Cops think the brass is out of touch, that we're too old and don't know the streets. I wanted to let them know we were there. This was where we were going to be from now on, on the scene with the troops.

An officer was standing inside the station with a cigarette in his hand. I turned to Sweeney, half in jest. "How long are you going to allow that officer to stand there and embarrass your chief?"

Sweeney walked over. "Officer, what's the story?"

"What is it?"

"You know the rules, there's no smoking. There's no smoking in the subway, and there's no smoking on the job." The officer put out the cigarette and got to work. Word was going to get out fast.

But I didn't simply want to be some lurking manager walking the system, waiting to catch and punish bad cops. I like cops, I understand them, their hopes, aspirations, and frustrations. I wanted them to do well, and I found it very important to support my troops. Transit is every bit as tough as the street, only in an enclosed area, and I understood what my people needed. From weapons to vehicles to equipment to sweaters and jackets, I provided for them so they felt good about coming to work. That was one key. Another, most important, was to provide leadership.

When I arrived at the MBTA, there were sixty-five transit cops, seven vehicles, and two motorcycles. The vehicles were junk, all beat to hell. It was demoralizing just to sit in one of them. We needed new wheels. The good news was, we could get some. The bad news was, they were going to be crummy cars. During the early-eighties gas shortage, rather than purchase the larger and more roomy Ford Crown Victoria or Chevrolet Caprice, the MBTA had bought the more economical Ford Fairlane. The prototype arrived, and it was small and uncomfortable. Our six-foot cops sat scrunched up in the front seat, their knees on the dashboard. Prisoner cages severely limited seat maneuverability. The union was hollering. I told them, "We're going to get bigger cars." I went to Jim O'Leary, who told me, "As a matter of policy, we're not buying the bigger cars, we're going to stay with the smaller ones."

Okay. I had been encouraging O'Leary to come out on the system, ride the trains with me, see the cops in action, and also take a ride-along in our cars. "Why don't you come down Friday night," I said to him, "do that ride-along we've been talking about and get some hands-on experience with some of the issues we're facing."

After riding the trains, we went back to headquarters and got into one of the Ford Fairlanes. I had already had the front seat pushed up as far as it would go and then rigged so you couldn't push it back. I put O'Leary in the front seat; I was driving. O'Leary was up against the dashboard with his knees banging. He said, "Jeez, this thing's cramped."

"Jim, this is a cop's office for eight hours. This is where we put our police officers every day, three shifts."

I purposely hit every bump I could find, and each time O'Leary hit his head on the roof and his knees on the dashboard. Finally, he said, "Okay, okay, I get the point. What's the difference in cost between a Ford Fairlane and a Crown Vic?"

It's one thing to sit up in the general manager's office and say, "I can save $4,000 per car by buying this smaller car. I drive a small car, what the hell's the difference?" But then you get in as a cop with all this gear on, and there are prisoners in the backseat, and the difference is clear. Also, the image was clear. All the other police departments were riding around in bigger cars, and we were putt-putting in our Fairlanes.

Over three years, we increased the MBTA police force to a 110-person department with fifty-five vehicles. You might ask why vehicles were so important in a transit system; we were a multicounty, seventy-nine-city-and-town transit system, and while we used police on the subway cars, it was critical that we had the ability to move quickly around our territory.

Equipment helps cops do their jobs, and it makes them feel good. I fought for these resources, and it worked. If people feel you'll fight for them, they'll work for you. If you work for them, they'll take risks to move the organization forward. "He's meeting me halfway, so I'll do it for him." And once your people see that your ideas work, and they are praised and rewarded for carrying them out, their work becomes easier and gets done better. If you earn their loyalty, not demand it, you'll get results.

When I first arrived at the MBTA, their operational plan was just to go out on patrol. I asked the officers, "Where are you going? What's your assignment?"

"Out."

"Where?"

"Out in the system."

"How do we get in touch with you?"

"We'll call in."

But their radios were so old and beat-up, they didn't reach into or out of the subways. As a result, once they entered the subway system, they were totally out of touch with headquarters. That had a strong impact on their safety as well as our operational control of our resources. As part of our seven-point plan, we spent four million dollars on the most compre-hensive subway radio network in the country. For the first time, MBTA of-ficers could reach their dispatchers, they could relay information, get backup, call for help. Their lives became safer, their jobs more manageable. We coordinated the system with the Boston, Cambridge, and Somerville police so their cops could enter the subways and communicate directly with our dispatchers, facilitating joint policing efforts.

There is a strong link between looking good and feeling good. I wanted my cops to have pride in their uniforms and I went about improving their look: new uniform items, new markings and logos on the cruisers, and a new identity to go with their newfound success.

The cops worked, the crime rate in the subways dropped, and an obscure, backwater police department that for years had received nothing but negative publicity began to receive a series of very positive stories. We also got some breaks. During my time at the MBTA, we became aware of the largest corruption scandal in the organization's history.

All the revenue coming into the MBTA went to a money room in Charlestown. Our special investigation unit was approached by a person who worked in that room who described an ongoing scheme and said most of the people who worked in the money room were stealing. We put people in undercover, and the information checked out.

Working with the state's attorney general, we put together a comprehensive, yearlong investigation involving dozens of hidden cameras throughout the system. We wired up the money rooms in all the bus depots and train yards, we put cameras into the central money room itself, and we caught these guys, on camera, stealing. A joint force of seventy-five state police and seventy-five of my people—the state police wanted to do it all themselves, but I insisted on our involvement in cleaning our own house—raided the money room while simultaneously arresting money-truck crews out on their routes and off-duty employees at their homes. Of the seventy people working in the money room, we arrested thirty-eight. Some of the people we locked up had money stuffed into their pockets and boots.

It was a TV bonanza. *The Boston Globe*'s lead story centered on how the MBTA had investigated and cracked the twin problems of crime and corruption, and I wasn't too disappointed to find my picture on the front page, hands on hips, stone-faced, watching handcuffed money-room employees being loaded into police wagons.

Unlike many chiefs, I enjoyed interacting with the media. It's one of the ways a leader can move his organization. I've always believed that an organization is a reflection of its leader, and if that leader is well respected, his organization will be well respected. I like being known in a positive way. The MBTA Police was a relatively obscure department, and I was able to increase both its visibility and mine as we became more successful. I might have been accused of having a big ego or a desire for publicity, but I don't see how you can move an organization forward quickly without capitalizing on your own persona and attracting attention. The media enjoys and needs a focal point, and a good manager gives it to them. Lee Iacocca almost single-handedly, through his persona, resurrected Chrysler. He told its story; he was its story. Who ever heard of

Perdue chickens before Frank Perdue got on the screen and told us about them? I came from the Steve Dunleavy school of marketing. I was able to link my organization with my persona, and we both moved forward.

Jim O'Leary was a remarkably honorable person, and I liked and learned from his management style. His basic philosophy was that you pick good people and let them do their jobs. He was the boss, there was never any question about that, but he gave his people room to maneuver. It was a strategy that turned the responsibility back onto the worker.

Some bosses, through heavy-handed threats, actually put a cap on creativity and encourage the people under them to underachieve. "This is what he wants, the son-of-a-bitch boss? I'm giving him this and not one iota more." It's up to the manager to identify good workers and support them, and this was one of O'Leary's strengths. Many people are capable of producing at a greater capacity when they are given greater authority. I certainly was. He trusted me to do my best, and I went out of my way to live up to that trust. If I failed, I would have failed both him and myself.

From 1983 to 1986, crime on the MBTA decreased by 27 percent. Ridership also rose as the system modernized and the police department expanded. We applied to the National Commission on Accreditation for Police Agencies and met eight hundred standards of excellence to become only the thirteenth police department in the country to be accredited. In many respects, it was like getting a college diploma to hang on the wall; we were a certified professional police organization—quite a turnaround in three years.

Unfortunately, Mary had been right: My job took a toll on our marriage. In the summer of 1983, only a few months after I'd been sworn in, we separated. We made several attempts at reconciliation, but we were going in very different directions and we were ultimately divorced.

While our divorce was pending, I attended a reception to honor the Suffolk County district attorney Newman Flanigan, held at Anthony's Pier 4 restaurant on Boston's waterfront. While circulating, I ran into a cop who had worked for me at District 4, Frank Dewan. Dewan had been partners with a cop I'd come on the job with named Joe Fiandaca. While Dewan and I were talking, we both couldn't help but notice three very attractive young women talking across the room. The one with her back to us turned, saw the two of us, and smiled.

What an incredible smile! Was she smiling at me? I thought so. This extraordinarily beautiful young woman walked over, and I straightened my tie. She said hello and gave Dewan a kiss. Dewan is about six foot two, this woman was five feet, so he had to lean way down to accept it. I was crest-fallen, but only for a moment. Dewan introduced us.

"Bill, this is Cheryl Fiandaca. Cheryl, Bill Bratton."

"Oh, I know who he is," she said. "How are you?" I must have looked startled. "You don't remember me, do you?"

"No," I said with a laugh. "And I don't know why!"

"Well, we met one time before."

"When was that?"

"Oh, 1970." That was thirteen years ago. From the looks of this ex-tremely attractive woman, she must have been about twelve at the time. "You and my brother Joe came on the job together."

Then it clicked. I was immediately smitten. She was just so beautiful, so vivacious, so alive. We talked for a few minutes, and then she excused her-self and walked into the next room.

I watched her go. "Frank," I said, "excuse me." I followed her.

She was standing talking to some other guy when I came up and said, "Hello again." She made the introductions.

"Can I get you a drink?" her companion asked her. She said sure. He went off.

When I was a teenager, I had never gotten up the nerve to ask out Camille Grasso, and for one long summer I had sat next to Irene Walsh, another teenage crush, and hadn't put my arm around her, let alone kiss her. But with this woman I was different. We began talking, and I couldn't stop. When her companion came back, I took her drink from his hand, thanked him, and gave it to her. He got the message and didn't stick around. Cheryl thought that was the greatest move.

When the function ended, we went to the upstairs lounge and stayed for another two hours. I did most of the talking. When it was time to leave, I walked her to her car. It was her father's car, a big old blue Chevy. We exchanged phone numbers. She stood up on her tiptoes and gave me a kiss on the cheek. "I'll call you," I told her. I had been struck by the thunderbolt.

Cheryl went home and told her mother, Lucy, "Mom, I met the guy I'm going to marry."

"Really."

"Yeah. He's going to call tomorrow. I think I'll wear my new light-blue suit."

I called the next day, of course, and invited her to lunch at Tia's on the Waterfront, a new restaurant. She had me pegged. Cheryl was going to law school and working at the district attorney's office, and when I saw her walking down the hill from the Suffolk County Courthouse, she was dressed to the nines. All I could think was "Wow!"

I don't think I saw the same outfit on Cheryl more than once during the first year we dated. What I didn't know was that she and her four sisters were all the same size, so they had five wardrobes to go through, and maybe fifty different pairs of pumps. Cheryl always looked great. She was also smart, funny, ambitious, supportive, and totally wonderful. She came from a large Italian family. Her mother, on a moment's notice, could prepare a meal for from two to twenty people. Her father, Joe, was the popular first magistrate of the East Boston District Court. Cheryl and I married in 1986.

Chapter 8

Joe Jordan was in trouble. He had a drinking problem that was having a disastrous impact on his ability to run the department. He had checked himself into a detox center in Rhode Island. Someone tipped off the press, and it became a front-page story. Jordan was evidently a closet drinker, after working hours; I had shared an office and bathroom with him for over two years and never suspected. Once again, speculation was high that Jordan would step down, but Mayor Kevin White talked him into staying, at least through the end of White's third term in 1985. Mayor White was leaving after three terms to accept a teaching position at Boston University.

Ray Flynn, a former South Boston city councillor and a long shot in a crowded field of candidates, was elected Boston's new mayor. Flynn wanted to appoint his own commissioner, but Jordan's term didn't expire for almost a year, and he wasn't moving. The city was unwilling to expend funds to buy him out, so they were stalemated. Boston had a new, progressive mayor and a status quo, lame-duck police commissioner.

My longtime friend and confidant Jack Gifford became a key player and Flynn advisor in the selection process for Jordan's successor. Gifford told me my name was being floated. I had the background. I had been screwed by the outgoing cabal but had showed the proper humility and proved my loyalty to the organization. I had turned around the MBTA and increased my recognizability, credibility, and professional credentials.

I was fairly confident I was going to get the job of my dreams and be the new commissioner, and I wanted to hit the ground running. I started putting my team in place, my closest friends and members of my study group during all these years. Jack Gifford would be my chief of the Bureau of Field Services. Al Sweeney would come over from the MBTA and be executive superintendent. I put a lot of time and attention into producing a detailed manifesto outlining exactly what should be done to turn the department around, in expectation of meeting with Flynn. I tried not to get my hopes up, but there's only so much negative thinking I'm capable of. I am more likely to be an optimist—Yes, I *am* going to be police commissioner!—and rather than prepare for the worst, I prepared for the best.

Ray Flynn appointed Mickey Roache, my old sector-car partner, my old college classmate, the guy I had encouraged to take the sergeant's exam, the guy I'd brought into headquarters. Roache was an acting lieutenant, not even a deputy superintendent; this was a tremendous jump. This straightforward, priestlike, kind of naive, hardworking Caspar Milquetoast guy was going to be in charge of the Byzantine backbiting empire that was the Boston Police. Everyone was flabbergasted, nobody more than me.

It turns out that Mickey Roache and Ray Flynn were lifelong friends. They had played stickball together in Southie. ("South Boston boy, your honor.") Mayor Flynn justified his choice with Roache's hard work, his loyalty, and his continuing success with the Community Disorders Unit. What Flynn was really looking for was a guy he knew, a guy who would be very responsive to him, a guy he could trust, a guy who was not going to give the mayor any problems. From Flynn's viewpoint, since I was known as an independent who was comfortable in the public eye, perhaps I wasn't that guy.

So Mickey Roache became police commissioner. Who does he go to for his top command? My team, my friends, my guys. Roache named Jack Gifford his superintendent-in-chief. He named Al Sweeney superintendent of internal affairs. Sweeney and I loved working together, and we were doing a great job at the MBTA, but I couldn't blame him for going back. Didn't I want to go back? Mickey MacDonald was appointed chief of the Bureau of Field Services.

Roache had the right guys, but he put them in exactly the wrong positions. I knew these guys extremely well. I had studied with them, I had worked with them, and I had planned for years how I would deploy them if I became commissioner. Al Sweeney was one of the nicest guys in the world, but the secrecy and edge of internal affairs requires a hardnose. He was too caring, too sensitive, not hard enough for the investigations he had to run. Jack Gifford was a hardnose when he needed to be, and one of the smartest people I'd ever met, but also one of the most *disorganized* organized people I'd ever met. He had file folders, plans, charts, and maps, but he went in fifty different directions and often couldn't control the things he set in motion. He would have been an excellent chief of BFS, controlling the patrol forces, or head of internal affairs. Sweeney was incredibly well organized and had the ability to control large amounts of information. With my systems, Sweeney's organization, Gifford's control of the streets, and the seasoning and maturity that Mickey MacDonald would bring, we would have had a tremendous effect on the Boston Police and the city itself.

I was desperate to get in. There I was at the MBTA, and after all the planning and dreaming, there was my team running the Boston Police Department—*without me!* Gifford and Sweeney arranged for me to meet with Roache to congratulate him and throw in my two cents about what could be done in the department. I'd been looking at the BPD for ten years, I had a few ideas. I let it be known that, if he was interested, I was willing to step down as chief of the MBTA to be appointed as a superintendent in some capacity in the Boston Police.

Roache and I were friendly, but Flynn quickly surrounded him with City Hall cronies. He was going to run that police department from top to bottom. As much as I was willing to give up my own shop to work in someone else's—for the reason that some day, some way, I wanted to run that department—nothing was offered. My impression was that I was viewed as perhaps too independent, too much of a fox in the henhouse. I was on the outside looking in: It was the ultimate irony.

With the Boston Police Department out of my reach and my position at the MBTA rapidly becoming a maintenance job, I set my sights on another turnaround and career-advancing opportunity: the Metropolitan Police. The Mets, as they were called, made up the third largest police department in Massachusetts behind the BPD and the state police. They were a division of the Metropolitan District Commission, a state organization responsible for parks and reservoirs and for policing many of the beaches, parkways, and highways in the eastern part of the state, particularly in the greater Boston area. The MDC's dynamic new commissioner was Bill Geary. I had been watching Geary, and I was very impressed.

For many years, the MDC had been under attack because of its inefficiency and incompetence, and Geary had set about to change its image. I
started seeing stories about the organization and their new police cars.
That kind of approach paralleled my own. I knew the cops would work
better in more functional surroundings, and that if they looked better, the
public would give them more attention and respect. Some years back, the
MDC cars were orange and blue; the cops looked like they were delivering for Howard Johnson's. Who would put cops in HoJo cars? No wonder
the cops hated working for that agency. Then, because the MDC was a
parks agency, the cars had been repainted green and white. They still
looked awful. Geary had taken the old green-and-white monstrosities
and brought in an outside consulting company to completely redesign
them. The new design, markings, and blue-white-and-gray paint scheme
gave the Mets the best-looking police cruisers in the state. Cops liked
them and began to work better as a result. Geary got press coverage on
both the design change and the results.

Geary was very much like Steve Dunleavy in his sense of marketing
and organization, and as he went about the business of reengineering the
MDC, he paid a lot of attention to appearances. It was the kind of thing
you'd notice when you were driving on MDC-policed roads: new and attractive signs signifying that someone new and improved was in charge
and paying attention. Also like Dunleavy, Geary knew how to market his
organization. He always got good stories on TV and in the papers about
his new signs. Geary was a master, and I watched him to pick up pointers.
Like Jim O'Leary, he also picked good people, and although more hands-
on, let them run their divisions.

In 1985, MDC Police Superintendent Tommy Keough resigned. I had
two years at the MBTA, my reputation was solid, and I fully expected to
be interviewed as his successor. I was very disappointed when Geary decided to stay in-house and promoted as superintendent Nelson Barner; I
thought I had positioned myself for the next step, that I'd at least get
an overture. I continued about my business, but 1985 was a year of
discontent.

I didn't have to wait too long. In 1986, major corruption scandals unfolded within the Metropolitan Police. Captain Gerry Clemente was the
man in charge of the Metropolitan Police at night. He had the keys to all
the state office buildings and, among other crimes, broke into the Civil
Service Commission offices, stole the department's promotion exams, and
was involved in selling them for around $3,000 a pop. Many senior people
in the Mets were thought to have attained their positions by buying those

exams. Clemente was a real rogue. As well as stealing the exams, he changed the test scores of people he didn't like. Clemente was also involved in a major bank break-in in Medford over the Memorial Day weekend. Superintendent Barner was convicted of perjury and sentenced to four years in federal prison for his involvement in the exam controversy.

I got the call. Bill Geary asked whether I would come onboard. I jumped at the chance. The MBTA was in good shape: Crime was down, the force had been doubled in size and was well supplied and accredited. I had turned it around, could accept a thank you, and leave. In June 1986, I resigned as chief of the MBTA Police to become superintendent of the Mets.

I was going to another state agency, still working for Dukakis, whose stock was high, and who was gearing up for a run at the presidency. My promotion was well received by the media, I was the guy coming in to straighten out another troubled police department. Turnarounds had become my specialty.

I had thought the MBTA was a tough department. The Mets were head and shoulders the worst police department in America. They lacked everything: systems, equipment, accountability, procedures, protocol, discipline. Their headquarters were on the ground floor of an old stone building on Beacon Hill. It must have been the last building in the continental United States still running on DC current. And my immediate predecessor was going to jail. It was an ideal department for me. Everywhere you looked there was something to do.

Bill Geary supported my decision to make key personnel changes at the command staff level. I designated Chief of Detectives Tommy White as my number two. I reassigned the deputy superintendents of patrol and administration and brought Kathy O'Toole from the Boston Police as deputy superintendent of administrative services. O'Toole had been a sergeant in the Boston Police Department and on the career fast track but had been bypassed. I was glad to get her. She was an extremely capable woman and really knew the legislative process; that strength was crucial in getting us our equipment. I promoted Al Seghezzi, who for some reason had been demoted by Keough to the rank of captain, to chief of patrol. He was another Mickey MacDonald for me; he was widely respected and truly welcomed the opportunity to be born again. Several years earlier, I had met a young Northeastern University student named Peter LaPorte, who had worked under me as an intern on a state criminal-justice subcommittee. He was a real go-getter, and Peter shaved off his beard and signed on as my staff assistant. These personnel moves were far-reaching, and my working relationship with Bill Geary was so good he completely supported them all.

My personal life was also moving. Cheryl and I were married in a wonderful ceremony at the Four Seasons Hotel, overlooking the Boston Public Garden. Geary, in his capacity as a justice of the peace, officiated. Al Sweeney was my best man. My life was really coming together.

For the first ten months of my administration, we extensively analyzed the entire department. It was worse than I'd thought. Some of the physical facilities were so poor—including leaking roofs, buckling walls, and falling plaster—that one squad room was actually heated by a fireplace. Our radio system hadn't been updated in several decades, leaving Met officers less able than cabdrivers to communicate with their dispatchers. Our walkie-talkies were so old and beat-up that walking and mounted officers couldn't receive calls for service and had to rely on cops in cars to look in on them once in a while to see if they were all right. Prisoners' short-term detention, processing, and housing areas did not meet proper safety standards. There was a severe shortage of locker rooms and showers for female personnel, while the men's facilities were in deplorable condition.

One of the lingering effects of the examination scandal was that many of the bosses were believed to have obtained their promotions by buying them. At the very least, most of the rank and file thought the brass was not supervising them closely and that they could get away with just about anything. The Mets knew their careers were going nowhere, and that dead-end attitude was reflected in their work. They had always been something of an invisible department, and many of them preferred to keep it that way.

Though one of their primary responsibilities was the control of traffic and the investigation of traffic accidents, the Mets never really investigated accidents involving their own vehicles. One of the reasons the fleet looked so bad was that no one was held accountable, and few officers were ever disciplined when they were at fault. As a result, we were suffering a chronic shortage of equipment because they were smacking up the cars left and right. The traditional July Fourth concert, with a half million people watching the Boston Pops play the *1812 Overture* on the Charles River Esplanade, capped by a fireworks extravaganza, was going to be my first big event as Mets superintendent. I had seen the old cars, some with trunk lids held down by rope, and I mandated that we would police the event only in cars with the new markings and without body damage. We were on display, and we were going to look good.

It was a measure of how bad things were that, out of the Mets' 113 marked cruisers, we could not come up with 25 that fit that description. Twenty-four of our cars had been totaled, another 35 were out due to breakdowns, the rest were overused and beat to hell. We were supposed to keep order on the roads; this was an embarrassment.

Working with Bill Geary, we immediately put a major effort into getting state money to upgrade our fleet, but I didn't want the cops to wreck the new cars. I installed a system of discipline. If an officer was found at fault in an automobile accident, he or she got at a minimum what was called an oral reprimand. I was going to get the cops' attention. Oral reprimands were given for a wide variety of infractions, from involvement in a car accident to an officer's not having his patrol guide up-to-date. I meant to instill accountability.

Oral reprimands were controversial with the union because they went into a cop's personnel file. We had big debates, their point being, "How can it be an oral reprimand when it's in writing?" It was just wordplay. A written reprimand, I told them, was given when an officer was found to be at egregious fault and was much more serious. I demanded all personnel orders and discipline be read at roll call, including oral reprimands. I installed Billy Boards in all station houses and posted the reprimands there as well.

We gave out more oral reprimands in one year than had been probably given in the hundred-year history of the organization, but not long after they were instituted the auto accident rate began to drop significantly, and the injured-officer rate took a nosedive. You know you've been accepted when the good-natured jokes start to appear. The Mets gave me a T-shirt that read: "I Survived the Reprimands of 1987."

When I arrived, the Mets were a dispirited, reactive, day-to-day operation with no direction, goals, or vision of its future. I was living in Revere at the time, and I arranged to be picked up and driven to work by different Met officers from the local district each morning. On our way in, I asked each of them for their ideas and their sense of the organization. This was a department that was lying down dying, and I needed to know why and how. We wanted our officers to participate in the life of the Mets, not just mark time there; we wanted them to believe in the Mets, because they were the Mets.

In order to jump-start this rusty machine, my staff and I came up with a forty-six-page plan of action. We identified the department's major strengths and weaknesses, defined its role within its parent agency, iden-

tified the changes needed to bring the organization into the m
world, and, most important, developed a written statement of its values.

Metropolitan Police Values

- The Metropolitan Police Department exists to protect and serve the public.
- The Department and its members will maintain the highest ethical standards of conduct.
- We will treat all citizens with dignity, respect, and courtesy.
- We will safeguard each citizen's rights to free expression, movement, and constitutional liberty while within the Metropolitan District Commission jurisdiction.
- We will use only minimum necessary force when performing our lawful duties.
- In applying the law, we will exercise discretion with consistency and equitableness.
- We are committed to giving each employee the authority to make decisions and to hold them accountable for their actions.
- The Department is committed to creating an environment that is productive and satisfying and of which its members can be proud.

We focused quickly on the department's vehicles and received $800,000 in state funding for thirty-nine cruisers, eight Suburbans with pushbar bumper plates to push disabled vehicles off the highways, five patrol wagons, and a dozen motorcycles. A hundred more vehicles and a $700,000 helicopter arrived within the year. After heavy lobbying, we got $2.5 million for a new state-of-the-art radio system including computer-aided dispatching and data processing and a citizen emergency call-box network, plus mobile data terminals in our cruisers. As a gesture of partnership and cooperation, we offered to share this with the state police. My team and I explained the virtues of this new technology to their representatives. They said they didn't have a need for it.

I established a uniform committee and instructed the department to get input from all levels of the organization. Promotion ceremonies, which had become tedious affairs, were reinvigorated and infused with pomp, circumstance, and significance.

I was learning how to inspire and motivate the rank and file by instilling discipline, by dealing with corruption, and by giving them better equipment with which to do their jobs and more satisfaction when the job was done well. For the men and women of the Mets, all of a sudden good work got rewarded and was more enjoyable.

In 1987, I received the second annual Gary Hayes Award from the Police Executive Research Forum, in recognition of my turning around two different police forces and actually having an effect on crime. The award was a tremendous honor. In the late 1980s, very few people in- or outside the policing profession thought such a thing was possible.

PERF convened its members several times a year for seminars and discussions. It was a unique professional organization. The notable names in the business attended as guest speakers and presenters: Ben Ward, police commissioner of New York; Lee Brown of Houston; Daryl Gates of Los Angeles; New York's former commissioner Pat Murphy; academics such as James Q. Wilson, George Kelling, Bob Wasserman, and Herman Goldstein; public officials such as Bob Kiley, then of New York's Metropolitan Transit Authority; President Reagan's attorney general, Ed Meese. Members had to have a college degree, and they had to believe in, create, and host research in the field of policing.

There were other advanced centers of police thinking. The Police Foundation was the godfather of the field, and the Executive Session on Policing at Harvard University's John F. Kennedy School of Government was developing the community-policing concept. I stayed involved with them all.

This was an interesting period in policing because the big-city chiefs opened up their doors to the research community. PERF and the Police Foundation let these social scientists, who ten years earlier they would have locked up for demonstrating outside the Chicago convention, into their station houses to interview prisoners and riffle their files. As a result, the field of policing included a generation of social scientists many of whom probably never thought they would get involved in this world. And, in an extremely conservative and intentionally isolated profession, the idea of the professionally informed and educated police chief began to emerge.

James Q. Wilson and George Kelling had written an important article entitled "Broken Windows" in the March 1982 issue of *The Atlantic Monthly* in which they'd said, "If police are to deal with disorder to reduce fear and crime, they must rely on citizens for legitimacy and assistance." In 1988, Kelling had delivered a paper to the Harvard Executive Session called "Police and Communities: The Quiet Revolution" that advocated a return to what he called "community problem-solving" policing. Kelling articulated and put into beautiful words what I had found from experience. I supported what he wrote because I had already lived it. The Boston-Fenway Program had convinced me of the absolute wisdom of that approach.

Meanwhile, between 1986 and 1989, the Mets turnaround was so successful that the state police wanted to take us over. They were the larger, more traditional, old-line organization of troopers, and they had become very jealous of our increasing visibility and success. Three years earlier, they had been the established power, and we'd been less than nothing. Now we were modernized and retrained and reinvigorated. We had better technology than the state police, better equipment, better cars, better uniforms. We had worked very hard to use the media to advance our image, and we were getting better press than they were. We had computers in our cars; they were still back at headquarters doing things with pen and paper. The state police was a good old-line organization, but in three years we had surpassed them in many ways, changing the Metropolitan Police from a dispirited, do-nothing, reactive organization with a poor self-image and an even worse public one to a very proud and proactive department. We were the Cinderella department.

What the state police did have, however, was a union with phenomenal political clout. Connected to Governor Dukakis and his Secretary for Public Safety Charles Barry, as well as the Massachusetts legislature, the union waged an aggressive political campaign to do away with us. The state police plan, in effect a hostile takeover, was to merge all six hundred Metropolitan police, plus four hundred Registry of Motor Vehicles police and a hundred Capitol police, into their own organization. They would have preferred to get rid of the personnel from all three organizations, but politically, the best they could do was a merger.

I fought that battle for an entire year. I didn't feel my agency was being treated fairly, and I didn't think the state police were in any position to run our operation as well as we did. It was a bitter fight in which we were outmaneuvered and ultimately beaten. Despite my good relations with Dukakis, he sided with the state police, a decision, I believe, he subsequently came to regret. Legislation was passed in 1990 to merge the four organizations into one.

The irony of the merger, particularly for the Mets, was that many of the state-police systems were not compatible with our computer systems. After the merger, many of our computers were effectively unplugged, and we went back to paper and pencil for such things as payrolls and attendance. It was a very discouraging movement back.

As a result of the merger, I was certainly going to lose my command and, at best, could hope for a second- or third-level position in the command staff of the Massachusetts state police. I was not very interested. Fortunately, in the spring of 1989, in the middle of all this political maneuvering, I got a call from Bob Wasserman and George Kelling. Would I meet with them over breakfast?

Bob Kiley, who had served as Boston's deputy mayor and head of the MBTA, had moved to New York in the eighties to accept the position of chairman of the New York City Metropolitan Transit Authority, the agency responsible for the New York Transit Authority (TA), Metro-North, the Long Island Rail Road, and a number of the city's bridges and tunnels. Along with Kiley, the president of the Transit Authority, David Gunn, had hired Wasserman and Kelling to research New York's subway system to develop solutions to its considerable crime and disorder problems.

The New York City subway system was a horror. Crime was skyrocketing, fare evasion was epidemic, graffiti was rampant, the fear underground was overwhelming, and as a result, ridership and public confidence were plummeting. Despite significant improvements in the condition of the trains, stations, and infrastructure, the continuing crime problem led Mayor Ed Koch to support the concept of merging the Transit Authority Police into the NYPD. Wasserman and Kelling had been hired to study the idea. Their research indicated that merger was not in the best interests of the Transit Authority and that the TA Police was an organization uniquely positioned to test many of their most progressive theories. What it needed was a leader, a new chief. I had turned around the MBTA Police. Bob Kiley had pinned the PERF Gary Hayes Award on my lapel. He knew me and he trusted Kelling and Wasserman.

We met for breakfast at the Bostonian Hotel, and Wasserman and Kelling immediately set about recruiting me. Would I be interested in heading the New York Transit Police, with four thousand people, twice the size of the Boston Police? Yes, I'd be very interested.

That summer I met secretly with David Gunn at his mother's house in Medford, Massachusetts, and in the fall he invited me down to New York to tour the system and continue our discussions. It was only when I got off the shuttle at La Guardia Airport that I began to realize what a hellhole New York had become.

In the baggage-claim area, four different limo drivers were haranguing exiting passengers, arguing over who was literally going to take us for a ride. I ran their gauntlet before I hopped into a grimy, dilapidated licensed yellow cab. The highway into the city was covered with dirt, grime, and litter so thick it looked like it hadn't been cleaned for decades. The medians between east- and westbound lanes were filthy, and when traffic slowed to a crawl there was little to stare at but debris. Abandoned cars were stripped and strewn along the side of the road like rat-eaten carcasses. The walls lining the road were scrawled with graffiti.

We came out of the Queens-Midtown Tunnel and were double-teamed at the stoplight by men with filthy rags demanding money, the official New York City greeters, the squeegee men. Welcome to New York. On Fifth Avenue, I saw table after table of unregulated peddlers; the great New York thoroughfare looked like a Third World Casbah.

We went down into the subways. Reality outstripped even the vivid descriptions Kelling, Wasserman, and Gunn had given me. After waiting in a seemingly endless line to buy a token, I tried to put the coin into a turnstile and found it had been purposely jammed. Unable to pay the fare to get into the system, we had to enter through a slam gate being held open by a scruffy-looking character with his hand out; having disabled the turnstiles, he was now demanding that riders give him their tokens. Meanwhile, one of his cohorts had his mouth on the coin slots, sucking out the jammed coins and leaving his slobber. Most people were too intimidated to take these guys on: Here, take the damned token, what do I care? Other citizens were going over, under, around, or through the stiles for free. It was like going into the transit version of Dante's *Inferno.*

On the platform, while we waited for the train all the benches seemed taken by people stretched out sleeping. At one end of the station, there was a cardboard city, homeless men and women camped day and night in packing boxes. Then we got on the train, the doors closed, and things got worse.

Now locked inside with no place to go, we couldn't help but observe the people splayed over the seats asleep, most riders giving them a wide berth. One foul-smelling sleeper could take up a quarter of a car by himself. No one made eye contact. If you could have held your breath for the entire ride, you would have. A parade of aggressive beggars was sliding open the doors between cars and tramping from one to another. "I've got TB," "I've got AIDS," "I'm going to breathe on you," "Give me money." It didn't quit. The entire ride was unnerving. I was not unhappy to get above ground. David Gunn, understandably, was not happy with what he had shown me, but he had made his point. All the improvements he was making in the conditions of the cars and stations would be for nothing without a turnaround in the system itself.

Gunn indicated that he was interested in bringing me in, but as with

Jimmy O'Leary and the MBTA, there was a lag time. Before a decision was made, he resigned and was replaced as TA president by Alan Kiepper, who had been recruited from Houston. I interviewed with him as well. Kiepper wanted three problems addressed by police: fare evasion, disorder, and crime.

I began to look closely at New York.

I was living north of Boston in the seacoast town of Marblehead. Each morning, I drove to work through the Sumner Tunnel, took a sharp right turn into the North End, and headed for the Freedom Trail Coffee Shop, a hole-in-the-wall luncheonette with a Formica counter and five vinyl-covered booths next door to the historic Paul Revere House. The Police Academy had been right down the block in 1970 and, a creature of habit, I'd been eating breakfast there ever since.

Most days I ate my bacon and eggs and read the *Herald* and the *Globe* before going to the office. In the summer of 1989, I began to read *The New York Times* and the *New York Post*. The *Times* influenced the decision makers, the *Post* was read by the cops. I was looking for the issues. How was transit being covered? Who were the players? Which reporters covered transit? And, as important, who were the usual cast of characters the press would go to for comment on the Transit Police? If I took the job and successfully turned that department around, I could legitimately begin positioning myself as a contender for the number one job in American policing, New York City police commissioner. It would require gaining high visibility and success very quickly in the country's most complex city and toughest media environment.

I found that New York newspapers report obsessively on subway issues. Three and a half million people ride the subways every day, another million and a half ride the buses, so literally the majority of New York's population had a personal interest in the chief of transit's job every day. And crime, fear, and disorder were going through the roof. It was the ideal situation.

For six months I studied the New York Transit Police, and finally, in April 1990, I got the job.

Chapter 9

ALAN KIEPPER GAVE ME MARCHING ORDERS. CRIME STATISTICS, HE TOLD ME, were grim. Robberies in the subway system had risen 48 percent over the past two years, far more than in New York City as a whole. Crime was causing fear; fear was causing abandonment of the system. "Your performance," Kiepper wrote in his letter welcoming me to the Transit Authority, "will be judged largely on whether you can show significant improvement in the reduction of crime and in the restoration of confidence."

I had three major issues to deal with:

Fare evasion. Fare beating was epidemic. People were entering the transit system without paying at a rate of about 170,000 per day, costing the city about eighty million dollars a year. Token scams were running wild. Fare beaters were pulling back the turnstiles and sliding through—a little New York dance step that everyone had gotten used to seeing—or jumping and pushing their way through the slam gates, and nothing was being done about it. Legitimate riders felt that they were entering a place of lawlessness and disorder. They saw people going in for free and began to question the wisdom of abiding by the law. Some were angry, others were disgusted, others just gave up and felt the entire city was out of control. Still others got the brilliant idea to jump the turnstiles as well. It fed on itself. The system was veering toward anarchy.

Disorder. Aggressive panhandling and vandalism was undermining rider safety. The threatening spiel had become part of the daily ride. People just didn't feel safe on the subways, and large numbers of New Yorkers were finding other ways of getting around. The fact that there were an estimated five thousand people living in the subway stations and tunnels was both a safety and a health hazard.

Crime. Frightening face-to-face crime was becoming more violent as juvenile robbers operating in gangs, or "wolfpacks," increasingly used firearms and assaulted their victims. Surprisingly, the transit system generated only 2 percent of the overall reported crime in the city, at its peak maybe fifty-five robberies a day. Nevertheless, fear of crime had become a major deterrent to use of the system, especially at night and particularly for women.

And while the transit system was becoming more dangerous and anarchic, the 3,500-person Transit Police was probably the most demoralized police force in America. Their work environment was awful, their equipment was semifunctional and obsolete, their morale was miserable, and it seemed that no one but their union cared. They had no champion. They were also the only police department in America that drafted officers into its ranks. New York City police applicants did not pick their own department—they took a civil-service exam and then by lottery were sent to the NYPD, transit, or housing police. Those who went to transit didn't want to be there. As the number of younger officers grew, the union leadership supported the concept of merging with the NYPD, which most of the transit cops wanted to join anyway. It was the only police force in the United States trying to merge itself out of existence.

Transit cops were known as the "Ohhhh" police. For generations, they had been treated as part of a second-class operation. People would ask cops in social situations, "What do you do for a living?"

"I'm a police officer."

"Oh, where?"

"City of New York."

"No kidding! I've got a brother who's a cop. Where do you work?"

"Uh, I work in Manhattan."

"Oh, yeah. What precinct?"

"I'm with the Transit Police."

"Ohhhh."

The "Ohhhh" Police.

Compounding the problem was the fact that several of transit's most

recent chiefs had not come from within the department but had tr
ferred over from the NYPD at the end of their careers. It was widely felt
that these chiefs were more sympathetic to NYPD issues than to the organization they led.

There was also a culture of competition between transit and city cops,
and transit cops were losers. They had nothing, they were nothing, they
went nowhere. Unfortunately, when I arrived, a lot of them believed it.
They wanted out.

My first day on the job I got a glimpse of why.

I had been announced as the new chief at a press conference that
morning at Transit Headquarters in Brooklyn. (Cheryl and I had taken
the subway from Manhattan and had quickly managed to get lost.)
Afterward, I went to the second floor to meet my command staff in my
new office. Exiting the elevator, a security officer was stationed to screen
all visitors. This cop was sitting with his feet up, reading a newspaper.

"Who is that?" I asked.

"He's assigned to the office."

"Why is he here?"

"That's his assignment."

I was incensed. "That's the image we project? He's got his tie hanging
off, he looks like crap, people walk into the chief's office every day, and
they see that for our image? Have that officer removed. I don't want him
here when I come out of this meeting."

My command staff was reasonably apprehensive to meet their new
chief. I seized the opportunity to inject optimism into an organization that
was sadly lacking in good news. "I didn't come down from Boston to
lose," I told them. "I intend to win. I believe in working hard, and I am ex-
pecting all of you to work hard with me. I also believe that we should have
some fun. My intention is to succeed and to have fun succeeding. We
should enjoy our time here." They looked at me like I was nuts.

Cheryl had flown home. She had decided to stay in Boston and continue practicing law. We would see each other on weekends. Around five-
thirty in the afternoon, I left the hotel where I was staying for my first
month, around the corner from Grand Central Terminal, and went out for
a walk in my new neighborhood. I got a big kick out of being in New York.

I was strolling west on Forty-second Street across from Grand Central
and the Grand Hyatt Hotel and I saw a cop leaning against a building. As
I got closer, I saw that he was very disheveled. He had shaggy hair and
looked as if he hadn't shaved that morning. His shirt was wrinkled and his

clip-on tie was pinned off to one side on his collar, a particular pet peeve of mine. His gun belt, which had originally been black but was now brown from wear, hung from him like he was Mister Goodwrench, and his hat was hanging from his holster.

You could differentiate transit and housing cops from the NYPD by which shoulder their patch was on; the NYPD wore theirs on the right. His was on the left—he was one of my men. Even his patch was beat-up, the corners curling and the stitching starting to fray. I walked over, identified myself, and stuck out my hand. It was something I did thousands of times: Look at the nameplate below the cop's shield, stick out my hand to shake theirs, look them in the eye, and say, "Hi, Officer Smith, I'm Chief Bratton, how're you doing?"

The officer straightened up a little.

"What's your post?" I asked. I expected he would tell me something like "Forty-first to Forty-third streets between Madison and Lexington."

"Right here, sir," he said.

"Right here?" He was standing in front of an office building. "What are you doing here?"

"I'm guarding the token booth, sir. That's my responsibility."

"Where's the token booth?"

He pointed down a marble corridor to an entrance forty feet away inside the building.

"If you're supposed to be guarding the token booth in there, what are you doing out here?"

"My radio doesn't work in there."

In that one conversation, all the problems of the Transit Police officer were clear. Zero morale, the absolute hatred of his assignment, the feelings of being disrespected by his organization, the feelings of disrespect for his organization, the lousy equipment, the lousy uniforms. He put on his hat, pinned up his tie, tucked himself in, and went back to his post.

I made it a point to get out and around the system my first several weeks on the job, and as I talked to more cops, I started to see things for myself. I didn't like what I was seeing.

Imagine the sheer drudgery and boredom of being a police officer in uniform assigned to stand in one place eight hours a day, day after day, just so people don't jump the turnstile or rob the booth. Cops being cops, they wanted to focus on crime: robberies, assaults, muggings. They hated being assigned to prevent fare evasion because they saw that as protecting the Transit Authority's money—not their money, not the taxpayers' money, or the city's money, but the Transit Authority's money. They felt they were being misused by the Transit Authority. The Transit Authority was the enemy.

On top of that, I only had four hundred cops working patrol at any one time, and there were over seven hundred entrances. How was I supposed to keep them all covered, let alone fight crime inside the system? Anyone who wanted to ride for free who saw a cop at one booth could walk down a block and jump the turnstile at the other entrance. The whole idea of planting a cop at each station wasn't going to work. And that's not even taking into account the deadening effect of the no-win job on cops who already felt they were in a loser's organization.

Two-thirds of what the Transit Authority wanted to make our main focus—fare evasion and disorder—cops didn't want to spend time on. They wanted to reduce crime. But absent getting my force inspired to deal with all three, we were never going to reduce any of them. I had to put together a transit team that was capable of setting goals, reorganizing and inspiring the department to meet those goals, and improving morale and confidence, while fighting the promerger stance of the union and the newly elected mayor, David Dinkins.

Kelling and Wasserman had given me the names of several talented people in the organization and I sought them out. The first was Dean Esserman, a young man in his early thirties who had gone to New York City private schools, graduated from Dartmouth, interned at PERF, gotten his law degree, become an assistant district attorney, and then general counsel to Transit Police Chief Vinny Del Castillo. Not your normal Transit Police career path. Esserman was a progressive thinker whom I could bounce ideas with, and I kept him on as both my chief counsel and policy adviser. He was very smart, well networked in the city, and extremely helpful. He had one of the most extensive police libraries I had ever seen, and his knowledge of New York City police history was nothing short of phenomenal.

Mike O'Connor, transit's chief of detectives, was also on Kelling and Wasserman's list. O'Connor had the reputation for being a real tough guy; they called him "Iron Mike." O'Connor was outside the power circle that was running the department when I arrived. He was on vacation the week I took over and was not there for my initial meeting with the chiefs, but when he got back he knocked on my door. I was interested in meeting this guy whom Kelling and Wasserman had thought so highly of. Right away, he said something I responded to.

"If you want to get out into the system," he told me, "I'd be more than happy to show you around. Night or day, I'd be available to you."

That impressed me. In my dealings with all the other incumbent transit chiefs, I had come to realize that they never actually went out and rode the trains. They had desk jobs, they were never seen by the troops, and they liked it that way. I liked O'Connor's direct approach. In fact, we did tour the subways and as I put together a planning group to set goals and reorganize the department, O'Connor became a confidant and an indispensable part of the brain trust. He was very creative, very ambitious, loved the department, and, most important, felt he could do a much better job. The fact that he was one of the department's most highly decorated members also gave him great credibility.

Al O'Leary was my director of media services, and he gave me a quick and important education in how to deal with New York's vaunted press. "Don't play games with them," he told me. "Don't deceive them. Tell it to them the way it is. Always tell them the truth." I liked O'Leary. He was personable, widely respected by the press, and a straight shooter. Since the press was essential to my plans, it was important to start off on the right foot with them. With Al O'Leary, I was assured of that.

Phyllis McDonald was the director of planning. Phyllis had been a deputy chief in Dayton, Ohio, as well as an academic, moving through both worlds as a consultant. She had been hired by Del Castillo at Wasserman's recommendation about a year before I was approached for the job and had been very frustrated at the slow pace of change in the department.

I brought with me from Boston for the transition period a woman named Athena Yerganian, a computer whiz who had worked with me at the MDC. She produced a lot of the analytical data, organizational charts, and color diagrams that the brain trust found so helpful in reorganizing the department.

I commuted to Boston on weekends to see Cheryl, or occasionally she came down, so during the week I worked day and night. During the first several weeks of evaluation and transition, I frequently met in the evenings in my hotel room with Wasserman, Esserman, O'Connor, McDonald, Yerganian, and Kelling, and we'd cook up strategies. Wasserman and Kelling had been hired by the Transit Authority as consultants and were feeding me ideas and reading material. The more I thought about it, the more the place needed shaking up. "We're sloppy about everything," I said one evening. "We're sloppy in our appearance, we're sloppy always thinking the city cops are first-class and we're second-rate; we're not getting a handle on the violence or the robberies or even the graffiti. The place is a mess."

The Transit Police organization I inherited was less than efficient. Vinny Del Castillo had been very impressed with computers and installed a number of computer systems to manage the organization. They generated a phenomenal amount of information but didn't bring about any significant change in the crime or disorder situations. Like most of his command staff, Del Castillo very seldom went out on the system.

Shortly before my arrival, Del Castillo had brought in a new deputy chief, George Latimer, as his number two. Latimer, a black man, had been a captain in transit for a number of years before retiring because he felt he couldn't crack the old-boy network. Wanting a minority on the command staff, Del Castillo asked Latimer to come out of retirement, and he jumped at the opportunity.

Latimer had quite a reputation as a tough guy when he was in the Transit Police. He immediately began building a coterie of chiefs around him who figured that when Del Castillo either stepped aside or was moved out, their guy as heir apparent would move up, and they would move up with him. Unfortunately, they weren't doing a particularly good job. The department had spent millions of dollars in overtime the year before, and robberies had gone *up* 12 percent.

My first week on the job, I asked every commander above district level to prepare presentations, to come into my office after work and tell me about their command and what they did. In an organization that felt disenfranchised, I wanted to involve every level in its own turnaround. They gathered what facts they had and showed me. I got a quick but thorough overview of the people in positions of responsibility within the Transit Police as well as a better understanding of the organization.

Within two months of taking over, I proposed to Alan Kiepper a major organizational restructuring. He agreed. We reorganized the Transit Police into two bureaus: operations and administration. Instead of one chief presiding over everything, we now had two deputy chiefs. George Latimer became chief of administration. I made Mike O'Connor chief of operations and gave him full authority to run the department day to day. O'Connor had my trust, and I wasn't going to hang over his shoulder. The message was clear to the department and the rank and file: A new day was dawning for transit. With the department in good hands, I was free to concentrate on the big picture.

George Kelling had identified Captain Richie Gollinge as a creative and assertive guy, someone who was willing to stick his neck out, one of the few white shirts who was out in the system working with his cops. (Captains and above wore white shirts with their uniforms, others wore powder blue.) Gollinge was in charge of the Transit Police district located at Columbus Circle, one of the city's busiest stations, in the heart of Manhattan. He was a big, robust guy, very outgoing. O'Connor was impressed with him, too, and so was I. I moved Gollinge up from a captain to a deputy chief working with Mike O'Connor, a triple leap, passing over all deputy inspectors and inspectors. It was an unheard-of promotion. Gollinge himself couldn't believe it. He came out of my office after I'd promoted him and told Esserman and O'Connor, "Chief Bratton made a mistake. He meant 'deputy inspector,' he said 'deputy chief.' " They laughed. "No, he meant what he said."

Most of the transit brass never went on the system—they commuted to work in their authorized take-home cars, and even when they moved around the city they'd take cars. They referred to riding the subways as "going into the rat hole," or "going back into the hole." I told them, "Look, I'm going to be riding the system—in plain clothes, in uniform, all hours of the day and night—and I expect you to get out there and show our people some support, see what's actually going on." We called it Getting the White Shirts Out. Transit cops weren't used to seeing senior command staff at roll calls; they couldn't believe that in the middle of the night a call would go out and a white shirt was on the scene to assist. We weren't there to spy on them, we really wanted to see the conditions they were working under.

Each morning I was briefed by my administrative sergeant, Cal Mathis, who had recently returned from the FBI National Academy. Each morning it was his responsibility to give me an information snapshot of the previous evening's events: patrol strength, numbers of crimes, major incidents. Each week, I gathered the department's senior leadership in my office. After about a month, we began meeting daily so I could intensify my knowledge of the department and so the senior staff had more access to me and could really see the direction I wanted to take them. These meetings created a forum for commanders to talk to each other on a regular basis. Anecdotes, customs, methods of getting the job done, things that worked—I wanted to hear them. If they made sense and they were permissible within department guidelines, I began to institute them departmentwide.

Many leaders do not like meetings. I do. I find them a very useful means of establishing personal two-way communication, and they've always been a part of my leadership style.

At the same time as I was trying to reinvigorate my troops, the MTA was trying to reinterest the public in the transit system. They were preparing a $3.5 million advertising campaign for the subway system under the supervision of their director of marketing and corporate communications, John Linder. George Kelling said Linder was very smart and highly skilled, and he suggested very strongly that I meet him. He felt we would hit it off.

I certainly did want to meet Linder. Here for the first time in my career someone had expertise and a multimillion-dollar budget to market what I was doing. We met for dinner at an old, dark wood–paneled restaurant off Sixth Avenue that had all these single malts and fifty-year-old whiskeys that Linder liked, and we talked.

Linder was in his early forties. His curly black hair was graying. He was slight, thin, and always looked worried. He all but wrung his hands when he spoke.

Linder was a great believer in focus groups, he was constantly testing people and products. His major frustration in promoting the Transit Police was how to market the organization when crime is going up 25 percent and when the officers are demoralized and look awful and have been consistently ineffective in dealing with very visible issues.

Linder's focus groups told him that despite the fact that the TA had virtually wiped out graffiti on the trains, about 20 percent of the respondents said it was still there. Things had gotten so bad, people didn't even believe what they saw. In one set of focus groups, Linder asked women what percentage of the city's crime they thought was committed on the subways. They said 30 to 40 percent. Homicides? Forty to 50 percent. When he asked men, crime came back at 20 to 30 percent, homicides 30 to 40. In fact, 3 percent of the city's felony crime and between 1 and 2 percent of its murders happened on the subways. "What would you think if I were to tell you that 3 percent of the city's crime happens on the subway?" he asked the women. "Would that change your level of fear toward the public-transportation system?"

They answered, "Absolutely not."

The subways, he found, invited fear because, whatever happened, you couldn't escape. Anything could happen to you anywhere in the system. For the public and for us, it seemed there was nowhere to run.

Linder had also run focus groups with transit cops, and his findings

matched my anecdotal information: They were as demoralized and disheveled as any organization he had seen. They didn't want to deal with
fare beating because they had no interest in protecting the Transit
Authority's property; they didn't want to collar turnstile jumpers because
that had nothing to do with real police work; and they didn't want to deal
with the panhandlers and underground population because they didn't
want to put their hands on people who might have AIDS. They were
happy, however, to go after serious crime.

We brainstormed for many hours that night. The Transit Authority had
six thousand subway cars and a couple of thousand city buses Linder
could plaster with billboards. He had the budget to reach all of New York
on television and radio and the capacity to hire writers, designers, and
everyone else needed to put together an extensive campaign. He could
provide a design department to upgrade the Transit Police's in-house
image, to get the cops onboard.

———

People needed good news in a bad way. What story could we tell them?

In their 1982 *Atlantic Monthly* magazine article, James Q. Wilson and
George Kelling had outlined their "Broken Windows" theory. As synop-
sized by Kelling, its three major points were:

1. Neighborhood disorder—drunks, panhandling, youth gangs, prostitution, and other urban incivilities—creates citizen fear.
2. Just as unrepaired broken windows can signal to people that nobody
   cares about a building and lead to more serious vandalism, untended
   disorderly behavior can also signal that nobody cares about the community and lead to more serious disorder and crime. Such signals—
   untended property, disorderly persons, drunks, obstreperous youth, et
   cetera—both create fear in citizens and attract predators.
3. If police are to deal with disorder to reduce fear and crime, they must
   rely on citizens for legitimacy and assistance.

We began to apply this concept to crime in the subways. Fare evasion was
the biggest broken window in the transit system. We were going to fix that
window and see to it that it didn't get broken again.

The Transit Police was not arresting fare evaders in any great numbers.
It seemed like such a minor offense—tokens cost $1.15 at the time—and
it often took up to twenty-four hours for one cop to process one fare

beater. If he issued a summons or desk-appearance ticket, very frequently the person would not show up in court or pay the fine. A warrant would then be issued, but no one ever really tracked them down. If a cop made an arrest, by the time he did the paperwork, took the perpetrator downtown to Central Booking to be held for arraignment, sat at the courthouse until the man or woman was arraigned, then testified and watched as they either walked or paid a minuscule fine, he was out of the system for sixteen hours. It just didn't seem worth the effort. Once or twice a year my predecessors did major sweeps, rounded everybody up, and brought them out to Yankee Stadium for a big publicity splash. That was about the extent of attention paid to fare beating. Rather than make arrests, the Transit Authority's preferred action was to station a cop at the turnstile while spending millions of dollars to make turnstile arrays more difficult to climb over or under. Meanwhile, the system was being overrun.

Could we devise a plan that attacked fare evasion, attacked disorder, attacked crime, and also dealt with morale? We came up with the fare-evasion mini-sweep.

Some stations were being treated as if they didn't even have turnstiles. I put a sergeant and five, eight, sometimes ten cops in plain clothes at these problematic stations day and night, and they arrested the people who were streaming in for nothing. The cops nabbed ten or twenty jumpers at a time. They pulled these men and women in one by one, cuffed them, lined them up on the platform, and waited for the next wave. When they had a full catch, they marched them upstairs in a daisy chain and put them into wagons to be taken downtown for processing. We did this all over the city.

For the first time in a long time, the cops were making arrests. They were being cops! The cops were motivated and getting noticed. Twenty people handcuffed in a line is a sight that will attract attention in a subway station. Riders saw fare evaders getting arrested and thought, "Good. I pay a buck-fifteen, why shouldn't they?" They saw cops hauling long lines of folks out of the subways and said, "Go get 'em," "Great job!" "Way to go!" "It's about time!" When was the last time a transit cop heard that?

By assigning a sergeant, I was assured of supervision, our cops were doing what we wanted, and they were doing it according to Hoyle. Focus, direction, supervision.

We ran these sweeps day and night. Our undercover officers saw people come into the stations even at three in the morning, check that the uniformed police weren't there, then attempt to evade the fare. We'd nab them. We publicized our efforts, and over time word got out that the Transit Police were serious about fare evasion twenty-four hours a day, throughout the city. Of course, we couldn't be everywhere, but the tactic of plainclothes patrol, as opposed to patrolling only in uniform, created the impression that we might be there. The fear of arrest, the control of previously uncontrolled behavior, began to change behavior. Fare evasion began to decline significantly.

It also became evident that many of the people we were arresting were exactly the ones who were causing other problems once inside the subway system. By focusing on fare evasion to control disorder, we were preventing a lot of the criminal elements from getting on the trains and platforms in the first place.

An unanticipated by-product of the sweeps came when we checked the identification and warrant status of everybody we were arresting. During the early stages of the initiative, we found that one out of every seven people arrested for fare evasion was wanted on an outstanding warrant for a previous crime. One out of twenty-one was carrying some type of weapon, whether a box cutter, a knife, or a gun. As so often happens in policing, we had focused on one problem to the exclusion of others. Now we were beginning to understand the linkage between disorder and more serious crimes. We hadn't thought of it, but it stands to reason that someone coming into the system with the intention to commit a crime is not likely to pay for the privilege.

For the cops this was a bonanza. Every arrest was like opening a box of Cracker Jack. What kind of toy am I going to get? Got a gun? Got a knife? Got a warrant? Do we have a murderer here? Each cop wanted to be the one who came up with the big collar. It was exhilarating for the cops and demoralizing for the crooks. After a while, the bad guys wised up and began to leave their weapons home and pay their fares. If the cops were going to be out in force, it was better all around not to be armed on the subway. Fewer weapons, fewer robberies and armed robberies, fewer murders, fewer perpetrators, fewer victims.

We were changing behavior by using the police more efficiently. We were defying the common wisdom of the last twenty years that the most cops can do is to respond to crime. In the subways, we were preventing it. As the press and the public began to take notice, the cops began to feel better about themselves and their effectiveness.

The major problem presented by the sweeps was what to do with all these people once we had arrested them. It continued to take sixteen hours to dispose of a case, and even if two officers were now handling twenty at a time, the hours mounted up. We were still losing cops off the system like crazy when they transported arrestees to the Central Booking facilities. Esserman and I and several of my staff were in a meeting, talking about arrest processing and logistics, when the proverbial lightbulb went off over my head: We were in the transportation business. I said, "Why don't we bring the arrest processing to them?"

Probably a dozen people believe they were the originators of this idea, and that's fine with me. My basic concept of leadership is the ability to enthuse and encourage the people in your organization so highly that, whatever idea is put into action, they embrace it so fully they forget the genesis and assume it was their own.

Thus was born the Bust Bus. We completely retrofitted a city bus into an arrest-processing center. Four cops, several telephones and fax machines, fingerprinting and photo facilities, a holding pen, and we were in business. It was a mobile district station. We led our daisy chains past the law-abiding citizens and onto the Bust Bus, which we parked around the corner from the station. We called the men and women carrying weapons or with outstanding warrants "keepers" and shipped them downtown. If the others had proper identification, we gave them D.A.T.s and sent them on their way. Instead of sixteen hours, someone arrested for evading a fare could be in and out in an hour, still a significant inconvenience to them but not to us. The cops could stay downstairs and continue making arrests. Now, rather than throwing up our hands every time we ran into a problem, we began to solve it.

The Bust Bus got great press. The American Civil Liberties Union raised hell about the fare-evasion sweeps, so I invited the city's corporation counsel, Victor Kovner, and his assistant, Diane Volk, to ride along and take a look for themselves. We parked the bus down at the bottom of TriBeCa and set up shop. Esserman, O'Connor, and I each made a presentation.

"There's nothing unconstitutional about this operation," I told Kovner and Volk. "We're moving people around in daisy chains, but if they didn't evade the fare, they wouldn't be arrested in the first place, so what's the problem? We have a system that's designed *not* to detain them any longer than is absolutely necessary. If anything, by having a bus right there, we have reduced the amount of time they are detained. The city is saving a significant amount of time and money, and of course you currently are involved in a lawsuit with the Legal Aid Society concerning the forty-eight-hour time constraint in arrest processing . . ." I gave them a good dose of statistics to prove my case.

"How's this program affecting arrest processing, Dean?"

Esserman gave the legal perspective, which we had researched; we were on firm ground.

"Mike, would you give the big picture?"

"What we have effectively developed," O'Connor told them, "is a system that deals with fare evasion and disorder and crime at the same time. For example, our statistics show that a large number of criminals arrested for subway crimes in the borough of Manhattan are actually from Brooklyn." It was a variation on Manhattan District Attorney Robert Morgenthau's favorite theme: Manhattan makes it, Brooklyn takes it. "How do you think they come over? By subway! If we are able to arrest them in the act of fare evasion, they won't come to Manhattan and commit their crimes."

After the meeting, the five of us stood outside the Bust Bus among several cops. The sidewalk was cordoned off, as the arrest-processing activity continued. Civilians know what's up when they turn the corner and all these cops are standing around; they're both drawn to it and kept away. The more assertive ones saunter over. "What's going on?" It was clearly a crime scene. Prisoners in handcuffs snaked in a long line from the nearby station onto the bus. An officer stood on each side of the door.

An old woman pulling a wire shopping cart read the lettering on the bus: "Arrest Processing Center." "A jail on wheels!" she exclaimed. "Why don't you bring that on up to my neighborhood? You can lock 'em up all day!"

And so crime, disorder, and fare evasion began to go down. I'd always tried to obtain multiple benefits from my actions, and this had been a particularly successful operation. We had reduced fare evasion, motivated the cops, streamlined the arrest process, and increased police productivity; we had involved the public, increased their attention, and won their approval; we had controlled disorder and achieved a decrease in crime. All from arresting people for a buck-fifteen crime. We were proving the Broken Windows theory.

We were doing all this good work on a shoestring. As well as being demoralized and undirected, transit was woefully underfunded. If I was going to encourage cops to be more assertive and more proactive and to make more arrests, I had to be able to back them up. That backup would come from the city police, who would respond to the radio, but it would also come from transit. The districts were large—District 4, for instance, ran from Fourteenth Street up to 140th Street on the west side of Manhattan—and when you've got a prisoner cuffed on the platform and you're hanging around waiting for backup with a crowd gathering around you, it can seem like an eternity until the cavalry arrives. We desperately needed more cars to back up the cops as well as to transport the increased number of prisoners to the jails and courts. I doubled the number of each district's patrol vehicles to four. This meant not only were my officers more secure and backed up more quickly, but four more cops could now get a change of assignment. Multiply that by three shifts and ten transit districts and you have 120 more cops per day with a change of work environment. Once again, I was getting multiple effects: higher employee morale, increased efficiency, increased safety of officers, increased visibility of the Transit Police.

I had to fight like crazy to get those vehicles. The Transit Authority was adamantly opposed. They didn't understand the rationale; we were the subway police, we were supposed to be below ground, what did we need cars for at all? They were putting together a new capital budget, and I was lobbying for a new radio system and improvements to the facilities, but that was going to take a long time to come through. We needed a jump start, a quick fix. I was having critical funding difficulties, and no one in a position to do us some good was responding.

The white shirts hadn't been in the system in so long that many had forgotten what life below ground was like. The irony was that every boss had come up through that system, and indeed, as tough as conditions were now, they'd been worse twenty years before. Promotion may have seemed like an opportunity for them to escape the responsibility to deal with those conditions. They had made it out of the electric sewer and didn't want to go back. What you don't see and hear, you don't have to respond to, so rather than feel guilty the white shirts stopped watching and listening.

Since Cheryl wasn't in New York, I got used to roaming the system all night, sometimes with someone from the department, sometimes by myself. I'd just get on a train and go, learn my way around, much as I'd done in Boston as a kid with Franny McNulty. I got a sense of what it must be like for the cops, and I must admit, alone in the middle of night, the tension did begin to build. I loved to have the doors slide open, step into a subway car at five-thirty in the morning, and see the reactions of the cops on their shift as I said, "How's it going, fellas?" It became a matter of pride for cops to be able to point to my signature in their memo books and say the chief had given them a "scratch" at a faraway station at some ungodly hour.

I began to take my command staff out of headquarters and into the district stations so they could see how bad conditions really were. The Fourteenth Street–Union Square station, for example, is multitiered, and the District 4 station was buried deep in the bowels of the system. If you opened the fire-exit door in the locker room, you were on the tracks. The steel dust from the wheels grinding against the rails was inescapable. Our officers hung their uniforms in metal lockers with the little vents, and every shift the uniforms were covered with steel dust before they could be put on. At the end of the shift, after eight hours of riding the trains, my officers wiped their hands across their faces and got fists full of black dirt. By taking the bosses back into the districts, I was letting the cops know that we were aware of their problems and would try to do something about them. These district visits became a regular event.

My instructions to each of the ten district commanders were purposefully vague. I wanted to test their creativity and presentation skills. I told them I was bringing the transit command staff and the other nine district commanders along so everyone could see what their peers were doing. I also told them, "When we get there I want my head of the Bureau of Administrative Services to see the conditions you're working under. I want a briefing on the conditions on your system and also on operations, what you're doing about fare evasion, what you're doing about disorder, what you're doing about crime."

For starters, we all rode the train to the districts. The commanding officer at the first meeting was well prepared. He provided coffee and donuts and made a good presentation. He was on top of his assignment, and I praised him for it.

At the next meeting, several weeks later, the CO was more razzle-dazzle. He had seen an acceptable presentation, and he wanted to go one better. His figures were more up-to-date, his outlook more advanced, and with the coffee and donuts he also served bagels and lox.

It got to be a competition! Not only did the refreshments improve with each visit, the ideas did, too.

But how do you reach 3,600 cops working all hours of the day and night in forty different locations? I had my staff produce videos for distribution to all units of the Transit Police. We had tried written bulletins, but many of the cops had grown up not reading newspapers but watching MTV. They would probably not read or absorb leaflets or even single-sheet flyers concerning new department developments, but they would watch a video from the chief at roll call.

The districts busted their butts trying to outdo each other. I knew I had them when they began trying to show each other up. And the more creative they were encouraged to be, the more the ideas flowed. Captain Frank O'Hara of District 4 made a video that ran eight minutes and was one of the best I'd ever seen. And instead of coffee and donuts he served a six-foot submarine sandwich.

Mike Ansbro, with whom I had not initially been impressed when he interviewed for captain, turned out to be one of the best thinkers. He was kind of a rough and tough lieutenant, a real New Yorker who hid his significant intellect behind his bravado. But when he came in number one on the captain's test, he was sent to the district station at Hoyt-Schermerhorn, one of the major hubs in Brooklyn. There, he instituted a program of walk-throughs: his officers walked through the cars and corrected all conditions; if someone was sleeping, they woke him up; if someone was aggressively panhandling they ejected him. They dealt with what was in front of them, and the public saw them, or so Ansbro thought.

Ansbro, responding to my edicts to get out in the system and show the flag, would walk through the cars behind his officers. He noticed that no one was looking up. It's the New York attitude—you sit in the subway and do not make eye contact. He thought, "This is ridiculous. I've got two New York Transit cops in full uniform walking the length of the train doing good work, and nobody notices they're there. I'm not getting the benefit I'm looking for."

What causes people to look up on a subway car? The loudspeaker. When announcements are made, people look up; one, because it's hard to make out what's being said, and two, because they figure something bad has happened. Ansbro developed what he called Operation Glazier. Why "Glazier"? How do you fix a broken window?

He put a sergeant and four cops on the platform. Each time a train pulled in, the sergeant gave a printed card to the conductor to read over the train's loudspeaker system. "Your attention, please. The Transit Police are conducting a sweep of the train. There may be a momentary delay while they go through the train to correct all conditions. Thank you for your patience."

The walk-through took only a minute. His officers were instructed to say hello to people, to engage them in a friendly way. They got the drunks off the train, quieted down the kids who were acting up, and sent it on its way. People saw the police doing their job, and they felt safer.

This type of creativity was beginning to flourish all over the department. It was a transit renaissance.

Once I was satisfied they could handle the responsibility, I decentralized power down to the ten district commanders. I told each of them, "Here are the goals: reduce fare evasion, disorder, and crime. I have certain requirements, mostly a certain number of cops on the trains, but beyond that you make the decisions. How many cops do you want in uniform, how many in plain clothes? Your call. You be creative as to how you're going to use those cops. You supervise them, you make sure they're not being abusive, and you make them productive." All they had to do was produce and be able to answer our questions when we asked them. I gave them authority and responsibility but held them accountable.

One of the Transit Police's major problems was the radio communications system in the subways themselves. It had been designed for train operators, not for cops. The subway stations, made of concrete and steel, were a hostile environment for radio and were filled with dead spots. We had among the worst police-radio systems in the nation. As long as officers were near the antennas that ran over the tracks, they could have radio communications, but as soon as they walked any distance away, they had no expectation of their radios working.

One notorious dead spot ran for a couple of stations through the middle of Harlem, so if an officer on an express train got in trouble, he could be out of communication for many potentially life-threatening minutes. Being out of touch for ten minutes at three o'clock in the morning in the middle of a jam on the A train could cause serious problems. It was a wonder more transit police weren't getting hurt. Over the years, more antennae had been added in mezzanine areas and passageways, but this put an added burden on an already antiquated and overloaded system.

The Transit Police union had made the radio system an issue, and before I came onboard the TP's position was that the problem was not as bad as the union said. I walked into Al O'Leary's press office and said I wanted to do a story on exactly how bad the radio system really was. O'Leary thought it could do some good, but he said, "Keep in mind, you're going to alienate the people who hired you. You're pointing a finger and saying, 'You didn't give our cops what they need to do their job.' " I told him, "They recruited me. They've got to be nice to me for at least six months." We did the story.

David Gunn had a terrific reputation, but when I looked at previous capital program budgets to see how requests for Transit Police funding had been treated, I found that of the billions spent on transit, minimal resources came to us. Trains were bought, tracks were fixed, but the Transit

Authority leadership was focused on moving commuters, not protecting them. Unfortunately, Transit Police leadership over the years had not been effective in lobbying to make the case for what they really needed. Our offices got painted and other inexpensive cosmetic repairs were arranged, but no significant capital had been invested in improving the Transit Police. It reinforced the cops' attitude that the Transit Authority didn't care about them.

I had made a point of contacting certain notable figures in the law-enforcement field who I thought could help the department. Tom Reppetto, head of the Citizens Crime Commission of New York, was among the first. The CCC is a privately funded organization that comments on police and criminal-justice issues, and Reppetto was constantly being quoted in the papers. I had read and admired his history of New York policing, *The Blue Parade*. A former Chicago police detective commander, he was very smart and knew New York inside and out. I asked him to give me some background on how New York functioned and who the players were. Reppetto, it turned out, knew very little about transit; his focus had always been on the NYPD. I invited him to tour the system.

To increase the visibility of our organization and to demonstrate our needs, I began to conduct these tours regularly. Few in the city had a real sense of the dangers and difficulties facing the Transit Police day in and day out, and I wanted to show them. I invited significant business and government people, including Victor Kovner, and Queens District Attorney Richard Brown, as well as members of the media, specifically reporters who regularly covered the transit system. Some of these people were only vaguely interested; some were what cops call police buffs. We buffed them up real good. We rode them all over New York on a Disneyland tour of the subways.

I would invite seven or eight prominent people on each tour, men and women who were in the position to help transit if they understood what we were asking for. We would start at five o'clock in the afternoon in my office over pastry and coffee. I'd give them a briefing and off we'd go. Four hours later we'd discuss what we had seen over dinner.

First stop was the communications room, where I'd show just how poor our communications system was. I would explain the dangers that transit cops lived with every shift, then we'd go ride the trains.

I introduced our group to certain transit units. The canines would be in one station or on the trains. The department had one of the best canine units in the country and regularly used them for station and train patrol.

For law-abiding citizens, they are a very comforting presence; for the criminal element they were very intimidating. Then we would get on a train, and I'd ask my guests to pick out the members of our decoy unit from the regular passengers. They'd look around and see the usual assortment of New Yorkers in transit. They usually got about two out of eight.

Then we'd take them into the tunnels. Most subway passengers don't even think of the tunnels when they ride the trains, but my officers had to deal with them daily. We'd go to the end of the platform, step down a short set of stairs, and stand on the ground as the trains roared by. Equipped with flashlights and reflective vests and guided by Transit officers assigned to the Homeless Outreach Unit, we'd begin to walk the tracks.

It was dark as a coal mine, with low-wattage bulbs the only illumination. The cars look big enough when you're standing beside one on the platform, but when you're on the ground at track level, there's another eight feet of wheels and connecting rods as long as your arm; the doors you normally walk through are above your head, and everything is out of scale. Eight or ten cars is a real load. A train, it becomes clear, is a large and dangerous vehicle.

In the tunnel, rats scurry everywhere. A ferocious wind, swirling and thick with underground debris, is blown by the speeding trains. The expresses and locals barrel through, banging from side to side, and there's very little space between the cars and the tunnel wall itself. Pressing your body back against the tunnel's filthy sides doesn't seem certain to save you. The noise is overwhelming, disorienting, and in the dark you can't tell which way the train is coming.

We took our guests to the cul-de-sacs where people had set up homes. The smell of urine and feces and unwashed bodies was often overwhelming. Indeed, you could detect where people were living just by the smell. A population of several thousand people lived in various parts of the subway system. Mattresses lay on the ground, and syringes and crack vials littered the alcoves—watch where you walk. One night, on a three-foot ledge right adjacent to the tracks, a couple was having sex as we passed by.

One of the more intriguing parts of our tour was the "Condominium." Under an emergency exit down in SoHo, a character had set up a duplex, his bedroom on one floor and his kitchen and living room—with television—on the level below, his electricity bootstrapped from one of the system's light sockets. There was a world underground, filled with an unsettled and not necessarily lucid set of characters, and we had to police that too.

When Peter Stengel, former president of Metro-North, became chairman of the Metropolitan Transit Authority, we took him out on the tour. It was a hot summer night, over ninety degrees, horrific New York humidity. The air conditioning in the cars was a delight. Then we got off and waited on the platform. I got lucky, there was a delay. I always hoped for this kind of good fortune. It's the subway; trains are late for all kinds of reasons, riders and cops are always waiting for them. This time, the train took an eternity to come, and Stengel and I were standing there, covered in sweat, having trouble breathing, getting hotter and hotter.

There's an expression we didn't like much: Transit cops are like corks, they keep bobbing to the surface. Everybody always complained, "Oh, those damned transit cops, always standing on the street instead of being down there where you need them." Well, you try standing for eight hours on a sweltering platform in the middle of August wearing a bulletproof vest. Imagine what a cop feels like, 120 degrees and encased in Kevlar. Or, in the winter, standing from midnight to eight on concrete in five-degree weather inside what amounts to a meat locker.

The train came whooshing into the station like a traveling oasis. The doors opened, and the cool air just about sucked us inside. I think Stengel got the point.

We invited the press on ride-alongs. The press looks for its own angles, but by excluding them you lose the opportunity to demonstrate the dangers, satisfactions, and joys of being a cop. Many police officials worry about what a reporter might find; I had faith in my officers, and I knew that the net result of a reporter's night in the system could only benefit us.

I began an initiative, modeled after New York City Schools Chancellor Ramon Cortines's Principal for a Day program, called District Commander for a Day. I invited around forty business leaders to spend a day in our districts and various commands. They had a ball. They rode the system with our men and women and came back and told me, "You guys have so little to work with. Your equipment's awful, the conditions your people have to operate in are ungodly." Many were lifelong New Yorkers, some involved with the New York City Police Foundation and the Crime Stoppers Program, but it was the first time they'd had any exposure to the real world of transit cops. They were in awe of how much we could get done despite the lack of equipment and the sad state of the system.

Some managers might be embarrassed to show their organization's shortcomings. I wanted to hype ours to the skies. As I tried to lobby for board-of-director and legislative support for transit, I wanted business-people to see the burdens we were working under and to understand, when they chatted at their dinner parties on the Upper East Side and Park Avenue, what it's like for a cop trying to make sure all New Yorkers get home safely.

Chapter 10

JACK MAPLE WAS A WELL-KNOWN ECCENTRIC WITHIN THE TRANSIT POLICE. HE had signed on with the department before he'd been eligible to vote, and at twenty-seven he had been its youngest detective, having made some four hundred arrests. He looked like a tough guy, he would rumble with the best of them, and he had a smart mouth. He was a working-class guy with aspirations. Then the tunnel rat from Queens began a major self-transformation.

A solidly stocky five foot eight, Maple cultivated a taste for sartorial display. He actually wore a carnation in his lapel. Then, neglecting to inform his wife, he mortgaged his home and spent a substantial portion of the money buying clothes and a sports car and becoming a regular at the Plaza Hotel's famed and refined Oak Room. "I really believe," Maple said, "when I was born, they messed up and put me in a civil-service bassinet by mistake." When the cash was gone and he faced a future of eternal payments to the Money Store, he'd confessed. His Oak Room phase cost him his marriage, but his legend was secured when the writer Michael Daly profiled him in *New York* magazine and later used him as the model for a central character in his 1995 novel, *Under Ground.*

Getting written up in *New York* put Maple in a whole new league. Every month, a select group of politicians, press, and police types gathered over pasta at an Italian restaurant and bantered, off the record, about the events of the day. Maple, this Transit Police lieutenant, was now in the middle of it.

Police departments are not kind to eccentrics. I think it has something to do with order, obedience, respect for the chain of command; all the commandments that police professionals hold high are routinely challenged by eccentrics in the ranks, and anyone with a fresh perspective and the balls to say it out loud will pay a price. Maple was very ambivalent about the bosses. He was cop enough to respect those above him because they were above him, but enough of a loner not to give a damn what they thought of him. He was a wiseacre with a quick wit. He was also extremely smart, a thinking and creative cop. In 1988, when he got the top score on the lieutenant's exam, it changed his life and got him more serious notice within the department. Now, not only was he a personality, he was a presence.

Maple was in charge of the Central Robbery Squad when I came in as chief of transit. His squad loved him, they were called "Maple-ites," and they worked and drank and played together. He and Dean Esserman, tunnel rat and Ivy Leaguer, were unlikely friends, both single, both basically without a life outside of work. On three occasions they went out to serve warrants. One night, they were in East New York, a tough section of Brooklyn, with a bunch of robbery and warrant detectives, waiting for a suspect they were following to come out of a bodega. They thought the man had a gun. Maple, the tough guy, and Esserman, the preppy former prosecutor, were the first two through the door. Maple, clearly the more effective representative of the Transit Police in this situation, knocked the guy down and Esserman piled on. The detectives came running in with their guns drawn—the place was pandemonium. Maple got the guy in a headlock. It was Friday night, and Maple looked up at Esserman and beamed, "It's better than sex, isn't it!"

But Maple wasn't getting proper respect. He was a wild card, in favor with one chief, out of favor with the next. He would consistently put together ideas and presentations and proposals for his superiors, but he was a lieutenant, and in the world of policing he could only have a lieutenant's opinion. Still, he kept plugging away.

When I came on, Maple said to his executive officer Tommy Burke, "Let's see what this guy's made of." They sat down and wrote a ten-page document outlining his ideas for reducing crime and improving the department, put it in a binder and gave it to the chief of detectives, Mike

O'Connor. "O'Connor's got a coffeepot in his office," Maple said to him-self. "Any time Bratton wants coffee, he's going to go in there and get it. They're going to interact. This coffeepot is going to make Mike O'Connor a big shot." Of course, Maple already knew that O'Connor was clearly a rising star in the department.

O'Connor passed the package along. He said, "I gave it to Bratton. I didn't even look at it. But don't ever give anybody anything like that; they're just going to put their name on it."

Maple told him, "I don't give a shit."

A couple of weeks later, O'Connor introduced us. I remembered the package and asked O'Connor to set up a breakfast where we could dis-cuss Maple's ideas.

He had a million of them. He targeted fare beating, warrants, wolfpack robberies, interrogation, interviewing, crime analysis, and coordinated de-ployment between detectives and plainclothes and uniformed officers. He had so many ideas he gave me a headache. I told him, "The reason they brought me here is to reduce crime." Maple said, "If we go by this plan it's going to happen."

Not long after, Maple made a presentation to the command staff about an idea that he wanted to pursue. Always on top of the statistics, Maple said his figures showed that subway robberies against the entire popu-lation were up a staggering 60 percent but against Asians the jump was an extraordinary 210 percent. Since the Asian victims, particularly the Chinese, were in large part immigrants, often illegal, with little under-standing of the American justice system, Maple's sense was that what was being reported was only the tip of the iceberg. In fact, he felt the reason Asians were the preferred victims of crime was precisely that they were less likely to report it and that the language barrier made identifying their attackers even more difficult. Maple wanted to put together a decoy squad to focus on the problem.

I said, "Go to it." There had been a scandal years before in which plain-clothes officers were accused of arresting people simply to inflate their number of summonses issued, and the department had been accused of covering it up. Maple had been running a decoy unit and had been tar-geted for investigation. The unit had been disbanded, and WNBC-TV re-porter John Miller had tried to get Maple put in jail. Miller had pursued "the Evil Sergeant Maple," but Maple was clean. The incident had noth-ing to do with Maple's unit. I was willing to take the risk.

Esserman got the Manhattan district attorney's office to sign off on the

Asian decoy unit, and we reinstituted a regular, and highly successful, decoy operation.

Regarding fare beating, Maple emphasized the need for volume. Our minisweeps were good for department morale and publicity, but he felt we weren't getting enough benefit from our efforts. He suggested that we not only arrest these people, but that we check them for warrants.

"If you run a warrant check on everybody," he said, "there's a greater propensity that you're going to catch not only people with prior fare-beat warrants, but really bad people. It's going to knock crime down. And then you're going to create an environment in the subway where the criminal element is going to say, 'It's just not worth doing robberies there.' "

The goal was to check everyone we stopped for any violation whatsoever to see if they had a warrant out on them. At first, people were just being given summonses and sent on their way. We'd have felons in our hands and we'd shoo them along because we didn't have the capacity to check them out. "Check everybody for outstanding warrants!" Maple said. It seemed like an obvious idea; all good ideas are obvious after someone's come up with them. I also liked it because it would put some teeth in the Desk Appearance Ticket program—the so-called "disappearance tickets" that frustrated the cops so much.

Maple also proposed a more aggressive deployment of the warrant unit, which tracked down people who were wanted on warrants, had failed to show up for court, or were wanted for crimes. Maple figured that since these people have already committed crimes, let's serve the back warrants and get them.

The warrant unit pursued two classes of people: wants and wanteds. A want is a person whom the police would like to question relative to a crime; a wanted is someone for whom a warrant has been issued. Transit had a warrant unit, but it was under the control of the NYPD and was extremely ineffectual. They were hardly bringing anyone in, and Maple felt we were missing opportunities to increase the pressure on the criminal element. Many of the criminals felt that once they had been arrested and bailed out, we would never go after them. Transit crime was one big free ride.

Many of transit's functions and responsibilities had been assumed by the NYPD. They were the powerful parent organization, we were the stepchild. Maple pointed out that while we had upward of forty transit detectives assigned to the combined NYPD-Transit warrant unit, transit warrants were basically not being served. The city squad prioritized crimes and served warrants on the most significant cases, which were rarely if ever ours.

An additional problem was the NYPD bureaucracy. It could be four to six weeks from the time a warrant was issued until it got into the hands of a warrant officer. The paperwork was overwhelming; wire baskets were stacked three and four feet high with warrants waiting to be processed. Plus, the warrant squad wasn't working weekends. Warrants were served by the NYPD Monday through Friday, 8:00 A.M. to 4:00 P.M.—basically when no one was home.

I went to NYPD Commissioner Lee Brown and said, "We're taking our people back from the warrant unit. I'm going to set up my own warrant squad." The NYPD's first deputy commissioner, Ray Kelly, was not happy about that initiative. His response was, "Take them away, but we're no longer going to have anything to do with your warrants." That was fine with me. They weren't serving my warrants anyway.

First, we sped up the process by which warrants were processed. Dean Esserman dove into the basement of the courthouse and followed pieces of warrant paper from the moment a judge said, "Defendant didn't show up for court today; warrant ordered," to the day, thirty to forty-five days later, when that piece of paper ended up at the NYPD being sprocketed into the wire baskets as a "new warrant." Esserman used his contacts to stay with the paper and move it from the judge's signature to our office in forty-eight hours. We developed a computer program, believed to be the first of its kind in the city, that changed this warrant process from being paper driven to something more like electronic mail. Now, when someone defaulted or didn't show up, rather than being out in the street committing crimes for a month before the police even began to track him down, he had us banging on his door in two days.

The cops who returned from working with the NYPD weren't happy to be back home at the "Ohhhh" Police, but I put Maple in charge. He took this disgruntled group and transformed them. He changed the way we pursued criminals. We went after them seven days a week, starting at 3:30 A.M. The troops, supervised by a uniformed sergeant, gathered each morning in Maple's office to go over the game plan: Here are the ten or fifteen people we're after today; here's what they look like, here's what they're wanted for, here's the layout of the buildings they are in. At four o'clock, the sergeant and his squad of six to eight detectives, all wearing Transit Police windbreakers, started banging on doors very loudly, so the neighbors could hear.

If two cops in plain clothes knocked politely at ten A.M., no one would know they were there. If you're walking up to the building at four A.M. in legitimate pursuit of a person with an outstanding warrant—"*Transit Police! Open up!*"—people look out the window and say, "Jeez, here's these cops serving warrants." We made an impression. If someone inside said, "Dave's not here, man, haven't seen him for weeks," we couldn't bust into the apartment. But if we went back every morning, banging on the door, eventually someone in the building might drop a dime that Dave really *is* in there, or that we could catch him coming out the door at six at night when he headed out to do his dirty deeds.

Again, we got multiple benefits from this action. We picked up a lot of wanteds, and we alerted the neighborhood to the fact that the Transit Police were not playing games. We took low performers on our force and partnered them with high performers, under the direction of a supervisor; our sergeants established accountability, and our cops, who had worked solo for their entire careers, had the opportunity to be part of a team. They were making arrests and having fun. And most of all, by catching the bad guys, we closed the loophole through which people were disappearing from the justice system.

We started bringing more people to court than the system was used to handling, and it was my job to alert the D.A.s and judges. Once in court, we tried to get our warrants prioritized, to expedite the trials of bail defaulters and thieves and the rest of our prisoners. We tried to get the courts to hold them; after all the effort we expended to track these people down, we didn't want them running straight out the door.

To support the operation I had to muscle the NYPD and schmooze with the district attorneys. Crime went down, morale went up. It was a great success.

Wolfpacks were another tremendous source of fear among passengers in the transit system and the city at large. Gangs of kids, teenaged and younger, swarmed through trains robbing, mugging, and terrorizing riders. Sometimes we would catch one, but the rest of the pack usually got away. Under police guidelines, one arrest clears a crime; if you catch one lone wolf, your statistics look good, so cops had no incentive to bust their butts to nab any more. Meanwhile, half a dozen kids were out there preying on their next victims, and we had done nothing whatsoever about reducing crime. We wouldn't quit until we had gotten two, three, four, five in the wolfpack, all the way down the line. Once we got these wolfpack members to court, we tied them to multiple cases and showed Family

Court judges that these young kids were, in fact, repeat offenders and career criminals. Building strong cases against them helped assure convictions and stiff sentences, sending them away and deterring others. We dried up wolfpacks in the New York City subway because we were not going to hide behind numbers. We were going to get everybody.

Maple had charts on his wall much like the ones I'd had on mine in District 4. He was a great collector of statistics, and he recognized the tremendous potential that computerization held for the Transit Police. Maple was able to gather the information transit had in its various subsystems and, through use of the department's computers, bring it all into his office, where he analyzed it.

We had been operating the warrant squad, the plainclothes and decoy units, and the Central Robbery Squad as separate units. Now, we aimed to weave a seamless web through which no criminal could slip. Ultimately, it became clear that we should combine these operations under one roof with one man in charge. Maple was clearly the man. I greatly expanded the Central Robbery Squad, promoted Maple to detective lieutenant, and put it all under his command. In October 1991 I promoted him to special assistant to the chief.

Esserman had been doing some independent work on creating a joint warrant squad with the New York State Division of Parole. They didn't have vehicles, we didn't have office space. Esserman traded unmarked transit cars to them for the whole first floor of their building across from the Port Authority Bus Terminal on Forty-second Street. We were in business.

Central Robbery was Jack's life. He lived there. He used to walk around the squad room at night in his Burberry raincoat that doubled as a bathrobe.

Then Brian Watkins was killed.

Watkins and his family had come to New York City from Provo, Utah, in the summer of 1990 to attend the United States Open tennis championships. At 10:20 Sunday night on Labor Day weekend, they were standing on the uptown platform of the D train at Fifty-third Street and Seventh Avenue when a wolfpack of about eight kids robbed them at knifepoint. Watkins's father was slashed when they cut his back pocket to get at his wallet. His mother was punched and kicked in the face. His brother and sister-in-law were roughed up. When Watkins tried to intervene, he was stabbed in the chest with a spring-handled butterfly knife. He died that night. Brian Watkins was twenty-two years old.

The gang ran off with $203 and some credit cards. They were found two hours later dancing at the club Roseland.

This was a horrible tragedy for Brian Watkins and his family. It was also among the worst nightmares the city and the Transit Police could imagine. A tourist in the subway during a high-profile event with which the mayor is closely associated (Mayor Dinkins, a tennis fan, was instrumental in keeping the U.S. Open in New York) gets stabbed and killed by a wolfpack. The murder made international headlines. Through good police work, we made arrests within two hours, but that wasn't going to bring the young man back.

Two days later, I got a call out of the blue from Richard Girgenti, Governor Mario Cuomo's criminal-justice coordinator. The governor understood the impact this killing could have on New York tourism and responded. "Can you put together a proposal as to what you would do if we were to give you forty million dollars?" Girgenti asked. "Believe me," I told him, "I can get that together for you very quickly."

This was the turnaround I needed. Working with the MTA and the Transit Authority, Governor Cuomo was able to identify forty million dollars in the existing budget that could be immediately reallocated to the Transit Police.

I took the first ten million and bought each cop in the department a new, more powerful, and reliable walkie-talkie. Once again, I got multiple benefits: The cops finally got new equipment and I gained a significant amount of patrol time each day when they no longer had to stand in line, twenty at a time, signing their radios in and out at the end of their shifts. I had asked them to work hard, and I felt they should know I would deliver in return. I visited several commands and made ceremonial presentations of the new equipment.

We spent ten million dollars to repair some of the dead spots in the radio system; this was the quick fix we'd needed. A couple of million dollars went to the new vehicles I'd been looking for, which improved response time and production and department morale. Two million went to renovate and upgrade the Transit Police Academy. I put money toward a transition in armaments, should we get Transit Authority approval. Ten million went toward overtime pay, to put the equivalent of two hundred extra officers in the system.

Within a few months, due to our increased manpower, new strategies, better communications, and improved equipment, the crime rate began to drop like a rock.

The death of Brian Watkins was a terrible tragedy that, ironically, ultimately became the catalyst for the turnaround of crime in New York City. With his immediate offer of money that Bob Kiley was able to divert from other projects, Mario Cuomo was the primary sponsor of our efforts. The governor has never received the tremendous credit he is due for his role in the reduction of crime in New York City. The money that he and Kiley provided was the catalyst that significantly accelerated the turnaround of the Transit Police.

We had already begun to redesign the transit uniforms. High-quality and well-designed uniforms contribute to a cop's self-image and personal pride and to the public's confidence in its police force. I put together a uniform committee and encouraged input from all officers. The committee looked at many options and came back with new shirts, patches, and an interesting recommendation: commando sweaters, with epaulets, very military, very smart. I approved it immediately. They gave us a very distinctive look and were also practical, much better than the coats we had worn before.

Everything the Transit Police had done in the past had been an attempt to disguise its identity and to look more like city cops. Even our patch used to hide the word "transit." We redesigned it. We designed recruiting posters: "Second to None. Join the Force on the Move." Transit cops, known for generations as "tunnel rats," liked that.

We were taking care of their interests and they responded. "New uniforms? New cars? New radios? Yeah, I'll shine my shoes. I'll cut my hair. I'll go to the gym." They had regenerated their pride.

We established a Chief's Award; we generated a document on the computer, lacquered it to a walnut plaque, and I personally made ceremonial presentations to deserving officers. Al O'Leary in the media services office sent a picture of the ceremony to the press.

When one of our cops did something good, we brought the officer to the press office, and O'Leary called up reporters. "I've got Officer Smith here, the guy who saved that pregnant lady." Reporters used to tease him—in fact, they'd throw it in his face: "The NYPD won't produce their cops when they're heroes; over at the transit public-relations office you handcuff your cops to the chair."

The Transit Police, which had been the conscripts of the law-enforcement world, were becoming the Marine Corps.

I had earmarked a portion of Governor Cuomo's $40 million for the Transit Police's transition in weaponry from the .38 six-shooter revolver to the nine-millimeter fifteen-round semiautomatic. I thought the change-over made a lot of sense and gave us multiple benefits.

Cops in New York widely felt that their weapons were inappropriate for their environment. They felt they were being outgunned. Transit cops, in particular, patrolled by themselves in a workplace where communication was difficult and they were at risk. They didn't often have gunfights, but on those occasions they were going up against people armed with nine-millimeters or worse. The NYPD standard issue was the .38 six-shooter; the Transit Police standard issue was the .38 six-shooter with a less powerful bullet. It seemed very clear to me that a change was justified and due.

I invited a group of armorers to come for a two-day seminar. We found that more than half the U.S. police organizations, including thirty of the thirty-one largest, six major transit police departments, the FBI, and the Secret Service had made or were making the transition to the semiautomatic. It was more accurate and more reliable, had more capacity, and was easier to load than the .38. I wrote a letter to the MTA board of directors requesting the change.

The response was explosive. I had stumbled on a cutting-edge political issue much larger than I had realized. Mayor Dinkins was adamantly opposed to the change. NYPD Commissioner Lee Brown was opposed, as were Ray Kelly and various community groups. The New York Times ran editorials against it. All of them had their reasons.

I suspect that Mayor Dinkins and Commissioner Brown felt uncomfortable with the political ramifications of switching to the more powerful firearm. Ray Kelly, as a career NYPD commander, was concerned about the cost of retraining his entire department. The New York Times, and the community groups, which didn't trust the police to begin with, felt it was an unnecessary escalation of what they saw as the war in the streets of New York.

I also think it reflected the fact that the leadership of the NYPD wasn't comfortable with the professional abilities of the cops they were leading. They may not have trusted their own systems to train and supervise their people to use these weapons appropriately. These concerns overrode the safety issues that the cops were voicing. The cops, feeling increasingly unsafe on the job, felt that this administration did not care about them.

The combined forces of New York politics were aligned against us, and the MTA board was extremely political—some members were appointed by the mayor himself. In addition, the NYPD didn't have nine-millimeters, and transit never got anything better than the city police. These roadblocks made me even more determined.

I was careful and emphasized that my main concerns were public and police safety. NYPD cops travel in pairs, I told the board, so they always have at least two guns and twelve shots between them. Our officers work by themselves. In addition to the .38 six-shot, most were permitted to carry a smaller second weapon, often in an ankle or waist holster. We were effectively authorizing officers to carry two weapons totaling twelve rounds, while I was asking for one weapon that carried fifteen. In a struggle, current regulations were doubling the potential for a gun to be taken away. In addition, the nine-millimeter was more accurate. We had done the testing, and if you let a round go in a subway station, with its concrete walls and ceramic tiles and steel pillars, it could turn into a lethal game of pinball. There was less of a ricochet factor with the more accurate nine-millimeter and its increased stopping power.

I didn't duck the issues they raised. We discussed police shootings and civilian complaints. The semiautomatic sounds as if it could be used to spray indiscriminate fire, I acknowledged, but it does in fact require the shooter to pull the trigger for each shot. The round itself would not be the full metal jacket used by the NYPD but a slower, controlled-expansion round, which reduces the risk of ricochet damage. Our weapon would require more effort to pull the trigger for each round fired, the so-called "New York trigger."

The Transit Police, I told them, would adopt the semiautomatic over four years in a carefully staged and thorough training program that would qualify about twenty officers per week. Along with instructing officers in the maintenance and use of the weapon, the training program would reinforce and emphasize the principles of the department's deadly-force policy. Our highest priority was the protection of human life, and our officers were instructed to use every other reasonable alternative before resorting to firearms. The firearm was viewed as a defensive weapon, not a tool of apprehension. It would give officers greater control over violent incidents in the subway. The more control, the less likely the incidents would cause injury or death.

As a manager, I trusted cops because I trusted the training I would give them, something the NYPD leadership did not. I knew this because Kelly had raised the issues while arguing with me. I had confidence in my organization.

I quite consciously decided to give this issue a very high profile. My constituency, the cops, would appreciate my efforts because they wanted the better weapon and they liked to see the boss out there fighting for them. Managerially, I was on solid ground because I had great belief and faith in my organization. Operationally, I was investing in better equipment that would improve the safety and skills of my officers. Morally, I had the high ground; I was on the side of the safer weapon.

For some reason, Commissioner Brown did not come to the board of directors meeting and make a personal appeal. He was on record as opposing the purchase of nine-millimeters for his department, and he must have decided that was enough. I knew Brown through Wasserman, and I liked and respected him. I understood the power of his office, and I was pleased not to have to argue against him.

Both sides lobbied intensely. The little Transit Police took on the city's entire power structure, and we didn't back down. All the mayor's people voted against us. The decision came down to a single man: Dan Scannell, eighty years old, vice-chairman of the MTA, a former cop—who carried a nine-millimeter.

We won. I went down to my car and got on the radio. "Chief Bratton here. I just want to notify members of the department that the board of the MTA today voted to approve the issuance of nine-millimeter weapons to Transit Police officers."

The calls on the radio went wild. Around the districts, they were cheering in the locker rooms. From that day forward, they would have gone through brick walls for me because I had taken on the mayor, the NYPD, and *The New York Times,* and we had won.

The weapon we bought was the Glock semiautomatic. I was with Cal Mathis, out in uniform on one of my ride-alongs one night, when a couple of kids no more than thirteen years old eyeballed us. "Hey, man," one said as we walked by, "you guys got Glocks!" These kids knew the firearms just by looking at them. It became a big thing on the platforms. "Hey, Transit's got nines!"

Some in the media and around the city felt that my main impetus for championing the nine-millimeters was to improve Transit Police morale. The transit cops now had things the city cops didn't: better cars, commando sweaters, nine-millimeters, and a chief who trusted them. Critics found that reason insufficient and Machiavellian. They were wrong. It was, in fact, a better weapon for the subway. The fact that this was a safety issue is what ultimately won the day. After his appointment as police commissioner, Ray Kelly ultimately approved nine-millimeters for the NYPD.

Chapter 11

Don Imus doesn't make fun of just anybody.

John Linder, the Transit Authority's director of marketing and corporate communications, decided the TA was going to make me a New York household name. He knew from focus groups that if we told people that only 3 percent of the city's crime occurred on the subways, it would have no impact. He felt we should gradually assure people that real action was being taken to improve safety on the system.

Linder recognized that when I'd told the transit cops they were demoralized and looked like slobs and didn't feel like real cops, and then had presented a plan to engage them, I had instinctively followed the same guidelines he had discovered. I told the truth, got their attention, and then went about correcting the problem. He arranged for me to go citywide.

In July 1991, Linder's shop put together a series of radio ads seeded with negative images while at the same time presenting a positive message. The campaign was centered on the phrase "We're Taking the Subway Back—for You." Implicitly, we acknowledged that the subway had been in the wrong hands and that it had to be taken back. There were criminals on it, we admitted; people thought it was unsafe. Explicitly, we told how we were reclaiming it. We were adding 20 percent more cops, deploying decoy units, patrolling the trains with canine units, and sweeping up fare evaders and aggressive panhandlers. As a result of our efforts, crime was down, and we were continuing the fight.

One of my particular favorites was an ad called "We Know Who You Are." It was about the Wake Up Program.

Dean Esserman and Central Robbery's work with the Parole Department had produced results. Most bad guys have criminal records; a lot have finished their jail time and are still on parole and under the eye of the state while they're committing more crimes. They found that parole was required to give police a twenty-four-hour notification before a convicted felon was released into a town. It was upstate thinking; a parolee gets off the bus with his brown bag, and the sheriff is there to say, "Hey, Bubba, welcome back, be good." It turned out they had to talk to us, too. They asked whether there was a way for one computer to talk to another to establish that the officer whom the parolee must contact be a member of the Transit Police. There was. So began the Wake Up Program.

"Ladies and Gentlemen," intoned the announcer, "the chief of the New York City Transit Police, William J. Bratton."

Behind me, a tape of street noises made it sound like I was outside.

"Serious crime in the subway has gone down dramatically for seven months in a row," I began. My Boston accent never sounded so pronounced as it did on New York radio. New Yorkers, for some reason, love a Boston accent. "Robbery alone has fallen 12 percent. That's because there are a lot more cops in the subway, and because of the many strategies they are using to stop crime.

"Today, I'd like to tell you about one of those strategies.

"Our crime-analysis unit keeps computer files on everyone who has been arrested in the subway. We have their names, their aliases, and their jail time. And when they come home from jail, a transit cop goes to visit them.

"First, we wish them well. Then, we tell them we're keeping their pictures and records on file. We think that's going to prevent a lot of crime, because someone who has committed a crime in the subway—and paid for it the hard way—is going to think twice about doing it again if he knows we know who he is.

"That's one way we're working to take the subway back for you."

Our ads were all over the radio, an inescapable presence in the way all successful campaigns are. They certainly didn't escape the attention of Don Imus.

Imus is a take-no-prisoners radio talk-show host who takes great and humorous pleasure in insulting people. He holds forth on world events and local stories every morning, and everything is a source of commentary and amusement. He is forever coming up with oddball characters and voices. Imus is a New York fixture, syndicated around the country, and he doesn't give much of a damn what people think. He's also a very funny guy. So he took us on.

His announcer intoned exactly like ours. Then this character with an exaggerated, heavy Boston accent came on the air. They followed my script word-for-word until they got to the part about the visits to parolees, which were made, "usually about three in the mornin'. To throw them a little welcome-home party." Was it my imagination or was the accent getting thicker?

"Now, I know you're thinkin': Who's mindin' the store downstairs when the Transit Authority's got teams of officers up on the street makin' door-to-door social visits to paroled ex-cons?" Crime was down, in the world according to Imus, "because when a former felon's got a piece of pound cake in his mouth, he can't be down in the subway poundin' you in the mouth for your cake."

I thought it was hysterical. I was pleased and flattered that Imus thought I had high enough visibility to parody. Any cops listening would get a big kick out of it, and anyone who hadn't already heard the real transit ads was getting a heads-up about them.

We were making an impact on the city and on the law-enforcement community. George Kelling and Bob Wasserman were trumpeting our successes among the academics. I spoke about the Broken Windows concept before the Executive Session on Policing at Harvard. I had been excited to be invited to these conferences when I was on the rise, and now I took many people from my staff with me to tell them thanks, showcase them, and allow them to network. I was also invited by New York attorney Adam Walinsky to join a group of law-enforcement experts on a visit to Moscow after the fall of communism and consulted with Russian police officials on how to police in a democracy.

With NYPD Commissioner Lee Brown, I coordinated joint monthly meetings in which we and our staffs discussed and pursued common issues. My staff and I always came with a prepared agenda. The NYPD didn't. Their senior staff usually sat in stone-faced silence, waiting to take their cue from Commissioner Brown. I never forgot that. I also earned a degree of respect from the city's political community, both the administration of Mayor Dinkins and those who were trying to unseat him, like mayoral candidate-in-waiting Rudolph Giuliani.

But my professional success had its downsides. Cheryl was in Boston, and I had spent two years commuting back and forth every weekend to see her. I knew what the pressures of a job could do to a relationship, and that kind of separation is not good for a marriage. It was exhausting, both physically and emotionally. It was also expensive. We were paying for two residences, the cost of round-trip Boston shuttle flights was not going down, and we were going into debt up to our eyeballs. I had come into the organization at a significantly smaller salary than other senior vice presidents in the TA. (In addition to the title chief of police, I also held the position of senior vice president.) This was done initially at my request, so I would not make more than Lee Brown. But the deal was, if I delivered, I would be compensated accordingly, about another $15,000 a year, commensurate with the salary level of other senior vice presidents. True to his word, TA President Alan Kiepper supported that deal.

While I was doing my job, Bob Kiley had resigned as chairman of the MTA and been replaced by Peter Stengel. When Kiepper asked about my raise, Stengel said the MTA was under budgetary attack and had to reduce costs. When I arrived, subway crime had been rising for thirty months, with robbery growing two-and-one-half times faster than in the city at large. Our results included a 22 percent decline in felony crime, with robbery down 40 percent. We had reduced felony crime and disorder in the subways, fare evasion had been halved, and we had increased ridership and greatly improved rider confidence. We had turned around the entire Transit Police department.

Still, I was not going to get the raise because Stengel felt it was not politically feasible. I also sensed that Stengel didn't fully understand or appreciate how we had effected our turnaround. Our motivation techniques did not appear to resonate with him. Unlike Kiley, who had extensive police experience, Stengel was a railroad guy, and he gave me the strong impression that he wanted to return to the simpler operation and just post cops at turnstiles. All of these factors led me to begin looking for other opportunities.

Lee Brown seemed like he was going to stay for his full term, so the NYPD commissionership wasn't on the horizon. Los Angeles, however, seemed like a possibility. After the riots, its embattled police chief Daryl Gates was being pressured to resign, and I decided to get actively involved in the search for its next leader. The LAPD required exactly the kind of turnaround I enjoyed performing, and the challenge of trying to rebuild that department in particular would be extreme. The job paid $175,000 a year, the highest police chief's salary in the nation.

I put in my application, met with their representatives, and was on a select list of eleven candidates when I took my name out of consideration. First, it became obvious that they wanted an African American to head up the organization. The LAPD had been severely criticized for racism, and the people running the selection process felt they needed a black man in the position to answer that charge. It was also clear that Willie Williams, the police chief from Philadelphia, was going to be that man. Second, the selection process had been confidential, but word of the final candidates was about to reach the public, and if I had been on that list it would have damaged the morale of my department. I would have taken the risk if I'd thought I had a good chance of getting the job, but without an actual shot, why undermine transit and my continuing ability to lead the department?

I was in Boston for New Year's 1992, at lunch with friends in a little Italian restaurant in Wakefield, when I picked up the *Boston Herald* and read a front-page story that the St. Clair Commission, established to investigate the Boston Police Department and headed by President Richard Nixon's former counsel James St. Clair, was about to recommend that Mickey Roache be replaced as commissioner because of incompetent management.

I had been watching the BPD. Jack Gifford, who had resigned as superintendent and returned to the rank of lieutenant, was always very involved behind the scenes, and we'd kept in touch. I thought to myself, "This might be the opportunity." I excused myself and went across the street to a pay phone and called Roache.

It was New Year's Day, but I knew where he was: behind his desk, where he always was. Sure enough, he answered the phone.

"Mickey, how're you doing? Bill Bratton."

"Hey, Bill, how're you doing?"

"Mickey, I've been reading the paper, all the problems with the St. Clair report. I think I might have an option you might want to consider."

Mickey was interested. He'd been reading the same paper I had. We arranged to meet the following Saturday at a hotel in Brighton. I had been very envious when my old sector-car partner had gotten the commissionership, of course, but that was natural, and we both understood. We talked for a couple of hours.

I told him I was starting to look around for a new position. I told him about my frustrations with commuting back and forth to New York. "It strikes me," I said, "that I can do something for you and you can do something for me.

"I've got a pretty good reputation for turnarounds and management, and this place, according to the St. Clair Commission, needs to be significantly reorganized. I need to get back to Boston, you need the department put in shape. Would you consider bringing me into the organization as the number two?"

I saw it register. Roache is a smart guy. He understood his situation.

He had to bring the idea to Mayor Ray Flynn. I knew Mayor Flynn's closest adviser, Joe Fisher, and had let him know during the week that I might be available and would be meeting with Roache. Roache and I met with Ray Flynn at the Parkman House several days later. I came prepared with an agenda for addressing the commission's recommendations and reorganizing the department. By this time, I had a practiced game plan.

They made an offer. I would be superintendent-in-chief, a five-star uniformed super chief of the Boston Police. I accepted.

Mayor Flynn wanted to announce my appointment as quickly as possible to stop the bleeding in the department and in the papers, but first I had to go back to New York and inform Alan Kiepper in person. He had brought me to the city, I felt he should hear it from me directly. I did not want to be perceived for any time as a lame duck and have that reflect negatively on the department or myself.

We were going to announce my appointment on a Wednesday. Tuesday evening, we ran another of our subway tours. After these tours, we routinely invited our guests to dinner to discuss what they had seen. At eight o'clock, I broke away to visit Kiepper at his apartment near Columbus Circle. I sat in his living room and told him, "Alan, I'm leaving. It's going to be announced in Boston tomorrow." He was stunned. I explained my rationale. "Look, certain things were promised to me. They didn't happen. I have had an excellent time working here but, financially, this place is killing me. I recognize that the timing isn't very good, but this opportunity came up very fast, and I feel I have to take it." I suggested he promote Mike O'Connor to the position of chief to ensure a smooth transition. O'Connor was the man for the job.

Kiepper was understandably shocked and disappointed. They had invested a lot of money in me as their spokesman, and now I was leaving. I was giving him very short notice. All of this was true, but ultimately I believe he understood that I had to go.

Mayor Flynn announced my appointment and the Boston Police Patrolmen's Association immediately went to court to prevent me from re-

turning. During the Proposition 2¹/₂ era, I had become the face of the layoffs and had fought the union over the introduction of one-officer sector
cars, and they held a grudge. I was going to have to make many more
changes in the department as a result of the St. Clair Commission findings, and they did not want me back. The union felt it had great sway in
the department, and my return might change that. I had also left to work
for a number of different organizations, an act of disloyalty the union
didn't take kindly to.

I have to admit I was surprised at the scale of the union's objections because, only the year before, the New York City Transit Police Benevolent
Association had named me man of the year in recognition of my work on
their officers' behalf. The Boston union claimed I had resigned from the
Boston Police and could not be reappointed. The suit was expedited, and
the city won, but my relationship with the union did not begin well.

I was the number two in the Boston police again, a position I had held
ten years before, but this time I was older, wiser, and even better positioned to assume the top role.

But I had outsmarted myself.

The St. Clair Commission report was so damaging that I had thought
Mickey could not survive. I believed that after a month or two, he would
be eased out, and I would move up. However, Ray Flynn was exception-
ally loyal to his childhood friend, and ironically I had given Mickey the political leverage to hold on to his job.

I had to go through Mickey to get new ideas approved. Often, that
didn't work out as I planned, and differences of opinion sometimes hin-
dered implementing worthwhile programs. Roache went so far as to erect
a wall between his office and mine by sealing off the bathroom corridor.

When I arrived, I found the department was every bit the disaster St.
Clair said it was, but I made the commission understand that we were
turning the place around. I did the same with the media. I imported John
Linder, who had recently left the MTA and formed his own consulting
company, and George Kelling to help write a plan of action in response
to the St. Clair Report. We got the neighborhood-policing program up
and running. Between 1992 and the summer of 1993, using the same
techniques that had worked in New York, we began to bring the Boston
Police back.

Not long after I left for Boston, Lee Brown announced his resignation
as police commissioner. Although he didn't reveal it at the time, his wife
was dying of cancer, and he made the understandable choice to return

with her to their home and family in Houston. Ray Kelly, a career NYPD police officer and Brown's first deputy commissioner, was named acting commissioner pending Mayor Dinkins naming a permanent replacement to complete Brown's five-year term.

Over that summer, I interviewed secretly with Mayor Dinkins for the job. The Boston commissionership didn't look like it was anywhere in sight, and the turnaround of the Boston Police was going smoothly. The choice, as I understand it, came down to me or Ray Kelly. I got the call from Mayor Dinkins at seven o'clock one October weekday morning. Normally by seven I'd be on my way to work, but Cheryl and I love cats, and we had just taken in our fifth, an abandoned weeks-old kitten who needed medication and TLC. We were rotating feedings as if it were an infant, and I was bottle-feeding the kitten when the phone rang. I cradled the receiver in my neck, made sure the cat was getting milk, and said hello.

"Bill," Mayor Dinkins told me, "I wanted to tell you that I've just spoken to Commissioner Kelly and informed him that I'm going to appoint him police commissioner on a permanent basis. I wanted to thank you for participating in the process. I was very impressed with you but I think, at this juncture, the department needs continuity, and Ray, I think, is the man who can provide that and leadership."

"Thank you very much, Mr. Mayor. I hope it works out well for you. It's very kind of you to call me yourself. All the best." I was staying in Boston.

In March 1993, Ray Flynn announced that he was giving up the mayoralty to accept the appointment as United States ambassador to the Vatican. Mickey Roache resigned almost immediately as police commissioner and announced he was running for mayor. Commissioners are like that—we all think we can be mayors.

Flynn didn't indicate who was going to be Roache's replacement, but I thought for sure I had the job. After all my plotting and intriguing, a major career goal was within my grasp. I waited for the call for a week, but nothing happened. Then other names started to surface, and I started to get anxious.

At seven o'clock in the morning a few days later, I got a call from Joe Fisher. Could I see the mayor at eight?

I walked into Ray Flynn's beautiful office overlooking Faneuil Hall and found the mayor in shirtsleeves. He and Joe Fisher talked with me about what he had tried to do with the police department. Was this an explanation? An apology? After fifteen minutes, he said, "Bill, I'm going to announce your appointment as police commissioner later this afternoon."

I'm not an effusive guy, but I wanted to jump in the air. Finally! I shook their hands and settled for a big grin.

Flynn mentioned several friends in the department he asked me to be mindful of, but said, "I understand fully that after I leave you're free to do what you want. With a new mayor coming in, the reality is, for the next five or six months you're going to be on your own." The acting mayor would be City Council President Tom Menino, who was also running for mayor.

I called Cheryl, my parents, my son, my staff. "I've got it!" Everyone was buzzing. Peter LaPorte, Bob O'Toole, and Kay O'Leary were all in my office when I got back. I can hardly remember the details, everything was an overwhelmingly happy blur.

I was sworn in that afternoon in the fourth-floor conference room at police headquarters, in front of my family and friends and fellow members of the department. Word had gotten out, and the room was overflowing. Roache was there, and the mayor presided. I had contacted former superintendent Bill Taylor, who twenty-two years earlier had predicted that this event would occur, and he was there as well. I signed the ledger that had been signed by every police commissioner before me. My parents were beaming.

I had done it! This kid from Dorchester, who came in as a rookie and didn't know a soul in the department, had gotten to the top. There was a wonderful feeling in the room, a restrained euphoria. To get that badge and finally hold it in my hand: police commissioner. Who would've thunk it?

Finally, the Boston Police were going to get on the national stage and break out. We were going to be the department that my friends and I had dreamed of more than twenty years before.

The commissioner's office itself needed attention, and in order to get what I wanted done, I needed someone to stay on top of the details. I appointed Peter LaPorte chief of staff. LaPorte was a bright, fast up-and-comer, running my office by day, going to law school at night.

I reconfigured the storied sixth-floor administrative offices to make them more open and accessible. No closed choir practices for a few of the chosen soloists, as Joe Jordan had done. No closed-door isolation, as had been Mickey Roache's management style. I wanted a wide-open chorus of believers going in and out of my office.

Upon my return as superintendent-in-chief, one of the first initiatives we had been able to complete was the promotion of thirteen new captains. No captains had been promoted within the department since 1977. I was influential in ensuring that Al Sweeney was one of these new captains. Sweeney was not one of Roache's choices, and I fully believe his talents would have been overlooked. After a dispute with Roache over several of his actions, Sweeney had been returned to his civil-service rank of lieutenant. Very few of Roache's inner circle had survived. To ensure that the new captains were fully equipped to run the neighborhood-policing plan we were putting in place, we designed and put them through the most comprehensive three-week training session in the history of the department.

Now, as commissioner, I didn't have to spend days or weeks cajoling and working with Roache to get authority to make my moves. I had the opportunity to put the right people in the right places, and I took advantage of it. I immediately promoted Paul Evans to superintendent-in-chief. Paul had not been liked by Mayor Flynn or Commissioner Roache and had been, I believed, unfairly criticized by the St. Clair Commission. I had come to know, respect, and admire Evans and immediately moved him up as my number two. I installed Al Sweeney as commanding officer of the Academy to fully utilize his skills. I brought Jack Maple up from New York as my executive assistant to begin making changes in the detective bureau. I put Jack Gifford in charge of the Operations Division on the seventh floor so I could have him close at hand. Bob O'Toole was always at my side.

Many of my plans were already in the works. In response to the St. Clair Commission, the city council had made two million dollars available to the department and wanted to put fifty more cops on the street. Ask almost any citizen, "Do you want more cops on the street?" and they'll say, "Of course." Politicians respond to citizens, so this is a popular theme. Under normal circumstances, I would agree. But the St. Clair report had pinpointed significant deficiencies in the technology of the department. We could put all the cops we wanted in the field, but without modern support they would have a hard time making a dent. I argued for systems over cops.

We would be better served, I proposed, with a computerized case-management system and photo-imaging, on-line booking, and fingerprinting capabilities that had been designed by deputy superintendent Bill Casey. We needed a planning unit to research and analyze how the department went about solving the problems it faced. Within several years of acquiring the technology, the Boston Police would have the equivalent of eighty more officers because of the manpower savings the technology would provide. I was able to persuade the commissioner, the mayor, and ultimately the city council, and we won the funding.

Under Roache, I had been able to implement many good programs, including the addition of new technology, the development of the neighborhood-policing program, and the training of neighborhood beat officers. Now, I could stand on the platform we had built in those eighteen months and expedite the goals of those programs by putting my own team into place. During the mayoral campaign, I had an opportunity to move quickly, without the traditional bottleneck at City Hall.

I promoted James Claiborne as the department's first black superintendent, chief of the Bureau of Field Services. He would run all the uniformed operations. To run the day-to-day operations of the detective unit under Superintendent Joe Saia, I appointed Billy Johnson as a deputy superintendent. A maverick and risk taker, Johnson had been running the best investigations in the department as head of the Community Disorders Unit and had become nationally known for his effectiveness in dealing with hate and racial crimes. Once again, I received multiple benefits from one action: Both men were the best people for the jobs, and I very consciously sent the message that this was a new, more progressive generation in the Boston Police, with advancement open to all races and risk takers alike.

To his credit, Acting Mayor Menino didn't try to politically influence the running of the department while he was busy campaigning. As a result, my staff and I were able to deal directly with the office of the new governor, William Weld, and, more important, were able to open lines of communication with the White House, through the good work of Joan Brody, who had been a student of George Kelling at Harvard's John F. Kennedy School of Government.

President Clinton was pushing hard for a national crime bill. His key was the proposal to hire 100,000 more cops nationwide. As this bill was being hammered out, Brody called the White House with no prior contacts to lobby for federal assistance for some of our efforts. She developed a respected relationship with the White House Domestic Policy Council and the White House staffers working on crime issues, and when the president was preparing to announce the filing of his legislation, which included the Brady gun-control bill, Brody proposed that I stand with him in the Rose Garden, representing American police chiefs. She is the only person I know who went cold-calling at the White House and got in.

I informed Mayor Menino I was going. By currying favor with the White House, I said, we were advancing the interests of the city of Boston and its police department. As a Democrat, he agreed.

With an elected mayor in office, getting that clearance might have been next to impossible. The opportunity to appear beside the president on the national stage is political gold and would have been co-opted in a flash. Mayors, always eager to ingratiate themselves with their constituencies, understandably want the anticrime platform and major crime-fighting ideas for themselves. But with City Hall in a state of flux, we had a rare opportunity to deal directly with the White House, and we jumped at the chance.

There were several speakers in the Rose Garden that day, and by the time my turn came, I dispensed with rhetoric and went straight to the heart of the matter. I implored Congress, "This time, let's get it done. The American people need this legislation. Let's get it done, and let's get it done now."

The next morning, as I approached the entrance to the Sumner Tunnel, the kid I bought newspapers from every day saw me coming and pointed to the *Globe.* "Hey," he said, "congratulations!" There I was, in color, over the fold, at the podium in the Rose Garden with the president and vice president and attorney general of the United States in the background. Wow!

When the crime bill passed, Boston received significant federal funding for its initiatives. President Clinton had succeeded where his Republican predecessors had failed. He had responded to America's need for a strong federal initiative to deal with the country's growing crime problem. I also opened a relationship with the White House that would otherwise have been impossible to obtain. Joan Brody did a terrific job.

Maple, Linder, LaPorte and I were sitting in Florence's, a favorite restaurant in the North End, on election night, November 1993. The polls had closed. My driver, Quion Riley, came in. "Who won?" I asked.

"Menino won."

"Who won in New York?"

At that point, the race between Mayor Dinkins and Rudolph Giuliani was still too close to call.

My interest was more than idle curiosity. There was speculation that if Giuliani was elected, I might be asked to come back as police commissioner. I had met Giuliani once and discussed the transit turnaround, but

I had no inside information. Still, something was stirring. I had my dream job, but I found myself once again attracted to New York.

Despite the fact that Tom Menino would not become full-time mayor until January, in one of his first acts he announced he wanted undated letters of resignation from all department heads on his desk. He got every one but mine.

I had been appointed to serve out the remaining two-and-a-half years of Mickey Roache's term. I had a little less than two years left, and I felt it was in both my best interests and the best interests of the institution of the police commissioner not to concede. Around six o'clock Friday night, LaPorte got a call at the office from Menino's chief of staff, Peter Welch.

After some small talk Welch said, "We didn't get your letter."

"You're not getting a letter," LaPorte told him.

"You know, every department head has submitted one."

"The police commissioner's got a five-year term. Statutorily, he serves that term."

Mayor Menino and I were obviously getting off to a rocky start. That was unfortunate, because I am very much a team player and had every intention of working with and for Mayor Menino, who I respected, while protecting the validity of the police commissioner's five-year term.

A few days after the election, I got a call from Howard Wilson. Giuliani had won and Wilson was responsible for reaching out to potential mayoral appointees. He was rounding up candidates for the position of police commissioner and told me the mayor-elect was very interested in having me apply. I told Wilson I wasn't particularly interested. When I had interviewed for commissioner under Dinkins, I had been a superintendent. I was now commissioner, and I had additional concerns. Cheryl, a lawyer, was actively pursuing a judgeship. I had tried living in New York on a similar salary and had found it difficult. I was within eighteen months of eligibility for a 50 percent pension from the BPD, and Cheryl and I were in the process of renovating a house in Boston as part of complying with the residency requirement of my position as police commissioner.

Apart from these not insignificant personal considerations, I was also very concerned about the interview process. I was simply being offered the opportunity to apply, not the guarantee of being accepted. I was the newly appointed Boston Police Commissioner, a job I was thoroughly enjoying, and how might it look if I applied for another job and didn't get it? What loyalty and authority could I command within my own organization if I was ready to trade it for one chance in ten at the next job that came along?

Wilson told me I was highly regarded and well along in the process.

After a series of phone conversations, he invited me to come down and meet informally with the group of Giuliani insiders who made the influential recommendations concerning the mayor-elect's most important appointments. As long as it was understood that I wasn't formally applying for the job, I agreed. I expressed my concerns about the tremendous damage that could be caused if news of my appearance leaked, and he assured me that not only the contents of the meeting but even its existence would be kept strictly confidential.

We arranged for me to fly down late one weekday afternoon and return the same night. I drove myself to the airport. The idea of being police commissioner of New York was certainly appealing. The prestige was considerable, the work challenging, the payoff when I succeeded extremely significant. Boston was my hometown, and I loved it; I loved the Boston Police Department. But New York also offered its own unique set of professional challenges. New York was Broadway, the Big Apple, and the job of NYPD commissioner was the Broadway of policing, the most complex and challenging police job in America. It was difficult not to be interested or excited.

At the shuttle terminal, I was almost at the metal detector when I said to myself, "I can't do this."

I didn't know Giuliani from a hole in the wall. I had earned the job I'd wanted all my life. Great challenges still lay ahead for me in Boston. No matter what Wilson said, I didn't have a lock on the New York job. They had shown no signs of budging in terms of salary. Cheryl's career was blossoming, and while she put on a brave face, she really didn't want me to go. Why was I upsetting all this? For the first time in my career, why not enjoy the satisfaction of a quest achieved?

I drove straight to Cheryl's office in East Boston. "I'm not going to do it," I told her. "We've got too many considerations. It would mean upsetting your career goals and being apart, and I just don't think we should." Although she had said all along that she understood what an important job this was and would support whatever decision I made, I could see the relief on her face. I felt relieved as well. Now I could concentrate even more strongly on Boston.

I called Wilson and thanked him for the invitation. "I appreciate being considered, the job is certainly tempting, but I've thought it over," I told him, "and it's not for me."

I found out later that the *New York Post* had a photographer waiting at La Guardia Airport. Their sister paper, the *Boston Herald*, would have shot me coming back at Logan. So much for confidentiality. I don't know for certain whether there was a leak from within the Giuliani camp or if the *Post* has ace reporters, but there are two shuttles servicing Boston to New York and the *Post* had both my airline and my arrival time. Had I been discovered actively seeking the job, my hand would have been tipped. I had been placed very much on the hook and only by luck had I wriggled off.

With my name out of the running, I kept reading in the papers that several others were under consideration. I had no way of truly knowing how the selection process proceeded, who was for show and who was for real. I can't say I wasn't curious, but for several weeks I went about my business.

Maple was beside himself when I told him of my decision. His real reason for coming to Boston was to be in a position to lobby me to accept the NYPD commissioner's job if, as he expected, Giuliani offered it to me.

He and John Linder began conspiring. The Mollen Commission was investigating the depth of NYPD corruption. Maple knew Judge Milton Mollen quite well. "Judge," said Maple, "I think he needs a little push." Mollen called me saying, essentially, "What do we have to do to get you into this?" and we went back and forth for a few days.

The plot thickened. Howard Wilson called again. They had done more homework and were considerably more serious about encouraging me to take the job this time. I got the distinct feeling from talking to Wilson that the mayor felt I was the guy he needed. I had already proved I could succeed in New York, I had visibility, Howard told me I had stature, it would be a coup to entice me from elsewhere. But that was window dressing. The main question was: Could I get the job done? The new mayor had campaigned on the issues of crime and quality of life, and he thought I could be the man to help him. Giuliani understood that I had my own police-management ideas that I brought with me wherever I went. Wilson asked if I would care to meet alone with him and Adam Walinsky, now a Giuliani adviser, to discuss the possibility further.

Rather than applying, I was being recruited. It was clear to me that this time there was a job offer at the other end. I agreed to talk with them at Walinsky's home in Scarsdale, New York, on the day after Thanksgiving.

Cheryl and I drove down with my friend Bob Johnson and his wife, Sandy. Bob runs First Security Services, the tenth-largest private security company in the country, and had been a mentor, confidant, and good friend for a number of years. When I had returned to Boston he had served as a trusted adviser and member of my kitchen cabinet and had even created a Police Foundation, modeled after the one in New York City, to raise funds for the Boston Police Department. The Foundation's first donation was used to buy ten bicycles to create the department's first bicycle unit, which made its first arrest, a drug dealer, while peddling back from the ceremony announcing its creation. Throughout the process, Bob was always available to me as a sounding board.

They dropped me off at Walinsky's beautiful old farmhouse, and after a nice lunch we sat on his sunporch and talked. Walinsky, a protégé of Robert Kennedy, was a longtime advocate of the Police Corps, an organization he had proposed to train college students to become temporary police officers, along the lines of the Peace Corps. He was a one-man band on the subject, editorializing in *The New York Times* and keeping the idea alive in Congress.

Wilson, Walinsky, and I talked for about an hour and a half. They wanted to know what I would do to turn the NYPD around. Giuliani had been elected largely on the issues of crime and quality of life. People in New York were feeling increasingly unsafe and threatened and the newly elected mayor had made it his priority to reduce crime and make them feel better. How would I live up to that promise?

I outlined my basic policing premises, beginning with the Broken Windows concept, and included the ideas that had been developed successfully in Boston and with the Transit Police and were at the time being implemented at the Boston PD. I also discussed the need to completely reengineer the NYPD. They asked me what I would need to take the job, and I explained my concerns about choosing my own team and resources, and my personal needs in salary and benefits.

At around four-thirty, Wilson excused himself for a few minutes. He came back and told me, "I just talked to the mayor-elect, and he asked if you would be willing to come into the city to meet with him. Quietly. Now."

So there it was. I was bypassing the selection committee and going straight to the top. I said I would be pleased to meet with the mayor. After I updated Cheryl and the Johnsons, they decided to drive back to Boston without me.

We drove to the midtown Manhattan offices of Wilson's firm, which Giuliani was using to conduct some of his interviews. At around seven in the evening, the mayor-elect came through the door. He had a nice way about him, very warm and gracious. In close quarters, Giuliani can be quite charming and ingratiating when he wants to be. He thanked me for meeting him on such short notice and said he admired my work in transit. My approach had worked in the subways, but he wanted to know once again, would it work in the streets. I said, sure, it's the same thing. What had gone on below ground had been a coordinated effort; the cops had been motivated, equipped, energized, and directed, while the Transit Authority had cleaned the graffiti and the station managers had helped control the environment. To reduce crime in New York, I said, we would do very much the same thing: motivate, equip, and energize.

But the cops weren't the only ones to be held accountable, I added. We needed the Parks Department to clean up and change the appearance of the city, we needed the Transportation Department to deal with graffiti, we needed the commissioner of consumer affairs to work on regulating the peddlers. We needed the district attorneys and Corrections onboard. What was required was a coordinated government effort. The new mayor didn't need convincing—that's what he already had in mind.

Giuliani said he very much wanted me to put my name up for consideration and strongly implied that I was the candidate he wanted. However, he did say it would be imperative for me to meet with the selection committee. They were important supporters who had already met with several candidates, and he said he would be uncomfortable going outside that process; it would be a significant slight to them and the work they had already put in if I did not at least meet with them. Although he was not offering me the job outright, his intentions were clear, and he felt the best-case scenario would be if the committee supported his selection and recommended me as well.

I was still concerned about maintaining the confidentiality of our talks. The mayor said he could not guarantee silence; many people were involved in the selection process, and speculation about previous candidates was already getting out.

It was time to make a decision. I told the mayor I was interested but that I would have to talk it over with my wife.

What followed was a couple of days of shuttle diplomacy, as the committee decided whether they would recommend me, and I decided, if they did, whether I would take the job.

How could I not take it? My whole career had been about making it to the top, and New York was the largest, best-known police department in the United States. We decided to go for it.

Cheryl and I had many conversations about the changes this job would bring about in our lives. I told her I would not take it unless she was willing to come to New York. Cheryl knew I was facing the premier career opportunity, that her practice was also going well, and she was continuing to pursue a judgeship. She told me she was willing to put her career goals on hold to accompany me. She said it would be like the president nominating her for a seat on the Supreme Court and my saying I didn't want to move to Washington. I could not have taken the job without her support.

Word got out in a hurry. When I flew from Boston to New York to meet with the committee, the New York press was at the gate. I arrived back in Boston around eleven and was met by another set of cameras and microphones. I was the lead story on the Boston TV news.

It was exciting, and for a few days it was almost nonstop. This media circus was not without its tumbling acts, however. During the time, I went to Washington with a group from the U.S. Conference of Mayors and Police Chiefs to meet with the president about the crime bill, and at a stand-up interview on the front lawn of the White House, a local Boston reporter asked me, "Commissioner, what if you don't get the New York City job?"

I smiled. "Well, you know, Boston's a pretty good consolation prize."

It was an attempt at humor that failed miserably. I was just being glib. I prized the Boston commissionership so highly I had spent my entire professional life trying to obtain it; it was anything but a consolation prize. But that's what I said and, naturally, the quote made headlines in Boston. Boston has a competitive relationship with New York in the best of times, from the Red Sox–Yankees and Celtics-Knicks rivalries to the cities' clashing cultures, and for me, a hometown boy, to consider leaving Boston and then call staying there a "consolation prize" was truly foolish.

Of course, they went running to Mayor Menino, who justifiably failed to see the humor. The *Boston Herald* ran a great cartoon showing the mayor slamming the door on my butt as I was leaving, saying, "I want to wish you . . . ah, the hell with it!" My ill-advised attempt at a joke still haunts me.

I arrived at Giuliani's committee interview with solutions. I had prepared talking points dealing with both crime in the city and the state of the police department itself. I began by telling them, "We will win the war on crime. We *can* carry out the mayor's determination to dramatically reduce crime, disorder, and fear throughout New York. We will successfully move against street-level drug dealing within twelve months. We will reduce crime by 40 percent within three years. We will reduce public fear measurably within four years and let people feel that they can walk the city's streets.

"We will win by transforming the systems and practices of *all* the departments. We will empower and make precinct commanders accountable for all police activity in their areas. We will reward success, not merely the absence of public failure."

We would empower anticrime units to make drug/decoy arrests, encourage every uniformed officer to make drug arrests, keep cops on the streets by reducing their time in court. We would treat guns like drugs by interrupting their flow at every point of supply, sale, and use. We would pursue *everybody* involved in the commission of a crime with a gun. We would identify the source of the weapons in the city and use stings to attack dealers.

We would fundamentally change the way the NYPD ran its investigations. As we had done at transit when we hunted down the wolfpacks, we would stop clearing violent crimes with one arrest—we would get *every* perpetrator. We would look for connections between crimes and try to make three cases per perp instead of one. We would bring the innovations that had made the transit warrant unit such a success to the NYPD.

The entire culture of the New York Police Department needed to be transformed. We would concentrate on rooting out corruption by recruiting investigators from leaders within the ranks, by training supervisors to see signs of trouble and rewarding commanders for finding it. "The cops must know their mission and have the skills to carry it out," I said. We would train all officers rapidly and systematically so they would be committed to the new strategies and the new ways to do their jobs, then we would organize a full-press campaign for public support. But, I stressed, the change must come from inside the department first.

On December 1, I flew down to New York with Cheryl, Jack Maple, and Bob and Sandy Johnson. Cheryl and I met at Giuliani's law offices with his inner circle. Then Larry Levy, an attorney in the city corporation counsel's office, took down information for the necessary background checks. Finally, at around one in the morning, Mayor Giuliani offered me the job. They were going to announce my appointment the next morning.

I had won the big one: police commissioner of the City of New York.

Chapter 12

NEW YORK DEMANDS IMMEDIATE ACTION. I SPENT THIRTY DAYS PUTTING together an organization that would be working at high speed and efficiency the day I took office. Mayors and governors have transition teams, why not a police commissioner? The New York City Police Foundation funded the transition process. I assembled a team from all areas of my professional life to analyze the NYPD from top to bottom and formulate a plan for success.

Bob Wasserman was the leader of my transition team, which included Bob Johnson, Jack Maple, John Linder, Dean Esserman, Al Sweeney, Peter LaPorte, Joan Brody, and Bob O'Toole. Wasserman had an intimate understanding of the personnel and practices of the NYPD, having worked with Lee Brown and David Dinkins on the Safe Streets community-policing program. He had developed a thousand-page analysis of the department to support the need for six thousand new cops.

Wasserman offered several recommendations: Janet Lennon, a former special counsel under Lee Brown, and Mike Farrell, a special assistant to Ray Kelly. Wasserman also suggested I bring in Judy Laffey as my executive assistant. Judy had served in the same capacity under Brown and Ben Ward, and she ran a tight ship. She knew the commissioner's office inside out and knew how the department really worked, and she was known and respected within it. The police were her family; her husband John was commanding officer of the Operations Division. I had met her when I'd visited Commissioner Brown, and she was efficient and personable. People would tell me, "That woman who works with you is delightful to deal with." The ones who couldn't get around her were less complimentary. The more I worked with her the more I liked and respected her.

Wasserman focused on producing a comprehensive Who's Who of the NYPD and an outline of the key current and ongoing issues. He wanted to know what the priorities were and where things were going. I had a relatively limited knowledge of the personalities involved and, outside of my good relationship with Lee Brown, had not been particularly welcomed into the inner offices of the department when I had been at transit. Wasserman asked the fifty most powerful people in the department—the deputy commissioners, the bureau chiefs, the assistant chiefs, and the deputy chiefs—to provide us with their personnel files and a detailed report on the operation of their units. I intended to interview many people before making my command staff decisions, but I could tell, by the documents they produced, what they were like.

Wasserman also organized discussions of my entrance strategy. Clearly, the most controversial idea was to ask for the resignations of all the significant people in the NYPD, and it was hotly debated. On one hand, such a potential bloodletting could clearly destabilize the department. I would be throwing a hand grenade into a roomful of police careers. On the other hand, it was easier to start off with a clean slate and not have to worry about excising people later. Everyone would be on notice that we meant to change things drastically.

I had gotten the sense when I was at transit that the NYPD was a culture of its own, very resistant to creativity. It certainly did not take the crime issue seriously. At transit, when I had thought through the dynamics of crime and acted to bring it down, the NYPD had taken little or no notice of our accomplishments. They had not been interested in investigating new ways of considering the profession, even though we were in the same city and essentially sharing the same base of criminals. Despite our resurgence, we had remained tunnel rats to them.

Under Dinkins, Brown, and Kelly, the NYPD was committed to the concept of community policing. The 1991 Safe Streets law, championed by the Citizens Crime Commission and pushed through by Dinkins, established a city income-tax surcharge dedicated to hiring six thousand more police officers, and the community-policing program was based on the idea that this infusion of new cops on the beat would have a significant effect in bringing down the crime rate.

Mayor Dinkins made a major mistake, one that probably cost him the election, by spending two years' worth of Safe Streets money on social-service initiatives rather than immediately hiring cops. Those initiatives were important, but the public wanted to feel protected, they wanted to see more cops on the beat. If he had hired 2,000 cops in January 1993, they would have been through the academy and on the streets that summer, just in time to be a positive issue in the campaign. The streets would have been swimming with cops. To all those who felt Dinkins was soft on crime, he could have shown pictures of himself and 2,000 cops being sworn in at Madison Square Garden. The photos would have shown him doing something and might well have produced the small boost he needed to be re-elected. Instead, press coverage of the police focused, to his detriment, on corruption scandals, which ironically, in a courageous political act, he had effectively addressed by appointing a mayoral commission under the direction of his highly regarded deputy mayor for criminal justice, Judge Milton Mollen. Dinkins got no credit; most of the cops for whom he won funding didn't come on the job until after the election. This was very poor political planning. In the first six months of Giuliani's term, the new mayor attended two graduation ceremonies and implicitly took credit for 4,200 additional police officers.

The community-policing plan that had been put into practice when I arrived focused on the beat cop. Capital improvements were being planned that would have set up community-policing offices in each precinct. "Officer Friendly" would respectfully resume contact with the community, courteously listen to people's problems, and immediately find appropriate solutions.

In theory, that's fine; beat cops are important in maintaining contact with the public and offering them a sense of security. They can identify the community's concerns and sometimes prevent crime simply by their visibility. Giving cops more individual power to make decisions is a good idea. But the community-policing plan as it was originally focused was not going to work because there was no focus on crime. The connection between having more cops on the street and the crime rate falling was implicit. There was no plan to deploy these officers in specifically hard-hit areas (to win political support for Safe Streets, Dinkins had had to commit to deploying cops throughout the city, in both low- and high-crime areas), and there were no concrete means by which they were supposed to address crime when they got there. They were simply supposed to go out on their beats and somehow improve their communities.

The new beat cop was a kid. No twenty-two-year-old kid from Long Island was going to come to Harlem, Hollis, the Upper East Side, or East New York and solve that neighborhood's problems. The city's problems were complex and difficult for the most experienced police and social service experts; these kids were unprepared and ill equipped to handle them, and it was unrealistic to expect that they could. And even on the odd chance that some of the new cops were capable of getting significant results, they were never going to be empowered to follow through. The NYPD was a centralized bureaucracy that didn't give out power even to its precinct commanders, let alone the cop on the beat. So these kids were getting sent out to be the problem solvers, and the neighborhood was beating up on them. "Why didn't you prevent that break-in? Why did my car get stolen? Why am I getting panhandled and mugged? Why aren't we safe?" They had no answers, and pretty soon they would be as callous and demoralized as the rest of the force.

Everyone on the transition team had a specific task. Maple was primarily responsible for investigating personnel. He also focused on crime. Esserman reviewed corruption issues, LaPorte began to concentrate on the administrative details that would be his responsibility as my chief of staff, and Sweeney synthesized the information. We met two or three times a week in a corner of the Giuliani transition offices at 40 Church Street, and again at Bob Johnson's First Security Services offices at Logan Airport in Boston.

We began to develop the NYPD team. I was being brought in to breathe some life into the organization, not to manage a holding action, and I wanted the best and the brightest. I knew I wanted to promote Dave Scott, an honorable man with whom I'd had a good relationship when I was at transit, to first deputy commissioner. The first deputy is the commissioner's right hand; he watches over discipline, he participates in the placement of personnel, he advises on policy, and he keeps an eye on the budget. The fact that Scott was black also helped. New York had lost a black mayor and a black police commissioner, and I felt it was important to show that minorities still had a significant role model and advocate within the department. He was also the right man for the job.

Wasserman and Maple directed me toward the up-and-comers. Maple did not have the political debts or vested interests of an NYPD insider; we would not be redeeming old political chits. He and Wasserman began preliminary interviews. With Maple, pretty much any conversation is an interrogation, and he very soon targeted the stars and the duds. He presented me with his impressions.

"An obstructionist . . ."

"Good communication skills. Strong detective background as well as patrol."

"No ideas. No creativity, leadership. Has integrity. Not good under pressure."

"Leadership: None. Creativity: None. Commitment: None."

The two people in the department widely considered the most brilliant, the most visionary, were one-star chiefs John Timoney and Michael Julian.

Mike Julian began as a plainclothes cop in Crown Heights, Brooklyn, and had worked toward his law degree at night. As an attorney within the department, he had represented both police officers and the city, and he had prosecuted cops for misconduct. He was in his forties but looked younger, was articulate and argumentative, and didn't make concessions easily.

Julian spent a year in the Cadet Corps recruiting minority police officers, then, after riots broke out in the Ninth Precinct's Tompkins Square Park and police had used excessive force to put them down, was given that Lower East Side precinct with the mandate to calm the streets. At a time when three hundred men and women were living in Tompkins Square Park and anarchists were squatting in the surrounding buildings, the NYPD needed someone who could work with the neighborhood's active and very visible antipolice groups.

Perhaps because he was not knee-jerk in defending cops who went over the line, or because he was smart and good-looking and could talk up a storm, some cops thought he was an elitist, a glamour boy. Maple swore the anarchists liked Julian better than the cops did. That didn't concern me. Where many commanders get caught up in the daily details of policing, Julian had an understanding, an intellectual overview, and a real talent for creating problem-solving strategies. When Lee Brown came in with his focus on community policing, Julian was considered the man to run the program. His name was familiar because Wasserman, when he was consulting at transit, had once indicated to me that Julian was the brightest person in the NYPD.

Under Ray Kelly, Julian established policy advisory groups, analogous to John Linder's focus groups, to involve street cops in identifying department policies that interfered with high performance. Four cops from each precinct, covering all tours, were made advisers to the police commissioner and began to detail what systemic and organizational alterations they felt had to be made in order for the department to perform at its best. Kelly had started to make some of these changes before Giuliani was elected, and Julian had had a large hand in the beginnings of this transformation.

John Timoney, forty-five, was the prototypical New York cop. He was born in Dublin and never totally lost the brogue. On first meeting, it takes serious concentration to understand him, and when he gets excited, his words run together in a blur. A craggy-faced guy with the appearance of a man who had acquitted himself well in a series of fights, he was a marathon runner and looked like a million bucks in uniform. He walked on his toes, like James Cagney in *Yankee Doodle Dandy*, like a hoofer or a fighter in the ring. He and Julian were good friends. Maple's assessment said, "He looks and sounds like a tough Irish cop, but his message and his programs are extremely progressive."

He was also very smart. Timoney was the chief of the Office of Management, Analysis, and Planning (OMAP) under Ray Kelly. OMAP is responsible for reviewing department tactics and procedures, and making recommendations relative to new policies; it is effectively the commissioner's personal think tank. Timoney had been on the job for over twenty years, was thoroughly familiar with all the department's initiatives, and was respected throughout the department as a leader who always had its best interests, and those of his people, at heart. He also had a world of self-confidence. His career goal was to be commissioner, he knew his competition within the department, and he believed he was better than any person there. When I was appointed, he had expected a promotion.

"If they only bump me from one-star to two-star, there's no way I'm staying," he told friends. "One-star to three-star, maybe. But I won't just hang out." He let it be known within the department that "unless there's some super-duper offer, I'm going into business with Kelly."

Working from Maple's and Wasserman's lists, John Linder brought together several leading candidates for the top jobs. In his practice, he uses the motivational technique of "strategic intent," which calls for an organization's leader to create seemingly unreachable goals, what Bob Johnson in the business sector called "stretch goals," and then challenges himself and his subordinates to invent ways to attain them. I had announced that we were going to take back the city "block by block." Linder now told this group of NYPD chiefs, "Here's what we want to do. Over the next two years we want a dramatic decrease in crime. That's our focus. Can we do it?"

"What do you mean by a 'dramatic decrease'?"

"Ten percent the first year. Fifteen the next. Twenty-five percent in two years." We had looked at the figures, and these were our goals. We thought they were within our grasp.

Several chiefs simply said, "Can't be done." They thought they were already doing everything they could to bring down crime, and anything more was out of the question. "Dramatic? No. You can have decreases. Crime goes down 2 to 4 percent a year, and we can continue that trend. But 10 percent? No chance."

Ray Kelly had told Linder, "You want to reduce crime? I can reduce crime. You give me fifty men and suspend the Constitution, I'll reduce crime." That wasn't the way we were going to go about it.

Only Julian and Timoney thought the decrease was possible.

"Yeah, it can be done," said Timoney, "but you're going to have to change everything about this place. If you really change the whole department, you can bring it down significantly."

Julian told Linder, "This car is operating on two of eight cylinders. If you get it on *four* cylinders, you can reduce crime twenty-five percent."

Those were the answers I was looking for.

When I checked Julian's background, one of his innovations was to put cops on bicycles. Teddy Roosevelt, my much-revered predecessor, had first put cops on bikes one hundred years earlier, but in modern times it had never been done in a major northeastern city; it was a California idea and was anathema to the rest of the chiefs. They'd said, "This can never happen and will never happen. It's dangerous, the bikes will be stolen, we'll look silly." What Julian knew, and the rest of the chiefs either didn't understand or wouldn't consider, was that cops on foot disappear. Because of physical fatigue and boredom, a cop on foot does not do an eight-hour shift. Julian felt, as I did, that if you could make the job more interesting to a worker, he'd give you a better day's work. The chiefs couldn't understand this. Lee Brown challenged Julian, "If you can get the money yourself, you can do it."

Julian tapped manufacturers, the Police Foundation, community and business groups, and finally he succeeded; the NYPD now has one thousand bikes on the streets of New York. The cops cover more territory more often and get around more quickly, largely due to his efforts. "You fought everybody on that," I said when I interviewed him. "You went against the grain, you went against their direction."

He said, "Yeah. They were wrong."

"That's the kind of attitude I want. I want people who are not only going to think differently, but who'll be willing to go through walls to do it."

I asked Julian who were the stars in the department. Most ambitious people in an organization will nominate themselves first. Julian impressed me again. "The guy you need is Timoney," he told me. "Timoney has the leadership skills to get cops to enforce and obey the law."

Maple told me, "Julian is brilliant, you need him around. But the cops hate him. Why don't you make him chief of personnel or something. This way you have him close to you, right? No one likes the chief of personnel, anyway." So I did. It's a position in which he could deal with fundamental issues such as training, human resources, and support programs for the police (such as suicide prevention), as well as create ideas outside his immediate area and get them implemented. The issue of training was going to be critical to the direction I was intending to take the department. We were confident we could reduce crime and disorder, but if we did it by antagonizing the public, or in a disrespectful way, or in an abusive way, or in a way that alienated an already suspicious public—particularly the minority community—we would win the battle but lose the war.

Essentially, I made Mike Julian Chief of Big Ideas.

Then I met with Timoney.

The chief of department handles the day-to-day operations of the entire NYPD and coordinates the activities of everybody under him. The chiefs of investigations, patrol, and the Organized Crime Control Bureau all report to the chief of department. I was looking for innovation, but I needed someone who would engender fear and respect, a tough guy who would take charge, point us in the right direction, and have the troops do battle for him, as O'Connor had done for me at transit and Paul Evans had done in Boston.

After hearing from Wasserman, Linder, and Julian, I had been so predisposed to like Timoney that I was very surprised when sparks didn't fly. Timoney was tough, all right, but at our meeting he came off as cocky, which I didn't warm to at all. It is a function of how undistinguished that meeting was that I can't remember much more about it. Timoney walked into the room with a chance to make his career and walked out with nothing. Aside from the fact that we didn't click, his rapid-fire, closemouthed way of speaking was so thick I couldn't understand him. I told Linder, "The guy's from Ireland, I can't understand a word he says." Timoney went back and told Julian, "The guy's from Boston, he talks funny."

Timoney's strongest rival was a two-star chief from Staten Island, Tosano "Tony" Simonetti. He was an effusive, effective, take-charge guy, well respected in the department. I was leaning in his direction when we got wind of a small, unresolved cloud over his handling of an incident that the Mollen Commission was still investigating. I didn't know whether it would dissipate or turn into some thundering scandal. (It eventually proved to be without foundation.) I had good feelings about Simonetti's ability and honesty, but I couldn't afford even the whisper of a problem with my appointments, so I left Simonetti where he was. Which left Timoney. Two days later I brought him back, and this time I listened closely.

In the two intervening days, I had interviewed all the super chiefs, the five men at the top of the NYPD chain of command: chiefs of department, patrol, detectives, personnel, the Organized Crime Control Bureau, plus the deputy commissioner of internal affairs. I mentioned two who had impressed me.

"Well," said Timoney, "that's where you and I differ. If I get the job they're the first two fuckin' guys I'd get rid of."

"Why?"

"There's only one person in the city that can do anything about narcotics, and that's Marty O'Boyle. O'Boyle's a one-star chief who's wasting away, getting ready to retire because he's fed up. He's the most talented guy in the police department. Everybody knows that. People who *know* know that." Timoney's endorsement moved him far up the list. "He's kind of a laid-back guy, but he's the best."

I looked at Timoney for a moment. He was clearly convinced and convincing. "Listen," I said, "they're not *all* going to be Irish, are they?"

Two days later, I gave Timoney the job.

Timoney was a Bronx cop, a cop's cop. He was from the real world of policing, he knew what it was like out in those streets, and he brought that perspective to my inner circle. You had to understand the world cops were operating in to understand how they got themselves jammed up. He understood, as I did, that everything in the police world was not black and white. At a time when there was a great pressure from the district attorneys, the U.S. attorneys, the Mollen Commission, and Walter Mack at the NYPD's Internal Affairs Bureau to be holier-than-thou and cleaner than clean, I needed balance. Timoney spoke for the cops about what it's really like out there. The prosecutors had never really experienced the streets. They espoused high morals and ethics but were lacking in the human compassion they might have developed had they been there. I could not forgive truly dirty cops, but I could understand those others who found themselves jammed up for making a momentary mistake. What Timoney brought to the table was knowledge and compassion.

I told him, "I have things to do here, and I need people who will do them. I know the media and the press, I know how to change a large organization, but I don't know the nuts and bolts of the NYPD, and I don't have time to know it. You're the guy. I want you to run the department, the day-to-day operations. I'll do the other stuff." If I was going to be the CEO of the NYPD, he would be my chief operating officer. Timoney's chest went out. That kind of trust will empower a good man.

Timoney was my second major appointment, after Dave Scott, and word of it jolted the department. He was passing over sixteen of his bosses and jumping from a one-star to a four-star chief. He would be the youngest chief of department in NYPD history. It was a huge roll of the dice on a guy I'd met twice for a total of maybe forty-five minutes, but he had the highest recommendations, and once I could understand what he was saying, it turned out he made a lot of sense. Dave Scott was also very supportive and felt they could work well together.

We then focused on the rest of the department. It quickly became clear that in order to make the necessary policy changes, we would have to take out a large part of the department's senior leadership. The super chiefs were good people and good cops who had been on the job an average of thirty-five to forty years each. They were talented, but they were talented for another style of policing. Some of them were tired and wedded to the status quo. We were going to be moving fast, our goals were different from theirs, and it seemed some of them simply did not have the flexibility to change such long-standing status quo thinking on such short notice. I was going to demand results, and they had already told me, in the interviews with Linder, that they didn't think the job could be done.

Ray Kelly had tried to make significant changes in the operational practices of the department but had left the old guard at the top in place. Timoney had often joked with him, "Everybody's dragging their feet. What you've got to do is lob a grenade on the thirteenth floor," where most of the super chiefs were housed. But there was a tough mayoral election coming up, and maybe Kelly's hands were tied. Along with the corruption problems being investigated by the Mollen Commission, it eventually cost him his reappointment.

It was very easy for Timoney to give free advice to Kelly. But many of the super chiefs were Timoney's friends, and now he had to give me his recommendations on who we should move on. He stayed up two nights, anguishing. Finally, he made his decision: Many of them would have to go.

In the end, I chose Louis Anemone as chief of patrol, the person in charge of the day-to-day operations of the precincts. Anemone was a cop's cop. In his mid-forties, of average build, he exuded enthusiasm and confidence. After the Crown Heights riots of 1991, Kelly had appointed him disorder-control commander, and he put together a response mechanism for any riot or major disturbance that might happen in New York. Under his direction, the department routinely began to train all of its personnel to respond rapidly to any circumstances that might arise anywhere in the city. Nobody wanted another Crown Heights. My instructions to him were simple; in the same way he had focused on preventing riots and disorder, I needed him to prepare the department to reduce crime and fear.

I decided to retain Joe Borrelli, alone among the super chiefs, as chief of detectives and promoted Manhattan South Borough Chief Charlie Reuther to chief of the Organized Crime Control Bureau. I left Walter Mack in charge of the Internal Affairs Bureau.

I didn't think much of it at the time, but Giuliani did not seek a lot of input into my selections. He had said the police department needed major change, and I assumed he would get kudos, by extension, for bringing in a commissioner who was willing to make those changes. He did not get involved in the specifics; it was pretty much my show to run.

The only appointment I wanted his acquiescence for was deputy commissioner for public information (DCPI). City Hall was going to leave the decision up to me, but I insisted that they be involved. I didn't want them complaining later. The DCPI handles breaking news, manages all requests for interviews and information, and is intimately involved in the operational, administrative, and strategic decision making of the NYPD. The DCPI was our chief liaison with City Hall and needed to work intimately with the mayor's office to coordinate the constant contact between us, them, the press, and the Hall's own press people. I was leaning toward Al O'Leary, who had done such a fine job at transit. I was depending on using the press to get our message out, and I wanted that message delivered fully and with enthusiasm; I wanted someone the press would not feel was going to deceive them. Al was widely respected and I had great faith in his ability to do the job.

The Hall was less comfortable with O'Leary than with John Miller, a thirtysomething on-air investigative reporter for WNBC-TV who had done some favorable pieces about Giuliani when, as U.S. attorney, he had been walking brokers out of their Wall Street offices in handcuffs. He and the mayor were on a first-name phone-call basis. Miller had also become very good friends with Jack Maple, whom he had tried to get thrown behind bars ten years earlier. Miller and Maple were now renowned buddies and could often be found late at night at their favorite haunt, Elaine's. Both were known for their sartorial splendor (Miller preferred $2,000 Brioni suits and Dunhill ties) as well as their smarts. Maple was lobbying hard for Miller.

Miller was best known for walking up to John Gotti in the street and trying to get the organized crime don to talk. There was something very compelling about that brand of journalism, kind of like watching a man picking his way among vaguely tamed lions, and Miller obviously liked living with that edgy uncertainty. I interviewed him at my transition offices in mid-December. He walked in wearing an expensive suit and a big-shot attitude, behind which he unsuccessfully tried to hide his nervousness. He was interviewing for TV; he really didn't know how to interview for a civil-service position. I was worried about his ability to make the transition.

"Tell me again," I asked. "You make $600,000 a year and you want this job that pays $95,000?" You had to wonder about his sanity.

"I've got to tell you," he said. "This is something I've wanted to do all my life." I was familiar with that kind of dedication and felt an immediate rapport. Miller knew cops, he had worked with them on stories, he knew the life. He was single, willing to get up at two in the morning and go chase calls. He would rather hang out with cops than go home. A successful career as a reporter had earned him a city full of great sources. He was a good writer and a ready raconteur. Having covered so many press conferences, he knew how to prepare for them and how to give the press what it wanted. I was a commissioner who was more than happy to talk to the press, who wanted an open administration, and he wanted to be on the team.

Okay. Miller would work out. I notified the Hall.

My transition team sat around a table at Bob Johnson's First Security Services offices in Boston and reported in. Things were bad: A major corruption probe was about to break; department morale was terrible; the uniforms looked like crap; the budget was going to hell. Dean Esserman, who by this time was deputy chief of police in New Haven, Connecticut, said, "There are going to be two big differences from the last time you came to New York. Last time, no one knew who you were. You picked up a place, you put it together, and you couldn't do anything wrong. Now, you're coming back as the man who saved the New York subway system, the man who led the Transit Police to victory. How are you going to beat those expectations?

"Second," he went on. "Last time, you came alone. There was a rumor you were going to bring people with you, and everyone in transit felt like they were going to be replaced. This time you want to bring in some of your own team. That could be a concern."

Bob Wasserman said, "The five super chiefs run the department." He named them. "They're Ray Kelly's people. They're going to kill you. They will control your time from the moment you wake up until the moment you go to bed, to keep you busy and out of the running of the organization. They will front you for speeches and meetings. They don't want the police commissioner to do anything. They just need a front man. So unless you get control of your schedule, they will control you. They're waiting to set you up."

I heard everyone's report, then I slammed my hand on the table. "Listen," I said, "I've just heard all the problems with the NYPD and the obstacles that are going to overwhelm us. Very good. Now we're going to go back around the room and you're going to tell me the solutions to these problems. You're going to tell me what we need to do. The day I walk in, I intend to hit the ground running. I want all resignations on my desk before I arrive. I will put my people in place on many levels, so I need to know who those people are. They're in the department. I don't have them. You find them. And when we finish going around this table again, you're going to have solutions. That's why I brought you aboard, that's why you'll stay aboard. I don't intend to be overwhelmed by them or by this job, I intend to overwhelm them."

We weren't going to get killed, we were going to win. We would have a plan; they would contribute substantially to it, and they would make it work. I could feel the room go, "Well, all right!"

Maple, through his own sources and Wasserman's leads, had found a number of people in the organization who were well thought of as crime fighters. He organized secret meetings at the Sheepshead Bay Yacht Club, this old, broken-down place in Brooklyn where they weren't likely to be noticed, and he picked their brains. It was immediately clear that the New York City Police Department was dysfunctional.

First, it was divided into little fiefdoms, and some bureau chiefs didn't even talk to each other. OCCB didn't talk to patrol, patrol didn't get along with the Detective Bureau, and nobody talked to internal affairs. There was no coordination of effort. It wasn't even a priority. And it appeared that nobody in the department was dealing with the quality-of-life issue.

The organization was very military oriented, with a strict chain of command, and information didn't flow easily from one bureau to another. Each bureau was like a silo: Information entered at the bottom and had to be delivered up the chain of command from one level to another until it reached the chief's office. There it would wait to be dealt with. Even when a memo finally arrived, there was a less-than-acceptable level of cooperation between bureaus. At some point, it seemed like one would call another and have to take a number, like in a bakery.

"We have a drug problem up here in Washington Heights."

"Sorry, we'll get to you in a couple of months. Narcotics is very busy now."

Once the chief's decision was finally made, it had to be sent back to the bureau that requested the service and work its way back down that chain of command. It's a wonder anything got done.

When Maple analyzed the bureaus, the news got worse. How was the NYPD deployed? The Narcotics Bureau, he discovered, worked largely nine to five or five to one, Monday through Friday. The warrant squad was off weekends. Auto-crimes squad, off weekends. Robbery squads? Off weekends. The community-policing officers—those six thousand baby-faced twenty-two-year-olds who were going to solve all the neighborhoods' problems—off weekends. Essentially, except for the detectives, patrol officers, and some other operations going round the clock, the whole place took Saturdays and Sundays off. The criminal element was working nights, they were working weekends, they worked late shifts and legal holidays. They were working harder and smarter than we were. No wonder crime was up, and prevention was down.

The NYPD had people bluffed. They had the reputation as the greatest crime-fighting machine in the history of policing, but the big blue wall was a lot of blue smoke and a few mirrors. They were good at responding to crime, they just weren't very good at preventing it. They weren't even trying to prevent it. They were cleaning up around it. My administration was going to commit itself to crime *prevention*.

If the NYPD was a bigger problem than we'd thought, so was the city. We identified the major problems: guns, youth violence, drugs, domestic violence, quality of life, car theft, police integrity, and traffic. Then we set about to develop strategies to deal with them.

I tried to persuade Bob Wasserman to join me at the NYPD. I would have given him any position he wanted. His presence and progressive policing ideas would have been a tremendous plus for New York. Ultimately, he decided to go to Washington and be Lee Brown's chief of staff when Brown became President Clinton's cabinet-level drug czar.

Meanwhile, Giuliani's people had begun to push their agenda. Two of his representatives, Dick Koehler and Richard Schwartz, presented us with a sixteen-item list of campaign promises, including getting rid of the squeegee people, and said, in essence, "You need to do these things in the first ten days." I told them we had a series of initiatives to reduce crime and systematically move the organization forward, as I had promised at my announcement, but that I would handle some of their requests, particularly the squeegee issue, immediately. I wanted to keep them happy, but I was not about to let them even begin to micromanage my department. We knew what had to be done. More important, we knew how to do it. That's what we'd been hired for.

Chapter 13

THE MOSQUE INCIDENT OCCURRED MY FIRST DAY ON THE JOB AND GAVE ME A quick immersion into New York policing and politics. In my first week, I had already been threatened with being fired. The department was in transition, we had a mayor who clearly wanted a large hand in police matters, we were going to have immediate issues every day to deal with, but we were looking at the big picture. I made it very clear within the department that we would not be ruled by the crisis of the day; we would handle all the police emergencies for which New York was famous, but we would keep our eyes on the more significant goal of reorganizing the NYPD and bringing down crime.

John Miller got a call from Cristyne Lategano, Mayor Giuliani's communications director. "What's Bratton got coming up?" They were relentless.

"Well, he's got the Channel 7 show and the Gabe Pressman Sunday talk show . . ."

"No more profiles in the papers," she told him. "And cancel all those appearances."

I had already accepted an invitation to appear on WCBS-TV's *Sunday Edition* the following week, and the Hall decided I could do it because they couldn't provide a persuasive reason to cancel. After that, Miller spent much of his time trying to keep me out of the papers. It was not the job he had envisioned. "We are developing crime strategies," Miller told every reporter who would listen. "We came in and told the city what we are going to do. Now we are behind closed doors, and rather than talking about the strategies, we'll be working on them. There will be no time for the commissioner to talk to the press." We called it "taking the submarine under."

That worked for a while, but eventually reporters want to talk to a new police commissioner to get the department's plans and views. The media kept taking soundings, and after a while the enforced silence became more than uncomfortable. About two weeks had gone by when David Seifman, a columnist for the *New York Post*, called Miller and said, "We understand the commissioner has been muzzled."

"Whatever gave you that idea?" Miller told him. "Let me get right back to you."

Miller called the Hall. "Seifman's on the phone saying we've been 'muzzled.' What do I tell him?"

"Tell him you haven't been muzzled."

Miller called back with the nondenial denial. "Look," he said, "he's been the most high-profile commissioner you could imagine. He's been on the talk shows, he's been at press conferences, there's not a day goes by that he's not in the papers. If that's a muzzle, I don't know what a muzzle is."

I had intended to use the media to influence the public, the cops, and the bad guys. We had a message to get out, and I wanted it broadcast. This was going to present a problem, but first things first. I concentrated on the mayor's request. The squeegee issue was closest to his heart. It alone might have won him the election. The squeegee people were a living symbol of what was wrong with the city.

During the campaign, Giuliani hit Mayor Dinkins very effectively over the steep decline in the quality of life. The presence of squeegee people was one of the most visible and annoying examples of this decline. It seemed as if any time a driver stopped at a red light, men and women approached the car, wiping the windshield with squeegees or rags or newspaper or whatever they had in their hands . . . and asking for money. They seemed to swarm particularly at the entrances and exits to every bridge, tunnel, and highway going into and out of New York City, a thoroughly unpleasant de facto welcoming committee. Implicitly—and often not so implicitly—they threatened motorists. You didn't give them a quarter or a dollar at your peril; they were perfectly capable of hitting your window or scratching your vehicle if you didn't come across.

The general feeling was that there was nothing anybody could do to get rid of them. This was a big broken window that wasn't being fixed, and the more squeegee assaults you saw, the more you felt the city was being abandoned. This sense of futility festered into real anger, and Giuliani used it to his advantage. Dinkins was losing votes around quality-of-life issues, and the NYPD under Ray Kelly made fixing the problem a priority. George Kelling came down from Harvard, and Mike Julian developed a strategy to deal with it.

The police department had always thrown numbers at the community. "Look at all of our arrests, look at our activity." But the department only measured activity, it didn't measure results. Civilians who complained about the squeegee men were in the same situation as the guy at I Street and East Seventh in Southie who placed 1,300 calls to 911 and never got satisfaction. The cops were a powerful group who could walk into community meetings and say, "It's the criminal-justice system that doesn't take this seriously, it's the judges who let these squeegee guys go, it's the society who created them in the first place. Don't blame us." People would back off because numbers don't lie, and so nothing ever got done.

But it was a lie. The strategies the NYPD was using were not effective, and the department knew it. They'd go after squeegee people and for a month show substantial arrests and summonses, but there was no urgency. They'd go after them for an hour, once a week. It was the same as working with prostitutes; if you tell them "Friday is sweep day, I'm going to arrest you; the rest of the week you can make all the money you want," you are inviting failure. Success comes with constant attention.

Could we move the squeegee people? Isn't begging covered under the First Amendment's protection of free speech? In the past, when the police arrested the squeegee people for interfering with traffic, the New York Civil Liberties Union was prepared to step in with an injunction, and they would have been right because the cops were applying the wrong law. Julian's group found a law directly on point: Traffic Regulation 4–04, which prohibited approaching a vehicle to wash a windshield. The NYCLU backed off. Its outspoken executive director, Norman Siegel, said he didn't agree with the law, but the cops weren't acting illegally by enforcing it.

It became the policy of each precinct to check their squeegee corners every two hours to ensure that the people were either chased away, issued summonses, or arrested.

In the past, none of the squeegee people had answered summonses. If they were given one, they disregarded it. With Traffic Regulation 4–04 in hand, the cops changed policy by warning them that they would be taken to jail. This immediately reduced the number of squeegee people by 40 percent; they left. The 60 percent that remained got arrested. Of those, it was found that half had previous arrests for serious felonies: robbery, assault, burglary, larceny, or carrying a gun. Almost half had been arrested for drug offenses.

As soon as they got arrested, they didn't return. In a month, the squeegee people were gone. It turned out that, despite seeming to be everywhere, there had been only seventy-five squeegee people in New York. They had worked only in high-visibility clusters, and when they were gone, their absence was highly visible, too. Sitting at a light without being hassled reminded New Yorkers of what they had missed.

This turnaround was effected by Dinkins and Kelly. When I arrived, we kept up the police presence and pressure. Ironically, Giuliani and I got the credit for their initiative, but understandably Giuliani was happy to take credit for making squeegee people an issue during the campaign and spurring the action. I saw the squeegee population as a fitting symbol of the sad state of the previous NYPD. They had given up. It was a damning confession: The world's greatest police force hadn't been able to handle seventy-five street people toting rags and sticks. Only politics prevented David Dinkins and Ray Kelly from receiving their due.

With all the resignations on my desk, I replaced four super chiefs. Unfortunately, NYPD resignations take thirty days to finalize, and I had created an awkward situation in which three-star chiefs were hanging around marking time for a month while the younger one-stars who replaced them were eager to begin doing their jobs. I should have handled things differently. But with Timoney, Julian, Anemone, Borrelli, and Reuther in place, Dave Scott as my first deputy commissioner, Jack Maple as my deputy commissioner for Crime Control Strategies, Miller as my DCPI, and Peter LaPorte as my chief of staff, I had put together a Dream Team of police professionals that was experienced, energized, and full of good ideas.

While we were working on our new policing initiatives, I supported a proposal from John Linder that the Police Foundation hire Linder's firm to work up what he called a "cultural diagnostic" of the NYPD. He defined this cultural diagnostic as "an analytical tool that determines the cultural factors impeding performance and the corrective values that must be employed as principles for organizational change. . . . To this end, the analysis defines the cultural assets; cultural obstacles to change; inherited operating culture; inherited core identity; projected core identity; and value or values that must guide revision of key organizational systems to institutionalize a new, high-performance culture." We both believed that change can be brought about rapidly by the creation of and reaction to a "discernible crisis," which leads to self-confrontation and requires both strategizing and action to correct.

I appointed Pat Kelleher as director of the department's reengineering process. Kelleher, like Marty O'Boyle, had been identified as another superstar. Over time, I came to be extraordinarily impressed with Kelleher, and when Walter Mack was removed, I promoted him to head up internal affairs.

I involved more than three hundred people from every NYPD rank and bureau and formed twelve reengineering teams on productivity, discipline, in-service training, supervisory training, precinct organization, building community partnerships, geographical and functional organizational structure, paperwork, rewards and career paths, equipment and uniforms, technology, and integrity. They surveyed nearly eight thousand cops and eventually made more than six hundred recommendations, of which 80 percent were eventually accepted. What they found was striking:

- At the highest levels of the organization, the basic aim of the NYPD was not to bring down crime but to avoid criticism from the media, politicians, and the public. As one police executive put it, "Nobody ever lost a command because crime went up. You lose a command because the loudest voices in the community don't like you, or because of a bad newspaper story, or because of corruption."
- The greater the distance from headquarters, the lesser the trust from one rank to the next. Exclusion was the rule. Creativity was actively discouraged. One commander said of his troops, "I have three hundred potential [career] assassins in my unit."
- Police officers believed the department had not backed them up, even when their actions were warranted.
- The department was structured to protect its good name (and the careers of its senior executives) rather than to achieve crime-fighting goals.

- The Internal Affairs Bureau was seen as intent on tripping up officers for minor infractions rather than rooting out real corruption.
- The mayor and my strongly voiced support for the department had encouraged people throughout the organization, but they were waiting to see what we would do.

They found a wide disparity between what was said by the bosses and what the officers believed was actually wanted. Officers felt they were in a twilight zone where staying out of trouble—and thus keeping their bosses out of trouble—was more important than achieving anything concrete and measurable in fighting crime.

CONSIDERED BY OFFICERS MOST IMPORTANT TO THE DEPARTMENT
1. Write summonses
2. Hold down overtime
3. Stay out of trouble
4. Clear backlog of radio runs
5. Report police corruption
6. Treat bosses with deference
7. Reduce crime, disorder, and fear

CONSIDERED BY OFFICERS MOST IMPORTANT TO THEMSELVES
1. Reduce crime, disorder, and fear
2. Make gun arrests
3. Provide police services to people who request them
4. Gain public confidence in police integrity
5. Arrest drug dealers
6. Correct quality-of-life conditions
7. Stay out of trouble

Maple and Timoney became good friends, but they had it out. Maple had been quoted by the writer Jack Newfield as saying, "Those guys over there at the NYPD have given up on crime fighting." Timoney was livid and confronted Maple.

"When have you guys ever addressed crime?" Maple demanded.

"What the hell are you talking about? Operation Pressure Point. Operation Take Back. Ben Ward dealt with it seriously."

"No, no, the NYPD never focused on crime. What are precinct commanders judged on? Corruption. Always. If you keep your nose clean, stay out of trouble, and don't rock the boat, you're gonna get promoted. No commander is held responsible for crime figures."

Timoney took it personally. When he'd had the Fifth Precinct, he had concentrated on crime, but as a former narcotics cop that was his background.

"That's not the point," Maple argued. "I'm not talking about individual commanders, I'm talking about the department. No one is held account-able. If your crime rates go up, okay they go up, so what. If you've got any kind of answer, you're fine. You're not going to lose your command over crime out of control. But one corrupt cop and you're dead."

Timoney couldn't deny it. The department required each commander to produce a state-of-command report listing the five top priorities of their precinct. Ever since the 1970 Knapp Commission, which publicized the NYPD's institutionalized corruption and made Frank Serpico a household name, the number one priority was always controlling corruption. The rest varied from commander to commander, but crime was way down the list. To prevent cops from being corrupted, bosses took them away from temp-tation, which meant out of proactive situations. They might set up crime-fighting units, but they saddled the cops with so many constraints that they were effectively prevented from doing their jobs.

For instance, it's incredibly difficult for a police officer to make a legally sound drug-dealing arrest while in uniform. He or she might stumble on a deal, but by and large, who's going to sell drugs to a uniformed cop? When we set up drug-bust units, we need to allow cops to work in plain clothes. However, plain clothes is where corruption might occur, with an officer pocketing drugs or money, and commanders were more worried about their cops going bad and sabotaging the boss's career than about making good arrests. Therefore, the arrests didn't get made, or were made strictly for the numbers and without any real concern for eliminating the problem, the crimes kept being committed, the bosses kept moving up the ladder, the cops kept being frustrated, and the streets remained dan-gerous. While there were individual commanders who trusted their cops and made fighting crime a priority, the department was institutionally paralyzed.

"Tell me I'm wrong," said Maple.

"You know," said Timoney, "I hate you, but you're right."

Timoney, good Catholic that he is, believes that confession is good for the soul and allows you to start anew. He felt that before we could go

forward we had to make certain admissions. He made them in public fo-
rums and on television. He began speaking to cops and telling them, "The
NYPD hasn't done its job in twenty-five years. We failed. . . . I failed to do
this job. I made a lot of arrests, but you know what? I wasn't doing my job,
either. But I'm going to start doing it from now on."

Maple was a holy terror. Timoney called him a pit bull; he was absolutely relentless. Once he came up with an idea, you couldn't dissuade
him, you couldn't knock him off course. He knew the criminal mind—"It
isn't a very sophisticated mind," Timoney loved to add—he knew the bad
guys' vulnerabilities, he knew what made them tick.

I wanted to know the size of our crime problem. Maple knew New York
City's 1993 crime figures off the top of his head: 1,946 murders, 86,000
robberies, 99,000 burglaries, 112,000 car thefts. (Jack knew his figures cold.
People in the office started calling him "Rain Man.") He told me, "Look,
we've got to track something else here. How many people are shot in this
city?" We found that 5,861 people were shot in New York City in 1993. The
difference between a shooting and a murder is usually a quarter of an
inch; they hit an artery, or they don't. "Okay," he announced, "*this* is the
size of the problem."

John Miller had developed a system in which he could receive breaking
information over his beeper. Maple told operations, "I want a phone call
at home every time we fire a gun and hit somebody."

They were a little put back. "You know how many times we're gonna
have to beep you?"

"Yeah, I know exactly. There were 442 incidences of police firing their
guns last year, and I think we hit about eighty. Plus, I want to get beeped
from the detectives on every murder. I don't care what time it is, I want to
be beeped."

A few days into my term, I said to Maple, "You know, it doesn't seem
that busy around here." In my morning summary, I was getting reports of
a water-main break here, a power outage there, and a brief synopsis of
major crime events.

"Commissioner, are you jerking me or what? We're living in a fool's
paradise. It's like pulling teeth to find out how many people got murdered
last week."

"Louie," he said to Chief of Patrol Louis Anemone, "we need to know
where we're at, weekly, with the crime."

This was a first for the NYPD. They only compiled crime statistics for
Uniform Crime Reporting purposes, a collecting point for the FBI, and

then only quarterly. As far as the department had been concerned, statistics were not for use in combating crime, they were only for keeping score at the end of the year. Even then, the only statistics they paid attention to were the robberies. But even that was smoke and mirrors. Each precinct was required to send robbery statistics to headquarters, but no innovations came out of it. Nobody used them for anything.

"The first week they gave me a pile of papers that were written in fuckin' crayon," Maple complained. That just got him mad. Then Joe Borrelli's staff said, "The chief of detectives has decided you can only get this monthly."

"You know," he told them, "I'm not really concerned about what his thoughts are. We're gonna get this weekly now." Maple knew he had my backing. I had told the command staff that when Maple spoke, he spoke for me. I was sworn in on January 10. February 7, we began getting our full set of weekly figures. And, more important, we were going to use them.

Maple pored over the stats. "Louie," he said, "in every precinct they should have maps of robberies, of burglaries, of shootings, narcotics arrests, gun arrests, so they can see how to deploy. There's no maps in these precincts. Whatever maps there are are four years old. You gotta have them up-to-date. We've got a war on crime, how do you go to war without a map? Hannibal had a map and that was in 218 B.C." Needless to say, I thought this was a great idea.

The NYPD was a fearful, centralized bureaucracy with little focus on goals. We created a crisis of confidence and encouraged everyone in it to rise to the challenge. The NYPD was not nearly as good as everyone thought it was, and it certainly was not as good as my team thought it could be.

Our first initiative was the Gun Strategy. We expanded on the concepts I had presented to Giuliani when I'd been interviewed in November.

When we arrived, suspects arrested in possession of a weapon in New York City were not necessarily asked, "Where'd you get the gun?" You'd think it would be one of the first questions, but often it never got asked. There was an eight-page order stating precisely what an officer was to do with a gun suspect: Run the person's stats through a computer to see if he or she was one of the 33,000 known gun violators who had been locked up previously on weapons charges. If they were, a special team of detectives came down to interview them about the case—not about the gun and where it might have come from; about that particular case. If they weren't previous violators, the detectives didn't talk to them at all. Maple found that even once these reports had been taken, the department was six months behind in filing them. The order also said arresting officers were supposed to turn gun arrests into confidential informants (CIs).

Under the new gun strategy, we first tried to build a solid case and get the suspect's inculpatory statement. Then, *every* gun suspect was interviewed by a detective. This was an important innovation. Let's actually get some bad guys. The detectives and arresting officers pursued any and all accomplices. As at transit, we made it department policy to arrest everyone involved in a crime, not just one perp to get it off the books. It's a cop's assumption that someone involved in a gun arrest is likely not a first timer. As at transit, we checked for wants, and if we found them we called in complainants from those other crimes to pick the suspects from photo arrays or out of lineups. Last, but not least, we asked the suspects *"Where did you get the gun?"* and *"Do you know anybody else with more guns?"* Our policy was: "Just ask."

Maple understood that people like to talk. Often, by this time, the suspect was willing to deal. We then got search warrants, hit the houses where the other guns were kept, busted the occupants, brought in more guns and suspects, and started the process all over again. We matched guns used in more than one crime and traced them to illegal sellers across the country. It was elementary, but it had never been done.

Maple was excellent at devising strategies, but when he put them on paper something was missing. Assigned the task of creating the first strategy, he assembled the traditional NYPD bureaucracy, and after a week of hard work and bitter debate they delivered a document to me.

I was aghast. The document didn't state the problem, it didn't address the issues, it didn't present the vision I wanted to impart. It was quite clear that within the department there were those who resisted the idea of criticizing the organization or even endorsing the concept of great change, because that would imply criticism of the department and its past leaders. I was very disappointed. Maple had the concepts and could articulate them with great flair orally, but they did not translate onto paper. I turned to John Linder to take over the writing process.

After talking with me at length to find out what I wanted, Linder crafted a twenty-page booklet stating the problem and our current practice in dealing with it and then outlining our new methods of attacking it. Linder, Maple, and others on Maple's task force had heated disagreements over the language and presentation. Linder felt we couldn't write about new ideas without comparing them to the old. Maple felt that would be taking unnecessary swipes at previous administrations and at Ray Kelly in particular, many members of whose inner circle were now key players in my administration and found themselves in the difficult position of criticizing their former boss. They fought it out, the marketer and the strategist, and ultimately Linder won my support. We hammered out a strategy that said what it meant and would be clear to the cops. For example, after stating that in 1993, 11,222 arrests were made for crimes in which a firearm was confiscated and that it was department policy to try and turn those arrested into CIs, the written strategy said, "Fact: The combined efforts [of the NYPD detectives] yielded four confidential informants." It was brutal but effective.

We put the Gun Strategy on paper and sent it over to City Hall. All written strategies were to be approved by the Hall before they were announced to the public. The mayor had campaigned on the issue of crime reduction and understandably needed to be involved in the announcements of initiatives on the issue. It stalled. They questioned when we should do it, how we should do it, why we should do it. They nitpicked it endlessly without ever changing it substantively. The mind games designed to show who was in control had begun. Getting City Hall approval for each successive strategy was a tortuous process and to the best of my recollection never added anything substantive to the documents.

When they finally approved the strategy, Miller said, "If we're going to get this on the air and in the papers, we're going to have to put on a fairly decent dog and pony show." (Miller knew, as I did, that cops weren't going to get the news of the Gun Strategy from some interoffice memo; they were going to see it on TV or read about it in the *Daily News*.) He asked Ray O'Donnell, the day lieutenant who effectively ran the press office in Miller's absence, how many guns we could get. The answer from the property clerk's office was that they could probably put together around ten thousand guns. "What do ten thousand guns look like?" he asked. "A lot." We then got word from the mayor's communications director, Cristyne Lategano, "No guns."

"No guns!" Miller said. "What do you mean?"

"The mayor doesn't like guns."

"Well, we don't like guns either. That was kind of the point."

"He doesn't want any guns at City Hall. He's worried that people are going to ask him to hold one and it's going to look stupid."

Miller said, "Come on, Cristyne, this is the guy who rode around in a Hell's Angels jacket with Al D'Amato." (As U.S. attorney, Giuliani had gone undercover with New York's junior senator at a drug bust and was photographed looking like a cross between the Wild One and one of the Village People.)

"That's precisely what he's worried about."

"I'll tell you what. He doesn't have to hold any."

"No," said Lategano. "He simply won't do it."

Miller couldn't believe a strategy that would take guns off the city's streets would be delayed because the mayor was worried about a photo opportunity. "Why don't we have the press conference over here? That way we don't have to transport ten thousand guns to City Hall, and it won't be such a spectacle, but the mayor will have the backdrop and get the front-page picture he wants."

It was finally resolved to hold the press conference at police head-quarters, where we would lay out the weapons, but the mayor didn't have to touch any of them. That was fine with us. Always known for his pointed humor, Miller quipped, "The last guy we want running around head-quarters with a gun is Rudy Giuliani."

Chapter 14

I HAD FOUND ELAINE'S THROUGH MAPLE AND MILLER. IT WAS THEIR hangout. Elaine's is what's known in New York as a "watering hole," and its clientele is a mix of intellectuals, celebrities, and the press, particularly gossip columnists, as well as New Yorkers who want a good meal and an enjoyable place to talk. Maple the tunnel rat was pleased to be a fixture in such an in spot.

While Maple and Miller seemed to be there every night closing the place, Cheryl and I went once every two or three weeks. Word got out that we were hanging at Elaine's, and it added to our Runyonesque work hard/play hard image, but the reality was far less spectacular than the perception. People may have conjured the image of us all slugging down shots, but I'm not much of a drinker. I might go up for dinner and join the guys for a Diet Coke, but I'd be long gone and they'd continue their plotting and conniving. Maple and Miller knew they might get called to a crime scene at any time, and they tempered themselves, so they wouldn't be going out with half a load on. Maple usually drank cup after cup of double espresso.

One night as I sat with him, Maple was doodling on a napkin, trying to figure out how to stop crime. He decided it came down to four elements:

1. Where are the crimes happening? Put them on a map. What are the times by day of the week, by time of day?
2. Here are the crimes, you've got them on a map. Let's coordinate the efforts between detectives and plainclothes and get there fast so we can catch the crooks.
3. What are we going to do once we get there? Are we doing decoys? Are we doing buy-and-bust operations? Are we doing warrant enforcement? Quality-of-life enforcement? What works?
4. Is it working? The precinct commander is in charge of the plan to reduce crime in his or her area; is that plan being pushed forward? Did they know where the crimes were happening? Were the efforts coordinated? Were the tactics effective? Was crime going down?

Maple had captured on his napkin the essence of all our strategies. To control crime we must at all times have:

- Accurate and Timely Intelligence
- Rapid Deployment
- Effective Tactics
- Relentless Follow-up and Assessment.

These are the concepts on which the turnaround of New York policing was built, and they bear discussing. I had become a staunch advocate of using private-sector business practices and principles for the management of the NYPD, even using the business term "reengineered" rather than the public policy term "reinventing" government. We further defined these four crime-reduction principles:

Accurate and Timely Intelligence. If the police are to respond effectively to crime and to criminal events, officers at all levels have to have accurate knowledge of when particular types of crimes are occurring, how and where the crimes are being committed, and who the criminals are. The likelihood of an effective police response to crime increases proportionally as the accuracy of this intelligence increases.

Rapid Deployment of Personnel and Resources. Once a crime pattern has been identified, an array of personnel and other necessary resources are promptly deployed to deal with it. Although some tactical plans might involve only patrol personnel, for example, experience has proved that the most effective plans require personnel from several units. A viable and comprehensive response to a crime or quality-of-life problem generally demands that patrol personnel, investigators, and support personnel use their expertise and resources in a coordinated effort.

Effective Tactics. In order to avoid merely displacing crime and quality-of-life problems, and in order to bring about permanent change, these tactics must be comprehensive, flexible, and adaptable to the shifting crime trends we identify and monitor.

Relentless Follow-up and Assessment. As in any problem-solving endeavor, an ongoing process of rigorous follow-up and assessment is absolutely essential to ensure that the desired results are actually being achieved. This evaluation also permits us to assess particular tactical responses and to incorporate the knowledge we gain into our subsequent efforts. By knowing how well a particular tactic worked on a particular crime, and by knowing which specific elements worked most effectively, we are better able to construct and implement effective responses for similar problems in the future. The process also permits us to redeploy resources to meet newly identified challenges once a problem has abated.

Maple put it most succinctly. Think of the Battle of Britain: Germany was getting ready to invade the British Isles. The British had fled Dunkirk and had only 450 Spitfires to protect their cities, while the Germans had thousands of bombers able to attack anywhere in England. However, the British had one thing the Germans didn't: radar. Despite very few resources, the British knew where the enemy was. Using their radar information, they were able to mobilize the 450 Spitfires exactly against the German bombers. Timely, accurate intelligence; rapid response; effective tactics; relentless follow-up—that's what won the Battle of Britain and that's how we were going to win the battle of New York.

We rolled out crime strategies consistently for the next two years. The second was the Youth Violence Strategy. Juvenile crime was New York City's growth industry. Kids were attacking, robbing, and killing people, especially other kids, in epidemic proportions. Homicide was the leading cause of death for New Yorkers between the ages of fifteen and twenty-four. One-third of all arrests involving firearms in the first ten months of 1993 were for crimes committed by children between the ages of seven and nineteen. Violence inside the city's public schools was skyrocketing. JoAnne de Jesus, the mother of a twelve-year-old who had been cornered in a Brooklyn public-school washroom, said, "The problem is that students aren't fighting with their fists anymore. They're fighting with guns." I'm a great believer that all behavior is learned. Many New York kids were learning on the streets, which had become killing grounds.

We extended the four crime-reduction principles to this problem. We surveyed the statistics and found that fully 40 percent of crime committed during school hours was committed by kids under sixteen. We found that many of the daytime victims were kids, as well. But kids, by law, *must* attend school. If they're in school, they're not outside robbing people or being robbed. If muggers can't find a victim, there's no mugging. We made the public schools our focal point. We instituted a citywide truancy program in which we patrolled neighborhoods, swept school-age kids off the streets, and brought them to school where they belonged. We picked up so many, we had to set up "catchment" areas in school auditoriums and gymnasiums.

Timoney had worked on the truancy issue as a deputy chief in Manhattan South. He broke the truants into three groups. First there were the hard-core truants who would go out the door the next day no matter how many times we brought them back. No one knew the size of that group. Second were the kids who skipped school because there were no consequences for doing so. "Why not skip? Nobody's gonna bother us." When cops were outside to bring them back and call their parents, they would get discouraged. Third was the group that bolted because of peer pressure, the kids who didn't have an answer to the schoolyard question, "What's the matter, nothing's gonna happen, you got no balls?" Timoney's sense was that 70 percent of the truants fell into this third group, and we gave them an out. "The damn cops are out there, they're gonna grab me and call my mother. I'd book in a minute, but I can't." We created a situation that allowed that group to save face and stay in school.

As I had done in Boston, we created the position of youth officer and assigned three to each precinct to develop youth initiatives and to get to know the kids in the precincts and schools. We revised department policy by negotiating with the schools chancellor in an effort to ensure that all crimes in and around schools were reported to us so we could respond. We proposed creating a database cross-referencing juvenile reports, truancy, and gang information, for use by the precinct commander and Family Court. We expanded the training of our cops. We also used the media to deliver our message and presented Sergeant Helen Rossi, who had been doing this work for ten years, as the embodiment of our anti-truancy efforts and paraded her before the press. Now, not only Sergeant Rossi but the entire NYPD was after these truants. We got great headlines and sent the right message.

The New York Civil Liberties Union expressed some consternation the first few weeks we put the program into practice, but our strategy had an immediate and dramatic impact on juvenile crime, and the outcry subsided.

We systematically implemented and released the Drug, Domestic Violence, Quality of Life, Auto Crime, and Integrity (Anticorruption) strategies. All were filled with innovations, and all were operated on our four guiding principles.

Drugs. Previously, Tactical Narcotics Teams (TNT) moved into drug-infested neighborhoods for specifically limited periods, worked intensively, encouraged those in the neighborhood to give them tips on illegal activity, and then moved on. Personnel came to work on weekdays, made relatively few arrests after six at night, and were basically not there on weekends. *Fact: These hours became known to drug traffickers working the streets, who could easily ply their trade accordingly.* The department held meetings with the neighborhood groups in the targeted precincts before, during, and after TNT operations. Drug dealers sometimes attended these meetings and were able to adjust the places and times of their own operations.

We targeted open-air drug activity, driving it off the streets and then closing and, where possible, seizing the inside locations. We confiscated and traced the guns we found on drug dealers, put cops in those areas we knew to be drug markets, more aggressively targeted low- and middle-level dealers and suppliers, and coordinated our efforts with federal and state forces to get local high-level suppliers. We trusted precinct cops to work in plain clothes, and empowered precinct commanders to authorize them to make arrests seven days a week, twenty-four hours a day. Working with the D.A.s, we also authorized the precincts to get their own narcotics-search warrants.

Narcotics and guns are inseparable—find one and you find the other. Before, they had been designated as separate and distinct investigations. We began to use the gun strategy on narcotics collars. Ask them, "Where'd you get the gun?" Track the guns back, get more, keep going.

The concept that conquered fare beating in the subways was put to use against the drug dealers. We were working in partnership with the Drug Enforcement Administration at the time, and Maple said, "Why don't we go after drug dealers with the quality-of-life violations?"

The feds spoke to him as if he were just a little slow. "Well, Commissioner, we don't do things like that." Quality-of-life arrests were small potatoes to them.

"All right," said Maple, "amuse me, okay? Every drug dealer in the world has a phony cloned beeper and phony cloned cell phone. They cannot help themselves. If they have millions, they don't want to pay. Just like all gangsters use bad credit cards—they can't help themselves. Let's lock them up for the phony cloned phones and see what happens. And you might even hear more drug traffic on the phones you're listening to. We'll see. The people we arrest for the phones, they're not going to know it's a joke. Amuse me." So they grabbed a guy with a cloned cell phone, and he gave up a string of murders. It's the same concept as busting Al Capone for tax evasion.

Domestic violence. The department had no system to identify and track repeat calls, so there was no way to alert police officers in the field to locations that had numerous calls for help in the past or a history of violence. In 1993, there had been 178,000 domestic-violence calls; the NYPD had filled out only 58,000 reports and made only 12,000 arrests. We developed a domestic-incident report and tracked and monitored all instances of domestic violence, including crimes other than those defined in the law as family offenses. We gave a higher-priority response to calls involving violations of protection orders—that was a must-arrest. We trained officers to identify patterns of abuse. Even when the abused party didn't press charges, if the officer thought differently, an arrest was made. We insisted the detectives follow up and make arrests in situations where the violator had already fled the scene. We made it department policy to emphasize problem-solving tactics to enforce the law and deter family violence and held detectives accountable for follow-up on these cases. John Timoney personally directed this initiative. He was one of the top experts in the state, if not the country, on this issue.

Quality of life. Boom boxes, squeegee people, street prostitutes, public drunks, panhandlers, reckless bicyclists, illegal after-hours joints, graffiti—New York was overrun. We called Police Strategy Number 5 "Reclaiming the Public Spaces of New York." It was the linchpin strategy. Many have come to attribute the rapid decline in crime in New York City to the quality-of-life enforcement efforts, but that's simplistic. It was one of a number of strategies that were deployed.

My experience in District 4 in Boston had shown me the importance of cleaning up the streets and improving the quality of life. We could solve all the murders we liked, but if the average citizen was running a gauntlet of panhandlers every day on his way to and from work, he would want that issue solved.

Previous police administrations had been handcuffed by restrictions. We took the handcuffs off. Department attorneys worked with precinct commanders to address the problems. We used civil law to enforce existing regulations against harassment, assault, menacing, disorderly conduct, and damaging property. We stepped up enforcement of the laws against public drunkenness and public urination and arrested repeat violators, including those who threw empty bottles in the street or were involved in even relatively minor damage to property. No more D.A.T.s. If you peed in the street, you were going to jail. We were going to fix the broken windows and prevent anyone from breaking them again.

Time and time again, when cops interrupt someone drinking on the street or a gang of kids drinking on the corner, pat them down, and find a gun or a knife, they have prevented what would have happened two or three hours later when that same person, drunk, pulled out that gun or knife. We prevented the crime before it happened. New York City police would be about prevention, and we would do it lawfully.

"Your open beer lets me check your ID," explained Maple. "Now I can radio the precinct for outstanding warrants or parole violations. Maybe I bump against that bulge in your belt; with probable cause, I can frisk you." Again the word would get out, leave your weapons home.

Who was going to implement our new strategies? Our cultural diagnostic showed that most bosses stifled those under them. To shake up the old thinking that was preventing the organization from performing at top capacity, I flattened the organizational layer cake by eliminating an entire level of executive supervision.

For policing purposes, the NYPD had divided the city's five boroughs into seven patrol boroughs: Manhattan North, Manhattan South, Brooklyn North, Brooklyn South, the Bronx, Queens, and Staten Island. We went further, dividing Queens and its eighteen precincts into Queens North and Queens South. The boroughs were divided into divisions, the divisions into precincts. A precinct commander sent his reports up to a division inspector, who had a deputy inspector working for him. The division inspector sent it up to the borough commander, who had an executive officer. I eliminated the entire level of divisions so that the precinct commander reported directly to the borough commander.

I cut staff at headquarters and in the special units, such as the Detective and Organized Crime Control Bureaus, and added it to the precincts. In New York City, that's where the rubber hits the road. And the people who run the precincts are the precinct commanders.

Each precinct commander was college-educated, averaged fifteen years on the job, had risen to a significant position of responsibility (I intended to find those who hadn't made it on merit and replace them), and had the whole field of vision. They knew how to command resources and get things done. Each precinct averaged almost 100,000 citizens; each commander was running the equivalent of a small-city police force with two hundred to four hundred officers in his or her command.

I encouraged the precinct commanders to use their own initiative, and I told them I would judge them on their results. The day-to-day operations were to be managed at the precinct level. I did not penalize them for taking actions that did not succeed, but I did not look kindly on those who took no action at all. The precinct commanders owned the successes, were responsible for the progress, and were accountable for the failures. No passing the buck here.

Previously, precinct commanders had not been allowed to work on vice conditions, to go after drug dens or houses of prostitution or automobile chop shops or any similar locations. All vice and drug-related crimes had to be handled by detectives in the OCCB or the Detective Bureau's specialized vice or narcotics squads. Precinct commanders went to community meetings and got their heads handed to them about all the crime locations in their precincts, but they didn't have the power to address those issues; they had to go up the borough chain of command and then over to the OCCB or Detective Bureau chain of command to get the resources.

We changed that. We authorized the training of the precinct commander and his or her officers to handle such locations, and gave them attorney assistance to attack them on their own. To go after a drug den, a commander could use his own people to work with the D.A.'s office to get probable cause and search warrants. To go after prostitution, we trained his people in proper procedure as decoys. We did this on issues up and down the line. If the problem remained beyond their resources, they could then go to the specialized units for additional assistance. By the dual processes of decentralization and inclusion, we effectively made the precincts into mini–police departments.

One of the first and largest problems we ran up against was jurisdictional. The precinct commanders, who reported to the chief of patrol, had previously had no control over the detectives in their own precincts, who were run by the precinct detective squad commander, who reported ultimately to the chief of detectives. In fact, control of personnel was guarded jealously. Rather than focus on the greater goal of reducing crime, commanders had traditionally refused to cooperate and instead concentrated on maintaining the importance of their own commands. Precinct commanders also had no ability to coordinate activities with other precincts without going through division and borough commands.

It was a turf war. All the movies ever made about New York City cops show the detectives in plain clothes on the station house's second floor and the uniformed officers on the first, with no intermingling. (How many uniformed cops do you see regularly in the squad room on *NYPD Blue*?) We were intent on breaking that barrier down. Initially, we didn't get much help from Chief of Detectives Borrelli on this issue. In Maple's initial senior-staff assessment Borrelli had been described as a potential obstructionist. Maple and Borrelli fought pitched battles over how best to coordinate precinct detectives and precinct patrol commanders, along with the specialist detective units in the OCCB. Ultimately, I opted to hold off on complete implementation of this change—for the time being. However, I quickly made it quite clear to the super chiefs that while I would not organizationally put detectives under the direct command of the uniformed precinct commanders, if they did not cooperate fully with those commanders, I would remove them. That threat worked.

Having given the precinct commanders increased power, I had to make sure they were handling it properly through accountability and relentless assessment. I assigned that responsibility to the borough commanders and then brought those chiefs in to give presentations on crime in their boroughs.

They each spoke for about ten minutes and then Anemone and Maple debriefed them. We all had the crime figures in front of us. Maple probably had them in his head. "You have two murders here," he'd say to them.

"Yeah, we're actively investigating them."

"What does that mean, 'actively investigating'?"

"Do you really want to go into detail?"

"Yeah. Let's go into excruciating detail with this."

The borough commanders said, "Crime is down."

"How much?"

"We made a lot of arrests."

"How many is a lot? Is it a million? Is it fifteen? Is it ten?" Maple was not a master of tact. "I see that robberies in the Fifth Precinct are up fifty percent, chief," he said. "What's going on?"

"Uh, the word is there's a lot of heroin out there."

"What does that mean? Tell me what that means, chief. Where is the heroin? Who's bringing it in? Why does that bring up robberies? What about burglaries? Who are the people we have identified who are doing them? Are the people who are doing the drug dealing doing the robberies? What's the robbers' method of operation? What are the detectives doing? Who are the victims?" The borough commander didn't have any answers. This happened a couple of times, then Maple said, "These guys are full of shit. They're used to jerking people around."

Maple understood, as I did, that the biggest secret in law enforcement is that many police departments do not address crime. They are dysfunctional. Chiefs don't ask follow-up questions because they haven't been on the street in about twenty years, they don't know the answers, and they're afraid that in the fencing back and forth, their underlings are going to embarrass them. Rather than be made to seem foolish, they let themselves be given fantasy briefings.

Maple wanted answers. "The bulk of your robberies are in the evenings. When are your people working?" Not evenings. "Why aren't they working nights? Why aren't you putting them there?"

The strategies were in play but weren't being uniformly adhered to. From borough to borough, division to division, precinct to precinct, some commanders took the strategies as gospel while others thought, "Ah, this will go away, it's extra work; we'll do it my way." When it became obvious that the borough commanders couldn't answer follow-up questions, I directed they meet every two weeks with their precinct commanders for a briefing. Maple said to Anemone, "Let's make sure they're doing this. We'll have one of the meetings down here at headquarters. We've got to get these mugs in here across the table, and they've got to go over, day by day, crime by crime, what's happening. What are you doing about it? Are you following the strategies?"

We quickly went from one meeting a week to two. Timoney, as chief of department, remarked to Maple that these meetings were running very long, sometimes for as much as three hours. Maple said, "John, what I want to do is have two three-hour meetings a week. That's six hours. Do you think that's too much, to talk about crime for six hours? We stand like potted plants behind the mayor and the police commissioner at press conferences at least six hours a week. Do you think we could talk about crime for six hours?"

The sessions started at eight-thirty in the morning. It didn't take long for the commanders to start complaining. "The traffic is bad. . . . I've got a community-council meeting. . . . I've got to go to City Hall. . . ."

"Louie," said Maple, "let's make it easy for everybody. The meetings are at seven o'clock in the morning. Now, if they've got any conflicts we'll make them at five o'clock in the morning. Seven o'clock, okay? Do we have your attention now, gentlemen?"

As the months went by, our sophistication grew. Week by week, we gathered more data, and rather than report only to their immediate superiors, the precinct commanders were instructed to also report to my command staff. We expected every precinct commander to be present and prepared to participate. We started with a book of numbers and ultimately fed them into computers that spat out an updated set of weekly statistics. What we began referring to as "the crime meetings" evolved into computer-statistics meetings, or Compstat.

It started as the simple monitoring of a briefing. It became an extravaganza. We had started panning for gold and had struck the mother lode.

We held Compstat twice a week in the second-floor press room. We soon moved to the operations room—or the command center, as it was more commonly known—on the eighth floor of headquarters, a space large enough to hold a borough's ten precinct commanders, plus each precinct's detective-squad commander and key personnel, as well as my command staff. With only 115 seats, we often had as many as two hundred people packed in there, including people from the offices of the district attorney and the U.S. attorney, parole, schools, and the Port Authority police. This was an occasion to dress. Most of the people strode into that room in uniform, with brass polished, looking like they'd just walked out of West Point.

Until this time, a precinct commander would never in his or her career expect to talk consistently and directly to the chief of department, the first deputy, or the police commissioner, but there we were, sitting at the command table. As chief of patrol, Anemone chaired the meeting. Each commander was called upon to report on his precinct about once a month, and we had his precinct's numbers in front of us. So did everyone else in the room. Notable statistics were listed—murders, robberies, felonious assaults, cases cleared (listed by year and crime), integrity monitoring, domestic violence—and significant increases or decreases were printed in red. As time went by, we incorporated color photographs of the commander and his or her executive officer on the profile sheets. When it was their turn to report, each precinct's leaders came loaded with information, statistics, and ideas, ready to fire. We called that being "in the barrel."

Maple still wanted pin maps: murder maps, shooting maps, robbery, burglary, narcotics, car-theft, gun maps. He wanted precinct commanders up and down the chain to know when and where the crime was happening. He told John Yohe in the Compstat office to keep a map of the 75 Precinct in Brooklyn, the busiest in the city, updated daily for a month. Yohe reported back that the work took eighteen minutes a day. Then Maple told the meeting that he wanted each precinct to keep updated maps. There was a groan. "Do you know how long it takes to do these maps?" they complained.

"Yeah," said Maple. "Eighteen minutes."

The first maps were handheld, with acetate overlays for each type of crime. (Mayor Giuliani, in a bit of self-serving smoke and mirrors, had led the media and the public to believe he was not making significant cuts in the Police Department's budget while other agencies were being decimated. In reality, our budget for other than personnel was being cut by almost 35 percent at a time when our activity was simultaneously expanding. As a reflection of how tight our budget actually was, we could not afford to buy the acetate these maps were printed on. We had to get a grant of $10,000 from the Police Foundation.) Within a year, we had three huge eight-foot-by-eight-foot computer monitors mounted on the walls and could call up each map, each crime, by computer.

The maps made crime clusters visual. It was like computerized fishing; you'd go where the blues were running. The First Precinct had a car-theft problem, the Fifth was having robberies around the subway stations at Canal and Grand streets, the Seventh had problems on Delancey Street, the Ninth had robberies around the clubs at night, the Tenth had hookers, Manhattan South had robberies from Thirty-eighth to Forty-second Street on Eighth Avenue, Manhattan North on the corner of Forty-seventh Street in the diamond district. Maple, in particular, could visualize the maps and remember all the facts from one meeting to the next. At every Compstat meeting, we would develop and analyze more information.

The mapping progressed, and the intelligence progressed, and the questioning got harder and harder. As we used to say, we raised the level of Nintendo. Some commanders enjoyed it, others were intimidated, others annoyed. Some were good performers who enjoyed the spotlight, others were solid on substance but no good onstage, still others couldn't get it right. It was a process that quickly identified who the real stars were. If a commander wanted to get noticed, he did it at Compstat. On the other hand, one good way to bring your career to a screeching halt was to bomb there consistently. Compstat was police Darwinism; the fittest survived and thrived.

Sometimes the grilling got tough. You've heard of the good cop/bad cop routine; Maple and Anemone were bad cop/bad cop. You didn't want to lie or bluff at Compstat—you'd get caught and hung out to dry. The people who did best had given thought to solving their precinct's problems; the people who did worst tried to fudge them. "The two biggest lies in law enforcement," says Maple, "are 'We worked very closely together on this investigation,' which means they don't work at all together, and 'We're doing this as we speak,' which means, 'We haven't done it yet.' They're holding actions." Maple and Anemone sliced through whatever crap they faced.

For example, the maps showed a large number of narcotics complaints coming from the housing projects in upper Manhattan. They also showed that the narcotics arrests weren't anywhere near the projects. The NYPD was not consistently giving the Housing Police the narcotics complaints made to 911, and as a result no one was addressing the drug problem up there systematically. In effect, if you lived in a housing development and called in a drug complaint, nobody would come. Housing didn't have the funds or manpower to run buy-and-bust operations, and the NYPD wasn't going into the projects. One NYPD narcotics commander said, "Do you know how hard it is for our undercovers to buy drugs in those projects?"

Maple answered, "If you think it's hard buying drugs, how hard do you think it is to live there and raise your children?" He asked the room, "Does anybody have any thoughts on this?" They then devised a means of cooperation to deal with the problem.

Sometimes the meetings got abrasive. But it was our business to try to save lives, and if a few egos were bruised, so be it. Maple said it best: Reasonable people didn't change the world; the world was changed by unreasonable people, because when you were unreasonable you got reasonable results. Situations got most contentious when we asked people to do things and they didn't do them. Maple made it a point to get to the bottom of that. "Captain," he would ask, "what are we going to do about the shootings in those housing projects? How are we doing with the buy-and-busts? Are we debriefing the prisoners? When you have CIs, are you bringing them in to look at photos so they can give you the organizational structure of the criminal element in and about the housing projects?"

"Well, the buy-and-bust hasn't worked," the commander answered.

"What else have you done? Are we doing any quality-of-life enforcement? Are we doing warrant checks? Have you done the overlays from the computer with the people with active bench warrants and parole warrants and systematically gone through them, arrested them for warrants, and debriefed them to find out who was engaged in this activity? Have we done that, and if not, why not?"

There was a case in Queens in which a man was going around beating a number of senior citizens halfway to death. He was found in a store using stolen credit cards, with the victims' blood still on his boots. "Now," Maple asked, "do we systematically check the credit-card companies when victims' credit cards are being used and see whether or not they can ID?"

There was an almost imperceptible hesitation. Maple put his hand over the microphone and whispered to Anemone, "They're not doing it."

The commander was standing across the room. He leaned in to the mike and said, "Yeah, we are." Bad move.

"You are? You know something, I really don't have anything to do now. I put my boat up for the winter. I'm gonna go collect the cases where credit cards were in evidence and look at them and find out who called the credit-card companies. Now, do we do it or we don't do it? Tell me. Tell the Jackster." They hadn't done it. "Then let's do it."

Precincts sent out squads to check warrants and issue quality-of-life summonses. They gave out ten. Maple said, "You know, we sent out a squad of eight people in plain clothes. Now I know that's the only job they had to do, but we sent them to five different precincts and they were averaging one hundred summonses a night. You're averaging ten."

We issued an order that all prisoners were to be debriefed, and a lieutenant stood there and told us, "We're debriefing everybody."

"Really. You're debriefing all the prisoners, Lieutenant, is that correct?"

"Yeah."

"Well then I guess the books are wrong here. It says there were four thousand arrests made in your precincts and you debriefed three hundred prisoners. What happened to the other 3,700? Why is it that no one is making statements to your detectives, and yet. . . . Is the assistant district attorney from the Bronx here?"

A voice from the corner said, "Yeah."

"What percentage of felons make statements to you folks without a cop there, and you put him on video and everything?"

"Sixty-three percent."

"And of them, how many are inculpatory statements?"

"Fifty percent of them."

"So, here's the district attorney with a camera, asking them Q and A and getting these statements, and the world's greatest detectives can't do it?"

You walk into any precinct and see the sign: "World's Greatest Detectives." There was a drug dealer in Brooklyn who raised pigeons and was consistently eluding arrest. Maple tore into that precinct's commanders. "A guy that raises pigeons in an abandoned building is outsmarting the world's greatest detectives? Come on now."

Sometimes Maple and Anemone would torment people. The most notable bit of aggression came when Tony Simonetti, who had become chief of Brooklyn South, was reporting, and up on the projection screens behind him appeared a computerized drawing of Pinocchio with his nose growing. That went over the line. When I heard about it, I raised hell with the two of them. One of my main rules is: You don't intentionally humiliate people in public, and they had violated that, and they both apologized to Simonetti.

But it wasn't all calling people on the carpet. When someone did particularly well we told them, "You did an excellent job here." We made a point of sharing their good ideas with the rest of the commanders, first to spread good police technique, and second to encourage and motivate good workers.

Over time, commanders brought in beat cops from their precincts who had done an exceptional job, performed heroically, or run an exceptional investigation. They described the circumstances and heard the whole room burst into applause. You can imagine the effect on a young cop and his or her career to stand there and be applauded by everyone in the department from his commanding officer up to and including the police commissioner. Compstat became a rallying point to encourage and reward people for good work. As at transit, where district commanders had begun improving their presentation and showing off their troops, at the NYPD, while the food didn't get any better, the performances did.

We encouraged creative thinking and backed our people up when they practiced new technique. We freed them from old restraints, gave them responsibility, held them accountable, and were very pleased with the results. We were often amazed. Commanders came up with solutions and innovations that none of us on the command staff had thought of. It was great to watch their minds at work.

Mostly, we attempted to involve the commanders in one another's problems and share successful solutions. "Inspector Chan, Fifth Precinct,"

Anemone called from the head table. "Didn't you have a problem similar to this with the robberies around the Grand Street station? Weren't they following people home and doing home invasions? What were your deployment tactics there? Maybe you could tell us about them." There was a reluctance for one commander to criticize another, and in the macho world of policing, even volunteering assistance might be considered criticism. We tried to mitigate this problem by taking it out of their hands; if he was called upon by his superior to respond, one commander wasn't showing the other guy up, he was helping him.

"Captain Smith from the six-two. Wasn't there a problem with car theft around Sheepshead Bay? What were your tactics there? How did that work?"

"Inspector Dunne from the seven-five. Didn't you have a problem with burglaries there in sector George? Right? With those Nehemiah Houses? What did you do to address that?"

If this had been a football game, Anemone would have been the guy carrying the ball forty times. He has a tremendous work ethic.

Compstat cut through a lot of crap because everyone in the barrel knew they were coming back in four weeks. But despite warnings, sometimes we asked a commander three, four, five weeks in a row for action and it didn't get done. At that point, Maple would explode. "I want to know why those shootings are still happening in that housing project! What have we done to stop it? Did we hand out flyers to everybody? Did we put Crime Stoppers tips in every rec room and every apartment? Did we run a warrant check on every address at every project, and did we relentlessly pursue those individuals? What is our uniform deployment there? What are the hours of the day, the days of the week that we are deployed? Are we deployed in a radio car, on foot, on bicycle? Are they doing interior searches? Are they checking the rooftops? How do we know we're doing it? What level of supervision is there? When they're working together in a team with a sergeant and four cops, do they all go to a meal together? When they make an arrest, does everybody go back to the precinct or does one person go back? Are we giving desk-appearance tickets to people who shouldn't get them? What are we doing with parole violators? Do we have the parole photos there to show? Do we know everybody on parole? Parolees are not allowed to hang out with other parolees, they're not allowed in bars. Of the 964 people on parole in the Seventy-fifth Precinct, do we know the different administrative restrictions on each one, so when we interview them we can hold it over their heads? And if not, why not?"

No one ever lost his job over not having the right answers. No one got in trouble for crime being up in their precinct. People got in trouble if they didn't know what the crime was and had no strategy to deal with it.

There are four levels of Compstat. We created a system in which the police commissioner, with his executive core, first empowers and then interrogates the precinct commander, forcing him or her to come up with a plan to attack crime. But it should not stop there. At the next level down, it should be the precinct commander, taking the same role as the commissioner, empowering and interrogating the platoon commander. Then, at the third level, the platoon commander should be asking his sergeants, "What are we doing to deploy on this tour to address these conditions?" And finally you have the sergeant at roll call—"Mitchell, tell me about the last five robberies on your post"; "Carlyle, you think that's funny, it's a joke? Tell me about the last five burglaries"; "Biber, tell me about those stolen cars on your post"—all the way down until everyone in the entire organization is empowered and motivated, active and assessed and successful. It works in all organizations, whether it's 38,000 New York cops or Mayberry, R.F.D.

Chapter 15

WHEN I SEE NEW POLICE OFFICERS COMING ON THE JOB, I SEE A WORLD OF difference being made. Being a police officer is not easy, and people come on the force for many different reasons. Lee Brown once said something I found very appropriate: "We talk and preach service, but we hire adventurers."

Police departments have traditionally marketed the job as a civil-service position. Frequently, as well as the police exam, candidates will also take the fire exam. We talk about helping citizens and upholding the laws and getting good pensions. But the job is also marketed by forces we don't control—television, books, newspapers, the movies—and they do a more effective job. Young people coming on the force are attracted by the action, the uniform, the power. They want the action precincts. They want the police movie image, to throw the food out the cruiser window on the way to the next dangerous call. They want eight hours of nonstop excitement, the radio barking all night. They're action junkies. Then they get in the Police Academy and out on the job and find they've been fooled—the bosses don't want them running wild in the streets; it is about service after all—and they get very disappointed. Most recognize what the real world of policing actually is and eventually adapt.

It's like throwing seeds; some land on soil, some on rocks. Cops by nature have a strong need to be accepted by their peers—they often cannot tolerate being a pariah—and the controlling station house voice is almost always cynical, and unfortunately it's the most vocal, and it carries. That cynicism too often frames the new cop's response to the realities of the street. As a result, only the most idealistic cop will buck the trend and speak up and say, "No, it doesn't have to be this way." If he's lucky, a recruit will land a mentor with a positive outlook, but all too many new cops are immediately thrown in with veterans who have a jaundiced view of the world. Former NYPD Commissioner Ben Ward said that when he first came on the job, he was amazed to find all the wisdom of the world in the back of the station house. Just talk to the cops, they knew everything about every issue. But as he grew, Ward learned that they knew very little. They didn't care about the facts, they just knew everything.

Many good people who enter policing become cynics in a very short time. There are two schools of thought on how to deal with this. In my circle, they were represented by John Timoney and Mike Julian.

Timoney felt that in some neighborhoods people will not work with the police because they're scared to death. Violence, drugs, lawlessness, and retribution have combined to create a void where a sense of community ought to be. That leaves control of the streets in the hands of either the criminals or the cops. "You've got to get in the face of these drug dealers," Timoney said, "and just bluffing isn't any good at all. They'll see right through you. So, to establish that 'this is my block,' it may come down to physical force."

A cop will try and stay within the bounds of acceptable behavior, but sometimes, when he gets immersed in the job, he begins to identify more with the people in the street than with his own family and friends. The bad guys become reality. In high-crime precincts, cops spend a lot of their time dealing with hard-core criminals, sociopaths, and psychopaths. Timoney himself, when he was younger and worked the Forty-fourth Precinct in the South Bronx, began to feel that anyone who wasn't facing violence and street morality all day long was, in the language of the street, a *maricón*. He recognized a metamorphosis occurring in himself. He was living the nitty-gritty, everybody else was in some ivory tower. Even off duty and among friends, he was acting more like *them*. Timoney describes it as "going native."

Some cops will adopt a street morality. They're in a war on crime and are not above meting out battlefield justice. This also extends to their behavior in the court system.

Some cops lie. We as a profession have finally matured to the point that we can admit that dirty little secret. Cops often lie for what they consider to be the greater good. They lie to get around the exclusionary rule. The Constitution as interpreted by the U.S. Supreme Court has very specific rules concerning how evidence is gathered. Evidence obtained outside legal boundaries is excluded. In an effort to put bad guys behind bars, throughout history cops have gone outside that boundary, and the exclusionary rule is a court-designed remedy for these police violations of the law. It has never caused cops to follow the law; it has caused cops to violate the law and then lie about the laws they violate.

There's a perverse morality to this. Most good cops won't fabricate evidence. They won't say a suspect confessed when he didn't. They won't get a gun and plant it in a car. But if they know they've got a bad guy and they search his car and find a weapon, they will justify the search by saying they saw the gun handle sticking out from under the seat.

It's called "testi-lying." Nobody wants to talk about it, but it happens all too frequently. Cops think, "The exclusionary rule says that evidence doesn't exist when it does. I know he had the murder weapon, but the courts are saying he didn't have it, at least not for the purposes of determining his legal guilt or innocence. So the courts are lying, so I'm lying, so we're all lying."

Many cops have contempt for the exclusionary rule and the entire system that, supposedly to correct a cop, could set a predator free. Let's say the suspect is a child molester, and every time he goes out he's a serious threat to rape a child at gunpoint. The cop sees him with a child in the front seat, turns on his red light and stops the guy's car. By turning his red light on and pulling him over, the cop has violated the law, which requires probable cause to stop a suspect. If the cop admits that he pulled him over without reasonable suspicion, the courts would probably suppress the gun and let this guy go free, and any confession would not be allowed in evidence. If the cop had pulled the man over for a minor violation like going through a stop sign, it would be a good bust. The cop thinks, "This is insane. I've got a rapist here. I am preventing another rape. I'm going to create a violation to justify the stop." As far as the cop's concerned, it's what he has to do to get the job done.

But it's a slippery slope when you start picking and choosing which lies you're going to tell under oath, and as the Mollen Commission had documented, NYPD cops were sliding down it in increasing numbers. The more contempt they showed, the more they began to lie outright. Then they'd hang themselves. Cops lost sight of the fact that the end does not and cannot, under the law, justify the means. As I told them in videos and face to face at countless roll calls, you cannot break the law to enforce the law.

When I addressed the issue I told the cops, "People think you're all liars. The judges think so, the D.A.s think so, the public thinks so, the media thinks so. I'm going to try and change that image they all have of you, but to do that I need you to work with me. I can only tell the stories that you give me. If you give me stories of brutality, corruption, and dishonesty, those are the stories I'll have to tell. I'm not going to protect you. If you give me stories of courage, honesty, and hard work, I'll also tell those stories. It's up to you. And if you break the law, I'm going to fire you, I'm going to put you in jail. I've worked too long in this profession, and too many others have dedicated their lives, to have the profession dishonored by a few."

I would rather lose a hundred cases than have one cop arrested for perjury. If a cop tells the truth, that he made a mistake, and a criminal goes free, we still get that gun off the street, we still get those drugs off the street. We'll get another chance to catch the same bad guy next week. But if the cop lies, an absurd outcome is possible: We get the gun and the drugs off the street, the criminal walks, and the cop goes to jail.

Much has been made of the police profession's traditional "blue wall of silence." Judge Mollen was told by a cop at one of the commission hearings, "Judge, I don't think you should call it a code of silence, I think you should call it a code of reluctance." Most cops don't think informing on fellow officers is their job. "That's Internal Affairs' job," they'll tell you. "I didn't sign up to catch corrupt cops, I signed up to catch criminals." One cop may refuse to work with another he knows to be corrupt, and when he goes to his superior and says, "I don't want to work with Officer Spitz," everybody will know why without it being said out loud. And when the bosses do grab a bad cop, the others will silently applaud. But they will not usually turn him in themselves. Cops depend on fellow officers for their lives. They need to know when they go through a door that they will be backed up. Rather than inform and then worry that their back won't be covered, they leave the job for the bosses. That's unfortunate, but that's too often the reality. The ultimate irony is the singling out of cops for this problem. How many judges, lawyers, doctors, and teachers do you see turning in their colleagues?

Internal Affairs, the unit responsible for finding and disciplining corrupt cops, has not historically been effective. The cops feel they are overly punished for minor violations and that the bosses are less concerned with their doing a good job than with keeping their noses clean. No cop will turn in another when slapping a drug dealer in the face gets treated almost as harshly as stealing and selling his drugs. "Mortal sins and venal sins," says Timoney, "we've never been able to make the distinction."

As the Mollen Commission's investigation had so vividly revealed, the NYPD was in danger of "going native" when I got there. I felt the crux of the problem in developing a new kind of policing and a new department culture was to prevent this negative transformation. We sent kids into environments where they were coming in contact with awful people, and we had to train and instruct and supervise them properly with these realities. We could not allow another generation of police to plunge into the *Apocalypse Now* jungle and go Marlon Brando on us.

This is the challenge and dilemma of modern policing. How do we control our environment and at the same time train our people to work in the community's best interests? With its emphasis on treating people respectfully and as partners, on interacting with responsible community and religious leaders, and on understanding that even in the toughest neighborhoods most citizens are good and law-abiding, community policing offered the best hope for the department and for the city. Unfortunately, some of my predecessors had unintentionally mitigated the effort by refusing to trust the officers they sent out to do the job. They were putting these kids into the neighborhoods to be problem solvers, but they didn't trust them to enforce the laws without getting corrupted or to carry weapons needed to do the job properly.

During his brief time as chief of personnel, Mike Julian was instrumental in beginning to change the way we recruited, hired, and trained new officers. Too many police officers view their relationship with the public as "us versus them." Community policing had encouraged them to go out into the neighborhoods and talk to people, to work as partners with them. Well, sometimes they would get cursed out and treated with contempt, and the unpleasant encounters stick in the mind. Often a cop will think, "It's easier for me to go dead. I'll look stoic and tough, and I'll walk the other way when I'm approached, because when I try to be nice to people, look what happens." Sometimes the media, for its own reasons, will run a negative, exaggerated story about one officer, and then they'll all feel hung out to dry. And, of course, the basic job of apprehending criminals puts them in contact with some rough individuals. It mounts up.

Linder's focus groups and officer surveys had shown that 90.8 percent of the cops felt the public has no understanding of police problems, and only 23 percent felt the community had a good relationship with the police. So we were dealing with cops who had troubling feelings about the public.

Julian believed that we could develop a more positive police culture. We would put recruits through the five months of academic work at the police academy and then put them on the streets for a month, where they would face the realities of patrol. We would then take them back in and allow them to describe their positive and negative experiences. We would explore their feelings and the reactions that were common among their peers in the station houses. We expected to hear complaints about how people treated them poorly, how the media maligned them, or how the criminal justice system dismissed good cases. These are some of the negative forces that cause cynicism and insularity among cops.

Despite these experiences, many cops maintain professional attitudes through their long careers. We showed new officers that there are cops who have not lost their ideals after ten or even twenty years on the force. We wanted the cops to listen and talk freely in an academy setting because they won't in the street. We had to expose them to the street professionals rather than leave it to chance whether they rode with a cynic or a believer.

The question we asked and answered was, "How can you follow the law and still get your job done?" How could we do what Timoney said was needed without kicking guys in the balls? How do we get our cops to understand that citizens are entitled to respect while cops need to earn it?

Julian felt that cops were historically taught what not to do in difficult situations—don't use force, don't take bribes, don't lie, don't do this, don't do that—but had never really been effectively taught how to do their jobs. The strongest example of this was the admonition, "Don't use choke holds to subdue suspects." But the training didn't provide effective alternatives to choke holds. The department covered itself with a blanket rule, and the cops were left to fend for themselves on how to stop a violently resisting suspect.

Early in my administration, we had a problem with a death in police custody that led us to examine the entire manner in which our cops were being trained. In this case, in an action in a housing project on Staten Island, the police encountered Ernest Sayon, a man who was on probation for a drug conviction and resisting arrest and who was free on bail after being charged with attempted murder for allegedly firing twenty shots into a housing project. They arrested Sayon, he struggled, and during the course of the fight, he died. It was a DPC, death in police custody. The city's medical examiner decided Sayon's death was a homicide and that he died of suffocation caused by pressure on his neck and chest while his hands were cuffed behind him. The community took to the streets, it became a media cause célèbre, and we had a potential crisis on our hands.

I formed a task force led by Julian to come up with specific recommendations on how cops can restrain people without killing them or getting themselves hurt. The task force included among others, a civil rights attorney, the leading academic authority on police use of force, and the chief medical examiner. They asked the people in charge of training at the academy, "What restraint techniques do we teach cops?"

"Martial arts. We train them in arm and wrist holds."

Julian got agitated. "That's the problem! We put a cop in a situation where he has to make arrests and detain people, but we don't require a certain skill level before he leaves the academy, and we never retest the skills during his career. Anything he learned in the academy is gone a month later. Any martial-arts person will tell you, you've got to be constantly training to make this useful in an actual situation."

"Is that true?" I asked.

The academy personnel didn't know. I instructed Julian to find out, and he returned with records showing that six thousand cops and six thousand prisoners a year are injured in arrest situations. Cops die wrestling in arrest situations. Prisoners die under the same circumstances. The medical examiner reviewed the previous four years' files of DPCs and found that most died from cardiac arrhythmia—heart attacks. Others died from cocaine intoxication. There was no clubbing; police don't club people to death in this city. There was not one incident caused by a choke hold. Yet when we questioned cops on how they restrained people, each said, "I grab them around the neck and take them down."

We finally found out that people died from positional asphyxia. Cops, trying to handcuff violently resisting prisoners, got them on the ground and usually either stood or sat on their chest or back while struggling to get the cuffs on. The prisoner, often intoxicated or under the influence of drugs, continued to flail and the cop sat on him harder, trying to restrain him even more. The medical examiner said, "When the prisoner is fighting, sometimes it's because he has no air. He can't breathe, but you think he's fighting you more, so you put more pressure on him, and that causes him to fight even more. Sometimes the price of tranquility is death."

So we developed a video training tape that used attention-grabbing animation to demonstrate the deadly effect of sitting on prisoners when trying to restrain them. We advised cops to sit people up as soon as they were handcuffed.

Cops do not want to kill anyone. In the three years since the police were properly trained, no one has died in police custody from positional asphyxia.

We taught the cops what to do, and we saved lives.

———

The best cops are able to use communication skills to avoid the use of force. New York cops may not have the best equipment in the country or be the best trained, but New York's Finest are some of the best at talking to people, which is what a cop spends most of his time doing. No police officer in the world deals with as wide a variety of people as a New York cop, who encounters a diverse mix of ethnic groups at the highest and lowest economic levels in one of the most stressful environments. We wanted a program in place to increase communication between the cop and the public; an officer can defuse a situation by talking and by showing respect. We brought a man named George Thompson, a retired Albuquerque cop, to the academy to teach a course in "Verbal Judo," or how to use the confrontational behavior of people to the cop's advantage.

Thompson's approach used humor, which the best cops use to defuse the tension in a crisis. Mike Julian felt Thompson's humor was unfortunately sometimes directed at the public. Cops love to laugh at the public as a way of insulating themselves, but when the humor was directed at everyone in the situation, it worked better. Cops often don't like to laugh at themselves because they always want to be in a position of power, and they feel being the butt of a joke is the wrong end. But we had to make them understand that it's not about how you look; you have real power when the situation ends in your favor.

We also began to raise our standards. We raised the minimum age from twenty to twenty-two, which gave a prospective cop more life experience before he or she came on the job. Instead of a high-school diploma, we required two years of college. We also upgraded the physical standards. For ten years, no physical exam was required to enter the NYPD. According to Julian, the physical exam in place when I got there could be passed by a seven-year-old. We developed a finger-strength test that measured whether an applicant could repeatedly and successively pull the trigger of a gun and found that thirty candidates, who would otherwise have been hired, couldn't pass. The department had, in fact, hired several people who could not be issued a firearm because they did not have the finger strength to pull the trigger. They could not be out in the street with a gun but were nevertheless being given full pay as New York City police officers.

The Academy was upgraded, but no one in professional policing has been able to change the police officer's developmental pattern from idealist to realist to cynic. It's an age-old problem that many people think may not be correctable. I don't believe that; they said the same thing about crime. Julian said to me, "You did the easy things, you let cops fight crime. That's what they want to do. What cops don't like to do is deal with the community. Now, get them to respect people. That would be an even greater challenge." I stepped up to that challenge. I went after the culture to make the NYPD a more proactive police force and a more respectful one.

The department has a long tradition of teaching professionalism, but a checkered history of corruption and brutality. One of the reasons is that many cops did not trust the department. The honest cops are born or raised honest; others appear honest out of fear of being caught. But fear is ephemeral. Only cops with internal constraints and respect for the community, the department, or themselves will make the right choice under pressure when no one is looking.

We had a great advantage when we spoke and when we taught. The cops were listening. We demonstrated early on that we would support them when they were right and that we would lead them toward unprecedented achievements. When we then warned them against brutality and corruption, they listened out of respect and trust, not just fear. They believed in us and, by extension, believed in the professional principles that were always the guiding force behind our crime-control strategies. We had the first departmentwide opportunity to change the culture, to develop in police officers the internal constraints that would have them make the right decisions not out of the fragile fear of being caught, but out of deep respect for themselves and the NYPD.

Two words every cop should learn are "explanation" and "apology." If an officer is not in an emergency situation, he or she should always explain an action before taking it. The public is infinitely more likely to go along with an officer if they understand what he or she is doing and why. And if he or she has done something wrong, an officer should apologize. "Why should I apologize? I'm a police officer, I acted legally and had the right to do what I did. The fact that I had the wrong guy is not my problem." I am a firm believer in putting myself in someone else's shoes. I asked the cops to think if they or a close family member had been the guy who had mistakenly been run in, how they would feel, and how they would react. It certainly would have been a problem then. If the cop showed the average citizen the human respect of acknowledging an error, that citizen and everyone he or she talked to about the incident would carry more respect for that officer. This is one way to build trust and communication between cops and the community they serve.

The police can't take back the streets that were effectively depoliced for twenty years without being assertive. However, if they are heavy-handed, if they don't get the consensus of the community, if they don't get the leadership and supervision of their own command staff that is so essential, then there is the potential for an explosion like that in Los Angeles. That black kid in District 3 in Mattapan would be a lot less likely to hate cops if a cop hadn't verbally abused and intimidated him for trying to walk down the sidewalk.

———

The 30 is a precinct that went native.

The 30 Precinct runs from 133rd to 155th streets, between Bradhurst Avenue and the Hudson River in Harlem. When crack hit New York in the eighties, it hit that neighborhood particularly hard. The homicide rate soared and the 30 became one of the city's most dangerous precincts. Over time, a number of the cops started busting drug dealers so they could steal their money and resell their drugs. As the investigations by the Mollen Commission, Manhattan district attorney, and the U.S. attorney had conclusively shown, from 1986 to 1994 officers there systematically robbed drug dealers of drugs and money, beat up suspects, engaged in drug trafficking, extortion, assault, evidence tampering, perjury, civil-rights violations, and income-tax evasion. They didn't just steal from routine busts, they actively searched out known drug spots to rob them. There were ninety officers assigned to patrol the precinct; thirty-three were believed to be involved, including two sergeants. After my appointment, I aggressively encouraged the three investigative groups to bring their work to closure. Finally, after two years, there were going to be widespread arrests.

Dean Esserman told me, "This is a battleship coming broadside on you, and it's about to ram you. New York expects corruption scandals, the press gets involved in the bloodlust, they love it." He advised me to go to ground zero when the time came and be at the precinct when they made the arrests. Miller encouraged this line of thinking. It would be a way of ensuring that we were not seen as just being acted upon, but that Internal Affairs and the commissioner's office had been integral players in the investigation. It also allowed me to send some very strong symbolic messages, not only to the public and the media but, more important, to the cops. We ensured that members of the NYPD who were assigned to the arrest team—which was also made up of federal agents, Mollen Commission investigators, and personnel assigned to the U.S. attorney's office—were clearly identifiable, by either their New York City Police uniforms or windbreakers clearly marked "NYPD." All the media footage would show that we were locking up our own.

We were going to arrest what became known as the "Dirty Thirty" that night. Miller got calls from police reporters all day. "We hear it's going down tonight." It appeared that someone from within District Attorney Robert Morgenthau's office was calling newspaper editors and telling them, in essence, "A big case is going down in the NYPD, a product of our long and intensive work, so make room for it in your papers." The editors, in turn, were calling their police reporters, notifying them, "There's a big bust going to happen tonight." Because it had been known for some time that the 30 was the subject of investigation, it was not difficult for them to identify the likely precinct. Judge Mollen was also apparently getting calls from the editors indicating that the case was going down, and did he have any comment. Mollen was understandably perturbed to have media control of his long-term investigation slipping from his grasp.

My team and I discussed what my role should be. There were three significant heavyweights—Mollen, Morgenthau, and U.S. Attorney Mary Jo White—and we were newcomers. Even though the crimes predated my arrival, the headlines would read, "NYPD Corruption Scandal!" and in the public's mind it would appear that it was happening on my watch. Internal Affairs said they were going to arrest a dozen cops that night. Two of them were working, so those arrests were to happen in the station house at the eleven-thirty roll call.

Arresting a cop is a very unpredictable business. Miller had seen cops pull guns on investigators. He had seen cops pull guns on themselves and blow their brains out. He said, "I don't think we want the commissioner walking into the three-oh while some cop eats his gun for a late dinner and splatters his brains all over the desk sergeant's blotter with TV cameras outside." He asked Greg Longworth, head of my security detail, for his recommendations.

Longworth said, "We'll have the commissioner in the area. We'll effect the arrest, and when we know it's secure he'll come in, be briefed by the investigators, and he can take their badges right off their uniforms and put them in his pocket, if that's what he feels should be done."

Miller circled the precinct at around ten that night and the area was quiet. Ninety minutes later, there were TV satellite trucks and reporters and lights and the whole media circus except guys selling cotton candy.

I had the privilege of seeing the cops in handcuffs. I was disgusted. The idea of police officers selling drugs is repugnant to me, as it should be to any cop. The head of the arrest team handed the officers' shields to me.

I went back to the precinct and addressed the morning roll call. I said, "It is unfortunate that in this command for the last number of months many officers who wear that shield that you all so proudly pinned on your chests when you took the oath of office decided to use that shield for purposes other than those for which it was intended, specifically to protect and serve. Many chose to use it to rob, to steal, to beat, to violate the law. They have now been arrested, and many of them are going to go to jail for a long time.

"We are committed to ensuring that the New York City Police Department is one that can be trusted, is one that the public can feel comfortable will serve and protect. . . .

"We're going to have difficult weeks ahead, those of you who did not violate the trust, those of you who have been working under very difficult circumstances up here, knowing some of what was going on. I've been disappointed, being quite frank, that more did not come forward. There are any number of ways that you could have let us know of the frustrations and the problems. . . .

"This department will work very, very aggressively to seek those out from our ranks who should not be here. It is unfortunate that there are still people in this precinct who should not be here. We know who you are, you know who you are. We're probably not going to get all of you—that's unfortunate—but there are some of you that we can and will be able to get."

Prior to the press conference at the office of the U.S. attorney, there was heated debate between representatives of Judge Mollen and District Attorney Morgenthau as to the wording of the press release. The enmity between the judge and the district attorney had broken out into the open.

Mary Jo White attempted to do what she could to mollify both sides, and ultimately a press release was created that satisfied both men. However, at the press conference Mollen and Morgenthau both tried to put their own spin on their respective offices' roles in the investigation. It was pretty awkward. Timoney and Maple were beside themselves, like kids in the back of math class, trying not to laugh. Timoney, who was always candid about his frustration with prosecutors, said, "This is incredible. We have 'testi-lying' for cops? They're all lying to the press, this is 'press-ti-lying'!"

After the press conference at the U.S. attorney's office, I brought over four hundred police commanders, every NYPD captain and above, into the auditorium at headquarters. I walked in, opened my folder and tossed the shields of all twelve arrested officers on a table.

"These shields will never be worn by a New York cop again," I said. "They are tarnished. I am retiring these numbers so no cop will ever have to wear a disgraced number again."

I addressed the problem of rogue officers and rampant corruption through a policy of inclusion that brought my precinct commanders into the game. The precinct commander was the person I trusted not to go native. I needed him or her and their counterparts in the special units such as narcotics and detectives to work with the community and the criminal-justice system and to lead, control, supervise, and discipline the officers under them. They had not really been included by previous administrations in the fight against corruption. Their involvement would be essential in mine. To that end, early in my administration, I organized a two-day retreat at Wave Hill estate, a beautiful city-owned complex of buildings and gardens overlooking the Hudson River, fifteen minutes north of Manhattan in Riverdale. The function was funded by the Police Foundation, and I invited all borough commanders, super chiefs, deputy police commissioners, and unit heads—the top seventy-five people in the organization. I wanted everyone exposed to the basic theories by which I was planning to run the department. I suspected for some chiefs this would be the first time they'd heard them. I also brought a number of outsiders, including Frank Hartman from the John F. Kennedy School of Government, my close friend and confidant Bob Johnson, and members of the Police Foundation.

I began by stating my goals: a 10 percent reduction in crime in the first year. "These are the bars you have to clear," I told them. "These are my expectations." Eyes rolled. Jaws dropped. This was the end of March, I had been commissioner for less than three months and I was asking for the moon. To many in that room 10 percent did not seem obtainable. It had never been done. In fact, to my knowledge no commissioner had even set a number before. In policing, you don't set crime reduction goals. My strategic intent was to set a seemingly impossible goal and then achieve it. Bob Johnson referred to them as "stretch goals," a common practice in the private business sector.

I also made it clear that the NYPD now had a policy of inclusion. I was going to trust the precinct commanders, to empower them, while using Compstat to manage and monitor their progress. I mandated that they be briefed on all aspects of their command, including sensitive cases being run in their precincts by Internal Affairs. In some respects, it was as if the CIA had marched into the State Department and said, "You have to know what's going on in our confidential operations, and we are going to brief you."

Walter Mack bridled immediately. Internal Affairs had traditionally guarded its investigations and findings against the threat of exposure and shared its information only with the commissioner. If there was an Internal Affairs problem in a precinct, the precinct's commanding officer was usually not informed. The thinking was that few if any police personnel in a precinct could be trusted; if a cop found out, he would expose a corruption investigation to save his fellow cop. Timoney went right at him.

"You're wrong," he said heatedly. His brogue took on a life of its own. "You don't understand police work. If you think you can't trust a precinct captain and put him in the know about what's going on in his precinct, and you won't give him the authority or the information that you keep to yourself in the hallowed halls of One Police Plaza, then you're out of your mind."

"No, *you're* wrong," said Mack, a former U.S. attorney. "I've been in this business long enough to know the Michael Dowds of this world. [Michael Dowd was a corrupt cop who was the subject of some of the Mollen Commission investigations.] You don't understand how this works."

Timoney said, "We're eating our own. We spent the last twenty-five years doing nothing but worrying about corruption. We didn't do any police work for twenty-five years, that was left up to the individual cop. We knew there were cops out there taking opportunities, but you deal with them . . . the way the department's going, we're paralyzed. We're being driven by the political motives of the D.A.s without any concern for what's right and wrong, for the soul of the police department." I smiled at this comment, for I believed strongly that this was the crux of the problem at the NYPD, and one I intended to change.

Mack firmly believed that there was systemic corruption throughout the NYPD. He felt that this was a real problem and that we couldn't include the precinct captains, because they were too close to their people.

"Somebody's got to speak up for these cops." Timoney was in his twenty-seventh year on the force. "I'm not going to protect corrupt cops, but I'm gonna protect the department, and I'm not going to let people run roughshod over it. I'm not going to tolerate that. You don't get it, you don't understand the NYPD, you don't bleed blue."

Several chiefs pulled Timoney aside afterward and said, "Jeez, John, you ought to be more careful with what you say." It had been their experience that the organization had not treated candor kindly in the past. I was perfectly happy to let them go at it, so long as the argument didn't get personal. As commissioner, my job was to say, "Okay, I've listened to all of you. This is how we're going to go. If you can't deal with it, you're going to have to get out. If you stay, and I find you are still not with the program, then I'm going to have to get rid of you." That's what happened eventually with Mack. He was smart, dedicated, and I respected him, but he couldn't adjust to the idea of inclusion and trust that was essential to the way I intended to reengineer the NYPD. For that reason, as well as other concerns relative to his management of IAB, by early 1995 he was gone, replaced by Pat Kelleher.

If the precinct commander was going to be the person I trusted to keep the cops from going native, he or she needed to be aware of the symptoms of that disease when they first appeared. Internal Affairs had that information. It was as if the precinct commander were a family physician trying to treat a patient who has a number of tests done, but the lab refuses to share the results. How could you hold someone accountable for corruption in his or her command if you didn't provide the resources to deal with it and didn't share information critical to success? In my opinion, and in that of most of my inner circle, this had been a fatal flaw in the department's anticorruption efforts going back to the major reforms of Pat Murphy in the early 1970s. As in the fight against crime, we needed to include as many players as possible, not exclude them by effectively saying, "We don't trust you." How do you expect people to deliver when you send that message?

While informing the commanders of the IAB presence, and getting them personally involved in the investigations, we also greatly expanded random integrity-testing cases—things like sting apartments and sting cars and cops posing as drug dealers—to monitor the cops. In 1995 we conducted over 700 stings involving close to 1,200 officers. Union officials were advising their members to treat all calls as if they might be stings. Needless to say, we did not object to those instructions. I demanded increased cooperation between bureaus and units. Because the inclusion of precinct commanders could facilitate assigning suspect officers to designated locations, stings that had taken many weeks were being done in two. Corruption dropped. Normally, an organization dealing with corruption has a tendency to slow down, get its story straight, circle the wagons. We kept the line moving forward. We were aggressively going after the corruption while speeding up our crime- and disorder-reduction efforts. We also instituted Compstat-like briefings where Internal Affairs commanders were grilled with the same intensity as their precinct counterparts.

The rest of the command staff at Wave Hill responded exactly as I had hoped. I think many of the police bosses remembered their frustrations as precinct commanders. We were guided by the three Ps: partnership, problem solving, and prevention. We wanted community involvement, innovative tactics, and assertive policing, and a focus not simply on reducing crime but on not allowing it to occur. We outlined the strategies we had already announced and those we would continue to present to the public.

Within nine months, we replaced a significant number of the seventy-six precinct commanders, installing many new people who understood what we were asking of them and who had shown at Compstat that they were capable of doing the job. The reengineering of the NYPD was on its way. Risk taking was being encouraged and rewarded for the first time in the history of the department. I couldn't have been happier or more excited.

Chapter 16

THE OFFICE OF THE COMMISSIONER OF THE NYPD IS TREATED WITH REVERENCE by people in the department. Unlike in Boston, you didn't hear cops or their unions bad-mouthing the department or the commissioner. It's part of the tradition. The fourteenth floor of One Police Plaza was like the hallowed sixth floor of the Boston Police headquarters, only more so. Uniformed members did not appear there unless properly attired in their dress uniform. It was a sign of respect for the office and the person of the police commissioner.

As well as the commissioner's office, the fourteenth floor held the offices of the first deputy and the deputy commissioners of Legal Matters, Policy and Planning, and Trials. This was not a place for casual attitudes or casual behavior; this was the command center of the greatest police organization in America.

Judy Laffey, my executive assistant, kept my schedule tight and organized. Maple and Miller joked that she commuted to work on a broomstick, but she actually had a very sly sense of humor and was tremendously valuable in maintaining order in what might have been a chaotic office. Having served three of my predecessors, she was also the institutional memory of the Office of the Commissioner. Also, for someone like myself who maintained an open-door policy, she served as a very able traffic cop to ensure that the open door did not get clogged with too many coming through at the same time.

So everyone was on their best behavior, except Jack Maple. As deputy commissioner for crime-control strategies, and later deputy commissioner for operations, a position that gave him an operational rather than just a policy role, Jack's office was on the ninth floor but, Maple says, "Commissioner, secretly I knew you liked me best." Maple had some unusual habits, such as piling a dozen pairs of shoes under his desk and working out on the heavy bag he hung in the corner. (I gave him an office with a shower, a very important status symbol and public-health concession.) He would not stand on ceremony, he would float—if Maple could float—from office to office visiting senior commanders, talking up ideas, building consensus, saying, "Listen, here's a thought . . ." He would "pollinate" police ideas. He and I rarely met for more than a daily total of ten minutes outside of general meetings, but he would pop into my office ten times each day like a bee returning to the hive, tossing ideas for discussion and approval. I also used him to test the waters for me. When we did have sit-down staff meetings, the plans had basically already been formulated and could be put into effect immediately.

He was also an excellent leader. He took critical operations that had not been functioning properly, redirected them under his own temporary command, then handed them back to their original commanders to manage, while he went on to the next. He took the quality-of-life initiative and then the warrant unit under his wing.

His first project was the Detective Bureau. Maple and Borrelli butted heads many times as Maple sought to involve a notoriously aloof bureau in the coordinated activities that were essential to our success in reducing crime and disorder. Our lead team of detectives was very good—they could solve ten cases at a time. Below the first team, however, we found the detectives had real problems.

The NYPD was a very promotion-driven organization, and, as a result of union lawsuits and contracts, if an officer spent eighteen consecutive months in certain units, the department had to promote him or her automatically to the position of third-grade detective, with a significant increase in salary. (In some cases, the timetable was twenty-seven or fifty-four months, but by and large the promotions occurred after eighteen.) Many of these people had not been performing traditional detective work, which is to investigate and solve crime. They were working in other valuable areas, but they were not learning true detective investigative and interrogation skills. For instance, we had 1,500 people assigned to the Organized Crime Control Bureau, the entity that dealt with narcotics. But many of those officers spent most of their time on dangerous plainclothes assignments running buy-and-bust operations, trying to arrest drug dealers. They didn't participate in hard-core investigations like a "rated" detective does. Over time, the department found itself with many detectives who had a very limited number of years on the job and no schooling and no real expertise in detective work. We had some super detectives who had been excellent plainclothes officers—"white shields," they were called because they had traditional patrolman's shields rather than detectives' gold ones—but others were wannabes who had never worked the streets. Compounding the problem was a very high retirement rate among our more seasoned detectives.

The Detective Bureau was particularly adept at responding to high-profile crimes. During my time as police commissioner, very few of these "press" cases did not get solved. But in many of the more mundane cases, they were not doing the job as well as they should, or could. In some respects, it was "slide-show policing"; they would focus on whatever was on the screen; nothing else would get looked at. Unit after unit, crime after crime, problem after problem, there was often minimal coordination and cooperation between units. Even on homicides, they were satisfied to catch one perp and not necessarily all his accomplices.

When we arrived, there were 27,000 "wants" in the system, dating back a couple of years. The detectives said they had been hunting these people down and couldn't find them. Maple said they were full of crap. He told me, "I'd like to import a couple of people from transit, along with some NYPD people under Lieutenant Norris. We're gonna take a look at a couple of precincts to see how good they are at catching people."

Lieutenant Eddie Norris was a Maple protégé and in some respects a clone. One night at Elaine's, we looked up to see two Jack Maples coming in the door. As a joke, Norris had dressed in a topcoat, homburg, bow tie and spectator shoes. The only thing missing was the mustache.

They took the want cards, visited the addresses listed on them, and with a squad of three or four cops caught several suspects right in their houses. That got the attention of the chief of detectives.

Maple's shop became the hot spot for NYPD creativity. The tunnel rat showed up the rest of the organization. Of course, he was bringing well-trained people to do the jobs and giving them the support they needed. He was bringing in ringers. But he knew that if you make unreasonable demands, you will get reasonable results. As the man whom I had chosen to create the crisis of confidence that Linder and I felt was essential to turning the department around, he had his detractors, but he also had many strong supporters. He forged relationships with Timoney and Anemone, who, to their credit, quickly realized that the NYPD had not been living up to its true potential. Even Borrelli and Reuther came begrudgingly to respect Maple.

Maple had leaped from transit lieutenant to the man in charge of NYPD crime strategies—as he liked to describe it, "the biggest leap in the history of law enforcement"—and he had to win the respect of the more established command staff. He did it with street brains and levity. His humor was as constant as his policing, you just had to have an ear for it. Maple was gruff, like a kid pushing the big guys to see how far he can go. For instance, I used to talk about the "special environment" we had in the Transit Police, and NYPD lifers such as Timoney and Anemone would good-naturedly make fun of me behind my back. They made transit jokes all the time. Maple used to respond, "Gee, why don't you talk to the big transit cop when he walks in here? I think he's coming in in about a minute. Why don't you tell him that little joke?"

He used to delight in torturing Timoney. Any time I'd hear laughter in Timoney's office, I'd know Maple was in there, Robin Williams with a homburg. He would imitate Timoney's accent. "Oh, I know you, you're a big mahn, Timoney, you're a big mahn. Today it's 'Good marnin', Commissioner Maple. Sure an' that's a fine suit you've got, Commissioner Maple.' But when Bratton leaves it'll be, 'Where's your man Billy Bratton now, fatso?'"

In February, only six weeks after we took over, the preliminary numbers showed crime down for that period over the previous year by 16.8 percent. But the first month was easy—it just showed what the NYPD could do if it paid attention. In March, the numbers were down 14.1 percent. The 1992–93 reduction had been 4 percent. Four percent? We could do 4 percent just by getting the cops' hands out of their pockets. For the month of May, the city's crime was down 11.4 percent. Our reductions couldn't be considered one-shot cleanups now; month by month they were consistent, as they had been in transit. Conventional wisdom had it that police could have no effect on crime; we proved that wrong.

We were also having a very good time. My inner circle was becoming a tight group of good friends.

Every Sunday, Cheryl cooked dinner, and the single guys—Miller,

Maple, and LaPorte—gathered at our apartment along with their significant others of the moment. We ate and laughed and talked over the past
week and planned for the week ahead. They also spent many evenings at
Elaine's where the business of New York continued and where Cheryl and
I occasionally joined them. Each of these guys could have used a woman
in his life, and they were all out looking for her, as evidenced by the rapid
turnover in their girlfriends. At times, Cheryl and I felt like we were raising My Three Sons.

Cheryl was waiting to be admitted to the bar in New York State. She
was teaching at John Jay College and administering several federally
funded programs. Things were not easy for her at first; I had a dream job,
but she had to start all over. She never complained, but I knew she wasn't
as happy as she could be. However, her fortunes turned when the O. J.
Simpson case began to dominate the news. When she decided to discuss
the trial in her class, all the local TV stations and CNN showed up.
Afterward, the local ABC-TV affiliate and ABC national radio hired her to
do on-air commentary on the trial. She developed a real flair for television
and moved from O. J. commentary to a full-time position as a reporter at
WABC-TV. She was articulate, attractive, smart, and quick—perfect for
television. As her media career began to take off, I was understandably
quite pleased and proud.

Miller had contacts all over New York, from the influence makers to the
wise-guys. His years on television had made him instantly recognizable
to, among others, maître d's, cabbies, and organized-crime hit men. Cops
loved him because he understood and saw things their way. He was a
valuable source of information coming into the commissioner's office as
well as a master at directing the information coming out of it. I could find
out the tenor of a situation, how things were playing where it mattered,
from John. I didn't have to ask; Miller was a reporter, he reported. He was
also pretty good at picking out the best restaurants in town.

Timoney and I became good friends. Though I'd had a hard time understanding him at first, I very quickly came to really appreciate him. He
was one of the smartest people I'd ever met. I admired his willingness to
speak his mind. He was quite outspoken and not as politically circumspect
as he might have been, and it cost him from time to time. As much of an
ego as I have, I think Timoney has even more, yet he made great sacrifices
for his job. I could depend on him to steer me right about the department,
its customs, capacities, and capabilities. He didn't sweeten anything, he
was very direct and honest, and I appreciated that. I always felt when I

spoke with him that I was getting the unadulterated truth. I put a lot of trust in him and gave him great power. He was the NYPD personified. He was my rock.

Peter LaPorte and I went back to 1983, when he was an intern out of Northeastern University. He was smart and incredibly organized; people responded to him and liked to work for him. Some bosses will push things under the rug; LaPorte dealt with problems directly, corrected them, and moved forward. He had a phenomenal work ethic and was not shy about correcting people and telling them what was on his mind. As chief of staff, he became my right-hand man in the very complex commissioner's office, which he coordinated and controlled. He was the guy who dispensed favors, a master manipulator. Although he was barely thirty, people came to see him as a power. If people needed to get something in front of me, they went through Peter. In a department with more than its share of "rabbis," he was the grand rabbi.

I trusted LaPorte to deal with City Hall, to work with Peter Powers, special counsel Denny Young, and company, to do battle with them, if necessary, so the mayor and I did not have to do battle with each other. He was a master of nuances and had good insights into what was really happening, as opposed to what we were supposed to think was happening. LaPorte had an impressive array of sources and networks and ears like *M*A*S*H*'s Radar O'Reilly; you didn't want to be within fifty feet of Peter and whisper because he would pick up the conversation. In a sense he was my knight errant. LaPorte and Miller were my champions in dealing with the Hall: LaPorte kept Young and Powers away from me while Miller, and later Tom Kelly, had the unenviable task of dealing with their Madame Defarge, Cristyne Lategano (or as we came to call her, the Dragon Lady). When I had Maple, Miller, and LaPorte working for me, I had an incredible intelligence network. Peter grew in the job. He was my shield against the mind-numbing games and machinations continually flowing out of the Hall. I'll never understand how he didn't suffer a nervous breakdown.

Work and friendship merged quickly. Because I truly love what I do, I'm always on the job. I like the excitement of moving large numbers of people into action, and I like the adrenaline rush of success. I'm not the kind of person who will kick back and watch a ballgame with the guys; I am more likely to sit around and talk about the crazy scenes that happened during the day's work, the maddening politics and unique personalities that were getting in the way of eradicating crime in New York.

Most of what was getting in our way was City Hall.

Rudy Giuliani and I never had a cross word. It was arranged that way. We had weekly meetings—my senior staff and I, he and his—to go over a weekly report we prepared presenting information on major events of the past week, major events expected in the coming week, and future issues.

"On Friday, June 30 . . . an altercation occurred involving worshipers at the Elim International Pentecostal Church and Officers from the 79 Precinct. Members of the congregation attempted to prevent the officers from issuing parking summonses in front of the Church. Four Police Officers were slightly injured as a result of the incident and one arrest was effected. Meetings were held . . . at which representatives of the clergy, the community and the Police Department were present. These meetings produced specific plans to control the parking condition that generated this situation. No future problems are anticipated at this location. . . .

"As you know, there have been several recent incidents which have involved alcohol abuse by members of the Department. In fact, this problem has reached the upper echelon of the Department. At a recent Crime Control Strategies Meeting it was apparent that the Commanding Officer of [a] Precinct was under the influence of intoxication. I have relieved him of his command and he has filed for retirement. . . .

"[John Timoney] is finalizing his analysis and recommendations for a standard 9-mm round for all members of the agency. . . . I expect a draft of the report will be available for your review within the next two weeks. . . .

"Please let me know if you would like more information about these events or issues."

If there was going to be a battle, and there frequently was, it came during the preparation of this agenda, during the week, between our staffs. Issues that were generating friction at staff level were almost never discussed between me and the mayor. We both preferred to have them worked out at a lower lever. Peter LaPorte consistently duked it out with Denny Young, the mayor's consigliere. Ironically, they liked and respected each other.

We sent them crime strategies and they sat on them, ostensibly reviewing them. We were not empowered to implement these initiatives without the acquiescence of the mayor. For example, the Auto Theft Strategy was ready for months before they were finally able to schedule a press conference to roll it out. Because this was a comprehensive strategy, it ended up delaying many attendant initiatives, including one that was intended to address the problems of gypsy-cab drivers who were getting robbed. We devised a program under which the department would issue stickers that said, essentially, "If I look like I might be having a problem, feel free to pull me over and check out the taxi." The cop would not be accused of harassing the driver, and the driver would have the increased protection of the police. This was delayed while we waited for City Hall to get its act together; meanwhile, the crimes continued. The Hall was the black hole of law-enforcement action. Whenever possible, we would launch initiatives long before they were finally announced at City Hall press conferences.

Giuliani had worked long and hard to get elected mayor and understandably sought every occasion to present himself to the public in the best possible light. The Hall attempted to insert the mayor into every possible scenario and to ensure that the mayor received credit for the initiatives coming out of city agencies, including the police. While attempting to create positive coverage by controlling all media, they became paranoid about leaks. A source of increasing friction, suspicion, and hostility between us was the fact that these policies and strategies were delayed so long that they were bound to leak. That created particular problems in the police department because of my policy of inclusion.

I was not very concerned about the contents of our strategies leaking to the press; I was much more concerned about leaks relative to ongoing police operations in which lives would be placed in danger. The strategies were not kidnapping cases, they weren't homicide or terrorist investigations, they were development of public policy and I encouraged participants from a wide cross section of the department to be involved in their creation, development, and the announcement of the successful solution of crimes. If something leaked from so large a group, so be it.

Sometimes leaks, no matter how inadvertent, gave us a sense of how the plan might go over with the press and public. One of our potentially more controversial ideas—allowing local religious leaders to accept weapons from members of their congregations and turn them in to the police in return for the gun owner's anonymity—hit the papers and demanded comment. I said, "Look, I'm not going to license every minister in New York to become a collection point for Uzis. We need the police one step closer to that process." We created an amnesty program for people who turned in weapons at the precincts. A bad proposal leaked, but it didn't do us any harm, and it certainly didn't bother me. My concern was not that the public learn about these strategies, only that they worked.

But City Hall went wild over leaks. We heard it from the mayor's staff, including the mayor's criminal-justice coordinator, Katie Lapp: "I'm

......ng you, the mayor went ballistic!" And each time a strategy was announced and previews of it appeared in the papers the day before, we'd get the same accusation: We were leaking it to *The New York Times,* the *Times* was our paper, we were playing it.

The Hall demanded complete secrecy so Giuliani could take the lead in announcing these strategies to the public and assume credit for their initiation and development. From a political standpoint it was understandable; he would need to show success in producing on his campaign promises to be reelected. No matter who created the concepts or was going to run the operation, the public unveiling of any and all police strategies had to come from the mayor.

My staff began to take umbrage at the attempt on the part of the mayor's staff to rewrite history. The strategies and most of the ideas involved in them had been born within the Police Department, but some in the Hall asserted that they had created them. At some of the joint meetings to discuss finalization of the strategies, some of the mayor's staff actually spoke of themselves as the principal authors. We had sweat blood developing and writing these strategies; now they were drinking it. Most of the time, Maple and Timoney just rolled their eyes. They joked with each other, sat in a corner, and whispered: "When Rudy was a kid, did he ever once get to school with his lunch money?" Still, the Hall persisted.

One way to stop the leaks was to stop including so many people in the conception of the strategies. I refused. The policy of inclusion was a major component in my management practice, and I would defeat myself if I caved in and abandoned it. Why should I exclude many of the ideas that were, in fact, strengthening the strategies? So the leaks continued and so did the raging.

The mayor's aides burned up the phone lines saying Rudy was furious, and after some bruising conversations, Miller and Maple and LaPorte trooped into my office and told me, "They are so crazed over there that when we go to the meeting this week, we'd better be prepared," and they would click off the issues. They had devised a system to gauge just how irate the mayor was supposed to be: the phone-book scale—how many phone books they should put down their pants before they went to the mayor's office to take their beating. They had phone-book meetings and double phone-book meetings, white-page meetings and yellow-page meetings and yellow- *and* white-page meetings! They expected to go over there and have the mayor say to me, "Now, I think my people have talked to your people about this, but I want to go through it, you and me." But I

never heard about it from Giuliani. He never brought up the inflamma-
tory subjects at our meetings. "Meanwhile," said Miller, "our heinies
would be hurting for two weeks."

Another factor in the mayor's difficult romance with the police department was that we were quite obviously having fun. Giuliani was a former
federal prosecutor, and a large percentage of his inner circle had also come
from that world. They had had incredible intimacy with cases and investigations, and while their business was now politics, law enforcement was
what they knew, it's what they enjoyed. My job was fun, particularly dealing with my cast of characters. We briefed the mayor on some cases at the
weekly meetings—"We have to call the U.S. attorney on this," "We're implementing a unique strategy on that"—and it got their juices flowing. We
could see it. They had all the frustrations of dealing with the budget and
school issues and labor contracts, and when they got to the police, it was
like recess. Our work was important and exciting, and it made news, and
for the backroom boys at City Hall, it had the added benefit of being politically valuable.

The Hall's political radar was incredible. Whereas the Dinkins administration had been justifiably criticized for its inattentiveness to issues,
which was thought to have been a significant factor in the inept handling
of the Crown Heights fiasco, no one would ever be able to accuse Rudy
Giuliani of not being in the know. The fact that a black kid and a Jewish
kid might have an altercation after school in the 75 Precinct might not
mean much to the average person, but Rudy, clearly understanding the
significance in that very racially conscious area of the city, would recognize
its potential volatility and act accordingly. There were votes at play, constituencies in the balance; one teenage street fight could become a microcosm of the battle for recognition between large power blocs in city
politics. And judging from the riots in Crown Heights and Washington
Heights, it could all blow up any minute. None of that would be allowed
to happen in the Giuliani administration. To give the mayor his due, he is
one of the smartest men I have worked with, and his instincts and work
habits are incredible.

Giuliani, through his liaison Bruce Teitelbaum, had extremely strong
ties to the Jewish community, particularly the orthodox Hasidic community in Brooklyn. The Hasidim hated Mayor Dinkins for what they perceived as his indifference to their safety during the 1991 riots in Crown
Heights, which had begun when a car in a rabbinical motorcade acciden-
tally struck and killed a young black child. The rioting had gone on for

three days, during which the Jewish community came to believe that the police were instructed by the mayor and Commissioner Brown to pull back and let the anger burn out. During the riot, a rabbinical student named Yankel Rosenbaum had been killed by black rioters. The Hasidim thought of the Crown Heights riot as a pogrom. The Jewish community had overwhelmingly supported Giuliani in the following election and had his ear.

The Hall asked the department to issue licenses so the Hatzoloh ambulance service, a community organization that primarily served the orthodox Jewish community, could use lights and sirens on their private vehicles. Denny Young spent quite some time trying to convince Timoney that this was a good idea. "The mayor is very concerned about this," he said. Timoney was not having any part of it. "They're nice people," he said, "but they've been a headache from day one. They blow lights, they're in private cars, a number have been cited for inappropriate use of the lights and sirens, they have caused considerable tension and resentment in the neighboring black community." They had lobbied and received legislation recognizing their private cars as ambulances, but the NYPD didn't recognize them—we didn't want them going through red lights and causing accidents.

"This is the law," said Young.

"Fine. Have the Department of Motor Vehicles issue them licenses."

They couldn't come to an agreement, so a meeting was scheduled at four o'clock on a Sunday at City Hall with the mayor. "It's the Sunday afternoon meetings where they break your balls," says Timoney.

"Mister Mayor," Timoney said there, "you've got to trust me on this one. The department is the best friend you've got on this issue. It can only hurt you. You don't want to license the Hatzolohs."

The mayor looked around the table wide-eyed, as if he hadn't grown up in Brooklyn. He asked his aides, "What's a Hatzoloh?"

John Miller was in the mayor's office at another time when one of Giuliani's aides said, "[State Assembly Speaker] Sheldon Silver wants to know if we can get these people their lights and sirens."

"Which people is that?" asked the mayor.

"You know, the Hatzoloh ambulance people."

"Uh, have I heard about this before?"

I understand Giuliani spent much of the four years between his loss to David Dinkins in 1989 and his victory in 1993 studying Dinkins's handling of the city. Mayor Dinkins was viewed by much of the electorate as hands-off, aloof, not in touch with the day-to-day operation of his government and his police force, which he didn't trust. Giuliani, used to micromanaging his federal prosecutions, would not make that mistake. He was going to have his finger in everything. The Hall consistently read every incident for its latent political message and tried to capitalize on it. Their intelligence-gathering apparatus never ceased to amaze me.

We began to suspect that my rising popularity was beginning to cause some political concern, if not to the mayor then to his staff. In all my years in policing, I had never been part of a popularity poll. The transit ads had raised my visibility with New Yorkers several years before, but not once had I been put in the same league with the man in charge of running the city. In April, after the mayor's first one hundred days in office, a *Daily News*/WNBC Harris poll showed me with an approval rating of 62 percent, nine points above the mayor. The *News* headline: "Rudy takes backseat to Bratton in new poll."

As part of my ongoing efforts to improve the morale, self-respect, and public image of the department, we intended to capitalize on the 150th anniversary of the NYPD in October 1995. I put together a committee to plan a yearlong series of events and programs. One of the events proposed was a parade. The department's fabled Emerald Society Band, with its drummers and bagpipers, was sponsoring a convention, scheduled for the first week of October, with some twenty-five bands from all over the world coming to compete. We could use this gathering as a catalyst for a massive ticker-tape parade. How better to give the department the respect and acknowledgment it deserved on its 150th anniversary than to have the men and women in blue march through the fabled Canyon of Heroes in lower Manhattan like astronauts or World Series stars?

We began to talk to the unions, various retirement groups, and the Police Foundation, all of whom were enthusiastically supportive and agreed to raise funds and provide volunteers. I was very excited. Here was a way for the City of New York to say thank you to cops who were increasingly making the streets safer. My staff contacted the special-events office and found that, even though it was still more than a year away, the only date available for the parade was Saturday, October 6, my birthday. Was I unaware of the coincidence? No. Was I throwing myself a birthday party? Hardly. I actually joked about it when I first heard the date.

Miller and I and Joe Wuensch briefed the mayor in my conference room. He was enthusiastic. He understood that a parade celebrating the police and the historic drop in crime would accrue to his benefit. How impressive for the mayor to march up Broadway at the head of a ticker-tape parade, with twenty-five bagpipe bands blaring, in front of tens of thousands of police and hundreds of thousands of cheering spectators. This was going to be quite a bash. Giuliani subsequently denied knowing anything about it or approving it.

I mentioned the amusing confluence of dates on Roger Ailes's cable-television talk show. (Ailes was a strong Giuliani backer and, ironically, the appearance had been arranged by Cristyne Lategano.) I joked that I was going to have one of the biggest birthday celebrations in history. My quote got picked up by one of the newspaper police-gossip columnists, and someone in the Hall read it. It was no joke to them.

The mayor and Cristyne Lategano didn't take kindly to the idea of a police parade that fell on my birthday and would once again put him at a public-relations disadvantage to me. City Hall refused to authorize it. Lategano said some unpleasant things about us in the paper the next day, and Miller told her, "The mayor could have cut him some slack. He didn't have to squeeze him like that." Rudy got on the phone and yelled at Miller for criticizing Lategano, then hung up on him. Peter Powers called back and told Miller he was in big trouble, he'd better watch himself. Once again, they didn't say a word to me. Relations continued to go downhill.

When the New York Yankees and New York Rangers won championships, Rudy got personally involved in their parades. He didn't mind marching up Broadway with them, but he wouldn't do it with the cops he professed to admire so much. But here the NYPD was delivering a safer city—200,000 fewer victims of crime a year, versus 1990—and the mayor denied the cops a parade. I thought that was shameful. Sports teams contribute to the spirit of the city, but they don't save a single life. New York cops were saving thousands of lives and in the process sacrificing many of their own.

In late summer, we cracked a big case. The previous March, a couple from Potomac, Maryland, and their two daughters were visiting New York and shopping in the chic Upper East Side bridal boutique, Vera Wang. Two men entered the store at Seventy-seventh Street and Madison Avenue, robbed the clientele, stole the wife's diamond ring, shot both parents, and got away. It was a random act of violence visited upon completely innocent people, and the latest in a series of robberies committed by the same suspects, known in the media as the "silver-gun bandits." As they were wheeling her mother into an ambulance, the fifteen-year-old daughter cried out, "I hate this city!" It was a terrible tragedy, the kind many people around the country expect when they think of New York, the kind that are uncommon but can set national opinion. The Vera Wang incident was one of the most highly publicized New York shootings in ten years. It took us six months, but detectives working out of the Nineteenth Squad, assisted by a tip to the Crime Stoppers Hot Line, finally caught the shooters.

It is normal procedure to call a press conference when you crack a big case. Because this was such a media event and knowing that Giuliani would want to be there, we tried to contact him. We got no response. A big Yankee fan, Rudy Giuliani was spending that Saturday afternoon at Yankee Stadium with several members of his staff. Miller beeped, no answer. Miller beeped various people in his entourage and still didn't get a call back. Time was passing. TV news reporters have deadlines, and the family, who had come to New York to make the IDs, was anxious to return home. By the time we raised someone from the Hall, we had fifteen minutes until we were scheduled to begin. It would take considerably longer than that to get the mayor out of the stadium and into lower Manhattan. They started screaming and yelling to delay it. "Screw it," said Miller. "Fine. We'll wait. We'll hold the press conference whenever you say. I will go out there right now and put them on hold."

"No, go with the press conference."

"No, we'll wait. We're going to wait, it's fine."

"Do the press conference now."

We did. It was the lead story on the local news.

Miller got another call: Go to Gracie Mansion and wait for the mayor. I had left to attend a wedding in Boston. One of my security detail, Detective Jimmy Motto, took him. They were talking in the car, and Miller was trying to decide how many phone books this meeting would require. He was inclined to tell the mayor, "Listen, you're at a ballgame, your people don't answer, what the hell do you want me to do, hold up the whole world?"

Denny Young said, "Sit down." Miller felt like he was a mob soldier about to get whacked. "Now," said Young, "when the mayor comes here, I don't think you should explain what happened." Consistently, Young or Powers would soften up people before they got to see the mayor. They literally gave them the line—You have to apologize—so when the mayor came in it was all scripted. Giuliani does not like surprises. He does not want to walk into a room without knowing the script.

"Denny," Miller explained, "we beeped the mayor's press people, we called the mayor's press people, and we left a message for the mayor's press people. They didn't call us back. And when they finally did call back, the press conference was starting in fifteen minutes, and their suggestion was to tell the world press—who is on deadline for the six o'clock news— that the thing will begin at quarter to seven. What reason were we going to give them?"

"Please," Young said, "I know some of that may be true. . . . I really wouldn't argue with him about this because, you know, he's very concerned about this, he's very angry. I would just say, 'Sir, it went wrong, and it's not going to happen again,' and apologize."

Miller was thinking, "I've known Denny a long time, and I know him a little better than I know Giuliani. Maybe my pal's here to help me." Still, his first impulse, which he often acted on, was to tell the mayor the hard facts. He sat there on the Gracie Mansion back porch with Denny Young, being prepared for the slaughter.

The mayor arrived and slammed the car door behind him. An aide handed him a clipboard and said something to him. He winged it back. Jimmy Motto, sitting in the car in the driveway, saw this and thought, "Oh, God, Miller's going to talk back to the mayor. Look at the mood he's in!" Motto jumped out of the car, ran into the mansion, through the kitchen, and was about to go up the stairs to get to the back porch to find Miller when he heard the door slam and Giuliani say, "Where's Miller!" He snuck back to the car.

As Miller recalls it, Giuliani stormed in. "What the fuck happened?" he demanded. They were the first words out of his mouth. *"What the fuck happened!"*

"Well, Mr. Mayor . . . obviously something went really wrong, and it will never happen again." He was beginning to think the porch advice had some value.

"I want to know what happened!"

"Well, there was a little miscommunication." Miller decided he wanted to hold on to his job. He had to walk the thin line between "We didn't cut you out of it" and "It was your staff's fault." He couldn't say "Cristyne didn't answer her beeper"; he would get killed for blaming one of the mayor's people, particularly Lategano, and it was bad form.

"What miscommunication?"

"Well, you know, in our communications with your people . . . things just didn't get communicated." He went straight to gibberish. "But from now on we'll make sure that none of these things go forward before we're in touch with your people. But," he said, trying to salvage some sense of normality, "I just thought it was limited to a crime story, and it seemed to be in the department's purview and not an area of big concern to you." Miller knew that was baloney but he had to say it. It was the wrong tack to take.

Giuliani lectured him. "This is one of those stories that affects the economic development of the city. It was out-of-towners, they were tourists. People who think about coming here see these stories. I visited the families and showed concern, I have been involved since the beginning, and when something like this wraps up, it's not the place of the police department to say, 'Oh, we'll handle this whole thing.'

"You know, I have the distinct impression that *someone* over there . . . is putting someone *else's* agenda ahead of mine."

Giuliani did not say he was pleased that the cops who worked this investigation had strung together a series of minute leads to track down the criminals and make this case. No, he was apparently furious that the department and the cops, who did all that work, had the temerity to announce it to the press without his being present. This entire blowup was over who was going to stand in front of those bright lights and take the big bow on national TV.

We continued to meet weekly with the mayor. We asked City Hall to release the statistics to the media that showed that crime was going down. They refused. The mayor was very upset when I then announced them at a meeting of an association of business people. Miller got a call saying, "What the hell is he giving out good crime stats for?"

During the mayoral campaign, Dinkins had said he was winning the war on crime because his administration had experienced a 3 percent decline, and Giuliani had made the rounds saying, essentially, "Numbers don't matter, and crime stats don't count." So now, when he had great numbers and stats to work with, his problem was that he was on record as having previously disparaged their worth.

An article in *The New York Times* had noted that another city had put in place a gun strategy and their gun arrests were way up relative to ours. Maple tried to explain to the mayor that because of the success of our Gun Strategy, fewer people were carrying guns, and that the more we continued to pursue this strategy, the fewer gun arrests we could expect.

"No!" he said, gritting his teeth. "This number goes *down* and this number goes *up*!" Meaning, the higher the number of arrests, the lower the amount of crime.

Maple had spent many meetings sitting around saying, "What do you think about putting ten thousand people in Narcotics and putting on a full-court press against the drug dealers until they can't function? The game would be over if we did that. That's where all our crime is coming from, according to everybody." Now he had his chance. "Well, Mister Mayor," Maple said, "we could affect those arrest numbers to go up while these crime numbers go down, but . . . what do you think about throwing ten thousand people into Narcotics? I have a plan. You want to knock out crime? We can put ten thousand people into the Narcotics Division and take this place out. There will be no more crime."

The mayor blinked. "Well, I don't know about that. I'd think we'd have to talk about that." He had a budget to consider, he didn't want to spend the money.

"Well, that would be how to do it," said Maple. "When you want to do it."

Chapter 17

MAPLE WAS PUSHING A BATTLE PLAN THAT WOULD WIN THE WAR ON CRIME IN New York City, particularly drug crime, once and for all. When we came into the NYPD, Maple had gone "pollinating" among the chiefs. "If there were no drugs in New York City," he asked them, "how much do you think crime would go down?" One chief said 30 percent, another said 40, another 50, another 90. He took the most conservative estimate. "The NYPD thinks that thirty percent of the crime in the city is somehow related to drugs. Why is it," he asked, "that in an organization of thirty-eight thousand cops [he included transit and housing in his calculations] we have fifteen hundred people in Narcotics? Why do we have four percent of the department dealing with thirty percent of the problem? I don't understand this. This is not smart business."

Maple took a number off the top of his head. "Why don't we just put ten thousand people in Narcotics and blow this place up? That's the end of the game."

Maple says the chiefs looked at him like he was from Mars. We had already heard the mayor's reaction, so he just kept the idea to himself. Several months later, he asked Chief of Narcotics Marty O'Boyle, "Marty, under past programs like Pressure Point and TNT, the crime came down in the five- or ten-block area where we focused. Tell me what you would need to take out the whole city. I want to know. Is it ten thousand cops? Is it five hundred thousand? Is it a million?" O'Boyle looked at him. "No, I'm serious. Amuse me." They came to the conclusion that the task would take a little more than five thousand cops working full-time. We had the cops to do it; staffing level was at its highest ever.

Maple figured, "Okay, this is what we'll do. We'll take the city back borough by borough."

To take Queens, we needed about eight hundred people. We needed around nine hundred cops for Brooklyn North and six hundred more for Brooklyn South. Staten Island would take a couple hundred. The Bronx needed about 1,200 and Manhattan North 1,400. "You go into Queens," Maple explained. "You stay there for six months with eight hundred officers. There are some bad areas: the 103, the 110, the 113, the 114 precincts. You do everything that works: buy-and-bust operations, quality-of-life enforcement, warrants, guns, the whole thing. It works, we know it works. We do our job and take out the drug organizations and clean up Queens. Now we have it under control.

"After six months, you downgrade by about twenty percent, you leave six hundred officers in Queens as a standing army and slide two hundred over to Brooklyn North, plus another seven hundred. We give Brooklyn North the same treatment for four months, leave several hundred there and slide the rest to Brooklyn South and then Staten Island. When we've cleaned up there, we leave some and move to the Bronx. We finish with Manhattan. Within a year we kill crime in New York."

When Maple finally presented his ideas and numbers at a general meeting, we knew we had a winning battle plan for the war on crime. We arranged to bring it to Giuliani. We were certain he would enjoy being the mayor who ended drug crime in New York. We called the plan Operation Juggernaut.

There were several obstacles we had to overcome before we could get Juggernaut under way. In a perfect world, we could swoop down on the city all at one time and crush crime, and the criminal-justice system would be able to handle the volume of arrests our plan was going to produce. But we did not live in a perfect world, and we would have to deal with district attorneys and judges who have their own caseloads and work schedules, and with the limitations of jail space in New York's already crowded system. The criminal-justice system was not designed for a police department to be effective, in which case it would be forced to become a high-performance organization itself. The courts were semifunctional; if we showed up with thousands more prisoners, they could become paralyzed. We would have to reach some accommodation.

Budget was another factor. This would be an expensive operation. The city couldn't afford to promote and pay a large contingent of new detectives. But we had a cost-saving proposal. We would run Juggernaut and also allow these cops to bank upward of a year's time toward promotion before transferring them and their newfound expertise back to their precincts. Juggernaut would be a success, and I would have a total police force that was trained to deal with drugs. Dave Dinkins had bitten the political bullet and raised taxes to hire six thousand more cops. Surely Giuliani, who had campaigned on the issue, would do at least as much.

In early December, we invited the mayor and his inner circle to our eighth-floor command center, the Compstat room, with its bank of TV monitors and computer screens, and made a two-hour presentation. Maple and Anemone were the chief presenters. We reviewed the history of narcotics in the city and the NYPD's response to it. We organized our statistics and made our strong case. At the end, to leave them completely pumped up, Maple and Anemone's planning group, the Swamp, produced a war movie—"Operation Juggernaut"—with scenes of drug use, a background of stirring music, the NYPD busting down doors to get at drug dens, a daisy chain of perps being led away, happy kids of all ethnicities playing in cleaned-up streets, men and women in NYPD windbreakers doing the job. We were going to wage war on drugs in New York and win.

Prior to Juggernaut, the city's war on drugs had been our Vietnam; we were fighting a hit-and-run enemy and had gone in and made a lot of contact when we could, but we'd never held the ground. We didn't have the tactics or the will to win. Juggernaut was the Normandy invasion. We were going to overwhelm our opponents, take the ground and never leave, and systematically take them out. The focus of our effort was going to be on the source of the problem: the drug dealers. We weren't going after the users. We would systematically take out the low-level street dealer, the midlevel operator, and high-level kingpin. We would attack them consistently on all fronts at all times. If you were a drug dealer, you were a marked man.

Time was of the essence. In September 1994, the strength of the city's three police forces had reached its maximum manning level, 38,310 cops. We knew that we, along with the entire city government, were in for hard times with a shrinking budget. We also knew that we would not get any additional cops to replace those lost to attrition until the spring of 1996.

Compounding our staffing problem would be the loss of several thousand civilian employees as part of the mayor's reduction of the civilian work-force. The window of opportunity to use our expanded manpower would be between eighteen months and two years.

The mayor was impressed. "How much will crime go down?" he asked. "How would you process the arrests?" He was clearly enthused.

We followed this up at a meeting at City Hall. Maple, Timoney, Miller, and LaPorte were with me, and among the mayor's aides were Powers, Young, and Lapp. We brought in maps and charts and laid out the attack plan for the entire city. We produced budget people to discuss the financial details.

In our weekly Thursday meeting in the mayor's office, Lapp said, "Mr. Mayor, we're moving forward with this," and discussed the million dollars a month that would have to be budgeted for the Correction Department. The mayor said, "It's money well spent. Let's do it."

The next day, on a police boat coming back from a function on Staten Island, the mayor was still talking about the details and what a great plan we had designed. I was pleased that he was so enthusiastic. The NYPD and the city were going to have an excellent new year. We were going to overwhelm crime. Nothing quite like it had ever been proposed for any American city.

Sunday morning, Maple woke up and looked at the headline on the front page of the *Daily News.* "I knew the world was over," he said. He called and woke up Miller and read the headline to him. Miller started laughing—it was either that or cry.

In large, bold letters, with "Exclusive" slashed across its front page, New York's Hometown Newspaper said, "BRATTON'S JUGGERNAUT." The smaller headlines, each with an NYPD logo in front of it, read: "Cops pre-pared to invade Queens in '95 drug-war offensive" and "Commish's '94: Year of success & symbolism." My picture took up about a quarter of the front page.

Juggernaut was dead. The mayor and I never discussed it again. He told Miller, "I'm not sure about this plan. I think it's ratcheted way too high."

Two weeks previously, the *New York Post* had run an article under the headline "Rudy Plans War on Drugs," which had outlined much the same initiative. We'd gotten no static about it. Patrice O'Shaughnessy of the *Daily News,* having run a "first week" article when I'd arrived, wanted to interview me about my first year. She had read the *Post* article and wanted to know what our big plan for the new year was. It was the drug plan, only now it had a name: Juggernaut. "But it's already been in the *Post*," she told Miller. "If something is going to bring change," he told her off the record, "that will probably be it." Miller wasn't shy about discussing our new plan; many of the details had already been in print with the mayor's name attached, the mayor had been fully briefed and was completely onboard, preliminary discussions concerning the plan had taken place with three hundred people in the department. O'Shaughnessy made Juggernaut her lead, and the *Daily News* chose the headline.

Giuliani was on the phone with Miller: "If we put in all these cops to make all these arrests, where are these drug addicts going to get treatment? Where are the social services?"

"Mister Mayor," Miller said, "as I think Commissioner Bratton explained in the presentation, he doesn't care where they get their drugs, or if the price goes up, or if they can find treatment if they want it; he's worried about all the people they're victimizing every day. He wants to get them locked up. And if they get right out, he wants to get them locked up again until somebody in the drug-dealing community looks up and says, 'You know what? This is too much trouble, getting arrested every other day. I think I'm going to stop dealing. You win, I lose, good-bye.' "

The mayor said, "Well, I'm not really sure about this."

Miller thought, but kept to himself, "You said you were sure the other day at the end of the meeting."

"We can't have these leaks," the mayor said, returning to an old theme. "Where did they come from?"

Miller told him, "There are three hundred people involved in planning this program. They're training hundreds of undercover officers who have all been told where they're going and what it's about. They're requisitioning cars and office space from all over the department. There is no one who *doesn't* know about this. I think to say that this is being leaked by me or the commissioner or somebody on senior staff. . . . I mean, everybody in the job is now part of this. There was a presentation that you were present at that included one-hundred-plus people. And it was in the *New York Post* two weeks ago!"

"This isn't the way we do policy. It's a leak, and I want the people responsible found, and I want them dealt with."

The Hall was telling us, "It's a great plan, it's just not the time for it." But there wasn't anyone in my command staff who wasn't convinced that if the *Daily News* headline had read "Rudy's Juggernaut," the plan would have been in place immediately, and we would have been well on our way to historic crime decreases and a much safer city much sooner.

We could not move forward with the plan on our own; it required coordination with other city agencies, including corrections, the courts, and the district attorney's office. Without mayoral support, the plan was effectively dead.

(We continued to lobby for it, and some fifteen months later, on April 1, 1996, a modified version of Juggernaut was finally authorized as the Brooklyn North Drug Initiative. This time there were no leaks, and the mayor officiated at its announcement. As anticipated in the original plan, shootings and homicides in that zone were quickly reduced by 40 percent, an effect, but for politics, that we could have had eighteen months earlier. My one great regret is that the benefits we experienced in 1996 were not felt in 1995. The decline in crime for Brooklyn North in 1996 was 50 percent greater than in the rest of the city.)

As 1994 ended, Dave Scott and Joe Borrelli retired. I moved Charlie Reuther over from OCCB into Borrelli's spot and named Timoney my first deputy. Marty O'Boyle moved from chief of narcotics to head up OCCB. Louis Anemone moved up to chief of department.

First deputy commissioner is a civilian job, and I didn't know whether Timoney wanted to take the uniform off. I told him I was perfectly willing to change the organization and have everyone report to the chief of department, if that's what he wanted. Timoney's career goal was to become commissioner. He made no bones about it, and I supported him; he would make a great commissioner. (I couldn't help thinking back to 1982 and the *Boston* magazine article.) First deputy is the stepping-stone, and Timoney told me, "If I want to be number one, I have to be number two."

The announcement of Timoney's promotion was a proud moment. Here was an Irish immigrant, tough as nails, who had risen in the ranks to become the number two man in the department. Timoney and a half dozen of us went to the mayor's office, Timoney thanked him profusely, had a photo taken, then had the promotion announced in the Blue Room, where the mayor usually meets the press. The mayor spoke, then I spoke. Afterward, in answer to a question from a reporter, Timoney thanked me for the confidence I had shown in him. Timoney went back to the mayor's office and again thanked the mayor personally.

Peter LaPorte felt an edge in the air. Cristyne Lategano, he noticed, did not seem happy. I can't say I noticed.

Timoney was in the shower when he got beeped. Go to Gracie Mansion. No reason given. He was scheduled to be the keynote speaker that evening at the black-tie Friendly Sons of Saint Patrick's founders meeting. He put on a tuxedo with a red bow tie and cummerbund. He called me. I didn't appreciate their summoning my first deputy without notifying me first. I went to Gracie Mansion with him, uninvited.

We arrived and were ushered to the basement conference room by the mayor's security detail. Miller, Maple, Timoney, and I used to joke about this room being Rudy's Star Chamber. It was where one Sunday evening they had brought Schools Chancellor Ramon Cortines, who had made the mistake of arriving by himself and shortly thereafter was forced out of office. Presently, Denny Young and Peter Powers entered. They were not happy to see me. We sat across the table from one another. Powers said to Timoney, "You didn't thank the guy who gave you the job."

"I thanked him and shook his hand before the press conference, I thanked him and shook his hand after the press conference."

"Yes, but when the TV cameras were on, you didn't do it."

"What are you, nuts?"

"Look, we all owe our jobs to him."

"Are you kidding me?" Timoney was incredulous. Why was I not surprised?

I had sat there and watched my second in command get raked over the coals long enough. "I resent you reaching out to my first deputy and bringing him up here behind my back. Who do you people think you are?"

Powers snapped back, "Don't you try and change the subject. We'll talk about that later on."

"No, we won't." The idea that they would try to intimidate my most powerful aide was more than a little troubling. This was clearly a broadside at my authority, as well as an abuse of one of my men. Powers and I went at each other for a while. Powers had a choirboy public image, soft-spoken and almost deferential. In reality he was the mayor's hatchet man: assertive, demanding, and one of the toughest people I'd ever encountered in government.

Finally, playing good cop/bad cop in front of two cops—who did they think they were kidding?—Denny Young tried to act as peacemaker. "I'm glad we got together and got to iron this out."

"Iron what out?" said Timoney. "You're crazy!"

This had happened because John Timoney had not thanked Rudolph *i publicly.* No matter how well you did your job, in this administration that one act could get you added to the enemies list and eventually fired. If you were not part of the cultlike following, willing to drink Kool-Aid at a moment's notice, you were suspect.

Timoney was an excellent first deputy. He had a realistic view of police work and a great and sympathetic understanding of the rigors of the job. He knew the difference between the book and the real world; he was both a throwback and a progressive, a unique crime fighter with respect for both the letter and the spirit of the law. And he was always looking out for the cops. Maybe that's what did him in with the Hall; his allegiance was focused in the wrong direction. Giuliani and Powers had vowed to break the NYPD and bring it under their control and that effort was clearly continuing.

Our 1994 crime numbers came out. Overall crime was down 12.3 percent. Shooting incidents fell by 16.4 percent. Murders were down by 18.8 percent, 385 fewer murder victims. Our strategic intent had worked, we had surpassed our goals. It was time to set new ones. In 1995, I told the department we wanted a decrease of 15 percent; nothing less would be acceptable.

Our numbers startled the media. As it began to look like we had a new and effective way of handling this seemingly insolvable problem, we started to get noticed. The press office was deluged with calls.

Because the reporting on crime shapes fear, from day one I had intended to marry *The New York Times.* I wanted the paper of record to tell our story, and I went out of my way to make the *Times* understand what we were doing. Like Babe Ruth, we were predicting where and when we were going to hit the home run. Unlike the tabloids, which would generate great headlines and public support, the *Times* would reach the decision and influence shapers, nationally and internationally. In one of our first interviews, I encouraged Clifford Krauss, the *Times* police bureau chief, to pay close attention to what went on here; we were going to deliver on our promises, but the larger story would be how we did it. In November, Krauss had written a front-page story under the headline "Bratton Builds His Image as He Rebuilds the Police," which ran for almost a full page inside and was both a profile of me and my team and an overview of our techniques. Once again, City Hall was not happy.

As far as the Hall was concerned, Miller's office had become nothing more than a fifth column, undermining all the efforts to Giuliani-ize the city. They thought that office was my own publicity machine generating stories about me personally. In fact, the public-information office spent a significant part of its time fielding reporters' questions about the daily incidents of crime and special events in New York City, which is the lifeblood of the local television and papers: How many people were at the demonstration? When was the suspect arrested? Where was the shooter? They didn't go out of their way to create a media frenzy, they responded to news stories in an effort to help the many reporters who covered the crime beat, both in New York City and around the world. They also answered hundreds of questions from average citizens each day. It was one of the busiest offices of its type in America and, like the rest of New York, it ran seven days a week, twenty-four hours a day.

By keeping to accurate information, the media could also deliver our message to the public, the cops, the bad guys, the politicians, and the country, and we made it our policy to take every opportunity to have the message delivered properly. We encouraged ride-alongs, in which reporters rode with cops during their shifts. We trusted that when most reporters saw the conditions and pressures a police officer works under, they would identify with the cops and write their stories accordingly. Every ride-along had the potential to be a mini–*NYPD Blue*, get great ratings, and help tell our story. Nevertheless, City Hall felt threatened. In February 1995, they told Miller to cut his staff. It was the first broadside by the Hall in what was to become an unrelenting effort to micromanage the Police Department.

There were thirty-nine people in the DCPI's office, twenty-nine cops and ten civilians. Miller was told he could keep seventeen. (The mayor's press office employed eighteen.) LaPorte received that message from Denny Young. Then the message changed. Not only would the staff be cut in half, but all Miller's people would be reassigned, and an entire new staff, chosen by City Hall, put in place. They were attempting to take over the operation. I sent Timoney to City Hall with Deputy Commissioner of the Office of Management and Budget Joe Wuensch and his aide Mike Butler. They met with Giuliani's chief of staff, Randy Mastro.

Mastro was pasty-faced and not very diplomatic. "The mayor wants the staff cut in half," he told my guys. "We've got an operation to run."

Timoney is not an extremely politic man. "Who the hell do you think you're talking to?" John has what's known in our circle as the "Timoney look," the visual equivalent of his jumping over a desk and choking someone. Mastro said, basically, "Please, leave me alone. This is what the mayor wants." The mayor's staff at all times seemed very scared of their boss. "There's nothing further to talk about."

The next day, Mastro called Timoney. "We want that list of the people you're redeploying. We want to know where they're going."

"Fine," Timoney told him, "I'll talk to Miller."

"We want it in ten minutes." He sounded as if Giuliani were standing next to him, terrifying him with what Timoney called "Rudy rage."

"Get real. We're talking about people's careers here. We've got to find places for them to land. These are loyal cops, you're not going to just dump them out somewhere, that's not how we do business."

"We want it done in ten minutes!"

"Slow down. I'll get back to you." Of course, Timoney didn't get back to him.

An hour later: "I want this thing now!"

"Calm down."

I called Denny Young. "Denny, what's going on here? You want something done, we'll do it. We will carry out the mission to reduce crime and disorder, that's what we're hired to do. But why are we getting this kind of interference?" Young didn't have a satisfactory answer. We knew without having to be told. This was the latest in the continuing effort to bend the police department to total submission under their control.

Miller, Timoney, Maple, LaPorte, and I huddled in my office for several hours to discuss our options and didn't return calls from the mayor's staff. I had scheduled a meeting with the mayor for four o'clock. I'd say what I had to say then. People knocked on the door and called through, "City Hall says, 'Call immediately!' " Timoney piped up, "Tell them to screw themselves!" You can imagine the rage the Hall was in by then.

I said, "If they push this Miller thing, I'm going to resign. I'm not going to take this; this is getting crazy."

Up to that point, Timoney and I had had a good professional relationship. This made it personal. He said, "We should all resign. All of us. We should go over en masse and resign." I was taken aback. Why would this man be willing to give up his twenty-five-year career for my battle? But he was. Timoney was a moralist, and he was offended that the department was being usurped and treated with such disrespect. Maple and LaPorte followed suit, though more reluctantly. We all had tremendous financial issues at stake; none of us had money. To lose a good job with little possibility of immediate reemployment would have been very difficult.

LaPorte's intelligence sources were working overtime. Word came to us that the Hall would accept our resignations. "If you're thinking of resign- ing," he was told, "don't worry, your resignations will be accepted." We were giving the thought serious consideration.

Cheryl came into the office. Miller had called her and told her he was going to resign. She had then called me, and I told her I and the others were contemplating resigning also. "Don't do anything," she'd said, "I'm coming down." Cheryl was one of my most trusted advisors. She walked in with a tin of homemade cookies. We were sitting around, cursing and looking for a magic solution that would make City Hall act reasonably. She asked, "Are there any adults here? The testosterone level seems really high."

Miller disappeared. The meeting continued. LaPorte came rushing in. "Miller just resigned."

"What!"

"Yeah. Miller, he's downstairs resigning. He called Rudy a Nazi! It's on television."

Miller had called the in-house press up from the second floor to his DCPI office and told them he had an announcement to make. We watched from my office, mesmerized. He spoke without a script. He was choked up and close to tears. It was going out live on New York One, a local news channel.

"[City Hall] said," Miller told them, "because of what's been in the pa- pers, that the people here couldn't be trusted and that therefore we shouldn't replace some of the cops but all of the cops. They were going to ask me to throw everybody out of here.

"Now, loyalty is important. Loyalty runs up. I'm loyal to the mayor, I'm loyal to the police commissioner . . . but there were loyal Nazis, too.

"Loyalty runs down. I'm loyal to my people, and I'm loyal to the re- porters we're supposed to serve here, because we're all loyal to the public. Whether you're a cop or a reporter or a police commissioner or a mayor, we all serve the same public. I'm not going to let that stop. Not on my watch. . . . Very graciously, I have to say, people said they would do what they had to do. We said we'd find places for them to go. And we would have done it. But now they want to find places for everybody to go, [and] I thought it would be easier and more sensible if I was not the one to do this disloyal thing.

"So, what do they say, the captain is supposed to go down with the ship, right?" He had been crying, at times finding it hard to speak. He cried some more.

"I'm not crying 'cause it's the end of the world. It's not the end of the world. My world looks pretty rosy." He sighed. "But I'm worried about you guys because, you know, I love you.

"So, I'm not moving the cops out to downsize the office. And I'm not moving the other cops out to go along with this ridiculous request based on somebody's idea of what loyalty's about. I'm not moving *anybody* out. I assume that they will come for my badge, and they can have it.

"I think that I work for the greatest police commissioner there ever was. I even think the mayor's going to do a good job. I think he's going to take on the budget, I think crime is going to continue to go down. But I also think that there are other ways to deal with human beings, and there are other ways to deal with the process of getting out information.

"Somebody in this administration said, trying to summarize the company line, 'We want to have more control over the information.' I have to suggest to you that the information that we put out here is not information that we are supposed to 'control.' It's not information City Hall is supposed to 'control.' In fact, it's not the mayor's information, it's the public's information. That's why they call this Public Information. The mayor has his own press office.

"I think having said that, I want to thank the police commissioner for giving me the greatest year, or fourteen months, of my life. And . . ." here he broke down, "I want to thank you guys for making it. . . ." Miller walked aside, and the press room erupted in applause.

Timoney said, "They're going to be showing this in journalism schools for the next hundred years."

Miller came back upstairs to my office. He had seen that we were heading toward resigning en masse, he understood that this was the Hall's intention, and he had made the decision to fall on his sword to save us. While we were furious and emotional and felt very deeply for John, he made it clear that it was more important for us to accomplish what we had set out to do than defy this particularly unpleasant mayor. "Look, guys," he said, "don't you resign. That's exactly what they want."

The mayor got right on the airwaves and tried to both spin the situation and demean Miller. He spent a significant part of the day being interviewed and ended up doing a sit-down on a local station. Give Giuliani credit, he and his crew came up with a masterful spin. Their explanation had little to do with the real reasons for the purge of the entire DCPI staff, but it sounded good: "NYC captains, NYC lieutenants, NYC sergeants shouldn't be public-relations spokespeople. . . . I need them to be New

York City police officers who will arrest people for crimes. . . . We can't have twenty-nine cops playing public relations person." As I have explained, the importance of the media cannot be overstated in reducing crime and disorder in New York. Miller said, "I think that City Hall should understand that positive publicity for the police department reflects well on them." But the mayor conveniently overlooked those facts in his haste to explain away his behavior.

Giuliani went after Miller personally. It was unseemly.

"It is not a tumultuous day in New York City when the deputy commissioner for public relations [*sic*] in the New York City Police Department resigns. Big deal. . . .

"It seemed to me that John, uh, had difficulty accomplishing what is a very difficult management task. Uh, some people are very good at one thing, they're not very good at another. . . . Miller indicated that he was unwilling to complete that task, it almost seemed for emotional reasons. . . . He obviously was under a great deal of emotional stress."

One local interviewer referred to the NYPD as my police department. "The fact is," Giuliani insisted, "it isn't his police department, it's the mayor's police department. We have civilian control of the police department in New York City. The point is, under the law of the City of New York," clearly someone had been sent to research the point, "the mayor of the City of New York is in control of the police department. So I have to make the final decisions about the police department, [and] I am fully capable of doing it." That kind of talk cowed the interviewer.

The same day Miller took his fall, Giuliani purged the head press officers in four other departments and fired nearly three dozen press aides. One of them, housing's deputy commissioner Harry Rittenberg, said, "They want to control the information. This is like Rudy Giuliani's *Kristallnacht.*"

CBS News Vice President Jerry Nachman said, "It almost seems like this is some former East-bloc country that you're covering, in which the chairman's picture has to be in every story you do."

I had to consider whether I wanted to stay. Could I maintain sufficient autonomy to complete the work I'd started? I felt very bad for John. He'd had his dream job, he had done it perfectly, and it had been taken out from under him. But he would remain my friend while our team continued to reduce crime and disorder in the city.

Rudy Giuliani, in his haste to sweep up every crumb of credit, had disregarded reason, personality, and honor. The mayor was a prosecutor, and he used the same tone on Miller, a devoted employee who had given the city excellent and valuable service, as he did on his defendants. A more smug individual was hard to find on the news that night.

The attempt to discredit Miller and his "emotions" failed. Miller had been a respected reporter, and the emotions he showed came from his dedication to his job and the recognition that City Hall's interference would prevent him from doing it. Miller soon regained his position, renown, and salary at WNBC-TV. New York's government lost a valuable resource.

The Hall assumed control of press ride-alongs, demanding scrutiny and approval of each request, and refused to allow the department to hold any but the most cursory press briefings in our own house. All interagency press conferences and releases of police strategies came out of City Hall. We were permitted to be accessible to the press concerning the news or issues of the day, but all profile or policy stories, requests for my appearance on weekend TV news panels or radio shows, anything involving national media, had to be cleared with them.

They sent us an acting DCPI, Tom Kelly, who had headed up public information for the Corrections Department, no doubt thinking that his provisional appointment would make him beholden to them. Timoney said he was a good guy, which went a long way with me, and LaPorte was impressed with him. I was comfortable with Kelly and quickly recommended, to City Hall's surprise, that he permanently replace Miller.

The attacks didn't let up. Cristyne Lategano tried to demean our entire vision of public information. "Public relations was put before any kind of substance," she told *New York Newsday.* "When you put glamour over fighting crime, it leads to serious problems. Now it is the time to get serious. This is a reality check. We're here to fight crime, not to be Hollywood stars. This is real-life cops, not *NYPD Blue.*"

The mayor backed her up. "I think she put it quite accurately," he said. He called our press office "dangerous," "out of control," and too publicity conscious.

Of course, it was all self-serving bullshit. Crime was down 12.3 percent. Murders were down 18.8 percent. Perhaps it was the fact that I was profiled in *The New Yorker* the same week Miller was terminated. In her attempt to belittle our accomplishments, Lategano publicly embarrassed herself and further demeaned herself in the eyes of the press.

By clearing out the entire public-information office, the mayor decimated the department's institutional memory. Longtime press officers knew exactly where to go for information because they had internalized NYPD history, while the new people placed by the mayor were at a loss. Reporters were obviously aware that the process had slowed down, and some of them took it out on Kelly. I thought that anger was misplaced.

But more than institutional memory was at stake. The thirty-nine individuals the mayor displaced, and whose work he so casually belittled, were people who had put many years into the public-information office and were widely respected by the press. He needlessly caused havoc in their lives. This is a mayor who consistently talks about how much he loves cops, yet in his desire to get at Miller and me, he crudely damaged the careers and lives of these hardworking police officers and civilians. How is he ever going to look anyone in the eye and say with a straight face that he loves and respects cops when he has treated them so callously?

As for putting cops in the field and not having them "playing public-relations person," two years later, in Giuliani's police department the public-information office was staffed by twenty-four uniformed police—including one detective, four sergeants, two lieutenants, and one deputy inspector—and seven civilians.

The mayor met the press daily in the Blue Room at City Hall. I was surprised at how much deference they showed him. The vaunted New York press, who were supposed to be so tough in pursuit of news and dirt and scandal, rarely pursued a story vigorously in open session. Maybe they were concerned about the competition stealing their leads, but there was hardly ever an edge to their questioning, and even less follow-up. The mayor has notoriously thin skin, and when he got upset it always made for good TV and overheated headlines, so I was surprised the press didn't bait that bear more often. They also didn't get much more information out of him than he went in willing to give. Maple used to joke, "The press should do Compstat in the Blue Room." The thought of Maple getting Giuliani dancing in the hot lights—"Tell the Jackster. Tell the Jackster!"—always gave us a laugh.

While the Hall was vitally concerned with local and national media, they didn't seem to focus on the international press. I met with about forty foreign correspondents and discussed the New York success story. Their articles and reports appeared in England, Japan, Norway, Italy, and Brazil. Correspondents from China, Hungary, Germany, Switzerland, Portugal, the Netherlands, and Israel all visited Compstat. *The Economist* profiled my management techniques under a headline that read, "NYPD, Inc." *The*

New Yorker had called me "The CEO Cop." An article in *The Times* of London said, "In a city famous for its murders, muggings, ghetto gun-fights, subway anarchy, drug gangs, junkies, rapists, winos, pickpockets and every other form of seething urban desperado, Bratton is turning the tide."

Chapter 18

As Compstat became more sophisticated and computerized, we pin-pointed crime and attacked it immediately. In July 1995, Mayor Giuliani and I announced the semiannual crime figures:

- Murder down 31 percent over the same period in 1994
- Robberies down 21.9 percent
- Burglaries down 18.1 percent
- Motor-vehicle theft down 25.2 percent
- Felonious assault down 6 percent
- Overall crime down 18.4 percent

Criminologists apparently still had a hard time accepting the reality of our success. I made a conscious decision to take on the academics, to challenge conventional wisdom about crime in America and prove that effective policing can make a substantial impact on social change. They were delighted with our success, but many did not attribute it to the policy change at City Hall or the new direction, management, and operations techniques we instituted at the NYPD. "There's a miracle happening before our eyes," said Jeffrey Fagan, director of the Center for Violence Research and Prevention at Columbia University. "Cops deserve credit, but it would be a first in the history of social science for there to be a single reason for such a dramatic change in social behavior."

We began to shape the message. We lined up their alternate reasons like ducks in a row and shot them all down.

The drop in New York's crime rate reflected a national trend. We *were* the national trend. According to FBI figures, in the first six months of 1995, serious crime throughout the country went down by 1 percent, or about 67,000 crimes. In New York in that same period, there were 41,000 fewer crimes, a 16 percent drop. We were two-thirds of the national decline in reported crime.

New York's teenage population, which was responsible for a significant portion of the city's violent crime, was on its way down, and many of them were dead or in jail. "Jail? Who put them there?" asked Maple. "Did all the sixteen-year-olds suddenly become fifty?" The number of sixteen-to-nineteen-year-olds in New York City was actually going up, not down.

Crime dropped simply because we had more cops. The NYPD reached its staffing height in September 1994 and lost about 1,400 each year thereafter through attrition until the next recruit class replenished the previous year's losses. Overtime was slashed. We were losing people and crime was still going down in double digits.

The crack epidemic that fueled the crime wave had ebbed. Heroin, a depressant, was now the drug of choice. This was the "all the criminals are nodding" defense. We spot-tested regularly in Central Booking and found that the percentage of people who had cocaine in their system when arrested remained the same or higher than it had been at crack's height. In Manhattan in February 1995, that number was 78 percent.

It was a particularly cold winter, which traditionally holds down crime. Come on. All the criminals stayed indoors? It was cold up and down the Eastern seaboard and those cities' crime figures didn't vary drastically. Were Boston's or Washington's criminal element more hardy than New York crooks?

Homicides were down because all the gangs had made peace with one another. The DEA had listened in on over 400,000 wiretap conversations, and we had never heard a word about this supposed treaty. And if the gangs made an agreement not to kill each other over drugs, did they also agree not to rob anybody, or steal cars, or commit burglaries or shoot people?

———

Maple said, "They're the ones who tried to convince Columbus that the world was flat. Remember in *The Wizard of Oz*, when Toto pulls back the curtain and the wizard says, 'Pay no attention to the man behind the curtain'? And Dorothy says, 'You're a terrible man.' And he says, 'No, Dorothy, I'm a good man. I'm just not a very good wizard.' I think all of these experts are good people; they're just not very good wizards."

But even though we had a real handle on crime and were seeing great success in many areas, we still had pockets of concern. One of the major criticisms we faced was that in our effort to provide more proactive policing, we had encouraged more aggressive police behavior, particularly in minority communities. I addressed this in my first roll-call speech at the 103, we addressed it in training at the academy, and we made it clear at all times that we would not be successful in policing New York if we were perceived by law-abiding New Yorkers as an occupying army. "Police brutality" is a phrase I do not use lightly, yet we were being accused of exactly that.

It is important to define "police brutality." We defined brutality as unnecessary behavior that caused broken bones, stitches, and internal injuries. But those were not the figures that had gone up significantly. What had risen were reports of police inappropriately pushing, shoving, sometimes only touching citizens. We were taking back the streets, and it wasn't easy work. In the course of enforcing laws that had not been enforced for twenty-five years, we were being more proactive, we were engaging more people, and often they didn't like it. We were dealing with murderers, rapists, muggers, and felons, the most violent people in society, as well as more than the usual number of thieves, drug addicts, and drunks. A lot of the "brutality" was reported by those people engaged in illegal behavior and looking for a bargaining chit. In three years there had been over 15,000 complaints of all types: brutality, disrespect, etc. During that same period the department had made almost a million arrests.

But we were also coming into contact with law-abiding citizens, and it was those people we were also concerned with. A cop gets called in, you think he wants to get in a fight in which someone gets hurt? He'd rather not; he has been taught how to restrain himself and his suspects so that doesn't happen. Where some cops didn't restrain themselves was their mouth. They tried to be too tough, they were impatient instead of courteous, they intimidated instead of simply carrying out their business. Sometimes the attitude led to more pushing and shoving than was necessary. Was there lack of respect by some police officers toward the public? Yes. Was there abuse? Yes. Was there more abuse than in previous years or administrations? I don't believe so. The rise in complaints was commensurate with the rise in contact. It's an issue I was dealing with but which was by no means resolved. As I repeatedly told cops at roll calls, "We're going to get crime down in this city and be applauded for it, but if you don't win the respect of the people you're policing, you are going to lose."

In 1995 five thousand complaints were made against 38,000 New York City police officers in a city of 7.3 million people that expanded every day by 3.5 million additional people coming into the city. All five thousand complaints were investigated, and fewer than five hundred were actually substantiated. That's five hundred individual acts out of the literally millions of encounters each year between police officers and the public. There were also 389 fewer murders in the City of New York in 1995 than there were in 1994. Of course, no one knows who those murder nonvictims are; they're still alive. I'm sure if you ask the people who lived, plus their families and friends, whether the style of policing that saved their lives was worthwhile, they would say yes.

There has been continuing discussion of residency rules requiring cops to live in the city they police. I don't think they are necessary. I've lived outside the communities I've policed and that didn't stop me from developing an understanding and affection for those neighborhoods and giving 150 percent in protecting and serving them. Most people like to get away from work once the day is over; why deny cops that opportunity? In New York, there are the issues of taxes and schools and environment to consider. Many people know and love and contribute to New York and still commute to work. Cops can, too.

I don't think residency should be a requirement so long as we hire the right cops. One of the concerns we often heard was that the police department didn't look like the community it was policing. It didn't. In a minority-majority city split about evenly between male and female, the NYPD was between 25 and 30 percent black and Hispanic and 15 percent female. We lose about 1,400 cops of all races to attrition each year, and we hire the same number of officers to replace them. With 38,000 cops on the force, even if we hired *only* minorities, we would not catch up any time soon. I, of course, wanted the best cops, no matter what color. We recruited inside and outside New York, and about 50 percent of our recruits came from the suburbs and outside the city.

We began discussions to develop a career ladder for inner-city schoolchildren, beginning in seventh and eighth grades. During the summers, these kids would spend time with the police. For twelve weeks, they would work with our youth officers and get exposed to the NYPD: go to the police station, go to the firing range, do a ride-along with officers on patrol, see what police do. We would then encourage those kids to join our

Scout Explorer programs, which are run by every precinct in the city. During high school, these same kids would be encouraged to stay involved with our mentoring environment, which many do not have at home. We could provide them with an experience different from the one they might be getting in the streets. Since approximately 85 percent of New York City public-school kids are minorities, it stands to reason that 85 percent of our group would be minorities as well. Acknowledging that the minority population often has a lot of negative interactions with the police, we would now be working with kids who, since they were twelve, had interacted more positively.

At the end of high school and the Explorer program, we would encourage these young adults to go to a city college, preferably John Jay College of Criminal Justice. We would offer them internships during which they would work ten to fifteen hours a week for the NYPD as cadets, and we would find them paying jobs in the private sector, particularly in the private-security field. Now the recruits would have a salary, working as security guards; they would be required to continue their college education. Then, at age twenty-two, they would take the civil-service exam. As much as I was given credit for my college degree on the Boston sergeant's exam, they would be given preference in hiring as police officers because of their extensive previous training and education.

This plan would over time significantly change the makeup of the NYPD. The people in our program would all be city residents, 90 percent would be minorities. Forty percent of our recruit class usually lived outside the city, but under my plan that figure would fall dramatically because the inner-city residents would be moved to the top of the list.

I also wanted to involve the much-maligned three-thousand-person school police by putting them under the control of the NYPD, as we had successfully done with transit and housing. While the people in our program were waiting to turn twenty-two and come on the job, at twenty they could join that force. What better security personnel to interact with high-school kids than young men and women who have recently come through that same environment and chosen our road? With young inner-city kids causing so much of our crime problem, such a police force could really make a difference. Some of our new officers would stay in the communities in which they were raised, which would bring the cops home.

I was very enthusiastic about this proposal and still am. Despite my and City University of New York head Ann Reynolds's strong support, the Hall never embraced it, maybe because it didn't originate there.

The NYPD was extremely productive in 1995. The Transit and Housing Police were merged into the department, creating a force of 38,310, more than three times as large as any other in the country. As I had done at transit, we upgraded to nine-millimeter weapons for the entire force and garnered the same benefits. We policed Pope John Paul II's visit to New York and the convening of the world's leaders at the United Nations. We continued to roll out our strategies. And crime kept going down.

One of the priority initiatives that we aggressively pursued was the placement of women in significant command positions. When we created the new Queens patrol borough I promoted Gertrude Laforge to the rank of two-star borough chief, the highest uniformed rank ever attained by a woman in the NYPD. We also placed women in some of the toughest precincts in the city, where they excelled, frequently outperforming their male counterparts. It took women a long time to get into the police profession, but I enjoyed providing them the opportunity to advance up the promotion ladder and letting their outstanding performance silence their critics. During my two years with the department, I took the opportunity to promote more women to command ranks than had served in them at any time in the department's history.

The end of 1995 was a time of great excitement. Because of the intimacy of the crime-tracking methods we had developed, we knew we were going to surpass our goals. I had asked the department to produce crime reduction of 15 percent in 1995, and we had reached 17 percent. It was the first time since World War II that the city had recorded consecutive-year double-digit drops. Every precinct had experienced declines in total felonies, and in two years every precinct had seen double-digit declines in the overall crime rate. During the first two years of my commissionership, total felonies were down 27 percent to levels not seen in the city since the early 1970s. Murder was down by 39 percent, auto theft 35 percent. Robberies were off by a third, burglaries by a quarter. The crime drop had been relatively balanced in rich and poor neighborhoods across the city, if measured by percentage. But while a 60 percent decline in the murder rate on the middle-class Upper West Side meant four fewer deaths in 1995, a 51 percent decrease in the poorer East New York section of Brooklyn meant forty-four fewer people killed. For many years, minorities had been suffering way out of proportion to their numbers. Those communities were benefiting greatly from the decline in homicides and shootings.

We were even starting to win over some of the academics and criminologists. Harvard's Mark Moore told *The New York Times,* "New York has enjoyed a significant drop in crime that can't be easily explained by sociological factors. Therefore, the claim this might be the result of police activity looks pretty good."

"This drop exceeds any of the expectations we had when we first started," said the mayor. We were going to have a great New Year's.

On New Year's Eve, Cheryl and I hosted Jack Maple and Bridget O'Connor, the transit sergeant he was dating, and John Miller and his date at our apartment for dinner and then took the subway down to Times Square to see the ball drop. The transit merger had been completed a few months earlier, and I had several nice conversations with the cops patrolling the platforms and the trains. Miller eavesdropped on a pair of elderly women talking about how safe they felt on the train at eleven-thirty on New Year's Eve and how good they felt about the city.

In Times Square, the confetti was blowing, the horns were blaring, there were hundreds of thousands of people celebrating in the streets, none feeling better than I did. The ball had been refurbished and for the first time would be activated by computer. The mayor was preparing to do the honors, and my gang and I stopped (minus, understandably, Miller) to say hello. As we walked through the crowd, I received many friendly salutes from the cops on the scene and heard a lot of "Attaboy, Commissioner!" and "Great job!" from the crowd. After the ball dropped, we all headed for, you guessed it, Elaine's.

Time magazine was going to do a major feature piece on crime in America. *Newsweek* had spoken to Peter LaPorte earlier but had not put anything in motion. Our end-of-the-year crime figures came out and were impressive, there was some nationwide decline in criminal activity, and *Time* decided that community policing was the reason. They assigned Eric Pooley to report on the New York angle. Pooley had been a writer for *New York* magazine, and in his last piece before moving to *Time* had savaged Giuliani. He had quoted former Mayor Ed Koch comparing Giuliani to "Frankenstein's monster . . . you run at the sight of him." Pooley had written, "What *is* it about this mayor that he can wholly dominate the political landscape and at the same time repel most everyone who inhabits it? . . . Greatness from a public servant demands heart and soul as well as brains and brass. Those close to the mayor swear he's got the first two."

I understand *Time* or Pooley sent a researcher to interview the mayor, and I was not surprised to hear that she wasn't given much time by the

Hall. *Time* might not have been their favorite magazine; that summer, when our semiannual figures had come out, they had published a full-page article about New York's crime turnaround, centered mostly around Giuliani, but had run a picture of me, not him, standing with two cops in Times Square. Word got back to us that he had taken Lategano's head off over that gaffe.

When Pooley arrived we let him sit in on a Compstat meeting. Compstat is great theater; the interplay between the bosses and commanders is not unlike the tense parts of a cop movie. We also sat Pooley down with Jack Maple, an interviewer's dream who can fill a reporter's notebook with off-the-cuff remarks that are highly quotable, highly accurate, and highly perceptive. Within a week, *Time* called Tom Kelly asking for crime numbers and saying they wanted to take a photograph of me.

We shot it under the Brooklyn Bridge, at night, on the Brooklyn side, with the lights of Manhattan and the Twin Towers in the background. There was an icy wind whipping off the East River, and I had my trenchcoat collar up. Ten days later I was on the cover of *Time*. The cover line read, "Finally, We're WINNING the War Against CRIME. Here's Why."

Time hits the newsstands on Mondays. That Sunday, a blizzard hit New York and shut down the city. Roads were impassable, we were in a state of emergency. The mayor held his first press conference of the day in our Command Control Center with the NYPD logo behind him. Larry Celona of the *New York Post* showed him an advance copy of the cover. The mayor said it was great for the City of New York.

Time ships out of Connecticut, and because of the heavy snow its trucks couldn't get into New York City. The magazine didn't get any substantial distribution in our area until Thursday, the day Mayor Giuliani and I held our weekly meetings.

I hadn't heard anything from him all week, but that was understandable; he had an emergency to preside over. I was curious how he would handle the situation. An appearance on the cover of *Time* is mother's milk for American politicians, and I was sure he and his staff felt I had stolen it from him. Although I didn't read it this way, to some the cover line intimated that *I* was the reason we were winning the war on crime. That must have caused Giuliani some consternation; they had threatened to fire me for showing up on the front page of the *Daily News*.

The mayor never mentioned any of it. We discussed police matters regarding the storm and whatever else was timely. To the best of my recollection, Giuliani's only public comment on the matter was, "Nice trench coat."

Chapter 19

THE NEWS THAT I HAD SIGNED TO WRITE THIS BOOK FOR RANDOM HOUSE HAD been in the papers, and, although I briefed him on the contract, the mayor insisted on having Denny Young and the city's corporation counsel Paul Crotty review it, ostensibly to clear it with the city's Conflicts of Interest Board. "What I'm concerned about," said Giuliani, "is that it follow the ethical and legal guidelines that are set for this." There were precedents for city officials to write books—Ed Koch, for instance, had produced a best-seller while in office—and I did not immediately turn it over. I did not think it was necessary, and I wanted to get the project under way. I was concerned that I would deliver the contract and it would disappear into the black hole.

I also resisted what was clearly an attempt to embarrass me by questioning my ethics. I was the city's top law-enforcement official; for the mayor to imply publicly that I might have stepped outside the law was an insult apparently intended to impugn my character. The mayor could dismiss the police commissioner any time he wanted, he didn't need to read the fine print on my contract to know that; this public hand-wringing seemed calculated.

I concentrated on the work at hand, reducing crime and disorder in New York City. We had made remarkable gains, and 1996 was going to be the year they were both expanded and consolidated. It was the year we were finally going to launch Juggernaut (though the word had been banned in City Hall). To get that done, I needed to transfer some personnel. After consultation with Timoney and Maple and my gang, we came up with fifteen transfers in all. This personnel juggling was routine, the kind of organizational caretaking best left to the person in day-to-day charge of the organization, and I had made these kinds of moves many times before. The Hall held us up.

Over the course of several months, under the guise of tightening the municipal belt in an increasingly worsening budget situation, City Hall had wrested control of many budgetary and personnel powers that the New York City police commissioner had traditionally held as manager over his department. Early in the new administration they instituted what they called the Vacancy Control Board, headed up by the mayor's first deputy, Peter Powers. Approval for all hiring and promotions now rested with the Hall. In the past that approval had been pro forma if the managers stayed within their budgets. But now the micromanaging began in earnest.

They started by controlling the numbers, but eventually they wanted the names. They started demanding the lists of our discretionary promotions: who we were making first- and second-grade detectives. They sought to use these discretionary promotions in collective-bargaining negotiations with the unions. They kept pushing it. Over time, they wanted to see not only promotions, but senior-level transfers. The department had always run the movements of its bureau commanders by City Hall, more as a courtesy than for any approval, and the comings and goings of lower personnel had never been subject to their whims. Timoney told me that during the Koch administration, everything had been left up to the department. Now, we had to get the Giuliani crowd's approval on minor moves as well as major ones, and they took an inordinate amount of time getting back to us.

I was out of town so Timoney took our handwritten list of about fifteen transfers and promotions to the regularly scheduled meeting with the mayor, who looked at it and didn't comment. Timoney called Denny Young to set up a meeting to discuss them, and when I called Timoney and asked how it went he told me, "This hump won't even return my call. I don't know what's going on over there. I've left fifty messages." Finally, he made phone contact.

"Denny, we want to put these transfers through."

"Well, let's talk."

"What's there to talk about? We're shaking up the department."

"Humor me. Let's just talk." They set up a meeting. Timoney brought the list and began to go through it. Young refused the first promotion. Timoney presented the second, Young refused it. Timoney believed this was the largest transfer of chiefs in the history of the department, and Young was sitting there looking for all the world like he was going to nix them all.

The third proposed transfer was Deputy Chief Jules Martin. "He was Dinkins's guy," said Young. Martin had been commanding officer of the police intelligence unit that provided security for City Hall and Gracie Mansion during the Dinkins administration.

"What do you mean, 'He was Dinkins's guy'? *I* was Dinkins's guy."

"He's loyal to Dinkins."

"Nah, nah, nah. Denny, you guys still fail to realize we're loyal to the police department. You automatically get our loyalty because you're there. We were loyal to Koch, we were loyal to Dinkins, we're loyal to you. That's the way it works. Jules Martin is as loyal to you as anybody else on this list."

"Yeah, but, you know, he worked for Dinkins."

"Listen, I understand he worked for Dinkins. Now he works for you guys. He's been a good soldier, he's been real good, he deserves a shot. We need a black guy up there, it's Harlem, it's traditional, he's a lawyer, he's a terrific guy."

"You say he supports us?"

"Yes, of course."

"Has he made any public utterances in favor of the mayor?"

"Are you kidding me? We're police, we don't do that!" Timoney got disgusted. "I'll tell you what," he said. "We're not getting anywhere here. My twenty-fifth wedding anniversary is coming up, I'm going to Saint Lucia. Bratton's on the way back, you can deal with Bratton. It's his police department."

"No, it isn't," Young spat. "It's Rudy Giuliani's police department."

The next morning, *The New York Times* reported that the mayor had rejected several of our top-level personnel moves. We assumed it was leaked by the mayor's people to show his power over the department. However, the Hall apparently felt the article made Giuliani appear heavy-handed. They asked two *Times* reporters, Clifford Krauss and Steven Lee Myers, to present themselves at City Hall to meet with Powers, Young, Lapp, and me and my DCPI. Rumors of our difficult relationship were spreading, and

Krauss asked for an anecdote in which the mayor and I got along. I told him we were not close personal friends but that we shared a vision for policing the city. He reposed the question in slightly different language, and I said, "I don't profess that the two of us skip down the lane hand in hand."

By law, the New York City police commissioner's term runs for five years, and the term I was completing—begun in 1991 by Lee Brown and continued by Ray Kelly—expired on February 21. Under normal circumstances, my reappointment would have been routine. These were not normal circumstances. It was March 9. Krauss asked why I had not been reappointed. He was told words to the effect that they were just a bit behind in their paperwork.

After the meeting adjourned, Krauss and Myers were buttonholed by the mayor's inner circle and told that my reappointment was actually being held up because they wanted to see the book contract. I had given them an issue. I was not pleased to have my ethics impugned. Rather than fuel another week's headlines, I submitted the contract for review. (As of the publication of this book, I have still not heard from corporation counsel on the matter.)

There was another attempted embarrassment. When I first came to the city, Cheryl and I had met the financier Henry Kravis and his wife at a party given by one of the mayor's supporters. We had had dinner together a number of times, and they extended an invitation for us to join them, traveling on their private jet, on two vacation trips to their homes in Colorado and the Dominican Republic, which we had accepted. During the flap over my book contract, a gossip columnist for the *Daily News* mentioned in his column that Cheryl and I were vacationing with Kravis and his wife and created the appearance that this trip was inappropriate. It wasn't, but it gave the appearance of impropriety, and raising the question of my ethics once again was a plus for the Hall.

Upon my return, at the mayor's request, Paul Crotty came to talk to me. I was under the impression he was coming as my attorney to advise me on the appropriate course of action as it related to this book. However, as soon as he came through the door, he showed me a list of every official trip I had taken during my twenty-seven months as commissioner, all of which had been approved, as required, by the mayor's office. He told me we didn't need to talk about the book deal, they were already looking at the contract; he wanted to talk about all these other trips. Shortly after our meeting, I was disappointed to find that the content of that conversation made its way into the local tabloids. Needless to say, I was quite concerned that a private conversation between me and the city corporation counsel would end up in the media. The next time I met with Crotty, I brought my own representation, noted New York attorney Richard Emery.

These were prosecutors; they were familiar with creating damage through investigation. I had seen them do it at the U.S. Attorney's office, I had seen them hound Schools Chancellor Ramon Cortines out of office. It was not their practice to see opponents leave the battlefield with honor; for them, it wasn't over until you were carried off on your shield.

Reporters told us City Hall was shopping stories like crazy: "Check phone logs," "Check travel records," "Check . . ." They would find nothing damaging; there was nothing to find. Then the rumors began that I was going to, as Randy Mastro told *Newsweek,* "cash in" on job offers in the private sector. Supposedly, I was offered a high-level position at the Walt Disney Company. Despite my denials, that rumor persisted. There was nothing to it whatsoever, but they were trying to position me as a lame duck, which could seriously undermine my authority to run the department. To blunt the attacks, I surprised them all by publicly releasing information on all my trips, both personal and private, during the time I was police commissioner. I even took the additional step of reimbursing my hosts for several private trips I had taken. I could feel the skids being greased.

Despite their continuing efforts to stir up the media, they were still not in a position to ask me to leave. The decline in crime and disorder in New York was overwhelming and growing every day. Thanks to *Time* magazine, the issue of credit for that turnaround had been resolved. I had a team in place that was successful beyond anyone's hopes or expectations; to fire me and disband it because of personal ambition would have been seen as remarkably petty, not to mention completely against the best interests of the city.

However, it is very difficult to work effectively when you have lost the confidence of the people you work for. Giuliani had made it clear whose police department he thought it was. He had also made it abundantly clear that I would not be allowed to run it. There would be no coup de grâce for me. It was death by a thousand cuts: ethics investigations, constant headlines, meddling micromanagement, leaks, delays, disrespect. I observed the slow strangulation of my ability to run the organization. He created a situation in which I had no choice but to resign.

I had always intended to resign at the end of 1996, when everything I had planned for the NYPD would have been in place. But after that issue of *Time* came out, the pace quickened. We knew there was going to be trouble. I began to explore outside job possibilities and to speculate as to the appropriate time to take them. I consulted with several friends and advisors, including Dr. Dee Soder of the CEO Prospective Group, a career transition consultant for senior-level CEO's, and Bob Johnson, who provided significant assistance on the best course of action. There were certain things, some symbolic and some operationally significant, I still wanted to accomplish. I wanted the Brooklyn North Drug Initiative, the modified successor to Juggernaut, up and running during my tenure, so City Hall could not take credit for its creation and development. Brooklyn North was finally begun in early March and brought immediate results.

I also wanted to march in the Saint Patrick's Day parade with my father Bill and my son David; they had not been able to make it the prior year. It was a gathering of eagles. Bob Johnson and Bob O'Toole came down specially from Boston. Jack Maple, John Timoney, and Peter LaPorte all walked with me. My whole security detail came. Only Miller was missing, but he was there in spirit.

Finally, after a number of months of discussion with my inner circle, I now had a date set. For their purposes, I needed to let them know. This was not a surprise; we had discussed it over Sunday dinners. At four o'clock Monday afternoon, March 25, I called my inner circle into my office and told them, "I'm leaving." April 15 would be my last day. That evening Maple, Miller, LaPorte, Cheryl, and I went out to dinner. During the meal, we got word that an off-duty cop had been shot in a housing project on the Lower East Side. Maple left to investigate, I went to the hospital.

I really did not want to leave the job. We'd had many successes in my twenty-seven months as commissioner. Felony crime was down throughout the city by 39 percent, murders were down by 50 percent, and we were geared up for more. Our Brooklyn North Drug Initiative was producing immediate results, it would continue to prove a huge success, and I would have liked to have seen it through citywide. We had another initiative that would broaden hiring practices and make the NYPD look more like the community it polices. Against great odds, we had made New York a safer place to live, work, and visit, and we had convinced people that the police were making it a better city. We had not yet convinced them that this was being done by a department that was not disrespectful, and correcting that was high on my list of priorities. We weren't done yet.

Unfortunately, I was.

Rather than remain in an atmosphere of increasing siege, in an administration that was going to micromanage and interfere with the quality of our work, I decided to resign. I had scheduled a 10:00 A.M. meeting with the mayor the next day; I hadn't told him why, although I think he suspected. Giuliani doesn't like surprises, and during the preceeding weeks, as his staff, through their press leaks, tried to push me out he would repeatedly call me personally to check on the rumors his own people were starting. Even at the end, he did not want to be upstaged.

I watched the headlines on the eleven o'clock TV news and then took my dog Charlie for a walk. I did that every night, went out for *The New York Times* bulldog edition, came back, caught the tail end of whatever was on, and read the paper. Charlie and I walked around Columbus Circle, down Broadway past the shoe-repair shop and the jeans store, west on Fifty-seventh Street in front of Coliseum Books to the newsstand at the corner of Eighth Avenue. I bought the paper, put it under my arm and walked back. I remember its being chilly.

Years before, the city had installed pedestrian street lights on Central Park South, the wide crosstown boulevard where horse-drawn hansom cabs stand in front of an impressive lineup of well-known hotels. The three-block promenade between Columbus Circle and Fifth Avenue is a tourist haven, a destination, a showcase for upscale New York. That stretch of cobblestone sidewalks bordering the park would be very attractive all lit up, a nice place for the kind of charming stroll New Yorkers would like to take but can't often find.

Like so much of New York in the late 1980s, the lights had been broken and never repaired. They had been broken before I arrived, the large plastic globes smashed, the bulbs shattered, and in the two years I had lived there, no one had fixed them. I had reported them on several occasions to the transportation and parks commissioners. You'd think that in such a heavily trafficked tourist area, the city would take special care. It was a little matter, but it spoke to bigger issues, another broken window that hadn't been fixed. If the city wouldn't repair the amenities in such a lovely, wealthy, and highly visible part of town, what must it take to get something done in a poor neighborhood where only the locals are looking? I looked across the street at the darkness. Still broken.

The headline of the lead editorial read, "Thank You, Mr. Bratton." That sounded all right. It was clear that I would not be commissioner much longer, and I thought that was a proper response. But the editorial itself was not the one I wanted. The *Times* recognized the department's turn-around in reducing crime and disorder, but the editorial focused more on the difficulties between me and the mayor than on my team's accomplishments. It also included all the Hall's well-crafted criticisms of me. While I like good press, my style was really not to chase the newspapers, certainly not with the relentlessness of City Hall, who would spoon-feed selected reporters and then call editors immediately as they saw an unfavorable story and lean on them to make changes. I hadn't lobbied the *Times* to include angles that showed me to my best advantage. Perhaps I should have. I was disappointed. Still, the headline was good.

The next morning at six-thirty, my security detail, as always, was waiting downstairs. I said good morning, got in, and thumbed through the papers. "Well, would you look at this."

The *Times* had changed the headline. What at midnight had read "Thank You, Mr. Bratton" was now "Time to Move On." Had the Hall actually gotten to *The New York Times*? When they were asked, the *Times* denied it. It was, truly, time for me to move on.

The mayor called me in my office at about quarter to eight from the van he used for transport. He asked if I was resigning; he had heard it reported on the news. I told him I was and that I was sorry he had first heard about it through the media and not from me directly.

As Maple, Timoney, LaPorte, and I walked from headquarters to City Hall for the ten o'clock meeting, we were charged by a phalanx of media. John Miller was there representing WNBC-TV. Louis Anemone showed up at City Hall with his sidearm strapped outside his jacket. "I heard there was an unruly mob," he said. "It turns out it was the press."

There was nothing exciting about my telling the mayor I was resigning. We spoke briefly, I recommended that he promote Timoney to commissioner and Maple to first deputy, and then we met the press in the Blue Room. Nothing revealing was said there, either. Giuliani and I were both very politic and mutually complimentary. We even joked a little.

Timoney exited the press conference with a friend, *Daily News* columnist Mike Daly. He thought I had been too easygoing. "That was disgusting," he said.

Timoney deserved a shot at commissioner. He was completely familiar with every facet of our operation, and with him in charge the NYPD wouldn't miss a beat. I felt the job should go to someone inside the NYPD's new way of thinking. Timoney himself had said as much to the *New York Post*'s police-gossip columnist, Murray Weiss. "If I don't get it," he'd told Weiss, "I'm outta here." Maple and Anemone, who the papers reported were both on the mayor's shortlist of candidates, both tried to talk him out of it. Anemone said, "If I get it, you're not going to stay?"

"You're a great man, Louie, but I'm outta here."

Wednesday evening, the day after I resigned, Timoney had gone to bed about eleven. At one in the morning, Peter LaPorte called him. Maple's interview had been scheduled, Peter said, and Anemone's; Timoney's hadn't. He tossed and turned for several more hours, got up at five-thirty, ran twelve miles, and got to his office about eight. An hour later, one of my team came in and told him, "I just heard Peter Powers talking about Howard Safir." Safir was the fire commissioner, a twenty-year friend of Giuliani, a former fed who had retired from the U.S. Marshals, and another name on the shortlist. "Powers said they were going to announce Safir as commissioner," relayed the man. "Someone said, 'What if Timoney says he'll resign?' He said, 'Well, nobody's irreplaceable.'"

Timoney's phone kept ringing. Come to City Hall at quarter to eleven; then eleven-fifteen, then, a quarter to twelve. There was a feeding frenzy on the TV news. The new commissioner would definitely be Safir. Reporters were calling looking for comment, and Timoney started to stew. He didn't like being treated like a yo-yo. "If there's no chance, what am I going over there for? I'm not going over," he thought. "Screw him."

Miller called. Timoney asked, "What's going on over there, Johnny?"

Miller, who knows everything, said, "I think it's Safir."

"Well then, screw him. I'm not going to go over there if it's Safir."

"No, you can't. It's like an order. You're a cop, you can't say no."

"Well, if you put it that way. Okay, I ain't gonna be happy, but I'll go over there."

Good soldier that he was, Timoney arrived. The mayor said, "I've decided on Howard." Timoney began to see red. "I know you're upset, you're angry, but please, think about it. The cops need you, the citizens need you. . . . Don't do anything rash. Will you please think about it and talk to Howard?" The meeting was over in thirty seconds.

Back in his office, the reporters called and told Timoney all the things they'd known beforehand but wouldn't say, that the whole thing had been a done deal. One reporter said that a month or two earlier, Safir had told people in the fire department that he was going to be the police commissioner. Timoney was furious. He felt like a fool for even entertaining the notion that Giuliani might appoint him. "Who the hell does this guy think he is, treating me like this, treating the police department like this!"

Over lunch, as Timoney began talking with two old friends and retired detectives, things became clear. "I've gotta make a call," he said. He phoned a friend, *Daily News* columnist Mike McAlary. "Mike, I'm outta here. There's no way I'm gonna prop up some lightweight." He called Giuliani some names. "Put that in there," he insisted.

So Timoney called Safir a "lightweight" in the paper. I got a call from Denny Young. The mayor wanted Timoney out of the building immediately. Our sources told us there was serious consideration being given to breaking Timoney down to the rank of captain. "I could care less," he said. "I'm resigning, what's the big deal?" The big deal was his pension.

In the NYPD, your pension is calculated on the rank you hold on your last day on the job. We called the department lawyers and personnel administrators, who told us that resignations didn't take effect for thirty days, which meant that Timoney was vulnerable. Interestingly, they had been contacted by City Hall concerning the same issue. The rumors were true. If they busted him back to captain, his pension would decrease by $35,000 per year. Apparently, the mayor was prepared to cost Timoney $35,000 a year for the rest of his life for calling the new commissioner a lightweight. Timoney says this threat wasn't rescinded until Lou Matarazzo, head of the Patrolman's Benevolent Association, called Staten Island Borough President and Giuliani supporter Guy Molinari and told him that if the mayor took a run at Timoney's pension, there would be 20,000 cops on the steps of City Hall in the morning. City Hall denied the threat had ever been entertained, let alone made, but we knew different.

Timoney kept his rank but was gone by that evening. (Timoney came back one more time. We snuck him into the building for the final picture of our command staff. We took two photos, one regular and one with Timoney in disguise, wearing Groucho Marx glasses.) Four days later, Maple and LaPorte resigned.

One of the elements of the job I had enjoyed most was presiding over promotion ceremonies. A few days later I presided over my last one. Timoney and I received a standing ovation. He and I hugged. Timoney hugged Anemone and then kissed Maple on the cheek and hugged him, too. I addressed the troops.

"For the last twenty-seven months, I have been privileged and honored to have been embraced by the New York City Police Department. It is a very, very special place. [I want] to say thank you. To first say thank you to the leadership that you see up on this stage, each of whom has been selected by me to lead you, to work with you, occasionally to discipline you.

"There are several things that I always seek out in leaders. I seek out, first, a love of tradition. I seek out a love of city, I seek out a love of department, and I seek out those who love cops. Because if you don't, you cannot lead them, you cannot inspire them; you cannot, when necessary, discipline them. Each and every one of the people on this stage has a very different personality. Every one of them. But they work together as a team because we share so many things, and the number one thing that we share is a love of cops.

"There has been a great deal of media attention as to who gets credit for the change in New York City. The people who should get the credit are the people in the trenches, who are doing the work, whose story I get to tell. You're the ones who deserve the credit because you're the ones making this city a safer place. I thank you for the last two years, allowing me to tell your story about the successes that you have achieved.

"As I now, after twenty-six years, get ready to leave a profession I love and go into a new one, and to leave this organization that I dreamed about forty years ago and now for twenty-seven months have been embraced by, I also want to say a special thank-you to a man without whom a lot of what has occurred over the past two-and-a-half years could not have occurred. An individual who, for twenty-nine years of his life, was a part of this organization, who, like myself, will be leaving. But the leaving will be harder for him, because he has spent so much time here.

"He will leave a great legacy, a legacy that cannot be challenged or besmirched or belittled by anybody. Among all the accolades that he has received—sixty-five decorations, combat crosses—the thing that means the most to him is to think of him as a Bronx cop. A Bronx cop." The auditorium rang with applause. "Despite all the titles and awards and honors, one of the reasons I selected John Timoney to work with me was that despite all that he had become, he remembered from whence he had come. He remembered what it was like to be in those streets, in those buildings, to be out there where danger lurked behind every corner. And in the decisions he would make, I could trust that first and foremost, he would try to put himself in your place.

"Among the many blessings that have been bestowed upon me has been to have the friendship, the loyalty, and the support of this great man. The department will truly be diminished by his moving on, but the city will not, this department will not, because the legacy that he has left in place will remain for the many Bronx cops who come behind him.

"John, it has been a pleasure and a privilege. You're the best I've ever worked with." I choked up. "I thank you."

Timoney addressed the crowd. As always, he knew what was on the cops' minds. "I know the kids are tired and hungry, so I'll just take one second." He thanked me. He told this group of cops on the way up that we had put together "the single greatest crime-fighting team to lead this great department. All the credit goes to the men and women of the NYPD, who I love, thank, and am going to miss."

The Emerald Society Band piped us out.

I addressed my last Compstat and told the gathered commanders and chiefs and personnel, "You've exhibited a heroism of your own. . . . You don't shirk responsibility. You rush toward it, you grapple with it, you wrestle with it, and you get it done. It is a singular experience to sit in that chair, to work with people such as yourself. I hope that whoever ends up stepping into my place shares the love that I have for this organization and comes to love and respect and admire you as much as I have. It has been one hell of a ride . . ." I choked up and had to stop for a moment. The room was very quiet. "I'm going to miss all of you."

For my last roll call, I addressed the evening shift at the Midtown North Precinct, my home precinct, at the station house in the middle of Central Park. I told them I would miss them, but since I intended to live in the city, I would still be there to watch them as they continued to succeed in making our city a safer place.

Mayor Giuliani took charge of the seating chart at Howard Safir's inauguration.

A poll taken by the nonprofit Empire Foundation days after I resigned found my approval rating among New Yorkers at 71 percent. The NYPD had a 73 percent positive rating, up from only 37 percent four years earlier. A Quinnipiac College poll showed that 60 percent of New York voters gave me credit for the drop in crime, while 18 percent credited Giuliani. I was pleased with our accomplishments. I would like to have done more.

I joined the private sector as president of a newly formed subsidiary of my friend Bob Johnson's First Security Services called First Security Consulting. In addition, I was made vice-chairman of his parent company and served on the board of directors. Johnson's accurate business sense was that a consultancy could be very profitable, offering the crime-reduction techniques and systems that we had developed at the NYPD to other cities, countries, and companies.

The speeches I used to give to motivate the troops at precincts around the city, I now gave for a fee at business meetings and conferences around the country. I continued to do pro bono speaking and guest lecturing at the FBI National Academy and for other cities and towns. And if I didn't have the adrenaline rush of commanding 38,000 cops and 6,000 civilians and running an organization with a budget of $2.3 billion, I had the satisfaction of bringing my crime-reducing methods to cities and companies around the country and around the world. And for the first time in my life, I had financial security. We had developed a method to reduce crime and disorder that would work in any city in America—indeed, in any city in the world.

Then some people wondered aloud what New York would be like if I became mayor. The story hit the papers, and for a while the idea was widely discussed. The thought intrigued me. Coming into the private sector, I found new challenges and new goals, but I had been a public-sector person all my adult life. Despite my growing financial rewards, I missed the constant stimulation. The crises in public life are different from those in the corporate world, and the successes give a different gratification.

I missed my team. Miller was on television. LaPorte had moved back to Boston and been named executive director of the Massachusetts Emergency Management Agency, the man in charge of preparing for every disaster that could conceivably hit Massachusetts. (His dealings with City Hall had prepared him well.) Timoney was working part-time with Mike Julian running a promotional school for police officers and had been appointed to the Crime Commission in his beloved Ireland. Maple had retired to his boat in Montauk, New York, where he spent that spring and summer pretending to be Ernest Hemingway, before emerging as a consultant himself, partnering up with John Linder. After our success at the NYPD, I felt we could do anything we put our collective mind to. My gang wanted me to go for it; they wanted to return to Camelot.

It was a heady month. I had no difficulty envisioning my team continuing and expanding the revitalization of the city. I had the good will of the people, and I had the best interests of New Yorkers at heart. I dreamed what it might be like to Compstat New York City's government.

But it's one thing to be a good mayor. It's another to get to be a good mayor. Cheryl thought the race could not be won. I had changed my registration from Independent to Democrat during the 1996 presidential race, and before I got in the ring with Giuliani I would have to win the Democratic primary. I was a centrist candidate, the kind who might win an election among the general public, but who would have more difficulty fending off liberals in a primary that was traditionally dominated by liberal voters.

If I got past the primary, I would face Giuliani in the general election. It would be a bloodbath. I had gotten a taste of his tactics at the close of my commissionership, and I suspected he would feel even less restrained in a political campaign. I was prepared to deal with that element. I had no financial backing, however, and I was not prepared to spend a large portion of my time raising funds, although I was getting indications that if I decided to get into the race, a substantial amount of money might become available. Giuliani, on the other hand, already had a war chest in the millions of dollars. Nevertheless, I felt Giuliani was beatable. My approval rating was ten points higher than the mayor's, and the public, as evidenced by his poll numbers, was still not warming up to him personally. If someone else could produce the same results—and I was someone who *had* produced the results—they could then ask, Is that the kind of man you want for mayor?

Still, there was the fact that I was not a politician. I knew people in various fields, including finance, law, and the media, who were knowledgeable about the city, and with their help I was confident I could canvass the political field and bring people together in much the same way as I found the talent in the NYPD. But that would take time, and I was being asked to dive in *immediately.* I could learn politics, but out of respect for the office of Mayor of the City of New York, I didn't think I could learn it quickly enough.

Ultimately, I decided not to get into the race.

———

The system my team and I installed continues to bring success. New York City is a much safer place now and will remain so.

In terms of importance and potential and commitment, police in America are probably the most misunderstood entity in public life today. Old images exist, and, in truth, old-guard departments exist as well. But, as we approach the millennium, there is a new breed of police leader and a new breed of police officer. We need more of them.

I was privileged during my last half-dozen years in policing to work on the national and international stage, and I feel there is still more the police can do. The turnaround of the NYPD was the catalyst for the turnaround of New York City itself and offers a potential blueprint for the turnaround of the crime situation in the entire country. We clearly showed that when properly led, properly managed, and in effective partnership with the neighborhoods and the political leaders, police can effect great change. We have clearly shown that police ...

given up as lost for decades. The continuing ...

leaders is to take them back in a lawful and re...

behavior of the police reflects the civil behavior ...

citizens.

Even as the police continue to accept responsibili...

in finding new strategies to reduce crime and fear, tw...

intractable social issues are race and police behavior. Ju ...ed

the crime and drug problems, I believe the police can t... ...dership

role in effectively resolving these issues that have tradition...ly been con-

frontational flash points and have contributed so much to the negative

perception of police. How ironic if the police, perceived in many neighbor-

hoods to be part of the problem, turned out to be in the forefront of a

movement toward understanding and resolution.

As we have raised the age and education requirements of police appli-

cants in New York in response to the Mollen Commission, we must ad-

dress a broad range of cultural issues in the many diverse communities we

police. We must put on the streets cops who more accurately reflect the

communities they serve. Most police departments have failed to attract

sufficient numbers of minority police officers, particularly black males. In

the past thirty years, the percentage of black cops in New York City has

risen less than 4 percent. This dismal increase, in a city that is more than

25 percent black, masks a deeper failure. Black males make up the same 9

percent of the NYPD that they did in 1967. Without minimizing the con-

tributions and competence of black female officers, we must make a

special effort to attract black males for what they offer to policing and

what they can contribute to their communities as role models with steady

employment, able to raise strong families.

Police officers must at all times understand that while the public de-

mands respect, the police must earn it. We can effectively police America's

streets while continuing to reduce police brutality, disrespect, and misbe-

havior. Succeeding at both is the next frontier for American policing. I in-

tend to stay fully involved in the debate and shaping of that frontier.

Mutual respect is among the key issues that American society, along with

the police, must face. In the last twenty years the police have clearly

changed—and for the most part, changed for the better—in our willing-

ness to address the crime problem. That new openness and ability to

change will propel the police, and ultimately society, in new directions.

While leading their organizations forward and teaching their officers to

police leaders must place a similar emphasis and priority on
cops new forms of behavior and respect for the residents of the
munities they police.

Essential to resolving these issues is increased respect and understanding. For many people who live in the inner cities, almost the only whites they encounter are the police, and some white cops encounter minorities only on the job. Inner-city kids go to largely minority schools and might have some white teachers, but the neighborhoods they come home to are all minority; the stores are minority staffed, the life is a minority life. If police leadership and individual police officers do not understand and respect the social mores and cultures of the neighborhoods they are policing, cops will continue to provide the spark that ignites unfortunate flash points.

There is undeniably great legitimate frustration with the behavior and attitude of some individual cops in minority communities. However, if we reduce crime and disorder, while at the same time walking the streets in a respectful way, we can begin to help society deal with its racial tensions. There is a great amount of work to be done in this area, but the potential for success certainly exists. As police leadership has accepted responsibility for reducing crime and fear, so too must it accept responsibility for dealing with racism, brutality, and inappropriate attitudes in the ranks. The first step is to admit there is a problem.

Drug abuse was once felt to be largely a societal problem. The police were often told the most we could hope to do was contain its effect. However, because of strong political support and our willingness to stick our necks out, the police and our partners in the criminal justice system and the communities have begun to get drugs off the streets while reducing the violence associated with their sale and use. In city after city we have begun to return control of the neighborhoods to their law-abiding citizens. In much the same way that we have played a leadership role in dealing effectively with the issues of drugs and crime, American policing can and must be an essential and significant force in addressing the issues of race and police behavior. American police can be the instrument of government that really does light the way toward addressing these societal problems.

To achieve these goals it is essential that police identify and train new leaders. Under consideration is a national Police Leadership Institute, privately funded, that would identify a number of current and potential future leaders and provide training, operational, and educational experiences that encourage a broad outlook. Mike Julian often said, "We tell cops not to do the wrong thing; we need to show them how to do the right thing." We have become better managers, we have the potential to become much better leaders, but we need creative leaders who are able to see beyond their own police departments and the police profession and think nationally and globally. Leaders must keep their minds open, not move into rigid and predictable conservative or liberal ideologies, and be available to all ideas dealing with the crime problem, much as we were in New York. Everybody in the city, liberals and conservatives alike, benefited from the tremendous decrease in crime.

We will develop leaders by improving their selection, mentoring, and education so they fulfill the promise of community policing, in which they are a part of the community and act with it, not on it or for it. The Leadership Institute would focus on teaching managers to deal with crime, drugs, and fear reduction, but it would also expose them to the most advanced thinking on race and police behavior and attitudes. It would be a way of ensuring that the American democratic principles, which also have to be the foundation of policing, are fully understood, accepted, and practiced. It would present ideas that work and flag ideas that don't. Compstat, for example, is a reflection of this process. We provided an opportunity for people to come up with creative new ideas. We empowered them to do great things, and they did. Encouraging the ideas that will improve human interaction is my dream, and ultimately my goal.

There are not many optimists in this country. I am an optimist. An organization is always reflective of its leader, and if there is no belief at the top echelons, there will be none below. I fully believe that with able police leadership, political will, well-trained cops, and community participation, we can take back America state by state, city by city, borough by borough, block by block. And we will win.

Acknowledgments

WE WOULD LIKE TO THANK SEVERAL PEOPLE FOR THEIR GENEROUS AND GRA-
cious contributions of time, recollections, insights, stories, and good
wishes to the writing of this book: John Miller, John Timoney, Jack Maple,
Peter LaPorte, Dean Esserman, Bob Johnson, Judy Laffey, Mike Julian,
George Kelling, Bob Wasserman, Al Sweeney, Bob O'Toole, Dee Soder, Al
O'Leary, John Linder, Tom Reppetto, Tom Kelly, Bob di Grazia, Joan Brody,
Greg Longworth.

Ann Godoff, Ruth Fecych, Ed Hayes, and Esther Newberg were all instrumental and extremely helpful in making this story into a book, and we
appreciate their good work. Tim Mennel copyedited the manuscript. Tom
Perry, Carol Schneider, and Bridget Marmion encouraged you to read it.
We thank them all.

My relationship with Peter Knobler began as one of collaboration and
grew into one of friendship. I thoroughly enjoyed working with this former '60s rabble-rouser and hope I broadened his perspectives on the
world of cops.

INDEX

ABOUT THE AUTHORS

WILLIAM BRATTON is the former police commissioner of New York City and Boston. Currently working in the private sector, he is a frequent lecturer on the issues of crime-reduction techniques, management, and leadership. He lives with his wife, Cheryl Fiandaca, in New York City.

PETER KNOBLER wrote the best-selling political memoir *All's Fair* with James Carville and Mary Matalin. He has collaborated on the autobiographies of Governor Ann Richards, Kareem Abdul-Jabbar, Peggy Say, NYPD Lieutenant Remo Franceschini, and Hakeem Olajuwon. He lives with his wife and son in New York City.

ABOUT THE TYPE

The text of this book was set in Palatino, designed by the German typographer Hermann Zapf. It was named after the Renaissance calligrapher Giovanbattista Palatino. Zapf designed it between 1948 and 1952, and it was his first typeface to be introduced in America. It is a face of unusual elegance.